Essays in Celebration of
Ray S. Anderson

On Being Christian . . . and Human

✳✳✳✳✳

Edited by Todd H. Speidell

<u>*Wipf and Stock Publishers*</u>
150 West Broadway • Eugene OR 97401

Wipf and Stock Publishers
150 West Broadway
Eugene, Oregon 97401

On Being Christian and Human
Essays in Celebration of Ray S. Anderson
By Speidell, Todd H.
©2002 Speidell, Todd H.
ISBN: 1-57910-936-5
Publication Date: April, 2002

Table of Contents

I. On Being Ray Anderson

Foreword (Kenneth Surin) 6
Biographical Introduction (Todd Speidell &
    Luanna Young) 9
Ch. 1: Community in the Life and Theology of
    Ray Anderson (Daniel J. Price)..15
Ch. 2: The Evangelical Malignment of Barth and the
    Power of the Vulnerable Word (Roger Newell)................34

II. On Being Christian and Becoming Human

Ch. 3: "For I Do Not Do the Good I Want . . . and I'm
    Tired of Trying": Weakness and the Vicarious
    Humanity of Christ (Christian D. Kettler).........................51
Ch. 4: WIJD: What *Is* Jesus Doing? (Daniel P. Thimell)........70
Ch. 5: Sharing in the Divine Nature: Transformation,
    Koinonia and the Doctrine of God (F. LeRon Shults).......87
Ch. 6: Life in the Spirit and the Spirit of Life
    (Susan Buckles) 128
Ch. 7: CrossRoads: A Christian Understanding
    of Vocation (Michael Jinkins) 147

III. On Being Human and Becoming Christian

Ch. 8: Resisting Reductionisms: Why We Need
    Theological Anthropology (Gary W. Deddo) 168
Ch. 9: The Humanity of God and the Healing of
    Humanity: The Trinity, Community, and
    Society (Todd Speidell) 194
Ch. 10: John Macmurray's Influence on Object
    Relations Psychology (Trevor M. Dobbs).......................206

Table of Contents

Ch. 11: Speaking in Tongues: Language, Nationalism, and the Formation of Church Life (Willie Jennings) 224
Ch. 12: Human Conscience, the Divine Command, and the Eschatological Community (David Gilliam) 236

Appendix for Teachers and Pastors (Sermons and Materials by Ray S. Anderson, compiled by Allen Corben)

"On Being Christian" 255
"The Epistemological Relevance of Laughter" 262
Case Studies 267
Bibliography 280

Part One

On Being Ray Anderson

Kenneth Surin

Foreword: An Appreciation

I am grateful to Todd Speidell for inviting me to contribute a Foreword to this *Festschrift* for Ray Anderson. Had I remained in the field of theological studies I would have wanted to contribute something more substantial to this volume, since Anderson's *Historical Transcendence and the Reality of God* was one of the works that shaped, in very decisive ways, my intellectual formation as a theologian.

In 1975 I was finishing my Ph.D. thesis on the ontological argument while living at the Community of the Resurrection, an Anglican monastic order, whose mother house was in Mirfield, in the north of England. The thesis was a dreary exercise in a certain kind of analytical philosophy, and Mirfield was the start of an education for someone very new to theology. Rowan Williams, then teaching at the theological seminary attached to the monastic community, drew my attention to a book that had just been published called *Historical Transcendence and the Reality of God*. A work's merits are of course much greater than the impact it happens to have on any one individual (this impress on this or that person being largely a matter of historical inadvertence), and the significance of Anderson's book derives from its place in a very important theological conjuncture. I read the book, and then read it again. The prose was formidable, and the argument labyrinthine in its construction. But there was no gainsaying the book's theological importance.

In terms of the history of theology, Anderson was (among other things of course) addressing a very significant dialectic left us by the combined legacies of Barth and Bonhoeffer. We know the story in its outline. If Barth made an inexpugnable divine transcendence the starting-point of theological reflection, then Bonhoeffer, while accepting the necessity of a theological acknowledgment of this transcendence, took the reflection on God's immanence to be an indispensable counterpoint to, and in some sense a completion of, this divine transcendence. But the reception of Bonhoeffer's work seemed subsequently to ensue in an impasse, as it came to be trivialized in the work of 'the death of God' theologians (with the exception of Altizer who followed the logic of 'godlessness' to a certain rigorously Hegelian conclusion). Bonhoeffer also seemed to be bypassed by the theologies of the cross and the political and liberation theologies that emerged in the 1960s and 70s. These theologies invariably used the event of divine self-donation on the cross to cut (in

Foreword

effect if not in intent) the Gordian knot that lay at the heart of Bonhoeffer's thinking as his life was being taken away by the Nazis. Ostensibly, and very schematically, any immanence perforce compromises transcendence (or at any rate its notion), and the reality of an immanence is attenuated by transcendence. Bonhoeffer espoused a theology of the cross that became more central in his later thinking, but how does the theology of the cross differ in function from the Barthian *deus dixit*, which cuts this knot by inserting transcendence pointedly and surdly (the 'verticality' of the Word of God) into historical immanence? This theological crux preoccupied the imprisoned Bonhoeffer, whose very late writings referred increasingly to Barth's seeming short-cuts.

Anderson's book picked up this crux. Why should 'Godness' be linked in unbounded fellowship with the created order? Barth insisted that the answer to this fundamental question be left in the realm of the analogy of faith, since the counterpart of the *analogia fidei*, viz. the analogy of being, was for Barth too close to an unacceptable 'natural theology.' Bonhoeffer was increasingly troubled by this Barthian proposition, since it seemed to involve a de-emphasizing of the 'givenness' of the historical and the quotidian–grace too permeates these latter domains, and the question of how therefore we are to make sense of this divine efficaciousness in the realm of the historical cannot be obviated by a peremptory 'God speaks.' The analogy of being, in something like its traditional sense, was intended to account theologically for precisely this efficaciousness of grace in the created order. Anderson worked through this problem with an exacting logic. The analogy of faith and the analogy of being require each other, this seemed in effect to be Bonhoeffer's important insight as elaborated by Anderson, though the language used here is of course an amalgam of the Barthian and the Thomist traditions. The task now was to find a theological logic that would work out the (theological) terms and implications of this mutual requirement of the two structures of analogy.

Historical Transcendence and the Reality of God elaborated this logic by resorting to the principle of the divine *kenosis*, a doctrine that has enjoyed a certain saliency in the Anglican and the Orthodox traditions, but which was never really accorded an explicit doctrinal centrality outside these traditions. Anderson made it central. He also gave it a new (for me) basis in ecclesiology. The church is the historical instantiation of this divine self-giving, and it does this by becoming the place of Christ in the world. (This, for Anderson, was also the core of Bonhoeffer's 'discipline of the secret.') The theologies of the cross of the 1960s did not on the whole make this move into ecclesiology, though Moltmann was later to formulate an ecclesiology that was approached by him primarily through the doctrine of the Spirit. The details of this logic and their implications are best left to the essays in this volume. Suffice it to say that Anderson set out a paradigm for theological reflection, in which Hegel's problem of history becomes the

Foreword

decisive question for the life of the church and the life of the church is in turn the place where the conundrum of history is worked through in the spirit of a demanding reticence called for by the 'discipline of the secret.'

Historical Transcendence and the Reality of God is certainly much richer than this schematic outline is able to indicate. To engage with it drew one inescapably into a profound and powerful theological thinking. Ray Anderson has of course done a lot more than write this important and exemplary book, as will doubtless be indicated by the contributors to this volume. I have never met Professor Anderson, but this takes nothing away from the wishes tendered here for a happy and productive retirement.

"BOUND TO GIVE THANKS"

"It is bound to be!

The lavish love of seed for soil

Produced a far too potent ecstasy

For dampened darkness to overthrow

It was bound to grow!

    For locked into the sense of seed

    Lies the extravagance of harvest

I am bound to see!

The seed of faith honestly sown

Bears forth the sower relentlessly

To the harvest heart of overflow

I was bound to know!

    For locked into the grief of grace

    Lies the eventuality of gratitude—

        bound to give thanks."

            Ray S. Anderson, *Soulprints*

Todd Speidell & Luanna Young

Introduction

The boy trudged along the edge of the dusty field peering ahead through the summer heat waves to see his father behind the horse-drawn plow. He always looked forward to this special time with his father when he learned from him the mysteries of growth, seed, seasons, and patience, all his father's unspoken wisdom. His father's words, sparely measured yet with deep conviction, established the boy's treasury of knowledge.

The father pulled the hand of the boy and plunged it into the overturned earth. "Son, this soil is part of your life," he spoke with quiet certainty; "you take care of it, and it will take care of you." This and other micro-lessons received and nurtured in the bosom of the earth's creative process all through the days of his own growing years gave the son of Albert and Alma Anderson a defined passion to take care of the soil of his life.

When Ray Anderson turned eighteen in 1943, he enlisted in the Army Air Corps, but when the war ended two years later, he returned to the fields of South Dakota to begin his life's work, taking care of the soil. He married his high school sweetheart, Mildred Babb, in August 1946, and graduated from South Dakota State University in 1949 with his Bachelor of Science degree in animal husbandry.

For seven years, farming was for Ray confirmation of his heritage and training, yet he had much time while on the plow when his thoughts were directed toward another destiny. After regularly listening to "The Old Fashioned Revival Hour" with Charles Fuller in the radio pulpit, Ray felt called to a new kind of training, theological studies at the newly founded Fuller Theological Seminary. In 1956, the Andersons sold their farm, despite his deeply rooted life of farming, and moved to Pasadena, California, where Ray began his studies.

Ray was quickly noticed among his classmates as intensely motivated and earnestly willing to participate in the life of the seminary. He was elected student body president, and he accompanied Dr. Fuller to promotional events. At times he felt frustration when certain professors were unavailable to students who desired personal interaction and mentoring, so he united the student body to request that faculty would have open office hours to be available to students.

One Fuller professor in particular, Edward John Carnell, shaped Ray's theological mind during his seminary studies, especially Carnell's

Introduction

contention that love--not pure, abstract, or impersonal thought--is the focal point of theological truth. The legacy of Carnell may be seen throughout Ray's theology of proclaiming God's love as expressed in human life, binding a person into a community of faith and hope and healing.

After graduating in 1959, Ray became the first pastor of an Evangelical Free Church in Covina, California. Ray summoned up his Norwegian Lutheran heritage to minister to this congregation of largely Scandinavian background, and he negotiated a way for this young congregation to buy property. He also retained and intensified for himself Carnell's interest in Kierkegaard, whose works sustained the young pastor in the early years of his ministry (see Ray's *Soulprints*).

The focus of Pastor Anderson's ministry was "exploration into God," a suggestive phrase taken from the English playwright Christopher Fry. His gift of relating the human dimension of suffering to the healing reality of Christian community brought into the church a significant number of "seekers," who experienced the reality of Michael Polanyi's words, "Our believing is conditioned at its source by our belonging."

Eleven years of leading a new church in theological reflection, incarnational witness, and the "exploration into God" led Ray, Mildred, and their three daughters, Carol, Jollene, and Ruth, in a new direction. In 1970, Ray became a doctoral student at New College, Edinburgh. Under the guidance of his mentor, Professor Thomas F. Torrance, Ray wrote his dissertation, *Historical Transcendence and the Reality of God*, in two years (published by Eerdmans in 1975). Ray's incarnational theology led him to argue that the transcendence of God is his being with us in and through the man Jesus, the Holy One in our midst.

In 1972, two years after moving his family to Scotland to complete his Ph.D., Ray became a professor at Westmont College in Santa Barbara, California. At Westmont, he became aware that many students were sent to this Christian college by their parents, whose Christian convictions they did not share. He invited these and other students to come to his home on Sunday evenings for informal theological conversation. This Sunday evening fellowship concluded each week with the sharing of communion elements to all present, since Ray insisted on Polanyi's priority of belonging before believing. This experience of belonging became the lived expression of Christ's body given for all, the therapy of relating and re-presenting Jesus' ministry to the Father for the sake of the broken-hearted.

In 1976, after four years of a teaching ministry at Westmont College, Ray joined the faculty of Fuller Theological Seminary in Pasadena, California, and soon thereafter also assumed the pastoral leadership of Harbour Fellowship in Huntington Beach. Ray, after all, had not left his pastoral position in Covina in order to become an armchair theologian removed from the reality of the world! This pastoral role provided a context for Ray's prodigious contributions as a professor, administrator, and author of numerous publications during his tenure at Fuller (see the Bibliography), and yet he never forgot his own advice to seminary professors to keep their office doors open for students! His teaching ministry, enriched by his personal quest and pastoral ministry, has touched and renewed countless lives around the world, who have been influenced and guided by Ray's pioneering and integrative work as pastor, theologian, and scholar. He has done his voluminous theological writing during the small spaces in his overload of classes and pastoral responsibilities without ever taking a sabbatical. During his thirty years of teaching, he has called on the same energy that led his father to tell him to work slower while baling hay because the hired men said he worked too fast!

The farm boy who believed his hand was rooted in the soil of South Dakota found a destiny where his heart for God is bound to his hand in the soil of many lives. The contributors of this volume offer a heartfelt word of gratitude, no doubt on behalf of many, to Ray Sherman Anderson, our mentor, pastor, and friend.

Acknowledgements

Luanna Young (member of Harbour Fellowship and graduate of Fuller Theological Seminary) deserves the first word of thanks, both for her artwork displayed on the front cover of this volume and for researching and writing the first draft of the Introduction to this volume. Webb School of Knoxville student Stephanie Helwig converted Luanna's artwork to a computer-formatted design, and computer consultant David Pierce of Webb School of Knoxville provided the technical support that facilitated the transfer of many files to prepublication form. Chris Kettler of Friends University merits an acknowledgement for offering sound advice on many key points related to this project. Allen Corben of Fuller Theological Seminary very helpfully and valuably transcribed various primary source materials by Ray Anderson to produce the Appendix. Jon Stock and Jim Tedrick of Wipf & Stock Publishers, who have published Ray Anderson's *The New Age of Soul* (2001) and *Dancing with Wolves While Feeding the Sheep* (2002), also warrant our gratitude for producing this book.

Finally, the following list of contributors comprises those who gladly gave of their time to write pieces that celebrate the influence of Ray's teaching ministry on their lives and recognize the occasion of his retirement from Fuller Theological Seminary:

Dr. Kenneth Surin, Prof. of Literature & Critical Theory (formerly Prof. of Religion), Duke University

Introduction

The Rev. Dr. Daniel J. Price, Pastor, First Presbyterian Church of Eureka, CA

The Rev. Dr. Roger Newell, Asst. Prof. of Religion, George Fox University

The Rev. Dr. Christian D. Kettler, Prof. of Theology & Philosophy, Friends University

The Rev. Dr. Daniel P. Thimell, Assoc. Prof. of Theological & Historical Studies and Chair of the Dept. of Theology & Missions, Oral Roberts University

The Rev. Dr. F. LeRon Shults, Assoc. Prof. of Theology, Bethel Theological Seminary

Dr. Susan Buckles, Adjunct Prof. of Theology, Fuller Theological Seminary

The Rev. Dr. Michael Jinkins, Assoc. Prof. of Pastoral Theology, Austin Presbyterian Theological Seminary

The Rev. Dr. Gary W. Deddo, Assoc. Editor for Academic Books, InterVarsity Press

The Rev. Dr. Todd H. Speidell, Ethics & Philosophy of Religion Teacher, Webb School of Knoxville

Dr. Trevor M. Dobbs, Psychoanalyst & Prof. of Marriage & Family Therapy, Pacific Oaks College

The Rev. Dr. Willie James Jennings, Academic Dean & Asst. Research Prof. of Theology & Black Church Studies, Duke Divinity School

The Rev. Dr. David Gilliam, Senior Research Engineer, California Institute of Technology, Jet Propulsion Laboratory (JPL), under prime contract to the National Aeronautics and Space Administration (NASA)

"A real Christian must also be
a genuine human being."
Ray Anderson[1]

---

[1] From the expanded lecture notes of Prof. Anderson's "Theology of Christian Community and Ministry" course, and originally from a series by Pastor Anderson at Covina Evangelical Free Church, Spring, 1970.

Daniel J. Price

Community in the Life and Theology of Ray Anderson

Ray Anderson is a theologian fully immersed in what it means to be human. So it comes as no surprise that his theology has been profoundly committed to the importance of Christian community, not merely as theory but also as practice, or as he would say, "praxis."[1] Ray has been the instigator of several Christian communities both before and since my wife, Karen, and I grew to love and respect him as our theology teacher. In the context of one of these communities from three decades ago he mentored us in faith, served communion for us at his home, performed our wedding ceremony, and later helped to launch us on a prolonged adventure overseas. Through many years and considerable distance, Ray has managed to keep in touch especially when we needed him, thus sustaining community in spite of modernity's odd distortions of it. We are not alone among those whom Ray has included in one form or another of Christian community.

Occasionally we replay the tape of our wedding recalling Ray's words over 25 years ago when he invoked the presence of the triune God and then encouraged us to remember that we were standing before a community of family and friends. With regard to that community he said that the bride and groom were:

> not to be separated from it, but to be given a place within it. Only we can give you that place. You have not only come to us as a community, to your family, but you have come to God's house, God's people. For human community is not enough. It is not enough that we bind ourselves to each other. For we recognize that we must always meet each other in the forgiveness and grace of Jesus Christ, in the reality of God's love. We say to you that there are resources in human love, and there is a resource in God's love and forgiveness to cover every eventuality. Thus we are now going to create that space of belonging for you, and that will be in the midst of us.

---

[1] See *The Shape of Practical Theology*, p. 23. "Theology is not simply something to be known; theology is something lived and experienced by a particular community." Anderson defines praxis as essentially "action" that is "profoundly saturated with *meaning*." *Ibid.*, p. 47. See also pp. 48-60. Hereafter, *Shape of Practical Theology*.

Twenty-five years later we appreciate even more fully the meaning of Ray's words. Many of our wedding gifts have long since tarnished, broken, or been given away. Ray's words are still something we treasure.

Ray has gifted many students with his words -- words that can make community happen. In part, the faith communities Ray fostered were due to his personal charisma. His active mind, strong physique (I used to admire how much he could bench press at the Pasadena YMCA), and unusual ability to connect with people on a personal level, made him the type of person we looked to for leadership. But the chief attraction for students like ourselves were words, not his own, but a new and refreshing vocabulary that reflected the living Word--the Word become flesh.[2] For evangelical students often raised on theologies of sterile abstraction or comfortable defensive posturing, Ray's words were a breath of fresh air. His classes were full of a type of Socratic dialogue that was stimulating and challenging. He pushed us to think and provoked us to act and be Christian outside of our comfort zones. Even in this so-called postmodern intellectual climate, many seminary and religious studies professors exult in tearing down the faith of conservative students. I have come to appreciate that Ray challenged us, not from a place of skepticism, but rather from the very depths of his profound respect for Trinitarian orthodoxy.

Perhaps because he was first a tiller of soil on a farm in South Dakota, then a pastor, and finally able to turn over the soil of his fertile mind on a third career as theologian, Ray has never been content to let theology disengage from other disciplines. He promoted practical theology before there was such a deep divide between systematic and practical theology. It is difficult to see the rise of practical theology as due to anything less than the sad realization that systematic theology is now perceived to be remarkably 'academic,' indeed impractical, to many in higher institutions of learning--let alone the person on the street.[3] After September 11, 2001, Americans are once again asking theological questions, yet some lament the fact that few theologians are willing or able to be consulted.[4] This lament could not be less applicable to our friend

---

[2] John 1: 14. In Anderson's theology, the Word, Spirit, and Father form a triune community of eternal love: the original community upon which all others are fashioned. See *Shape of Practical Theology*, p. 114.

[3] See *Shape of Practical Theology*, pp. 7-8.

[4] See, e.g., *The American Prospect*, vol. 13, issue 5, March 11, 2002. Charles Marsh opens with the following sentences: "There was once a time when American Protestant theologians were a vital part of the national civic debate. In recent decades, however, theologians have steered their discipline toward a quest for academic respectability, choosing narrow specialization over efforts to influence a wider public. It is a remarkable fact that today, even in a time of terror and warfare, when religious questions once again fill the public square, no one turns to our theologians for help."

Ray, who has spent his 'academic' career bringing theology to the church, street corner and counseling office.

Ray has provided wise counsel at crucial times in our lives. His capacity to tune in to the problems and dilemmas facing the Baby Boomer generation helped many of his students to forge their way forward in the later twentieth century and emerge in the twenty-first with a sense that God has something to do with our lives. In the early years of our acquaintance he helped us through a maze of interpersonal struggles that came from the surprising exigencies of living in a Christian college community nestled in the foothills of Santa Barbara. For example, as faculty advisor Ray gave practical guidance to Karen, who was the editor of the college newspaper at the time. He counseled her through the responsibility of reporting on a leadership crisis precipitated by the sudden resignation of a third college president in four years. It was our good fortune to have Ray more or less "graduate" with us from college and follow us to Fuller Seminary. A few years later our problems reflected those of our larger society: how to juggle career goals with the prospect of having children? Again, Ray was able to assess the competing calls of a new generation and offer suggestions that would get us through: "Get far enough through the Ph.D. program that they have a significant investment in your graduation. Then get pregnant." We followed his advice. It worked.

Ray's life was so visibly shaped by the theology of Thomas F. Torrance that he was able to inspire a number of us to likewise trek across the Atlantic and study with either "T. F." Torrance or his brother James, whom we affectionately came to know as "J. B." These Scottish adventures had costs to be sure, but they were well worth it for the benefits -- I'd guess we speak for many in saying so. Having traveled far from sunny California, we found ourselves studying theology on foreign soil where fog, wind and rain knew no bounds. In that cold climate, the theologies of Barth and Bonhoeffer, Torrance and Ray Anderson, began to take on living flesh in the form of an intimate expatriate community.

One of the ironies of community is those who need human community most desperately, can either reject it or push it away inadvertently. Ours was an experience infused with grace, for while we arrived in Scotland in desperate need of a place and people to whom we could belong, we experienced several profound levels of community. We were warmly welcomed by a surprising number of theology students from many corners of the earth. Our group of aspiring theologians was nestled in a friendly Scottish community that treated us like kin; it was greatly appreciated and surpassed anything we had expected.

Community in the Life and Theology of Anderson

Incarnational Community

Fresh off the boat from studying with T. F. Torrance, it is not surprising that "incarnational theology" was the first theological term out of Ray's mouth; he shared it enthusiastically with us at a dinner one night when he was being introduced as our school's new theology professor. Initially, I was skeptical. I doubted that he knew what he was talking about since I hadn't heard the term "incarnation" used by his predecessor--a popular recent graduate from Harvard Divinity School who had been abruptly fired for being too "neo-Orthodox."

It turns out, Ray *did* know what he was talking about. Further theological developments in his thinking have built upon the incarnation and driven home its importance as (among other things) the linchpin of community.[5] The church is in fact an incarnational community, *the* incarnational community which participates in the reconciling ministry of the Father, Son and Spirit.[6] Our service witnesses that Christ is in our midst; apart from the incarnational community Christ becomes an abstraction.

In Ray's life and writings, incarnation means that the ideas of faith are meant to be lived; theological convictions are meant to be enfleshed in the days and hours of our lives. It is compelling to know a person like Ray who takes theology to heart. He practices what he preaches; he preaches what he practices. For example, for many years he has maintained his role as a pastor and preacher at Harbour Fellowship alongside his substantial teaching load. In spite of his academic brilliance, Ray never allowed cleavage between theology and practice, theory and community. He has honed his theology on the stone of pastoral experience and was well respected for his years in pastoral ministry. One never got the feeling about Ray that like many ex-pastors he was removing his collar in order to do something more interesting. Why he pursued not merely a second, but also a third career is best explained by his drive and calling. Perhaps, C. S. Lewis would say it best through his children in Narnia, Ray desired to press "further up and further in." Ray's life reminds us that theology is a heavenward calling, and yet, the heavenward call is not one of escape. Theology puts words to the faith that will guide and direct the Christian community into costly discipleship.

The practical nature of Ray's theology is further illustrated by his willingness, indeed eagerness, to engage theology in dialogue with other disciplines. My wife and I have been repeatedly encouraged by Ray's

---

[5] See especially the introduction *of Incarnational Ministry: The Presence of Christ in Church, Society, and Family,* ed. C. D. Kettler and T. H. Speidell (Colorado Springs: Helmers and Howard, 1990), pp. xii-xvii. Hereafter, *Incarnational Ministry.*
[6] *Shape of Practical Theology,* p. 114.

eagerness to listen to cross-disciplinary ventures between psychology and theology. Ray's writings contain almost constant dialogue with the human sciences, as well as practical insight into the nature of family, society and the church. Again, theology that is incarnational is always looking for fertile ground in which to sow seeds and take root.

Incarnational Theology and Continental Thinkers

At first Dr. Anderson, as I called him so many years ago, struck me as amazingly bold in his pedagogy: serving us not mere historical surveys of others' theologies, but actually weaving around us the spell of his own theology with its many esoteric words and phrases. The intriguing effect of Ray's pedagogy was this: his words were engaging from start to stop. Many of us hadn't a clue at first what Ray was talking about, but we knew it was something real and powerfully instructive. This was true for a wide spectrum of students from a variety of backgrounds. I will never forget the number of African American students at Fuller Seminary who were enthralled with Ray's teaching. To say he spoke their language does not quite describe the picture, although he connected with them on a deeply personal level to be sure. Other teachers did this also, but there may have been this sense once again that beneath Ray's words was the reality of the living Word. His classes were not just instruction in doctrine, but also preparation for life and ministry. Maybe it was the canny, street-wise nature of his lectures that we could take and use Sunday morning for sermons, and then again Wednesday night for prayer meeting or small group discussion.

As I digested Ray's theology I slowly began to realize there was a wide range of thinkers behind Ray's thinking. Ray thus became a kind of midwife who helped many of us give birth to new ways of thinking about the faith. One of the benefits of cutting my theological teeth on Ray's early works was the opportunity to meet a number of authors who had been largely unexplored by young theological students who had tended to read theology with the blinders of American Evangelicalism. True, there were some early references to E. J Carnell and other American theologians who helped us feel safe. It was Dr. Carnell, I believe, who first encouraged Ray to think about the primacy of love and its need for tangible expression within community.[7] But the real adventure came, for Ray, and later for many of his students who studied overseas, when we began to explore the continental thinkers like Barth, Bonhoeffer, and John Macmurray. These were names that became familiar to us as we read *Historical Transcendence*

---

[7] See *Historical Transcendence and the Reality of God* (Grand Rapids: Eerdmans, 1975), p. 206. Hereafter *Historical Transcendence*.

and the Reality of God. These were the thinkers who helped Ray to expound his theology of community.

For college students it was a lot to digest: Ray's words about life and faith, alongside these new theological faces from the European continent. I will never forget a faculty colloquium where one of the philosophy professors at our college challenged Anderson to define his terms in a particular discussion. I was uncertain what "terms" his colleague found objectionable: perhaps something like the frequent use of 'ontic,' 'noetic,' 'inner logic,' or something similar. The philosopher was coming from the influence of later Wittgenstein and linguistic analysis, so for some reason he needed to put Dr. Anderson in check each time he used a theological term. But to those willing to work with the inner logic of Ray's own logic, it rarely disappointed because his was a theology to feed both the mind and spirit. It was a theology spun from experience--a theology reflective of the community from which it came and intended to be taken back to that community for further refinement.

For me, the thread that continually pulls together Ray's theology is "community." It is my suspicion that this theme is not only a key ingredient to Ray's theological cookbook, but also strikes a lost chord for many of my generation.

The Isolated Individual in Western Church

To a large degree Western culture has built on the foundation of the sanctity of the individual, on the one hand, the rights and privileges of individuals are the pillars that have upheld Western culture the past two centuries and kept it from crumbling. On the other hand, this individualism has tended to extremes and thus created a modern (some would say postmodern)[8] world where the solitary individual has experienced enormous separation and isolation. Individualism has permeated the church too in some pernicious ways: it has distorted our theology and undermined our attempts at building authentic community. It has focused our attention on salvation as something we know more than something we do. It has led to a pervasive notion among modern and postmodern Americans that says, "I can be a good Christian without church." Pastors who try to gather the flock on Sundays know this statement is almost axiomatic for modern Americans, and especially for absentee males. The easiest thing for the Christian today is to be isolated from a community, and the Christian community itself to be isolated from other communities. Ray Anderson provides a healthy antidote to the pronounced individualism of much Western and especially Evangelical

---

8 For a brief but penetrating analysis of postmodern thought and contemporary theology, see Anderson's, *Shape of Practical Theology*, pp. 17-21.

theology with statements like the following: "Too often, evangelism takes place outside the event of community, where there are no rituals of reinforcement and no context of belonging."9

Much of Anderson's theology has been road-tested by my pastoral experiences of a quarter century; both serve as a reminder that it may be easier to make converts than to keep those converts together in a community that claims to mirror the love of Christ. For this reason the formation and nurture of Christian community has become my passion and life work.

Where is the authentic community of Christ more needed than in twenty-first century American culture? One cannot help but contrast today's American mega- church with the early church members: the former coming to worship through a maze of freeways, sitting in their comfortable pew, and returning home for the rest of the week with little or no contact with brothers and sisters. The latter church met in homes, where they were a community composed of small groups by default. I mention this to draw attention to my belief that a lamentably large proportion of preaching today exacerbates the individualism that it claims to cure.

Fortunately, in recent years many churches are rediscovering the small group as a building block, indeed the cornerstone, for community. It is not by chance that Anderson's theology has provided the theological underpinnings for many small group leaders and teachers.

Yet, "community" is no panacea. Even vibrant communities can sow seeds of hatred, some covert and accidental, others more overt and intentional. For example, there are in America today great numbers of communities of a Christian nature that are so tightly knit that they can become ingrown cliques. These are communities of exclusion that seldom venture outside the walls of the church. The need to cluster with like-minded persons and fence out the world is understandable, perhaps as the reaction to modernism's enormous and sweeping cultural change, but the tendency is ultimately pernicious. These are the communities that have spawned their counterpoint communities with their liberal nostrums like "inclusive" and "diverse." The sentiment among the liberal counter-reactions is also understandable, for the true community of Christ cannot become self-righteously exclusive or even inadvertently closed.10 This would violate everything Christ came for and taught. However, many of the recent theological reflections of the liberal left have been vague and innocuous. Warm spun theologies of "justice" have failed to support the reality of an "inclusive" community. My experience with liberal churches is that they like to talk about diversity and inclusivity but their lack of

---

9 *On Being Human*, p. 189.
10 Many Biblical passages come to mind, most notably Matthew 25:31-46.

Christopraxis lures few people of racial or ethnic diversity. Diversity for its own sake is too weak a principle upon which to found a community.

The theology of Ray Anderson and others like him helped me to see the importance and challenge of building community *of* and *by* the church, but not necessarily *for* the church in an exclusive sense. More will be said about this below.

Individualism and the Therapist's Couch

Psychology too has needed to traverse the incline slope of individualism. From the outset one thinks of Freud's couch as the paradigm of modern therapy. Individualism reigns here. The classical analyst as an individual helps the client as an individual: the former taking copious notes, the latter free associating about the experiences of childhood while hardly making eye contact. Both are isolated from their communities in order for the healing moment to take place, much like the surgeon and patient lying on the operating table. This therapeutic practice should not to be altogether dismissed; it is, however, truncated. The healthy individual who has no one to go home to is a person who has found a solution and still needs a cure. I think many would prefer to live as a neurotic who is nevertheless loved by a caring community, rather than a psychologically "healthy" hermit.

Anderson puts his finger on the "narrow individuality" of modern psychology:

> The distinction between social and psychological is intended only as a logical distinction appropriate to the true form of humanity. If existence with the other, or social existence, is determinative of existence as a singular being, then discrete individuality in abstraction from the other is already a symptom of disordered humanity, not the beginning of a cure. To some extent, deprivation of social encounter constitutes privation of humanity, with at least psychological consequences. Psychotherapy, then can be construed as a systematic limitation of attention necessitated by the sociopathic condition.[11]

I will never forget my conversation with a man whom, until recently, served as the Bishop of the Church of South India. He learned that my wife was a clinical psychologist, and when we asked him about the state of psychology in his country, he grinned and revealed to us that

---

[11] *On Being Human*, p. 49. Anderson does not seem to be using "sociopathic" in any clinical sense, but rather theologically to describe the symptom of social brokenness in our respective communities.

except for pockets of heavy Western influence, there were no practicing psychologists in India. These kinds of problems are handled through the community and families, he told us. This led me to reflect upon the fact that while Western countries may have an edge in psycho-pharmacology, there is not much to brag about when a rich country like America has so many mentally ill wandering aimlessly in our city streets. It should also give us reason to pause and reflect for a moment on the sorry condition of our communities, or lack thereof, in the affluent West today.

Fortunately, modern psychology has come a long ways since Freud. Few therapists make their clients lie down on a couch any more (except for a handful of psychoanalysts mostly around urban New York), and in North America the psychological inroads have resulted in an almost limitless supply of small groups and Twelve Step programs for every ailment of mind and body. Group therapy has become a huge phenomenon in America today and that is not by accident.[12] Nor is it at all unusual for large churches or church communities to have counselors or psychologists employed to help people with specific emotional problems in their church and local community.

What about contemporary Christian theology? Have we overcome the pernicious effects of individualism? For the most part I would say, 'no.' We are still propping our theology up with the individualism of the egocentric and individualistic philosophers. Ray Anderson takes exception to theology's proclivity for pronounced individualism. Let us then trace the thoughts of some of the seminal thinkers who helped Professor Anderson develop his articulate and passionate understanding of community, paying attention to Anderson's own discussion and theological development along the way.

The Seed of Community in the Philosophy of John Macmurray

It took many years of study to come to a full appreciation of Anderson's insight into the thought of people like John Macmurray. My prima facie reading of *Historical Transcendence* only hinted at Macmurray's importance. In 1987 I concluded my first term of ministry in Fresno and decided to study with Rev. Prof. James B. Torrance, who had studied philosophy at Edinburgh under Macmurray and others. We launched out for Scotland with haste, knowing "J. B." would soon retire. In Scotland I re-discovered the writings of John Macmurray and was taken with the profound novelty

---

[12] In all fairness to those who labor in the psychotherapeutic community, I must say that those who do their job well as therapists are actually working with a small community, though partly in absentia, through establishing the appropriate psychological transference. Few patients do therapy without reference to a community either of family and or friends, both real and psychologically represented in the therapeutic process.

of this philosopher: one of the few to consciously incorporate the insights of modern psychology into his philosophical perspectives. Because we combine the theological and psychological disciplines in our marriage and education, I found Macmurray to be an exhilarating breath of fresh air.

Macmurray was one among several thinkers to share the insight that the tradition of Western philosophy had for too long seen the individual as an isolated thinker. Descartes' *cogito ergo sum* comes quickly to mind as the prototype of individualistic rationalism. Professor Macmurray developed his Gifford Lectures of 1953 [13] largely from the problems inherited from a lengthy tradition of philosophical speculation. Macmurray propounded the idea that the self is an acting agent rather than solely a thinking mind. With this seminal thought in place, Macmurray developed a model that was able to explain not only thought, as the subordinate component of human agency, but also human action or behavior. Anderson summarizes Macmurray:

> the self as agent cannot exist in a personal sense in isolation; action will be impossible in the complete sense because apart from the Other, who is also an agent, there will be no 'resistance' to the self of the kind necessary to produces a personal act. Without resistance, which Macmurray defines as the core of tactual perception, the self as agent cannot experience itself, because there will be no 'other' than self to constitute a limiting factor to the movement of self. This opposition, which comes in the form of that which is Other than the self, constitutes the unity of the experience of the self as Agent.[14]

Anderson then quotes directly from *The Self as Agent*: "The distinction of Self and Other is the awareness of both; and the existence of both is the fact that their opposition is a practical and not a theoretical opposition."[15]

Where did Macmurray get this idea that "tactual" resistance is absolutely essential to the development of the self? It is likely that he was influenced by the insights of post Freudian psychology.[16] The de-emphasizing of the visual, and explicit emphasis upon the importance of the tactile sense in Macmurray's thought helps us along the way toward rediscovering community. This is because the tactile resistance

---

[13] These were published in book form as: *Self as Agent* (London: Faber and Faber, 1957) later republished in 1963 with the same pagination, and his 1954 Gifford lectures became *Persons in Relation* (London: Faber and Faber, 1961). In my view, these two books are some of the most overlooked philosophical works of the past century.
[14] *Historical Transcendence*, p. 194.
[15] *Self as Agent*, p. 109.
[16] At the University of Aberdeen students and faculty acknowledged the influence of Macmurray's wife, who had been a psychologist.

emphasized by Macmurray breaks through the isolation of the thinking individual and compels us to understand that emotional and intellectual development is essentially communal and physical from the earliest experiences of infancy.[17] The mind is not in a box as Descartes conceived it, but develops in dynamic bodily interaction between self and other. It is not surprising, then, after dealing with many of the epistemological problems created by philosophy, that in his second volume Macmurray develops a theory of person based on community. He summarizes the second volume of his lectures with these words:

> The theme of the present volume can be stated simply. The idea of an isolated agent is self-contradictory. Any agent is necessarily in relation to the Other. Apart from this essential relation he does not exist. But, further, the Other in this constitutive relation must itself be personal. Persons therefore, are constituted by their mutual relation to one another. 'I' exist only as one element in the complex 'You and I'. We have to discover how this ultimate fact can be adequately thought, that is to say, symbolized in reflection.[18]

Macmurray follows out the implications of his profoundly relation-oriented philosophical revolution as he contrasts a 'community' with 'society.' He states that a society is a grouping of people who come together for utilitarian purposes. "A community, however, is a unity of persons. It cannot be defined in functional terms, by relation to a common purpose. It is not organic in structure, and cannot be constituted or maintained by organization, but only by the motives which sustain the personal relations of its members."[19] Anderson is quick to draw out the implications of Macmurray's comment above, "Because the self is basically

---

[17] The primacy of the interpersonal in human development was emphasized by L. W. Grensted in his Bampton Lectures of 1930 when he stated: "The belief that a knowledge of things is in some way prior to the knowledge of persons is sheer delusion. In the analysis of life we cannot start from the solid world about us, for both its solidity and its apparent self-existence are mere interpretations of our experience, and the experience from which we set out to interpret the world is not simply our own. It is and was from the very first a corporate existence, in which we are intimately interrelated with others like ourselves. The contact of spirit with matter constitutes a problem of apparently insuperable difficulty. The contact of spirit with spirit is a primary and uncontrovertible datum." *Psychology and God* (London: Longmans, Green and Co., 1931), p. 81. It is unknown whether or not Grensted influenced Macmurray's thought, but, it seems likely even though Macmurray interprets the primacy of the interpersonal less dualistically than Grensted.
[18] *Persons in Relation*, p. 24.
[19] *Ibid.*, pp. 157-58.

an agent who acts, personhood can only exist when there is a community of acting agents who intentionally relate out of love."[20]

Macmurray has provided Ray Anderson with some seminal ideas that refocus our attention on the communal character of being human. However, Macmurray developed his idea of community from philosophical speculation, not from any Biblical or Christological perspective. To fill this lacuna Anderson looks to two very eminent theologians of the twentieth century.

Community Rooted in Christ: Bonhoeffer

Other influences upon Anderson's view of Christian community are found in Dietrich Bonhoeffer and Karl Barth. Let us first take a look at Bonhoeffer.

It is almost startling that a twenty-one year old German man who wrote a doctoral thesis at the University of Berlin exploring the sociological categories of theology could write this profound treatise. Such was the gift to the church of the short life of Dietrich Bonhoeffer. Why Bonhoeffer chose to explore such an important topic is beyond the scope of this essay, but we can be thankful he did. Certainly his thesis, later published in various editions as *Sanctorum Communio*, has laid the foundation for much reflection upon the idea of Christian community ever since, including the writings of Ray Anderson. Bonhoeffer's key idea here is that the church (*Kirche*) is "Christ existing as community (*Gemeinde*)."[21] Anderson picks up this theme again and again throughout the course of his writings: applying it to his theology of the church, ethics, and pastoral care.

It is somewhat surprising that Bonhoeffer was interested in the sociology of the religious community, given his historical setting and family. He was the son of a well-established Berlin family, his father a prominent psychiatrist of the pre-Freudian type. At first glance the Germans do not seem nearly as community oriented as some peoples living further south. While they are not always gregarious toward the visitor, the concept and practice of community are very important indeed to Germanic peoples. Having lived in a German speaking country for several years, I was constantly impressed with how many activities, events and political expressions sprang from the local *Gemeinde*.

But the dark side of the *Gemeinde* is those who are excluded--or worse. Bonhoeffer's courage in swimming against the tide of fascism created a theology of paramount importance to the church. His *Sanctorum*

---

20 *Historical Transcendence*, p. 248.
21 *Sanctorum Communio*, tr. J. Soosten, ed. C. J. Green (Minneapolis: Fortress, 1998) p.141 and 121. The editors translate *Christus als Gemeinde existierend*, 'Christ existing as church-community.' Cf. p. 303.

Communion laid the foundation for nothing less than his profound later writings and his dissent from the inhuman directives of the Third Reich.

In his later work about community drawn from the underground seminary at Finkenwalde, *Life Together*, Bonhoeffer reminds us that the ideal of community can become a dangerous thing.[22] By this Bonhoeffer means that disillusionment can form when the idealistic dreams of a community rub against the complex interpersonal realities of a community. Disillusionment with others, and finally with self, then make room for the grace of God to establish a real Christian community, rather than the community of illicit dreams.[23]

Anderson too reminds us throughout his writings that the community of God is not a lofty ideal, most especially not an ideological community that attempts to wall others out. This is why the community that is alive in the Spirit is best described as a *kenotic* community: that is, a community that empties itself out in love and service both to insiders and outsiders.[24] This is the community that participates in the self-emptying love of Jesus Christ; a community rooted in sacrificial love, not dreams or ideals. It is a community that is incarnate--it is a flesh and blood community infused with the Spirit of Christ and therefore Christ-like service.

In his earlier work, Anderson reminds us that the community of the Spirit is both kenotic and "ek-static." Anderson coins the latter hyphenated phrase consciously so as to make clear that the ek-static community is more than "ecstatic" in the sense of being beside oneself. Rather, a community is ek-static when it dares to reach outside itself as a witness to what lies within.[25] In other words, the church community is ek-static in as much as it re-presents the person and work of Christ in its concrete actions in the world.

Both Bonhoeffer and Macmurray were influenced by the I and Thou (*Ich und Du*) philosophy of Martin Buber, even though the extent of Buber's influence is not always clearly stated.[26] One thing, however, seems clear: both thinkers built upon Buber but developed his ideas in slightly different directions. Whereas Macmurray takes Buber's I and Thou and translates it in the context of developmental psychology, thus emphasizing the

---

[22] *Life Together*, tr. D. W. Dobberstein (New York: Harper and Row, 1954), p. 26f. Cf. *Sanctorum Communion*, p. 199.

[23] Bonhoeffer here documents the influences of St. Paul, Luther, and Barth, and we may infer, Kierkegaard. See *Sanctorum Communio*, 199f.

[24] See *Historical Transcendence*, p. 229ff. Anderson's term, *kenotic* is a biblical one, taken from Philippians 2:7. With this word Paul describes Christ's self-emptying, incarnational love.

[25] Following Dr. John Zizioulas' work, *Being As Communion* (London: Darton, Longman and Todd, 1985), Anderson here defines ek-stasis as "a question of the movement (ek-stasis) toward community in God . . ." *Historical Transcendence*, p. 240 n. 29.

[26] See *Sanctorum Communio*, pp. 5f., 54ff. Also *Historical Transcendence*, pp. 202 n. 42, 248f.

tactile and interpersonal, Bonhoeffer took hold of Buber's I and Thou and interpreted it in terms of the ethical responsibility entailed by such encounter. In a sense, in the scope of his total theology, Anderson combines the best of each of these thinkers. With I and Thou, Buber sought to enhance personal interaction and intimacy; he wanted to prevent us from treating the Other as an "It," thus depersonalizing and objectifying fellow humans. Bonhoeffer, on the other hand, pulls out the ethical imperatives that stem from I and Thou. Macmurray places I and Thou in the context of developmental psychology and from it spins a theory of self, knowledge and community based on practical philosophy (in the Kantian sense). All these have influenced Anderson's theology of community in the direction of the personal. But his studies with T. F. Torrance and of the mighty works of Karl Barth were needed in order for Anderson to root the Christian community in the incarnation as kenosis.

In a Western Europe where the church had been so immensely influential but by the early twentieth century was threatened by its own irrelevance, Barth and Bonhoeffer both developed a passionate theology to keep the church from becoming closed off from the pain and hunger of the world outside its walls (*extra muros ekklesiae*). Today with the ever-growing disparity between have and have-not peoples, the challenge to love the neighbor outside our church walls has grown even more urgent. The danger that community--even the community of Christ--can close itself off from the pain, suffering and injustices outside the community is one that must be guarded against in each generation. As a pastor I see this subtle distortion of community happening almost inadvertently and unconsciously. The poor, lonely and estranged can sit at the gate like Lazarus outside the rich man's house seldom being noticed, or an even more sinister face can frown upon any community in the form of antipathy, competition or even hatred and violence between communities.[27] Such communities are fatally closed, and as such they cannot be the community of Christ.[28]

Bonhoeffer's influence on Anderson here is palpable, as Anderson himself suggests:

> Practical theology in the mode of *paraclesis* is a summons and invitation for humanity to become truly human; it is an exhortation to move out of the place of sorrow and humiliation into a community of reconciliation, peace, and dignity.

---

[27] Lately our minds do not turn only to Northern Ireland to see examples of religious and sectarian violence. The Balkans, Middle East, India, Pakistan, Kashmir and other places also come to mind as communities where the glue of heavy handed government has recently been withdrawn and the respective societies are now in conflict.
[28] See *Sanctorum Communio*, p. 272f. n. 430.

Christopraxis as a form of the real presence of Christ is a pledge of comfort and consolation to the oppressed and broken. It may have to take the 'worldly' form of the presence of Christ in many cases, or the 'nonreligious' form of Christ's presence in the world, as Bonhoeffer came to see it. The praxis of forgiveness must first of all be a praxis of reconciliation and restoration of humanity in the world before its authenticity can be affirmed in the liturgy of the church.29

Building on the work of Bonhoeffer and creative employment of the terminology of John's Gospel, Anderson also develops a theology of pastoral counseling that includes community. The Holy Spirit is the 'paraclete,' the Called-Alongside-One who abides with the believer and the church.30 Anderson's *paracletic* community is thus a community of caregiving patterned after the care given by Christ through the presence and power of the Holy Spirit. Anderson states, "The role of the caregiver as moral advocate is an extension of the body of Christ. The pastoral care that provides this intervention and advocacy should be offered in such a way that the primary caregiver is not the sole advocate. A model of caregiving then would include the following guidelines."31 These guidelines include connecting the caregiver and the caregiving network to the Christian community.

Community Rooted in Cohumanity: Karl Barth

If Bonhoeffer lays one cornerstone, Barth provides another for Anderson's theology of community. Anderson is clear, both in his writings and some recent communication with this author, that he has been greatly influenced by Barth's understanding of "cohumanity."32 Cohumanity begins with Barth mapping out his anthropology in terms of Christology; we peel to the core of Barth's anthropology in his section under "The Basic Form of Humanity." Many have read this penetrating section in the *Dogmatics* and

---

29 *Shape of Practical Theology*, p. 203. See especially his important chapter, "The Humanity of God and the Soul of the City," pp. 178-186.
30 See John 14:16-17. The Spirit is called upon by the believer; but is sent by the Father and Son.
31 *Shape of Practical Theology*, "1. The caregiver operates within a network of Christian community so that her or his spiritual and personal life is nurtured and affirmed as belonging to Christ and indwelt by Christ's Spirit." Four more categories of pastoral care guidelines are given with each couching the pastoral care in the context of the Christian community--yet with sensitivity to such potential problems as preserving confidentiality and surrounding the individual with the right, i.e. carefully selected, caregiving network. p. 222f.
32 The German term is *Mitmenschlichkeit*, normally translated by Bromiley et al. as "fellow humanity." Anderson uses the more up-to-date term, "cohumanity," although he also seems to use these two terms interchangeably. See, e.g., *Shape of Practical Theology*, pp. 136ff.

others have commented on it at length.³³ So I will highlight just a few key ideas here.

Barth sees the humanity of Christ as axiomatic for a Christian anthropology. He draws out the implications of Christ's true humanity (*verus homo*) in the following statement:

> The humanity of Jesus consists in His being for man. From the fact that this example is binding in humanity generally there follows the broad definition that humanity absolutely, the humanity of each and every man, consists in the determination of man's being as a being with others, or rather with the other man. It is not as he is for himself but with others, not in loneliness but in fellowship, that he is genuinely human, that he achieves true humanity, that he corresponds to his determination to be God's covenant-partner, that he is the being for which the man Jesus is, and therefore real man.³⁴

Barth derives his anthropology from the Bible, and from the I and Thou of Martin Buber. This is particularly true of his section where he describes our fellow-humanity as being in encounter.³⁵ Note the way Barth builds on Buber, and developing his thought in the direction of the obligation that any I and Thou encounter entails: "'I am'--the true and filled 'I am' -- may thus be paraphrased: "'I am in encounter'." Barth continues to remind us that this being in encounter is not optional but ontological:

> Nor am I in encounter before or after, incidentally, secondarily or subsequently, while primarily and properly I am alone in an inner world in which I am not in this encounter, but alongside which there is an outer world in which amongst other things I certainly come up against being, against the being of the Thou. No at the very root of my being and from the very first I am in encounter with the being of the Thou, under his claim and with my own being constituting a claim upon him.³⁶

Among Anderson's many fine summaries of Barth, his outline of Barth's anthropology in his chapter, "The Concept of Neighbor in the

---

33 See, e.g., Todd Speidell, "Incarnational Social Ethics," in *Incarnational Ministry*, pp. 147-150. For an extensive treatment of Barth's anthropology see my book, *Karl Barth's Anthropology in Light of Modern Thought* (Grand Rapids, Eerdmans, 2002), especially pp. 138-164. Hereafter, *Karl Barth's Anthropology*.
34 *Church Dogmatics*, III/2, p. 243.
35 See *Karl Barth's Anthropology*, p. 139 n. 155.
36 *Church Dogmatics*, III/2, p. 247.

Ethics of Karl Barth"[37] is both profound and helpful. Here he helps us tounderstand Barth's determination to root Christian ethics in revelation and ultimately in Christology as the basis for creation. The fact that ethics are drawn from Christology and not from an abstract doctrine of creation reminds us that Barth here has much in common with Bonhoeffer: for both thinkers the Other whom I encounter as my neighbor creates an ethical obligation. This sense of ethical obligation to the neighbor is something that Barth constantly attempts to establish by pulling ethics away from universal or abstract ethics and grounding it in revelation--specifically in my neighbor as the representative of Christ. Anderson traces the development of Barth's earlier lectures at Göttingen and *Ethics*[38] to his later dogmatics, observing:

> Theologically, Barth argues, the concept of right (or law), falls under the concept of reconciliation, not that of creation. At this point, while still wishing to hold to some form of orders of creation, a concept he later rejected, Barth clearly sees this order as grounded in God's determination that humans exist as fellow humans and that rights are contingent on this divine determination. What is right is grounded in what actually is in fact the case--though this can only be known with certainty and clarity through revelation--that human beings exist for and with the other as neighbor.[39]

Anderson traces the narrowing of Barth's ethics from revelation in general and natural law to Christology, and then he makes an important observation:

> The church, says Barth, must always be a missionary community. By that he means that the church must be an open circle, not a closed one. The neighbor as criterion of Christ for me cannot be identified only as a fellow member of the church. It may be that the one who stands outside of the church is precisely the neighbor of the church and therefore the criterion of Christ for the church as well. If I refuse to meet this neighbor, even though he may appear to be ungodly to me, says Barth, I may deny the Christ living in me.[40]

---

[37] *Shape of Practical Theology*, pp. 132-160.
[38] *Shape of Practical Theology*, pp. 141-146.
[39] *Shape of Practical Theology*, pp. 144f.
[40] *Shape of Practical Theology*, p. 146.

An important conclusion can be drawn from Anderson and his following of Barth's understanding of cohumanity, and Christology as the basis of ethics. While a finely focused Christology bears increasing weight in Barth's theology through his theological development, it does not narrow, but rather broadens the scope of Christian ethics. The community of Christ therefore becomes the very embodiment of the triune God's love for the whole world.

Barth is often accused of being Christomonistic. Actually, in Barth's theology we see the Trinity guiding every aspect of his thought. The triune God of grace thus becomes the paradigm for his doctrines of God, the Word, Creation and Reconciliation; it is also the foundation for Christian anthropology and hence the community we call the church. The *ad intra* and *ad extra* triune community of the Father, Son and Holy Spirit provide the occasion for human community and the reality of the church community. Here we gain insight into the dynamic nature of all human and divine interactions. The pre-existent community of Father and Son in the Spirit provides the basis for the incarnational community of the Church. The Church is not the same as the original, but rather a reflection of the original love of Father and Son in the Spirit.

Conclusion

I have traced the logical necessity of community developed in the thought of Macmurray, then compared its similarities and dissimilarities to the theology of community found in Bonhoeffer and Barth, all the while showing how these thinkers profoundly influenced the theology of Ray Anderson. It would miss the point to belabor the obvious and propose that the arguments or ideas promulgated by Ray Anderson must be given a foothold in today's seminaries and churches. I obviously think this should be the case.

Anderson himself might prefer that I put it this way: the only conclusion worthy of such a study on community is to point out that those who follow Christ must participate in the love of Christ within the church in order to proclaim it outside. In our preaching, our liturgy and fellowship, is laid the groundwork for our mission and service. No single person can accomplish this, for sin crouches at the door wherever we seek to let divine love become incarnate. By grace alone the community of Christ can become the living Body of Christ.

How desperately needed are Barth's, Bonhoeffer's and Ray Anderson's theology of the church. This may be especially true today when sectarian violence and inter-religious warfare have reared their ugly heads, not just in little pockets within the countries of the East and West, but between East and West. But even more needed are men and women of the church like Karl Barth, Dietrich Bonhoeffer and Ray Anderson.

So far, as we strain our eyes to see into the distant horizons of the twenty first century and beyond, we have little empirical reason to hope that the twenty-first will be any less bellicose or bloody than the twentieth. Yet, for those who look beyond the earthly horizon to the heavens and seek truth from a source beyond, there is every reason to hope that the church can be an agent of reconciliation and hope, helping us to rebuild the fractured communities of our world for Christ. In the course of the twenty-first century the world may yet again look to the church, not only because we preach Christ, but more likely because we embody the Christ we preach.

Roger Newell

The Evangelical Malignment of Barth and the Power of the Vulnerable Word

Background: The Evangelical Malaise

Many of Ray Anderson's students are indebted to him for deepening our attachment to the evangelical faith by introducing us to a positive and not a polemical conversation with Karl Barth. And even as our commitments to our various ecclesiastical traditions have deepened over the years, our identification with the adjective "evangelical" remains strong. The Scottish missiologist Andrew Walls casts fresh light on our affection for this gospel word when he describes it as a protest against a nominal Christianity.[1] As such it stands in a long tradition of protest movements against superficial Christian profession, "going back to the fourth century when the desert fathers turned their backs on the attractive commodity then for the first time widely available--Christianity combined with self-indulgence." Formal religion alone was inadequate. The need for inward religion, real as distinct from nominal, was urgent. Wearing his hat as a historian of world missions, Walls assesses the Evangelical Revival of the eighteenth century as perhaps the most successful of all the reformulations of Christianity in the context of changing Western culture. Though not identical among its exponents, its message included a deep call for radical discipleship, a retaining of the central medieval concern for atonement, and further extended the notion of a life of holy obedience in a secular world.[2]

Crucial to its achievement, Walls insists, was the refusal to abandon the recognized established churches, but instead to combine traditional loyalties with "a serious recognition of individual selfhood and personal decision . . . That reconciliation bridged a cultural chasm in Christian self-identity. It helped to make evangelical religion a critical force in Western culture, a version of Christianity thoroughly authentic and indigenous there."[3] As the missiologists say, evangelicals contextualized the gospel

---

[1] Andrew F. Walls, "The Evangelical Revival, the Missionary Movement, and Africa," *The Missionary Movement in Christian History* (Maryknoll, New York: Orbis Books, 1996), p. 83.
[2] *Ibid.*, p. 82.
[3] *Ibid.*, p. 84.

for the northern Protestant world.⁴ Walls suggests that the crisis in Western Christianity today is closely connected with the attrition of this historic evangelical achievement, the weakening of the ethical influence of institutional churches, and the increasing efficiency of the state coupled with the relegation of religion to the private sphere of personal judgment and individual decision. Given our present situation, in which "Christianity combined with self-indulgence" has never been more epidemic, and with Christianity increasingly privatized by our social and educational structures, we are now more than ever in need of a robust evangelical recovery of faith in the gospel.

If the need is anything like I've described it, why have evangelicals made so little common cause with the renewal of evangelical theology forged amidst the fierce persecutions of German National Socialism? Why has its primary theological mentor, Karl Barth, too often received a lukewarm response from the American evangelical church, ranging from curt dismissal to cool reprimand? Through his longstanding dialogue with Barth, Bonhoeffer, and of course, his doctoral mentor, Thomas Torrance (himself Barth's student in Basel), Ray Anderson has helped three decades of North American pastors and theologians pay fresh attention to an alternative vision of evangelical theology, to recover and not dismiss Barth's work as both an evangelical protest against and bold engagement with modernity--amidst the assault of German Fascism. For the rest of this essay, I would like to explore both theologically and historically why this resource has received such a limited reception and what strengths Barth may yet contribute to the evangelical witness.

Let us remember that following the victory of the Allies in World War II, Barth never joined the camp followers who identified the triumph of Western democracy with the triumph of the gospel. He chose instead to maintain an even-handed conversation with ideological socialism *as well as* ideological capitalism and to identify the gospel with neither. Barth's independence from the American hegemony may well be a sufficient answer to our first question. Consider: if a highly nuanced advocate of Western democracy such as Reinhold Niebuhr could be frustrated with Barth's unwillingness to denounce the communists as he once condemned the fascists, small wonder lesser commentators found it so easy to ignore or dismiss this awkwardly neutral Swiss.⁵

---

4 Certainly, as Walls elsewhere remarks, "There is nothing wrong with having local forms of Christianity--provided that we remember that they *are* local." "The American Dimension of the Missionary Movement," *The Missionary Movement in Christian History*, p. 235.

5 For Niebuhr, here was a clear case of democracy versus totalitarianism. In contrast, Barth's notion of democracy was influenced by the Swiss tradition of Christian social egalitarian democracy (including Kutter and Ragaz) and hence was more complex than simply the right to vote. Cf. Reinhold Niebuhr, "Why is Barth Silent on Hungary?," in *Essays in Applied Christianity* (New York: Meridian Books, 1959), p. 187.

A Sampler of Barth Critics

With these questions before us, let us turn to the three representatives of evangelical theology which Ray Anderson has used as case studies in his essay "Evangelical Theology": G.C. Berkouwer, Carl Henry, and Helmut Thielicke.[6] I wish to pay special attention to where each diverges from Barth and consider the resulting implications for a witness to the gospel. In his introduction, Anderson deliberately includes a broad canvas to paint his evangelical family portrait, including Jonathan Edwards' "old school Calvinism," Charles Finney's pragmatic revivalism, the Princetonian orthodoxy of Warfield and Hodge, as well as Darby and Schofield's Dispensationalism. Like Andrew Walls, Anderson identifies a cluster of evangelical concerns, but lingers specifically over three items: orthodoxy in doctrine rooted in the Reformation confession of *sola scriptura* and *sola gratia*, biblical authority as an infallible guide to faith and practice, and personal experience of salvation through Jesus Christ.[7] (A most problematic absence from Anderson's short list is Walls' attention to social manifestations of discipleship. This absence of a clear witness to the social justice component of the gospel will be considered later.)

Berkouwer: The Triumph of Doctrine

Anderson describes Berkouwer's theological method as the articulation of correlations between the divine word and the responding human subject. Instead of the liberal tendency to make the human subject the criterion for divine revelation, and unlike Orthodoxy's tendency to make abstract doctrinal constructs the center of faith and thus ignore human experience, Berkouwer describes the very nature of revelation as the Word of God spoken *and* heard in Holy Scripture. Thus embedded within Scripture lies the true correlation between faith and knowledge, subject and object.[8]

From this frame, Berkouwer finds Barth's theology of the atonement wanting. Barth's error apparently is the Orthodox penchant for constructing abstract doctrine, in this case, of "grace" as a principle of divine triumph. Barth thereby eliminates the human response, since grace by definition always triumphs over sin, but Berkouwer finds this a hollow victory since the dignity of our human response has been disrespected. Further, this commits Barth to an unbiblical universalism in which human response is swallowed up in divine activity, history devalued, and evil is

---

6 Ray S. Anderson, "Evangelical Theology" in David F. Ford, ed., *The Modern Theologians* (Oxford: Blackwells, 1997), p. 483.
7 *Ibid.*, p. 482-4.
8 *Ibid.*, p. 486.

no longer taken seriously. "Grace" becomes a theological principle abstracted from Scripture and used to subjugate and thus reduce all else barely to a cipher.[9]

Barth's reply to these charges may be expressed with a series of questions. What if sinful humanity both in its inflated self-righteousness and deflated despair is overcome by the human obedience of Jesus, the divine intervention of the Son of God? What if the human and divine at-one-ment is first and foremost not a doctrine, nor a principle of correlation, but the very person, Jesus himself? What if the sheer Word, the Word of God in Jesus, in vulnerability and limitation as the person Jesus was and is, what if Jesus is in fact the divine and human presence where correlation or to put it more biblically, where reconciliation occurs? What if Scripture is a written witness to this reality? What if Barth, like his pastoral guide, Blumhardt, is faced here with the issue of obedience to the real presence of Jesus? Is Barth's teaching really about doctrinal dominos in which the grace domino rightly positioned topples all others and sweeps the board?

Berkouwer does not recognize that he mistranslates Barth's refrain (which Barth learned from Blumhardt), "Jesus is Victor." Berkouwer's proposed "Triumph of Grace" is itself an abstraction, a depersonalizing of Jesus the merciful and holy One. It amounts to a stripping away of the sweet exchange between our sin and God's righteousness inherent in Jesus, the personal Word. By turning from the personal Word made flesh, Berkouwer flattens the victory of Jesus into a principle of grace and then labels Barth as a necessitarian universalist. However, for Barth, this reduces Jesus' personal (and personalizing) victory into a theological abstraction, and can only be rejected as utterly contrary to his method.

As I stated earlier, Barth's inspiration for trusting God's victory in and through Jesus is Pastor Blumhardt, who chose to cry out to God for the deliverance of what he could only describe as a demon-possessed member of his parish. Unforgettably Blumhardt dared pray to Jesus to deliver this person. Barth clearly describes the personal nature of this trust.

> We can trust a person, and in the case of this person we must do so unconditionally and--with final certainty, as Blumhardt did when he accepted that battle . . . Blumhardt never even dreamed he could control Jesus. He did something which is very different, and which is the only thing possible in relation to this person. He called upon Him . . . He did so with absolute

---

[9] This is Barth's paraphrase of Berkouwer's *The Triumph of Grace in the Theology of Karl Barth*. Cf. Karl Barth, *Church Dogmatics, The Doctrine of Reconciliation* (Edinburgh: T&T Clark, 1976), Volume IV,3,1, pp. 172-180.

confidence. But he still called upon Him. It is thus a matter of confidence in this person, of His free act, of calling upon Him.[10]

When evangelical theology listens once again to the lesson Barth learned from Blumhardt, it will find itself connecting theology to prayer in an organic way, akin to J. B. Torrance's paraphrase of P. T. Forsyth: "Prayer is to the theologian what original research is to the scientist."[11] This is no theology of logical dominos. This is being true to the truth of the Word amongst us. This is calling upon and trusting this Name and none other.

Carl Henry: Guardian of Reason

For Carl Henry, as for his mentor, Gordon Clark, Christian faith must be rationally defensible in terms of the criteria by which all truth is verified. Otherwise, our truth claim reduces to existential and subjective experience. Henry is confident in his belief (his presupposition) that Aristotle's laws of non-contradiction are the test of all truth, including Christian revelation. Though divine revelation is the source of all truth, the truth of Christianity included, reason remains the instrument for recognizing it. Authority must be grounded in absolute certainty. The means of knowing certainty must be logically verifiable and rationally accessible to every one. Anderson concludes that Henry's approach leads to "orthodox doctrine rather than a compelling experience of God himself" as the basis of evangelical theology.[12]

What further shall we say in defence of Barth's scandalous refusal to grant Aristotle a veto on Christian truth claims? Certainly here is no scandal-making for its own sake or to thump an existentialist drum. Barth wonders how can that which is conceived by the Logos be illogical?[13] Yet can it be admissible for abstract philosophical principles to have the status of final judge of the truth of Christ? Is Aristotle's logic really the silver thread we must spin to heaven? Is not Jesus our connection to heaven-- God's logic (Logos) who descends to us and summons us to the rationality of discipleship? Surely the one (Logos) has priority over the other (logic). Thomas Torrance has demonstrated repeatedly how the case for scientific credibility can best be made when theology pursues its own axioms and methods in conformity to its own field and reality. This is a more rigorous

---

10 *Ibid.*, p. 176.
11 P. T. Forsyth, *The Soul of Prayer* (London: Epworth), p. 117.
12 "Evangelical Theology," p. 491.
13 Karl Barth, *Anselm: Fides Quaerens Intellectum* (Richmond, Virginia: John Knox Press, 1960) p. 22.

approach to rationality than seeking to defend theology before external criteria.[14]

Henry represents an ongoing tendency within various forms of evangelical theology to assume some kind of pre-understanding or philosophical *a priori* through which the Word of God must be sifted before it can articulate the Word meaningfully (rationally) to culture. However, the epistemological conviction which enables Barth to cast aside this dependency is his belief that the Word, despite all its vulnerability, is inherently articulate and not dependent on ancient or modern paradigms of plausibility to anchor this claim. Barth insists that the proper study of theology is God, the concrete, living Word, and not abstract propositions about God. This disparity between Henry's method--abstract, *a priori* principles of logic, and the object of his study--Jesus the Christ, the concrete, historical person, the Word made flesh, is stark. From Barth's perspective, Henry has simply deferred to abstract philosophical categories, allowing these to sit in judgement on God's truth made flesh. Despite its evangelical clothing, we have here the liberal tradition in a nutshell: to make human culture and its plausibility structures (ancient or modern) the final criteria which examine and judge the revelation of Christ. The temptation that follows is to tailor our witness to Christ in a manner which gives least offence to whatever the prevailing *zeitgeist* affirms.[15]

With equal clarity Barth saw the political disaster of deferring to non-biblical sources of validation. Perhaps he first learned his lesson when battling the "German Christian" movement. These accommodators sought to show how Christianity did not trespass against but truly fulfilled the Hitlerian renaissance of German culture: "The Swastika is a sign of sacrifice which lets the cross of Christ shine out for us in a new light."[16] It was only those like Barth and Bonhoeffer, deeply convinced that the truth of the gospel involves crucifixion as well as fulfilment, who would insist that the cross of Jesus is in fact the final criterion of truth. The cross is not simply a principle of sacrifice to partner with or translate into other symbols as if this guarantees the gospel's relevance, lest its advocates be found guilty of special pleading before the bar of modern reason. The point made at Barmen was one which Henry never grasped: "We reject the false doctrine that the Church could and should recognise as a source of its

---

[14] Cf. T. F. Torrance, *Theological Science* (Oxford: Oxford University Press, 1969) and *Divine and Contingent Order* (Oxford: Oxford University Press, 1981).
[15] Lesslie Newbigin has done much to expose the shared apologetic intention of both fundamentalism and liberalism to fit Christian faith into reigning "plausibility structures" current in the culture and thereby to establish the truthfulness of the Christian faith. Cf. Lesslie Newbigin, "Mission in a Pluralist Society," *A Word in Season*, (Grand Rapids: Eerdmans, 1994), p. 164.
[16] Quoted in Ebehard Jüngel, *Christ, Justice and Peace* (Edinburgh: T&T Clark, 1992) p. 23.

proclamation, beyond and besides this one Word of God, yet other events, powers, historic figures, and truths as God's revelation."[17]

Barth would, I believe, concur with Jüngel's assessment of Barmen that there can be "a more natural theology than so-called natural theology: a natural theology which knows Jesus Christ as the one who has reconciled both human beings and the world (2 Cor. 5:19)."[18] This is not to deny value to Aristotle's logic nor usefulness in the distinctive features of our culture that have instructed and formed us. Again, says Jüngel, the world has its own lights, it own glories. They are, after all, "refractions of the one light . . . the lights and truths of the *theatrum* of the *gloria dei.*"[19] However, no *a priori* standards and guides, no worldly principles which purport to transmit the meaning of the gospel to modern life, should be granted independent status for interpreting and screening the Word of God.

Let us stay with the political implications a moment longer. Was Carl Henry's conscience at all uneasy following World War II as he recited the addition "*under God*" in our pledge of allegiance or sat in American churches, gazing at the American flag standing tall at the front of our church sanctuaries? Was he not even a little reminded of Herod's posting of the Roman eagle at the entrance to the Temple in Jerusalem? What did (and does) it really mean to declare proudly, "In God we trust," on every penny we earn (or spend)? Is it not a highly ambiguous witness for the evangelical church to be the most visibly successful contextualizer of the gospel to American culture and simultaneously the tax-exempt chaplain to our nation? Who more obviously than the evangelical churches of our leafy suburbs has accommodated to "Christianity combined with self-indulgence"? In our adaptation to modern Western democracy, with our liberal market philosophy, where is the message of the cross, the summons not for self-fulfilment but for death to self, dying to the world and its principles which precede any resurrection? As we take pride in our global leadership have we any space to hear of a different kind of leadership based not on self-aggrandizement but on the cross, where Jesus empties himself of everything but love and carries the strategy of the Sermon on the Mount through to its final climax of sacrifice--even for his enemies? Will this ever fit the plausibility structures which our Western democracies find reasonable? Will not this call to discipleship always shake us to the core and ask us the fundamental questions about our deepest loyalty? An evangelical theology which has listened carefully to the church struggle against National Socialism will not be shy about asking Good Friday questions to the various capitalist nations, including those who pride themselves for being democratic and pluralist.

---

17 The Barmen Theological Declaration, quoted in Jüngel, p. xxiii.
18 Jüngel, pp. 26-27.
19 *Ibid.*, p. 29. Quoted from *Church Dogmatics, IV,3,1*, pp. 152-153.

There are other issues to address, if only briefly, in this context. Barth himself challenged the American church to discover a ringing affirmation of freedom cleansed of its Pelagian self-confidence. This reflects this same fundamental Gospel paradigm shift at work in Barth's method: to redefine our notions of freedom, even as we redefine the meaning of rationality, *in the light of the gospel*. Freedom from self-contradiction cannot be accepted as an *a priori* criterion to evaluate the gospel, for unless I am willing to lose my life, I shall not find it again. When Jesus declares that it is in dying that we live, it may seem to be a contradiction, until we encounter the logic of discipleship.

Here I shall be specific. At this late hour (specifically the aftermath of September 11, 2001), shall Western culture learn how to become peacemakers? Unless it does, it cannot discover the liberty of the children of God, nor become aware of the presence of the gospel seed growing secretly among us. In addressing America's "war on terrorism" Former U.S. Senator from Oregon, Mark Hatfield, reminded his audience that the biblical "shalom" is more than the absence of war, but has to do with a sense of well being and fulfilment. Such an "enfleshed" peace is more than spiritual, for it includes diet, health, a place to live, clean water, etc. What threatens peace? All that impedes this lack of fulfilment, including poverty, lack of health care, etc. In the world today, 500,000 children under fifteen are impressed into the military, 900,000 children in the Middle East will never have the opportunity for education. Deny these opportunities and you have the seeds of war. Maldistribution of opportunity leads to war. Hatfield asked, "Will America's current war on terrorism address these issues?"[20] I ask, "Will evangelicals throughout Western society raise such "Kingdom of God" questions or will Hatfield remain an eloquent but isolated voice?"

Helmut Thielicke: No Retreat

Anderson's final evangelical case study considers Helmut Thielicke and his division of modern theology into Cartesian and non-Cartesian camps. For Cartesian theology, the human person functions as the criterion to which the Word of God must be appropriated. So Schleiermacher and Bultmann both use the self-consciousness or the existing self as the criterion for revelation.[21] From our sketch of Carl Henry, we should not be surprised when Thielicke includes in this circle the conservative orthodox theologian for whom the objective truth of revelation is determined by the criterion of human rationality. Anderson surmises that these seeming opposites share

---

[20] Mark Hatfield, public lecture entitled "America's War on Terror," October 24, 2001. George Fox University. Newberg, Oregon.
[21] "Evangelical Theology," p. 488.

a hidden Cartesian method, for both seek to "appropriate the Word of God to the primacy of the human subject whether through an intuitive principle, an ethical principle, an existential principle, or a rational principle."[22]   Thielicke is confident that the Word of God does address and create a point of contact with humanity. Both here and in the very categories of Cartesian and non-Cartesian, one clearly sees the influence of Barth. However, there are two areas where Thielicke parts company from Barth. First, there is his rather muted affirmation of the virgin birth. Yes, the doctrine serves as a theological warning against any notion of adoptionism, as if Jesus somehow earns his way up the divine ladder through his exemplary God-consciousness. Like all adoptionist christologies, this subverts the gift of God into a human achievement, but Thielicke sees this doctrine as potentially contributing to a commonly docetic habit of distancing Jesus from our common humanity. It has no doubt contributed to the unhealthy use of Mary as our mediator to advocate on our behalf with her son. Barth, however, declines to see this teaching in such a problematic light. He insists instead that the sign of Christmas, like the empty tomb as the sign of the resurrection, should never be separated from the reality of God's redemptive coming among us.[23]

The mention of docetism anticipates Thielicke's most serious concern regarding Barth's theology, *including* the Barmen Declaration. Writing in his autobiography shortly before his death, Thielicke says that for all Barth's powers of theological formulation, Barth's "attention was fixed on issues whose only relevance was to the inner life of the church."[24]   Had Hitler impugned the Heidelberg catechism, then Barth and his followers would have "willingly allowed themselves to be burned at the stake," but the Nazi bosses had no interest in such internal church affairs. Among other exceptions, Thielicke acknowledges Bonhoeffer as one who early on realized that the church needed to offer resistance more broadly. Thielicke also readily acknowledges that from 1937 on, Barth made a "theological *volte-face.*"[25]

What shall we make of Thielicke's complaint against Barth?   In retrospect Barth himself was critical of his unwillingness to confront

---

22 *Ibid.* Cf. Anderson's earlier comment, Scripture without its transcendent authority in referring to the historical reality of God collapses into either an existentialist or a rationalist theology. Ray Anderson, *Historical Transcendence and the Reality of God* (Grand Rapids: Eerdmans, 1975), p. 270

23 Helmut Thielicke, *The Evangelical Faith* (Grand Rapids: Eerdmans, 1977), Volume 2, pp. 410-413. Cf. Karl Barth, *CD*, 1/2, p. 193.

24 Helmut Thielicke, *Notes from a Wayfarer, The Autobiography of Helmut Thielicke* (New York: Paragon House, 1995), p. 68.

25 *Ibid.*

National Socialism, particularly its racist brutality towards the Jews. He candidly admits the Church struggle

> confined itself to the Church's Confession, to the Church service, and to Church order as such. It was only a partial resistance. And for this it has been properly and improperly reproached: properly---in so far as a strong Christian Church, that is, a Church sure of its own cause in the face of National Socialism, should not have remained on the defensive and should not have fought on its own narrow front alone; improperly--in so far as on this admittedly all too narrow front a serious battle was waged, at least in part and not without some success.[26]

Elsewhere Barth explicitly confesses his greatest regret concerning Barmen: that he had not made the Jewish question "a decisive feature" of the text. "Of course, in 1934 no text in which I had done that would have been acceptable even to the Confessing Church, given the atmosphere that there was then. But that does not excuse me for not having at least gone through the motions of fighting."[27]

Thielicke accurately diagnosed in Barth a disinclination to commit the church to addressing the concerns of the world *theologically*. There was within Barth a reluctance to go beyond the critique-and-clarify task of theology to ensure that the preaching ministry of the church stay true to the content of the Word of God. To his credit, Barth does not excuse but confesses his hesitation. Did Bonhoeffer's own willingness to leap across this reluctance nudge Barth towards a more direct engagement with the social components of evangelical theology? Certainly the political engagement that Bonhoeffer (with fear and trembling) ventured upon has come to be seen as an essential development of the Barmen declaration, urging a more direct encounter with social and political reality.[28]

Anderson concludes his essay with both an affirmation and a challenge to evangelicals. He affirms evangelical theology for breaking free from the "theological tragedy of fudamentalism without capitulating to the theological fads of postliberal radicalism."[29] (Let us give Carl Henry credit for his contribution in this regard.) However, I believe Barth's initial hesitancy fully to engage the world at Barmen has for too long been echoed in evangelical theology as a whole, as if we have never seriously taken stock of Barth and Bonhoeffer's breakthrough. Anderson's measured

---

[26] Quoted in Arthur C. Cochrane, *The Church's Confession Under Hitler*, (Philadelphia: Westminster Press, 1962), pp. 40-41.
[27] Eberhard Busch, *Karl Barth* (London: SCM, 1975), p. 248.
[28] Cf. John W. DeGruchy, *Bonhoeffer and South Africa* (Grand Rapids: Eerdmans, 1984).
[29] "Evangelical Theology," p. 494.

words sum up our dilemma: "evangelical theology remains more concerned for the spiritual and intellectual aspects of salvation than for the social and physical needs of people."[30]

By the end of the tragic thirties, Barth definitely did not ignore the "social and physical needs of people." Yet sixty-five years after Barmen, the inclusion of issues surrounding social justice remains highly problematic for evangelicals. On the one hand (as Walls has pointed out), since the days of Wesley and Wilberforce, not to mention the desert fathers, evangelicals have been deeply concerned with issues of social holiness. But on the other hand, Western individualism combined with the private sector mentality has inclined evangelicals to find its niche most comfortably in a modern, suburbanized version of Luther's two kingdoms. Perhaps evangelicals have so domesticated ourselves therein, we find an incapacity or even a disloyalty in raising social issues. Dom Helder Camara, Roman Catholic Archbishop of Recife, used to say, "When I feed the poor, they call me a saint. When I ask why are they poor, they call me a communist." Evangelical theology has commonly failed to ask such questions, as if to ask them is either to be disloyal or to posit discredited Marxist solutions. What keeps us from raising these questions has to do with a certain comfort in restricting theology to one's private life only. Certainly there is a lack of hermeneutical consensus on how one applies a high view of Scripture to the everyday complexities of social and political reality. Indeed, given our real and genuine contemporary disagreements over specific issues of "social justice," we can be more sympathetic as to why no mention of the Jewish question or the Aryan paragraph ever appeared on Barmen's printed page. Nevertheless, in retrospect Barth was correct to insist that there was no excuse for not attempting. Evangelicals may never have a consensus on a proper social witness to the gospel, but if we are simply mute and fail to address major social issues, our witness hovers docetically disincarnate and deservingly lacks credibility.

If evangelicals have been reticent to explore the social and political realities of the gospel, we are not unique. After all, though Barth's decision to address the world directly had its roots in the inadequacy of Barmen's church-centric strategy, it had a much longer gestation than simply the launch of National Socialism. Prior to this he saw the gospel co-opted to defend the militarism of Kaiser Wilhelm, rendered socially irrelevant by Pietism's reduction of the life of faith to a privatized religious experience and even overly systematized by Ragaz's "religious socialism."[31] Only after experiencing multiple false paths, a full four years after Barmen's inadequate response, after the unprecedented military build up of Germany, after his personal deportation from Germany, then and only

---

30 *Ibid.*, pp. 494-495.
31 Busch, p. 78.

then did he decisively move to interpret matters of social justice within the defining context of justification by faith. In this way he made christology determinative for social as well as personal righteousness.³² For evangelicals Barth's decision to address social justice issues christologically, remains to be explored in a thoroughgoing way, but Barth has bequeathed us with a framework well worth further consideration. In the meantime, evangelicals have also been left to ponder the prophetic question posed by Lesslie Newbigin: "How often does today's evangelical preaching of Christ as Saviour distort the gospel? A preaching of the gospel that calls men and women to accept Jesus as Saviour but does not make it clear that discipleship means commitment to a vision of society radically different from that which controls our public life today must be condemned as false."³³ Newbigin touched another nerve when he asked whether evangelicals have far too often been seduced into "a mental separation between righteousness as an inward and spiritual state and justice as an outward and political program?"³⁴

Power and Poverty

The challenge before evangelical theology is to invigorate the church through the power of the vulnerable Word and not to worry overly much about fitting the good news into dominant paradigms of plausibility. I choose the adjective "vulnerable" to remind us that Christianity began its life on the public stage when Jesus in weakness and risk commandeered the cross as a symbol of power and transfigured it into the victory of God. He met this dominant symbol in the most vulnerable manner possible, accepting the consequences of its cultural authority fully, yet in such a way that did not simply defer to its predetermined meaning. Through the sheer impress of the Word's willing sacrifice, Jesus effected a transfiguration of symbolic meaning. The Roman cross would no longer represent Imperial dominance over the ancient world. The ancient British poem "The Dream of the Rood" evocatively depicts the new situation: "On me the Son of God suffered for a while; therefore now I tower glorious under the heavens, and I may heal every one of those that hold me in awe ... The Son was victorious in that foray, mighty and successful."³⁵

Is this not the heart of the evangelical vocation--to proclaim the triumph of the Son of God over all principalities and powers, to declare the Lordship of Jesus to the very foundations of culture through the message

---

32 Karl Barth, "Church and State" *(Rechfertigung und Recht,* 1938), in *Community, State and Church* (New York: Anchor, 1960) p. 101.
33 Lesslie Newbigin, *Foolishness to the Greeks* (Grand Rapids: Eerdmans, 1996), p. 132.
34 *Ibid.*
35 "The Dream of the Rood," *Norton Anthology of English Literature* (New York: W. W. Norton and Company, 1968), Volume 1, pp. 28-29.

of the vulnerable Word? Shall the church not bear such a risk-taking, vulnerable witness to a culture of power? This way of asking the question reflects the praxis perspective that Blumhardt taught Barth to incorporate into theological epistemology. In other words, one cannot simply sit back and observe culture wind its way down to the crasser expressions of practical atheism, self-indulgence, the punitive neglect of the least among us, and the identification of cultural strength with militarism. Blumhardt asked a question which Barth has since posed to us: "Is it a tolerable theological notion that 2,000 years ago the glory of God was proclaimed over the darkness by signs and wonders, while today patient resignation in the power of darkness is to be the last word?"[36]

Unless the church participates in "Christopraxis," the world cannot know or understand the nature of Christ's self-emptying embrace of the world. Earlier, Ray Anderson challenged evangelical theology to explore questions of praxis.

> Again, in practical terms, as well as in the most profoundly theological sense, the form of such an incarnational, evangelical existence in the world can best be expressed as *diakonia*, a transcendence of service. Thus more important than the *form* of the church in the world, is the *mode* of the church's existence in the world . . . *diakonia* is the gospel, for it is lived transcendence.[37]

As Jesus' culminating *diakonia* of the cross was enacted before the cultural powers of his own day, so faithful praxis will enact parables and announce today the moving of almighty God in a manner strange to our expected ways of authority and power. Here I wish to mention two forms of Christological praxis on behalf of the poor in our time. For over thirty years Jean Vanier has declared the good news of the vulnerable Word by sharing in weakness and community with the mentally handicapped and their helpers amidst a culture of achievement, status and success. In France and in communities planted throughout the world, Vanier has prayed, played and served with these poorest of the poor, bringing them into the very heart of a common life together in the gospel. Vanier simply reports, "I began l'Arche in 1964, in the desire to live the Gospel and to

---

36 Karl Barth, *Protestant Theology in the Nineteenth Century* (Valley Forge, Pa: Judson Press, 1976), p. 649.
37 Ray S. Anderson, *Historical Transcendence and the Reality of God*, p. 275. For Anderson's discussion of "Christopraxis," see "Christopraxis: The Ministry and the Humanity of Christ for the World," in *Christ in our Place: The Humanity of God in Christ for the Reconciliation of the World. Essays Presented to Professor James Torrance*, ed. T. Hart and D. Thimell (Exeter: Paternoster Press, 1989), pp. 11-31.

follow Jesus Christ more closely."38 Like all true parables, Vanier's way of pastoral praxis summons us to decision about whether we shall walk past on the other side of the poor or like the good Samaritan, stop and tend their wounds.

An evangelical praxis grounded in the vulnerable Word will lead us to an encounter with less subtle forms of poverty as well. N. T. Wright, the Anglican New Testament scholar, has brought before us the following challenge: just as the church has established baptism and communion as visible reminders of preparing the way of the Lord, so in the light of Jesus' own words, "forgive us our debts as we forgive our debtors," let our witness to the gospel include a clear summons, both symbolically and practically, to release the millions of desperately poor children, women and men throughout our world from their international debt. Wright is referring to the huge debts, often contracted under former military regimes purchasing large quantities of Western armaments, who have no legal means of declaring bankruptcy and starting over. This has left countries in Latin America inheriting indebtedness of $640 billion. Sub-Saharan Africa owes more than $216 billion to the world's richest nations and financial institutions. Interest payments alone on these loans makes basic health care and education beyond the remotest possibilities of these nations.39 For the nineteenth century American evangelist Charles Finney, the abolition of slavery became a defining expression of repentance and faith in the gospel. Today's systematic and massive financial transfer of resources from these vulnerable millions and their descendents has reached an urgency such that the evangelical church must decide whether or not Finney's call for abolition be translated to the present situation, which is hardly exaggerated when described as a peculiarly post-modern form of slavery. Are the cries of the world's poor a witness to the groaning of the Spirit, reminding our spirit that this world belongs to God? Where are the evangelical declarations on behalf of these enslaved peoples? If we are unsuccessful in changing the policies of Western financial institutions, will our generation be excused for not even "going through the motions of fighting" on their behalf?

Concluding Unnecessary Postscript

As a young seminarian, I eagerly sought out the most meaningful articulation of Christian theology that I could find. Through the encouragement of Ray Anderson and others, some financial aid and sacrifices, I found myself in Aberdeen, Scotland, studying the theological epistemologies of T. F. Torrance and C. S. Lewis, under the wise and caring

---

38 Jean Vanier, *Community and Growth* (London: Darton, Longman and Todd, 1984), p. 11.
39 N. T. Wright, *The Millennium Myth* (Louisville: Westminster/JK, 1999), p. 103.

supervision of James Torrance. The debt I owe them all in various ways, especially pastoral ways, is beyond words. However, twenty three years later, I am drawn to recall a Day of Prayer, in which our invited speaker Roland Walls (no stranger to Ray Anderson) glanced up from his lecture notes, gazed straight at James Torrance and with soft-spoken intensity declared, "Theology is not a science. It's an art!" Sitting in the back of the room, I smiled at what had, in the Aberdonian context, a paradoxically iconoclastic effect. I knew almost at once that Walls had shown me how to frame my fledgling dissertation, and ground it with some degree of conceptual legitimacy. I embraced Wall's declaration as permission to explore the many connections and differences between Torrance the theological scientist and Lewis the theological artist, without trying to falsely convert the one into the other or grant either priority. I saw more clearly the theological validity of Lewis's depictive achievement in enabling us to taste and see the truth of the gospel through his literary art-- and that this could indeed stand alongside the interpretive achievement of Torrance's theological science.

Yet over the intervening years I have come to see how essential it is to weave one more thread into theology's tapestry. Walls was quite right to insist that theology is an art, though perhaps it was a bit of bravado to simply dismiss the scientific thread. Theology is more than an art, more than art *and* science. *Theology is worship.* And as the ancient prophets reminded Israel, true worship entails authentic service (praxis). As theological aesthetics rescues theological science from arid intellectualism, theology as praxis keeps both aspects honestly grounded in a discipleship of the cross.

Reflecting on his native Belfast and contrasting it with his adopted Oxford, C. S. Lewis once mused that moralistic Puritanism is the memory Christianity takes in an industrial, commercial society even as theological aestheticism is the memory it takes just before it dies in a cultured, fashionable climate.[40] Hence the recent and exemplary initiatives of theology through the arts in America and in Britain must be both welcomed and warned. The story told about Thomas Aquinas' visit to the Vatican is worth recalling here. The Pope, much enjoying the opportunity to escort his great theologian through the Vatican's splendor, could not help but boast to Aquinas, "No longer can Peter say, "silver and gold have I none!" Aquinas replied, "Nor can Peter now say to the lame man, "in the name of Jesus of Nazareth, get up and walk." A theological aesthetics must again and again humble itself before the sacrificial service of the Son of God, and kneel at that place where beauty was crowned with thorns

---

[40] C. S. Lewis, *They Stand Together, The Letters of C. S. Lewis to Arthur Greeves (1914-1963)* (London: Collins, 1979), p. 433.

and crucified.[41] George Macleod, the founder of the Iona Community, pled with the church of his day not to indulge in any romantic betrayal of the gospel:

> I simply argue that the Cross be raised again at the centre of the market-place as well as on the steeple of the church. I am recovering the claim that Jesus was not crucified in a cathedral between two candles, but on a cross between two thieves; on a town garbage dump . . . Because that is where he died. And that is what He died about."[42]

Having come too slowly to this position many years later, I now see what I had glossed over before, and that is Ray Anderson's consistent witness to a praxis of what he calls "lived transcendence" as the fruit and fulfilment through the Spirit of the mission of the Son of God.[43] "More important than the *form* of the church in the world is the *mode* of the church's existence in the world . . . *diakonia* is the gospel, for it is lived transcendence."[44] With all its academic and ecclesiastical complexities, its increasing intellectual sophistication and aesthetic sensitivity--*and despite its lack of consensus on socio-political commitments*—this prayerful task remains for the evangelical community: to enfold the way of service to the poor into the heart of our *theological* witness to the gospel.

---

[41] Hans Urs Van Balthasar, *The Glory of the Lord, A Theological Aesthetic, Volume 1: Seeing the Form* (San Francisco: Ignatius Press, 1982), p. 69.
[42] George Macleod, *Only One Way Left* (Glasgow: Iona Community Press, 1956), p. 38.
[43] *Historical Transcendence and the Reality of God*, p. 275.
[44] *Ibid.*

Part Two

✼

On Being Christian and Becoming Human

Christian D. Kettler

"FOR I DO NOT DO THE GOOD I WANT ... AND I'M TIRED OF TRYING": WEAKNESS AND THE VICARIOUS HUMANITY OF CHRIST

One of Ray Anderson's most creative contributions to theology has been in the area of theological anthropology. I can well remember the spiritual and theological excitement I felt when I first read *On Being Human: Essays in Theological Anthropology* (1982).[1] From issues of abortion to homosexuality, Anderson was right to see that the study of theological anthropology would be a crying need in the years ahead as a remedy for the continual confusion that the church faces in these areas.

A later book of Anderson's, however, building and elaborating on his theological anthropology, has not received all the attention it deserves. *Self-Care: A Theology of Personal Empowerment and Spiritual Healing* (1995) develops the profound implications of a theological anthropology in terms of both a theology of emotions, often sadly neglected in traditional theology, and in addressing existential crises such as shame and abuse.[2] My own work in recent years in drawing out the implications of the vicarious humanity of Christ for existential crises has found rich resources in Anderson's pioneering work. Among these issues is the problem of weakness. Early in Ray's theological career, the British theologian D.M. Mackinnon paid tribute to the "nervous, restless quality" of Anderson's writing and the "breadth and depth of his theological culture" that "entices the reader to engage himself or herself with the issues with which he is concerned."[3] This essay is one modest attempt to pay tribute to a career of "nervous, restless" theology, from which this writer has greatly benefited.[4]

---

[1] Ray S. Anderson, On Being Human: Essays in Theological Anthropology (Grand Rapids: Eerdmans, 1982).
[2] Ray S. Anderson, Self-Care: A Theology of Personal Empowerment and Spiritual Healing (Wheaton, Il.: Bridgepoint, 1995).
[3] D.M. Mackinnon, foreword to Ray S. Anderson, Historical Transcendence and the Reality of God (Grand Rapids: Eerdmans, 1975), ix.
[4] I would like to thank Todd Speidell for careful criticism of an earlier version of this essay.

THE PROBLEM AND DENIAL OF WEAKNESS

Self-esteem is a popular topic. Why shouldn't it be? Who can deny our need for self-esteem? Few among us have not been battered down by the criticisms and demands of others and ourselves. If we could just affirm our self-worth, perhaps we can live healthy lives, not haunted by the grim specters of our failures and our inability to live up to expectations often impossible for us to fulfill.

But why am I so susceptible to the accusing finger that tells me that I have failed? Perhaps it is because I am too aware of my weakness. I see myself in Bernano's country priest, the very picture of ineptitude. I see myself even at times as Green's "whiskey priest" in *The Power and the Glory*, living a life of hypocrisy. I see myself as Kafka's "K.," a helpless victim of the external forces of life and fate, which I can neither understand nor control. I see myself as King Lear, a prideful, self-centered king who tries to evade responsibility but wants the power and the authority and the acclaim at the same time. Scripture itself testifies that "while we were still weak, at the right time Christ died for the ungodly" (Rom. 5:6). The disciples only represent all of us when they fail to heed Jesus' instructions to "stay awake" in Gethsemane (Mt. 26:41). They do not, and only prove Jesus' following comment, "The spirit indeed is willing but the flesh is weak." But this can only reaffirm to me what a miserable creature I am. The result is that I almost drown in my weakness. I become a weak, pitiful figure.

How can I still say that I am a Christian? How can I live with myself in all this weakness? How can I expect others to like, let alone love, me in my weakness? And how can God put up with such a pitiful ambassador?

My weakness may take many forms. Paul's admonition to the Thessalonians to "help the weak" is probably engendered by their weariness in waiting for the Second Coming (I Th. 5:14; 4:13-18).[5] The physical existence itself is an obvious source of basic human weakness. Paul makes the point to the Corinthians that, even though there will be a resurrected body, first the body "is sown in weakness" and "dishonor" (I Cor. 15:43). Paul's "weakness of the flesh" (literally, Gal. 4:13) is probably not his emotional frailties but a "physical infirmity" (so NRSV).[6]

Such frailty is not simply physical. The physical and the emotional join hand in hand. The felt omnipotence of the newborn infant and its need for self-fulfillment is soon frustrated, as Ray Anderson points out.[7] The resulting sense of powerlessness may create antisocial behavior leading to

---

5 David Alan Black, *Paul, Apostle of Weakness: Astheneia and Its Cognates in the Pauline Literature* (New York: Peter Lang, 1984), p. 46.
6 Ibid., p. 73.
7 Anderson, *Self-Care*, pp. 101-102.

violence. Powerlessness cannot accept the dictates of delayed gratification, as it interprets the lack of self-gratification as the lack of self-fulfillment.[8] Our infantile sense of weakness breeds violence, a violence bred by negative self-esteem. With such a negative self-esteem, Anderson contends, there is no place to accept responsibility for being guilty of sin in a healthy way.[9]

Such an existence of weakness is found in the early moments of separation from the womb, a time that cries for immediate attachment, as contemporary "attachment theory" has shown.[10] With a "snip of the scissors, the human infant is set adrift both physically and emotionally on the ocean of humanity."[11]

As we progress through life, our weakness is expressed in a bittersweet way in relationships with others, some joyous, others bearing the fruit of betrayal. In such a moment of betrayal by a loved one, Anderson comments, "one has become vulnerable to all."[12] Because I have "let down my guard," I have shown to others as well that I can be hurt. I am weak.

But how easily I can deny my weakness! There may be good reasons to deny some traditional ideas of "Christian weakness." I surely should deny, with Bonhoeffer, the kind of Christianity that is based on making people weak, groveling in their sin, so that then the gospel can be offered to them as a solution.[13] "Religion" was a problem not a solution for Bonhoeffer and Barth. Religious people bring in God when their resources fail. This "God of the gaps" exploits the weaknesses of people but is thereby marginalized, since he is always on the boundaries, not at the center, of human existence.

Christian views of atonement readily speak of the vicarious *death* of Christ, and rightly so. In recent years, however, Thomas F. Torrance, James B. Torrance, and others have spoken of the importance of not just limiting the vicarious work of Christ to his death. No, from baptism to resurrection Christ lived a life for us in the entirety of our humanity. His vicarious work is a *vicarious humanity* lived for us and in our place, judging our attempts at religiosity and embracing us with a breadth and depth of love at the ontological level.[14] In this case, there is no "God of the gaps," but a God in the depths of our humanity, judging and affirming.

---

8 Ibid., p. 105.
9 Ibid., p. 114.
10 Ibid., p. 173.
11 Ibid.
12 Ibid., p. 177.
13 Dietrich Bonhoeffer, *Letters and Papers from Prison*, ed. Eberhard Bethge (New York: Macmillan, 1972), pp. 281-282.
14 The most important writings on the vicarious humanity of Christ are found in T.F. Torrance, *The Mediation of Christ*, revised edition (Colorado Springs: Helmers and Howard,

Certainly the reality of the vicarious humanity of Christ speaks of God displacing us in our religious "place," in order to meet us in the richness of our real existence. We may like to wallow in death and guilt, but even then Christ intervenes. Bonhoeffer's "religiousless Christianity" is an apt metaphor for the action of the vicarious humanity of Christ.

Bonhoeffer, however, can speak in another way of a genuine weakness in God. His poem, "Christians and Pagans" is a poignant testimony that the power of God is not necessarily found simply in God's availability to humanity:[15]

> Men go to God when they are sore bestead,
> Pray to him for succour, for his peace, for bread,
> For mercy, for them sick, sinning, or dead.
> All men do so, Christian and unbelieving.

Interestingly, it is "all men" that "go to God" in their distress in some way, Bonhoeffer claims, whether or not they are Christians. This is not what is distinct about Christianity.

What is distinctive is in the next stanza, where:

> Men go to God when he is sore bestead,
> Find him poor and scorned, without shelter or bread,
> Whelmed under weight of the wicked, the weak, the dead.
> Christians stand by God in his hour of grieving.

Here we have a suggestion of a "weakness" in God! God's weakness is seen in humanity going to God in his need. Why is he needy? Because of us, because of *our* weakness. God has become weak for our sake. This is not just a vicarious death, but also the entirety of the vicarious *humanity* of Christ. We are curiously invited to "stand by God in his hour of grieving." As the disciples were invited by Jesus to "stay awake with me" in

---

1992); "The Word of God and the Response of Man," in *God and Rationality* (Oxford: Oxford University Press, 1971), pp. 133-164; and James B. Torrance, "The Vicarious Humanity of Christ," in T.F. Torrance, ed., *The Incarnation: Ecumenical Studies in the Nicene-Constantinoplitan Creed* (Edinburgh: The Handsel Press, 1981), pp. 127-147. The implications of the vicarious humanity of Christ for contemporary views of salvation are discussed in Christian D. Kettler, *The Vicarious Humanity of Christ and the Reality of Salvation* (Lanham, MD: University Press of America, 1991). Elmer M. Colyer provides a helpful survey of the vicarious humanity of Christ in T.F. Torrance's thought in *How to Read T.F. Torrance: Understanding His Trinitarian and Scientific Theology* (Downers Grove, Il.: InterVarsity Press, 2001), pp. 97-126. Cf. Andrew Purves, "The Christology of Thomas F. Torrance" in *The Promise of Trinitarian Theology: Theologians in Dialogue with T.F. Torrance*, ed. Elmer M. Colyer (Lanham, Md.: Rowman and Littlefield, 2001), pp. 51-80.
15 Ibid., pp. 348-349.

Gethsemane (Mt. 26:38), so are we invited to participate in God's "grieving."

The poem is not at an end, however, because this weakness is the weakness of the cross:

> God goes to every man when sore bestead,
> Feeds body and spirit with his bread;
> For Christians, pagans alike he hangs dead,
> And both alike forgiving.

"He hangs dead" for both the Christians and the pagans. Our weakness, our going to him in our need, has been transformed in a wondrous way by the cross. He has shared the humanity of all, Christians and pagans alike, in order to take their place in the totality of their lives, *even in their weakness*.

God does not want us to start from our strength, to affirm robustly that we are made in the image of God and redeemed by the blood of the Lamb, by the cross of Christ. The weakness of God is an indictment of our unwillingness to admit our weakness.

Are we that willing, however, to be aware of our own weakness? Pascal stops us in our tracks:

> What amazes me most is to see that everyone is not amazed at his own weakness. We behave seriously, and everyone follows his calling, not because it is really a good thing to do so, in accordance with fashion, but as if everyone knew for certain where reason and justice lie.[16]

Pascal is amazed by something. It must have been quite a feat to amaze Pascal, given his scientific genius. What is he amazed at? He is amazed at human beings, human beings that are not amazed at their own weakness, their inability, their frailty, and their finitude. Tracy, Katharine Hepburn's character in the classic film "The Philadelphia Story," is an attractive, intelligent Philadelphia socialite who discovers on the eve of her second marriage her own pronounced character flaw: She cannot stand weakness in others. Her inability to love others for who they are is ironically her own weakness.

In the modern world, our ideas of "weakness" can easily become an excuse to avoid moral responsibility. The Hall of Fame baseball slugger Reggie Jackson quickly comes to the defense of Daryl Strawberry after one of Strawberry's many lapses back into drugs. "I used to think he was weak," Jackson concludes, "but now I know that it is a disease." Even if

---

16 Blaise Pascal, *Pensées*, trans. A.J. Krailsheimer (New York: Penguin, 1966), p. 37.

drugs and other kinds of addictions are diseases, how quickly do we moderns rush to deny any extent of moral responsibility that we are weak, especially in a moral sense.

We seriously live our lives presuming to know "reason and justice" (Is this the arrogance of Aristotle?). We very easily deny our weakness. How ironic, for it stares us in the face every day. As each day passes, I age; I gain one more fleck of grey hair . . . one more step into the grave. In the meantime, I stand puzzled about my humanity. In Pope's famous words,

> Know then thyself, presume not God to scan
> The proper study of manhood is man.
> Plac'd on this isthmus of a middle state.
> A being darkly wise, and rudely great;
> With too much knowledge for the sceptic side,
> With too much *weakness* for the stoic's pride,
> He hangs between: in doubt to act of rest,
> In doubt to deem himself a god, or beast;
> In doubt his mind or body to prefer;
> Born but to die; and reas'ning but to err;
> Alike in ignorance, his reason such,
> Whether he thinks too little or too much.[17]

I am puzzled by myself. I have too much knowledge, so the agnostic's cynicism is not possible. But I also have too much weakness, so that I cannot possess the stoic pride of a Zeno. Even the law of God, according to Paul, can become a part of "the weak and beggarly spirits" (Gal. 4:9) when it holds one captive to frustration and powerlessness (Rom. 7:23).[18]

I begin by denying my weakness. I proceed to a collapse of that "character armor" (Ernest Becker) and I react. I become resigned to my weakness. I become fatalistic. I realize that I am but like the remains of Alexander the Great, the one who once conquered the known world died and became a part of the earth, the earth that now is a part of a sod house *(Hamlet)*. Hardly an honorable fate for a world conqueror, let alone any person! In our weakness, we live lives full of "the sound and the fury," and after all is said and done, they signify "nothing."

What do I hear? Who do I feel? I feel blood and flesh, the blood and flesh of Someone like me, but also unlike me.

> The dripping blood our only drink,
> The bloody flesh our only food:

---

17 Alexander Pope, *An Essay on Man,* Ep. Ii (1733) 1.1, cited by *The Oxford Dictionary of Quotations,* third edition (New York: Oxford University Press, 1980), p. 379 (emphasis mine).
18 Black, p. 81.

In spite of what we like to think
That we are sound, substantial flesh and blood--
Again, in spite of that, we call this Friday good.[19]

We thought we were sound once. Certainly that is the lie of youth. Middle age shows the grey and the girth all too well. "In spite of what we like to think that we are sound . . ." It is the lie of religion as well, of having "sound doctrine." Yet in spite of that, there is the flesh of Good Friday that stands before us, dripping, bloody. This bloody flesh is weakness, too. Does it have anything to do with our all too temporal flesh?

THE *VIA NEGATIVA* OF WEAKNESS

"The acknowledgement of our weakness is the first step towards repairing our loss," said Thomas à Kempis.[20] I should not lie to myself. I may not be a tremendous success; there may be serious character flaws in my life. I may act like a jerk towards others. But this does not deny the importance of encouraging my self-worth. Acknowledging my weakness may paradoxically be one of the best foundations for developing my self-worth. To lie about my accomplishments may give me a "placebo" of self-worth, but lies eventually catch up with us. There must be a better foundation for self-worth. Can it come from acknowledgement of our weakness? T.S. Eliot is helpful again:

> In order to arrive there,
> To arrive where you are, to get from where you are not
> You must go by a way *wherein there is no ecstasy.*
> In order to arrive at what you do not know
> You must go by a way which is *the way of ignorance.*
> In order to possess what you do not possess
> You must go by *the way of dispossession.*
> In order to arrive at what you are not
> You must go through the way in which you are not.
> And what you do not know is the only thing you know
> And what you own is what you do not own
> And where you are is where you are not.[21]

---

[19] T.S. Eliot, "East Coker," *Four Quartets,* IV (New York: Harcourt, Brace and World, 1943), p. 16.
[20] Thomas à Kempis, cited by Tony Castle, *The New Book of Christian Quotations* (New York: Crossroad, 1982), p. 252.
[21] Eliot, "East Coker," *Four Quartets,* III, p. 15 (emphasis mine).

Weakness and the Vicarious Humanity of Christ

I do not want to go without "ecstasy" or live in "ignorance" or "dispossession." Eliot says I must. Weakness is a kind of *via negativa*. This may be a very personal, potentially embarrassing weakness.

> But he said to me, 'My grace is sufficient for you, for power is made perfect in weakness.' So, I will boast all the more gladly of my weaknesses, so that the power of Christ may dwell in me, . . . for when I am weak, then I am strong. (II Cor. 12:9-10)

This is the strength of the "weak" whom God has chosen in order to put the "strong" to shame (I Cor. 1:27).

I must stop at this point, though. This acknowledgement of weakness can so easily remain empty moral exhortation. It can easily degenerate into a demoralizing, dehumanizing self-hatred. "When I am weak, then I am strong." Paul did not say this apart from his consciousness of the vicarious humanity of Christ. The vicarious humanity of Christ does not just present an ideal or pristine humanity, as many immediately believe when they think of the significance of the humanity of Christ. The New Testament witness often declares the sinlessness of Christ (II Cor. 5:21; I Pet. 2:22; 3:18; I Jn. 3:5; Heb. 4:15; 7:26).[22] But this sinlessness is not a reality apart from his sympathy with our weaknesses: "For we do not have a high priest who is unable to sympathize with our *weaknesses*, but we have one who in every respect has been tested as we are *yet without sin*" (Heb. 4:15). As Ray Anderson comments, "When we begin with a view of the self as intended by God to be free of pain and impervious to loss, we end up with a caricature of both God and human beings."[23] Who is it that God loves? Only the potential me, once I have been "cleaned up" by Christ, once I have been made presentable? No, it is the present me, warts and all. That is why Anderson rightly objects to the cliché, "We must love the sinner, but hate the sin." He remarks,

> I wonder if people who say that have any idea of how destructive and downright ungracious that concept is. Whatever my sins and failures may be, that is who I am! You cannot love me without accepting the whole of me, painful and threatening as that may be.[24]

---

[22] G.C. Berkouwer, "The Sinlessness of Christ" in *The Person of Christ*, trans. John Vriend (Grand Rapids: Eerdmans, 1954), pp. 239-271.
[23] Anderson, *Self-Care*, p. 209.
[24] Ibid., p. 218.

"Unconditional acceptance" does not simply entail a moral imperative to get over one's problems, but solidarity with the sinner. This is the legitimate *via negativa* of weakness: "For while we were still *weak* . . . Christ died for the ungodly" (Rom. 5:6). The vicarious humanity of Christ displaces our ideas of our own pristine human perfection, which we demand of ourselves in order for God to love us.

Does such a view of weakness, however, create a *necessity* for weakness, as often some view evil and suffering as a way to achieve "the greatest good"? This is common in both lay and traditional theology.[25] Was the cross really a "necessity" for God, as is commonly believed?

"God lets himself be pushed out of the world onto the cross. He is weak and powerless in the world, and that is precisely the way, the only way, in which he is with us and helps us" (Mt. 8:17).[26] So says Dietrich Bonhoeffer from one of his most famous letters from prison. Bonhoeffer is saying something significant about God and the cross. As Anderson observes, beginning with a self free of pain and weakness is not just a caricature of human beings but also of God. Our "caricature" of God may include a God who cannot suffer, but as such is only the traditional "working hypothesis of God" which Bonhoeffer suggests that the modern world has rightly discarded. The cross then is not a "necessity" for God, in order to achieve the greatest good or for God to be reconciled to us, but instead is a demonstration of the power of God exhibited in his weakness. Indeed, is this not a greater power than sheer force, a power that is able to become weak? This is "the only way" that God helps us, according to Bonhoeffer, citing Mt. 8:17's quotation of Isa. 53:4: "He took our infirmities and bore our diseases." In Bonhoeffer's famous words, "Only the suffering God can help."[27] This is the difference between the Bible and other religions, Bonhoeffer claims. The God of the Bible is not simply the *Deus ex machina* that humanity yearns for because they have reached the end of their rope. The cross turns those aspirations of religions on their heads. There is a power here in the suffering of God. God's weakness is not the surrender of the Son to the helplessness of the Father, as Dorothee Sölle believes,[28] but it is a power we do not expect. Christ "was crucified in weakness, but lives by the power of God" (II Cor. 13:3-4). What is "sown in

---

25 See Norman L. Geisler, *Philosophy of Religion* (Grand Rapids: Zondervan, 1974), p. 376, and the self-styled Irenaean theodicy of John Hick in *Evil and the God of Love*, revised edition (San Francisco: Harper and Row, 1977). The recent essay by Ray Anderson, "Did Jesus Have To Die On the Cross?" provides a penetrating critique of the atonement as a necessary "work" of Christ, a cross without a resurrection. Ray S. Anderson, *Dancing With Wolves While Feeding the Sheep* (Pasadena: Fuller Seminary Press, 2001), pp. 69-78.
26 Bonhoeffer, *Letters and Papers from Prison*, p. 360.
27 Ibid., p. 361.
28 Dorothee Sölle, *Christ the Representative, an Essay in Theology After the 'Death of God,'* trans. D. Lewis (London: SCM Press, 1967), p. 150; cited by Paul Fiddes, *The Creative Suffering of God* (Oxford: Clarendon Press, 1988), p. 2.

weakness ... is raised in power" (I Cor. 15:43). The "weakness" of the faith of the Palestinian Jew Jesus, the historical figure subject to the shifting sands of historical contingency and skepticism, is nonetheless raised in power. That God provides the "religious" response in the faith and obedience of the Son is even more surprising and threatening.

Paul appeals "three times" to the Lord for the "thorn in flesh" to be removed. He did not want it.[29] But because it remains, he was able to hear from the Lord, "My grace is sufficient for you, for power is made perfect in weakness" (II Cor. 12:8-10). Acknowledging the grace of God in the midst of his weakness enables Paul to be "content with weaknesses, insults, hardships, persecutions, and calamities for the sake of Christ; for whenever I am weak, then I am strong." The "grace" sufficient for Paul is a grace of God coming into our existence in weakness, in order to be sufficient for us.

Acknowledging the *via negativa* of weakness is no compulsion upon God but similar to Socrates' teaching that the first step in knowledge is to realize that you do not know. Recognizing our weakness is such a step. There is no necessity here, but freedom, the freedom of God, the freedom of God to love, and for us to recognize that love.

What remains is the question: *How* does God's weakness help us? One answer may be found in the reality of God himself in Christ having faith for us and in our place, the vicarious humanity of Christ.

WEAKNESS: THE INABILITY TO BELIEVE

Self-Denial: Ours and Christ's

Acknowledging our weakness, as Thomas à Kempis says, can be the first step towards our restoration. But this is not the same as viewing ourselves as worthless. The vicarious humanity of Christ will not permit that. Commonly, our understanding of the process of salvation is to first feel miserable about oneself as a sinner before God and to be a failure in life and then find the grace of Christ as the solution to the problem. Experientially, that is true for many people. The vicarious humanity of Christ, however, interrupts a theology based on that experience. For such an experiential theology, as sensitive as it is to how the gospel meets human needs, can easily reinforce our sinful existence. The substitutionary atonement is not an act of Christ having to take our place because we are worthless. As Lewis Smedes puts it, we do not deserve salvation, but the

---

[29] *Contra* Black on II Cor. 12:9b: "So I will boast all the more gladly of my weaknesses, so that the power of Christ may dwell in me." Black concludes, "Therefore, rather than pray for the removal of his infirmities, Paul glories in those things which reveal his weakness and utter dependence upon God" (p. 156). If so, why would Paul pray "three times" for the "thorn" to be removed?

very fact of God's love in Christ means that we are *worthy* of salvation.[30] The longing for self-fulfillment, pleasure, and the consequent powerlessness we feel is not evil, as Ray Anderson reminds us.[31] Our desperate attempts to find that fulfillment in terms of self-gratification, particularly in the exploitation of others, are the evil. Original sin is our distorted sense of omnipotence, as bizarre as that sounds. If God has taken our place in Jesus Christ, then I do not speak the first word of my weakness. Jesus Christ and his grace speak it. As Torrance suggests, the vicarious humanity of Christ is a judgment upon our attempts to ground spirituality in either nature (Roman Catholicism) or our subjective, individual piety (Protestantism).[32] Even our weakness is not a connection to God that we can savor and nurture, to the point that God is always the answer to our need! Paul can say both "I can do all things through him who strengthens me" (Phil. 4:13) and admit his weakness ("For I do not do the good I want, but the evil I do not want is what I do" [Rom. 7:19]). He had hope in his "deeper identity," in the one who "will rescue me from this body of death" (Rom. 7:24).[33] The vicarious humanity of Christ meets our needs, but also reveals both needs we never thought we had as well as our "deeper identity."

"Self-denial" is a common category in spirituality, Christian or otherwise. Calvin calls self-denial "the sum of the Christian life."[34] Self-denial, however, is radically redefined by the vicarious humanity of Christ. Christ is the One who has already *denied himself* before the Father ("yet not what I want but what you want" [Mt. 26:39]). It is not left up to us to deny ourselves in order to reach God. If Christ has taken our place and represented us to the Father, how could we think that our attempts at self-denial would be meaningful? How would we even know what denial means? Yes, Paul can say "God chose what is low and despised in the world, things that are not, to reduce to nothing things that are" (I Cor. 1:28), but the purpose of this choice is "so that no one might boast in the presence of God" (I Cor. 29). Not even weakness, emotional, physical, spiritual, or economic, should be praised.[35] The rug has been pulled out from under us by the vicarious humanity of Christ. Christ calls me to deny

---

30 Lewis B. Smedes, *Shame and Grace: Healing the Shame We Don't Deserve* (San Francisco: Harper San Francisco/Zondervan), pp. 119f. Cf. Anderson, *Self-Care*, p. 161.
31 Anderson, *Self-Care*, pp. 100-102.
32 T.F. Torrance, *Theology in Reconstruction* (Grand Rapids: Eerdmans, 1965), p. 134.
33 Mark R. McMinn and Gordon N. McMinn, "Complete Yet Inadequate: The Role of Learned Helplessness and Self-Attribution from the Writings of Paul," *Journal of Psychology and Theology* 11, (Winter, 1983), pp. 304, 307.
34 John Calvin, *Institutes of the Christian Religion*, edited by J.T. McNeill, translated and indexed by F.L. Battles (Philadelphia: Westminster Press, 1960), 2 vols., Library of Christian Classics 20 and 21, III.7.
35 Black, pp. 99-100.

myself, but only because Christ has already denied himself for me. The burden is not on my ability to deny myself! What a tortuous experience the Christian life can be otherwise! "To learn what is new we have to learn how to forget," Torrance says, "to take a step forward in discovery we have to renounce ourselves."[36] Torrance hastens to add, however, that such a radical self-renunciation is only possible in Jesus Christ, "by making us share in His life and what He has done with our human nature in Himself."[37] Thus, the life of prayer is not a mark of the *homo religiosus*, the neurotic religious person obsessed with his self-righteousness who thinks that he can coerce his way to God, gain God's approval, and proudly display his spirituality publicly (Mt. 6:5,6). The prayers of Jesus were not an affirmation of the spiritual ego but a renunciation of the ego, the highest expression of trust in the Father.[38] Prayer is a kind of letting go, a release from our egos and our agendas. Prayer is admitting our weakness.

The Immobility of Failure and the Faith of Christ
Weakness is most deeply felt in failure. Whether it is moral failure, relational failure, or spiritual failure, weakness often results in failure. How can we cope with failure? Rarely do discussions of sanctification and spirituality involve a place for failure. The most terrible implication of failure is not the act of failure itself, but the results of that failure in the life of the person who failed, the legacy of betrayal, incompetence, and the lack of will power. How crushing is the loss of esteem in the eyes of friends, the public, and even in the destruction of our own ideals.

Jacob and Rachel have been crucial to the life of Mt. Zion Church.[39] Jacob has been a key part of the leadership team whose music has also contributed much to the worship team. His wife, Rachel, has provided leadership in Christian education. But Jacob has recently resigned from his position of leadership at the church. Jacob has just turned forty and seems to have hit the classic mid-life crisis. For years a smoldering resentment has developed against Rachel. A few years ago, an opportunity to advance to a more prestigious university was halted by Rachel's refusal to move. For Rachel, the recent years of the abortion debate have rekindled guilt about the abortion which preceded her marriage to Jacob. Jacob has now entered into a relationship with a young co-worker. Nothing physical has been done yet, but he has moved out of the house.

How can Jacob deal with such an obvious moral failure? Torrance says of the vicarious humanity of Christ,

---

[36] T.F. Torrance, *God and Rationality* (New York: Oxford University Press, 1971), p. 54.
[37] Ibid.
[38] John McLeod Campbell, *The Nature of the Atonement* (Grand Rapids: Eerdmans, 1996), p. 176.
[39] This case study was provided by an anonymous graduate student in ministry at Friends University.

> He believed for us, was faithful for us,
> and remains faithful even when we fail
> Him, again and again . . .[40]

But isn't this a recipe for antinomianism? Jacob has failed his wife. Jacob has failed the church. Jacob has failed God. Even if this crisis passes, what is to keep him from finding another "sweet young thing"? And are we so far from Jacob? Don't all of us have those failures that we try to hide in our closets?

If Christ believes for us, however, if he remains faithful for us, in his vicarious humanity, does failure really have the last word? From a secular perspective, we are what our choices make us to be. We choose to be a physician or a cab driver. We choose to go to Harvard or Slippery Rock University. We choose to go to a gay bar or to a church picnic. The world will say to us, "You have your freedom, now live with your choices." In some sense, God says the same thing. Adam and Eve had their choices, and they had to live with the consequences.

Adam, however, is not the last word about humanity. The Last Adam is (I Cor. 15:48). Yes, Jacob can be morally exhorted. The result is that he is thrown back upon his own moral ability. But the mid-life crisis is too strong. The sense of failure at mid-life can only haunt Jacob.

Christ, however, has believed for us. How can Jacob believe anymore? Christ has entered into a human existence filled with centuries of failure, our fallen human nature. That is the depth of his love. "What then are we to say? Should we continue in sin in order that grace may about?" (Rom 6:1). No, Paul responds. We have died and risen with Christ. He has taken our place. He stands before us, still believing, still trusting the Father, still possessing faith. Christ the believer, not just moral exhortation, is what will move Jacob to a repentance which penetrates to his ontological core, to the deepest recesses of his being. Even the law of God, Paul says, "weakened by the flesh" (Rom. 8:3), simply reveals our moral incapacity.[41] Christ's perfect obedience is always before us, becoming a constant reminder and prod to become conformed to him, to be "perfect, as your heavenly Father is perfect" (Mt. 5:48). Christ has already been faithful. He has not failed.

Therefore, our faithlessness, our failure, our weakness has been relativized. No longer does our faithlessness, our failure, our weakness

---

[40] T.F. Torrance, *Conflict and Agreement in the Church*, Vol. 2 (London: Lutterworth Press, 1959-60), pp. 81-82
[41] H.-G. Link, "Weakness," in *The New International Dictionary of New Testament Theology*, ed. Colin Brown, Vol. 3 (Grand Rapids: Zondervan, 1978), p. 995.

determine our present or future. The substitutionary work of Christ, the "wonderful exchange," includes not just the past, dying for our sins in the past, but also the present and the future as well. Jacob's failure in one sense is more terrible than he or the church believes. It is a sin against Christ, his suffering for Jacob's sake. But it is only terrible because the more glorious reality is of the one who believes and is faithful to us, incredibly, even when we are unfaithful to him.

How can Jacob's faith be restored, then? How can it be rescued, in spite of this failure? Is there a place for Jacob's faith if Christ has believed for him?

Christ's faith not only replaces the reality of Jacob's failure, but also *replaces his faith*! This is hard for us to accept. We want to hang onto our faith! Is there any place for individual responsibility then? But Jacob's failure has been replaced by the faith of Jesus. There is the loss of "the ground to do evil" when one looks at Jesus Christ, as Barth says.[42] There is an actual ontological replacement in Jacob's life because of the life of Christ. This is genuine conversion.

So Jacob's faith, too, is moved out so that he may truly believe! There is a place for Jacob to have faith, but only if it is faith devoid of any ground to stand on by itself.[43] When Jesus says, "This is my body," this has a power that does not need faith in order to give it meaning. Genuine faith can only confess the truth of Christ.[44] And this is no purely intellectualistic confession. This confession is a passionate confession, a passion that has yet to be fulfilled.[45] This passion cannot be quenched, no matter what spiritual disciplines we may fail to do, for this passion respects the faith of Christ, the one whose faith really matters. Ministry to Jacob should involve acknowledging his passion, the passion that became misdirected but should not be ignored. This is what Jesus did with the woman at the well (Jn. 4:11-26), according to Anderson.[46] "What others may have seen as promiscuous sexual passion, Jesus diagnosed as an unfulfilled thirst for a love that gave back as much as it took." So, her cry, "Sir, give me this water, so that I may never be thirsty" (Jn. 4:15) was a response to Jesus' sensitivity at the level of the physical (water, v. 7), ethnic (as a Samaritan, v. 9), and the relational (her "husbands," v. 18). He did not simply offer a pardon for sin without addressing "the restoration of the

---

[42] Karl Barth, *Church Dogmatics,* T. F. Torrance and Geoffrey W. Bromiley, eds. (Edinburgh: T. & T. Clark, 1936-1968), IV/1, p. 281.
[43] Ibid., p. 243.
[44] Ibid., p. 245.
[45] Karl Barth, *The Christian Life,* trans. Geoffrey W. Bromiley (Grand Rapids: Eerdmans, 1981), p. 111.
[46] Anderson, *Self-Care,* p. 47.

self," as Anderson puts it.[47] To do otherwise is to be guilty of religious malpractice!

Jacob's faith is "moved out" by the vicarious humanity of Christ. But it is only moved out *in order to be restored*. That is why the faith of Christ is vicarious, not just exemplary. Jesus lived a life of utter faith in and obedience to the Father, ministering in his name, teaching and healing. His healings were for the sake of empowering human beings to be truly human.[48] So when Jesus, having been touched by the sick woman, became aware that "power had gone forth from him," he commends the woman for her faith (Mk. 4:25-34). The vicarious faith of Jesus did not exist for himself, but for us, for our sake, in a vicarious sense, so that we too might participate in the quality of his relationship with the Father through the Spirit. This is the kind of faith which is passionate, which acknowledges the passions within us, like Jacob's, and seeks to redirect them to the Father's will. Why is it that we refuse to ascribe passion to faith? "Love, after all," Kierkegaard cries, "has its priests in the poets . . . but not a word is heard about faith. Who speaks to the honor of this passion?"[49]

I may wrong in large parts of my theology! I may suffer from theological weakness! Even Paul, however, said, "I am not aware of anything against myself, but I am not thereby acquitted. It is the Lord who judges me" (I Cor. 4:4). My faith and my hope in time of weakness and failure are in the faith of Christ. This is faith as a "new act each day and hour" because it is in constant dependence on the grace of God.[50] Grace becomes not the excuse for easy believism but rather the constant nourishment of faith, because it is the gift of *Christ's own faith* that sustains and restores us.

Our failures and weaknesses are so devastating that just the power to overcome them is not enough. Viewing the Christian life as simply empowered by the Holy Spirit is not sufficient. The Spirit indeed "helps us in our weakness" (Rom. 8:26-27). This is "the Spirit of Christ" (Rom. 8:9), the Spirit who enables us to participate in the life of Jesus. Christ does not simply enable us to respond. No, he acts on our behalf and in our place when our weakness is so great that we are unable to respond at all! Jacob's failure, therefore, should not be either rationalized or judged. It should be replaced ontologically by the faith of Christ.

The popular devotional story "Footprints" tells of a person looking back upon her life as footprints left in the sand. There are usually two sets of footprints, hers and the Lord's. But during her darkest days, there

---

47 Ibid., p. 9.
48 Ibid., p. 199.
49 Søren Kierkegaard, *Fear and Trembling/Repetition*, ed. & trans. H. V. & E. H. Hong (Princeton: Princeton Univ. Press, 1983), p. 62. Cf. Jack Rogers and Forrest Baird, *Introduction to Philosophy: A Case Study Approach* (San Francisco: Harper and Row, 1981), p. 32.
50 Ibid., p. 78.

would be only one set of footprints. Had the Lord left her in her time of greatest need? That appeared to be the case. God seemed silent. But what was revealed to her was the exact opposite. During those times in which only one set of footprints remained, the Lord had carried her through the valley of the shadow of death.

The vicarious humanity of Christ only takes this story one step further and deeper. When Christ is carrying us, he is also walking for us, in our place. We become like children, in utter dependence on our parents. To be like those children, Jesus said, is to enter the kingdom of God (Mt. 19:14).

God does demand. But he gives what he demands (Barth).[51] This is the vicarious humanity of Christ. The Christian life is not simply the "effect" of God's demand as a "cause." That would be the result of a doctrine of God as only a sovereign, omnipotent machine. "Command what you will," says Augustine, "and give what you command."[52] The relationship between Christ and the believer is much closer than a cause and effect relationship, much closer than we ever dared to imagine. Because the Christian life is already God's project, it becomes our project, through the gift of the Holy Spirit (Rom. 8:13). Otherwise, all that Jacob can say is, "Well, this was just the inevitable mid-life crisis. There is nothing I can do about it." We end up in rationalization, frustration, despair, and we eventually give up.

JESUS: THE ONE SPIRIT-LED BELIEVER

Jesus is a believer![53] How can we say such a thing? Isn't he the revelation of God, the very incarnation of God? Certainly to speak of him as a believer belittles the deity of Christ, doesn't it?

Jesus does believe, however, as is evident throughout the Gospels. He lives a life of faith in God the Father, a life led by the Holy Spirit (Lk. 4:1-14). In fact, his faith is a genuine faith, including temptations, (Mt. 4:1-11; Mk. 1:12-13; Lk 4: 1-13; Heb. 2:18; 4:15), the struggle of Gethsemane (Mk. 14:32-42; Mt. 26:36-46; Lk. 22:40-46), and the cry of abandonment from the cross (Mt. 27:46; Heb. 5:7). In Gethsemane, he counsels the disciples to "stay awake and pray that you may not come into the time of trial; the spirit indeed is willing for the flesh is weak" (Mt. 26:41). Jesus knows this because it is his experience.[54] He desires the disciples' presence because "I am deeply grieved, even to death" (Mt. 26:38). He invites them to share in

---

51 Barth, *Church Dogmatics*, IV/1, p. 280.
52 Augustine, *Confessions*, X.29.
53 Torrance, *Theology in Reconstruction*, pp. 153-156.
54 Ralph P. Martin, *Mark: Evangelist and Theologian* (Grand Rapids: Zondervan, 1972), pp. 119, 205.

his faith but is careful to counsel them that this is not a faith without struggle.

Instead of shying away from considering Jesus as a believer, the struggle of his believing may provide the key to the nature of *our* belief and the weakness of our unbelief. This may especially be true if we recognize that just as believers are indwelt by and led by the Spirit of God (Rom. 8:9, 10, 11), so also was Jesus. Is that significant in our attempt to understand and practice the Spirit-filled Christian life? I think so. Jesus, the one Spirit-led believer, believes *before* I do. To be Spirit-led is first of all Jesus' task.

The Holy Spirit is the presence and power of Jesus Christ. The Father sends him in the name of Christ (Jn. 14:26). It is because the Father sends the Spirit of truth to the disciples that they are not orphans (Jn.14:18). This Spirit will testify on the behalf of Christ (Jn. 15:26). The Holy Spirit needs flesh. He needs the flesh of Jesus Christ. As such, Christ is repeatedly considered in the Gospels as the One confirmed and led by the Spirit (Mt. 3:16; 4:1; Mk. 1:10-12; Lk. 4:1, 14, 18).

The Jesus who was led by the Spirit is a believer. As the Spirit is the continual presence of Christ indwelling believers, Christ must continually believe, performing the concrete actions which characterize genuine faith, "trusting and obeying, understanding and knowing, loving and worshipping."[55] Therefore, *our* actions are not just the "results and consequences" of his action, as Thomas Smail claims.[56] In *all* of our acts Christ takes our place. He *continues* to believe through the presence and power of the Holy Spirit even today.

The faith of Jesus may not seem like much. In a sense it has its own "weakness." Historically, many Jewish rabbis of the first century had faith. In fact, Jesus is "the defenseless Word," in Anderson's words.[57] Nonetheless, he has *exousia,* authority, an authority that is "exposing" instead of "exploding" (Lk. 4:36; 5:18-26). What his authority exposes is the judgment on our ability to judge, a judgment on our authority. As Barth remarks, his coming means our displacement.[58] We cannot truly know ourselves as sinners apart from this displacement. This is a part of his substitutionary work. "In that He takes our place it is decided what our place is." This faith with authority leads to him being sentenced for our sake throughout his vicarious life and death. His very meekness and holy love becomes an assault on our sin.[59]

---

55 Torrance, *God and Rationality*, pp. 145-146.
56 Thomas Smail, *The Giving Gift: The Holy Spirit in Person* (London: Hodder and Stoughton, 1988), pp. 109-112.
57 Ray S. Anderson, "Divine Reconciliation and the Incarnation of God," lecture notes, Fuller Theological Seminary, Winter, 1981.
58 Barth, *CD* IV/1, p. 240.
59 Anderson, "Divine Reconciliation . . ."

This One led by the Spirit believes before we do. This is true chronologically, but it is also true theologically. His belief is the ground for our belief in order for our lives to be filled with his Spirit (Rom. 8:9). "He believed for us, was faithful for us, and remains faithful even when we fail Him, again and again . . ."[60]

As the One who already believes, Jesus himself has fulfilled the two great commandments (Mt. 12:28-34; Lk. 10:25-28), as John McLeod Campbell observes.[61] The obedient Son loved the Father with all his heart, soul, mind, and strength, and his neighbor as himself. Jesus has *already* loved and *continues* to love God and his neighbor. What does that mean for the Christian life? It means that the Christian life does not *need* to be lived. It has already been lived. It *continues* to be lived by the risen, exalted Christ through the Holy Spirit. He is our High Priest who represents us before the Father.

The place for the seeking of power and authority, even the power of the Holy Spirit, has already been taken. Jesus possesses it. Authoritarian Christian leaders seek for a security that ignores the vicarious humanity of Christ, the faith of Jesus.[62] Jesus has lived the perfect life of sonship.[63] In that sonship there is acknowledged an abrogation of secular power, of privilege, even to the extent of death on a cross (Mk. 13:32; Phil. 2:6-8). The meekness of his vicarious faith becomes an assault on our ability to judge, our attempts at authority. Without the presence of this vicarious faith, the church degenerates into self-promotion and self-preservation. In opposition to this degeneration of the church is the authority of the kingdom of God as the presupposition of the atonement.[64] Ministry based on our own faith, and not the faith of Jesus, may proclaim pardon for sin, but only degenerate into the "religious malpractice" Anderson speaks of that does not involve the "restoration of the self."[65]

Because Someone has already believed, we now have a *source* for our faith, a source for our life in the Spirit. The Epistle to the Hebrews exhorts his readers to look to "Jesus the pioneer and perfecter of our faith" (Heb. 12:2). The emphasis is upon the faith of Jesus, since he is the "pioneer and perfecter," the one who *first* has faith. The context of 12:2 makes this plain. Having just finished the roll call of the great heroes of faith in Israel (ch. 11), the author continues . . .

---

[60] Torrance, *Conflict and Agreement in the Church*, Vol. 2, pp. 81-82.
[61] Campbell, p. 112.
[62] See Ray S. Anderson, "Leaders Who Abuse: The Misuse of Power," in *The Soul of Ministry: Forming Leaders for God's People* (Louisville: Westminster/John Knox Press, 1997).
[63] Ibid., p. 169.
[64] Anderson, "Divine Reconciliation . . ."
[65] Anderson, *Self-Care*, p. 9.

> Therefore, since we are surrounded by so great a cloud of witnesses, let us also lay aside every weight, and sin . . . and let us run with *perseverance* the race that is set before us, looking to Jesus the pioneer and perfecter of our faith, who for the joy that was set before him *endured* the cross. (Heb. 12:1, 2).

The same Greek word (*hypomeno*) is the root for both the *perseverance* of the Christians and the *endurance* of Jesus. There must be a connection of ideas in the author's mind that our faith is based on the faith of Jesus, the "author of salvation" (Heb. 2:10). This perseverance was based on his "hunger for an ultimate joy," as Anderson puts it.[66] "Without the hunger for an ultimate joy, He would have chosen a more accessible goal and settled for some form of immediate success." Jesus' faith was not fatalistic but had the content of hope. "Faith is a dangerous and destructive drive without hope to sustain its passion."[67]

There is an *actuality* of the faith of Jesus that dramatically and decisively creates the *possibility* of our faith.[68] Someone has already believed . . . for us! Someone has already believed, in spite of our weakness. Thus our rather comical and pitiful pursuits of power and authority pale beside what God has done and is continuing to do in the midst of our weakness. This is the power and presence of the Spirit, the Spirit who indwells in and is given through Jesus.

---

66 Anderson, *Self-Care,* p. 48
67 Ibid.
68 Cf. the comment by Ray S. Anderson: "The actuality of knowledge of God (in Jesus Christ) precedes the possibility of our knowledge of God." Lecture notes, Fuller Theological Seminary, Fall, 1979.

Daniel P Thimell

*

WIJD: What *Is* Jesus Doing?

One of the most profound statements I have ever heard Ray Anderson make concerning the nature of ministry was spoken before a Systematic Theology class: "We must take the shoes off our feet and stand within the logic of Father, Son and Spirit in order for knowing to take place." Ray has a way of tossing out to his students such compressed, meaning-laden comments which are, at first glance, inexplicable (I seem to recall a monk from Downside Abbey in Ireland describing *Historical Transcendence and the Reality of God* as "infuriatingly obscure"). It brings to mind a remark of John McLeod Campbell's father to the former, "you have a queer way of putting things."[1] They demand a certain disciplined pondering in order for understanding to proceed.

And yet his comment is, as the Scots would say, 'spot on.' Knowing does not take place from some autonomous vantage point. Meaning is not conferred by the knower. It is determined by the object, which, in this case, is God himself, the Triune God, who has given himself to be known in the humanity of Jesus. A Trinitarian-incarnational perspective takes as its dogmatic starting-point the self-disclosure of God in Christ. Too often, the Scriptures are treated as a goldmine of information and principles for 'successful living,' which are then subject to the control, interpretation and implementation of the knower. In some churches, information is gleaned from a disciplined, grammatical-historical exegesis of the Biblical text and then handed out in a piecemeal 'expository' fashion.

By this I do not mean to suggest that one need not be concerned with the rights of language or of the morphology and syntax of the text in its cultural and historical setting. My concern is rather with the preoccupation with the individual trees at the expense of the forest. The whole of Scripture is greater than the sum of its parts, and that wholeness can only be seen in the light of Christ, who is its Subject and its Interpreter.

The challenge of theological hermeneutics, often described by James Torrance as the correlation between the Truth of Statement and Truth of Being, points us in the right direction. God's self-revelation in Christ is mediated in and through Holy Scripture. The Written Word possesses no revelatory power in and of itself. It is as Christ, the Living Word, shines

---

1 Edgar P. Dickie, Introduction, John McLeod Campbell, *The Nature of the Atonement*, 4th ed. (London: James Clark Ltd., 1959), p. xx.

through the Scripture by the cleansing and renewing operation of the Holy Spirit upon the human heart and mind, that revelation takes place. After the crucifixion, Cleopas and another disciple were trudging dejectedly toward a village called Emmaus. Then a stranger joins them and asks the reason for their despair. They tell how their hopes were dashed by the execution of Jesus. But the One Whom they do not yet know takes them through a reinterpretation of all the Scriptures in the light of himself. Soon, their eyes are opened and they are given to recognize the Crucified One, now risen and standing in their midst (Luke 24:13-35). We, too, must walk the Emmaus Road with Jesus if we wish to understand the Sacred Writings.

Anderson points us in the right direction when he says: "The on-going ministry of Jesus Christ gives both content and direction to the Church in its ministry. Jesus is the minister *par excellence*. He ministers to the Father for the sake of the world, taking the things of God and disclosing them faithfully to sinners, and taking sinners to himself and binding them graciously in his own Sonship to the Father."[2] The central thesis of this paper is that the Crucified, Risen and Ascended One lives and moves at the center of Christian ministry. Whether we are preaching, leading in worship, or engaging in pastoral care, the Living Christ is the only one who does these things in any significant or life-changing manner, and thus our ministry must be a partaking in his. *Christian ministry is the gift of participating in the ministry of Christ in his offices of Prophet, Priest and King.* What follows is not intended to be a comprehensive investigation of this theme; it is too wonderful for me, I could not hope to sound its depths. This is offered as a mere sketch of some possible directions, a précis, which is to say, an outline, of some implications of ministry understood as a sharing in the threefold ministry of Christ.

Preaching as Participating in the Prophetic Ministry of Christ

Jesus Christ is the One True Prophet. "In many and various ways God spoke of old to our fathers by the prophets, but in these last days he has spoken to us by a Son" (Heb. 1:1,2).[3] The divinely inspired testimonies of all the prophets who went before receive their true light and focus and meaning in the light of Christ. The Sacred Writings of the Old Testament are a finger pointing forward to the coming of Christ, but we only see that from the perspective of their fulfillment in him, as his followers discovered on the Emmaus road. Because Christ alone has come to us from the bosom of the Father, having dwelled with him and the Holy Spirit from all

---

2 Ray S. Anderson, "A Theology for Ministry," in Anderson, ed., *Theological Foundations for Ministry* (Edinburgh: T & T Clark, Ltd., and Grand Rapids: Eerdmans, 1979), p. 8.
3 The Revised Standard Version will be used except where noted.

eternity, he only can make him known (Jn. 1:18). John the Baptizer knew this. In his preaching, he described himself as a "voice" who had no calling to promote himself or to contrive his own empire. He was a voice *directing the attention of the people away from himself to Christ* (1:23).

His theme was simply this: "among you there stands One Whom you do not know" (1:26). His theme was Christ. His obsession was Christ. The interpretive framework for his preaching was Christ. Even his frequently misconstrued call for repentance was not a summons for people to place themselves into grace by their efforts at self-conversion. In Matthew's account, he says, "I baptize you with water for repentance, but he who is coming after me is mightier than I . . . he will baptize you with the Holy Spirit and with fire" (3:11). In other words, If you want to repent, all I have is water. But Jesus is mighty to save, to transform you from the inside out, and give you repentance through the cleansing fire of the Holy Spirit. *Repentance is a gift of Christ.*

If Christ is the One True Prophet, if he alone can reveal God to us in a life-changing manner, then our proclamation, our preaching of the Written Word must always be grounded in the Living Word. Karl Barth insists that, "It is not the function of the preacher to reveal God or act as his intermediary. When the Gospel is preached, God speaks."[4] The message of the reconciliation God has accomplished in Christ is entrusted to us, but as we proclaim it, we find that the living God speaks through our human words: "So we are ambassadors for Christ, God making his appeal through us" (2 Cor. 5:20). True preaching is a participation in Christ and takes Christ for its central theme. Paul Scherer, the great Lutheran preacher of a generation ago, admonished divinity students at Yale,

> The *glad, good news* (Romans 10:15) is not *about* Jesus; it *is* Jesus–who judges life, ransoms life, and sets life upon its feet again . . . Let me beseech you therefore, wherever you take your text, make across country, as fast as ever you can, to him! That is Spurgeon's phrase: unless it becomes our practice, we shall be giving men a stone, when it is bread, only bread, they need! Usher men into his company. If we fail in that we have failed indeed and betrayed our trust beyond all remedy. It is Christ who must "confront the demons"; it is Christ who must stand "in the midst of conflict" so that no one can escape him. Else all your pains have gone for naught, and God's word is that day,

---

4 Karl Barth, *Prayer and Preaching,* tr. Sara F. Terrien and B. E. Hooke (London: SCM Press Ltd., 1964), p. 67.

for all you have done, unspoken in the ears of your congregation.⁵

Too much preaching in our time is not Christ-centered or grounded in the kerygma. Proclamation rather feeds on the felt needs of the audience, offering emotional healing, psychological adjustment, self-improvement, or methods for materialistic acquisition. God becomes a call-in psychologist who dispenses cures in the form of three-step plans, or a cosmic Ann Landers whose agenda is to offer do-it-yourself advice for solving our problems. Ironically and tragically, behind this seemingly benign God who doles out these goodies lurks a Lawgiver whose blessings or curses are dispensed according to our performance. If a person doesn't feel better, if his marriage doesn't improve or his bank account doesn't grow, the blame lies not in the prescribed steps, the laws. It's his fault, described as a lack of faith, of effort, or of carefully following all of the laws. As Thomas Smail says, "the picture is of a God who lays all his blessings on a table [and] cries out, 'Come and get it—if you can!'"⁶

"This world," Eugene Peterson observes, "is no friend to grace."⁷ In a fallen world such as ours, a world captured by the myth of self-salvation, and the attempt to create one's own meaning and happiness in life, grace is always an alien word. The keynote to most national political campaigning in this country is "The American Dream," described in materialistic terms as a paradise reachable through sweat and toil by anyone, provided government either gets out of the way or provides the proper assistance (depending upon the ideology of the political candidate). We like to believe that. A narcissistic society such as ours believes that the proper 'self-help' formula will cure anything, from a bad marriage to poverty to sin itself.

Unhappily, much of our preaching echoes such myths. We preachers crave success as much as anybody, and so marketing shapes homiletics. Church growth consultants tell us that we need to tailor our ministries in ways attractive to the world. Some, motivated by a godly concern to spread the Gospel and evangelize in such a manner that new Christians are folded into the local church, have mistakenly reasoned *backwards* from the fact that, at Pentecost, 3,000 were added to the church, to the postulate

---

5 Paul Scherer, *For We Have This Treasure–The Yale Lectures on Preaching, 1943* (New York: Harper and Brothers, 1944), p. 95.
6 Thomas A. Smail, *The Forgotten Father* (Grand Rapids: Eerdmans, 1980), p. 155.
7 Eugene H. Peterson, *A Long Obedience in the Same Direction. Discipleship in an Instant Society* (Downers Grove, Ill.: InterVarsity Press, 1980, p. 11. Although Peterson helpfully describes the Christian life as a disciplined pilgrimage, I must part company with his suggestion that it begins in a transition from the "works of the law" to "justification by faith" (p. 16), as if the grace of the Gospel comes *after* a bit of law preaching to drive us to despair and then to repentance (pp. 25-26).

that the disciples must have followed a practical strategy wherein numerical growth is a primary criterion for evangelistic methodology.

Of course, numbers do matter. If heaven throws a party over one sinner who is brought back to the fold, then surely, the more, the merrier! If our hearts beat with the Father's, we cannot take comfort in the thought that our smallness as churches somehow validates our 'faithfulness.' Paul, constrained by the love of Christ, declared that he would become all things to all people in order to save some (I Cor. 9:22). Practical strategies are not inherently inimical to the Gospel. Yet Paul also renounced "disgraceful, underhanded ways," and refused to "practice cunning or tamper with God's word" (2 Cor. 4:2). Some ways of preaching are ethical; others are not. Some are faithful to the Word, while others are less so. In all too many messages offered from pulpits today, one would not even know that a sermon was being preached. Instead, hearers are offered the latest wisdom distilled from *Psychology Today* or *Reader's Digest* regarding how to be better organized, how to be more fulfilled, or how to raise better kids. Preaching should be practical, but abstracted from the grace of God in Christ, from the living Christ, practical "how to" sermons become another form of works religion.

In 1799 Friedrich Schleiermacher, the father of modern liberalism, utilized as his theological method presenting *Speeches to Cultured Despisers*.[8] But in his attempt to make Christianity palatable to sophisticated minds in his culture, he transformed it into something other than the "faith once for all delivered to the saints," a dehistoricized religion of symbolism and subjective God-consciousness, in which the principles of Jesus are decisively divorced from his Person.[9]

Ironically, the attempt to make Christianity relevant renders it irrelevant, when the Christian message is tailored to suit the preconceptions of a society seeking to live without God. It ends up telling the world what it has already been telling itself, and that message can only lead further down the road of sorrow and loss. God has already made himself fully relevant to humanity in the flesh of his Son, and any attempt by us to reshape teaching to make it more palatable can only result in another gospel, which is no gospel (see Gal. 1:6-9).

Both liberalism and conservatism can fall prey to this preoccupation with principles to the neglect of the Person. Liberalism may deny the final significance of the Person of Christ in rejecting his deity. All that remains are abstract concepts of Love, Peace, Justice and others that must be implemented by well-meaning individuals. Conservatism may affirm his

---

[8] The full title of his influential work is *On Religion: Speeches to its Cultured Despisers*, trans. John Oman (New York: Harper and Row, 1958).
[9] Cf. Alisdair I. C. Heron, *A Century of Protest Theology* (Philadelphia: The Westminster Press, 1980), pp. 22-32.

deity, his Person, and yet set the principles apart from his Person as laws to be followed in order to find fulfillment, peace, and success. These have become the staple diet of much preaching in this country today.

The problems with this approach are manifold. The God and Father of our Lord Jesus Christ is not fundamentally a Lawgiver whose grace is conditional upon our performance. And his agenda is not dictated by our daily 'wants list.' The great themes of biblical revelation center on the present and coming Kingdom of God, actualized by the mission of God in the humanity of Christ for the reconciliation of the world. This kingdom embraces the liberation of creation from its bondage to decay, pollution, and the destruction of species. It also means wholeness for individual persons who through the saving humanity of Christ are reconciled to God and one another and thus find their true being as 'persons in relation' (John Macmurray).[10] But it also includes the transformation of social structures. Canon Rex Reed says that he is "not very impressed with a God who finds parking spaces for charismatics but is not concerned about the agony of Rhodesia."[11]

"What Would Jesus Do?"

A place to begin, therefore, is with a proper doctrine of God. *The nature of God determines the way of knowing Him, and God has given himself to be known in the Person of His Son.* Among other things, this means that Christian life and ministry are centered, not in the autonomous individual, but in Christ. One of the most popular slogans in American Christianity is "WWJD." Whether plastered on bumpers, printed on t-shirts or fashioned into fine jewelry, it's an acronym, of course, for "What Would Jesus Do?" It is not altogether to be gainsaid. The original crafter of the motto was Charles Sheldon, a nineteenth-century Congregational minister who wrote a moving devotional book entitled, *In His Steps*. As the title indicates, he takes as his point of departure the admonition contained in I Peter 2:21 (KJV): "For hereunto were ye called; because Christ also suffered for you, leaving you an example that ye should follow his steps."

Certainly the imitation of Christ is an important concern for every Christian. We are called to be like Jesus, and Sheldon, to his credit, offers a stirring appeal to meditate on Jesus and follow the Spirit's leading in implementing what Jesus would do in the marketplace, the boardroom, and on skid row. In many ways, Sheldon anticipates the concerns of the Social Gospel movement.[12]

---

10 John Macmurray, *Persons in Relation* (London: Faber and Faber Ltd., 1961).
11 *Ibid.*, p. 15.
12 See James H. Smylie, "Sheldon's *In His Steps*: Conscience and Discipleship," *Theology Today* (April, 1975), 33-34. Smylie includes some helpful insights into the social concerns of

Yet, true as the call to emulate Jesus is, taken as the whole of the Christian life, it is a half-truth. Taken by itself, it is nothing more than another wise maxim to live by, alongside of the Golden Rule, and the call to love God and neighbor. But Christianity is not about maxims, not about rules of thumb, not about clever little keys to living which can be implemented by an autonomous actor untouched by the reconciling and revealing work of the living Christ. Justo Gonzales notes the danger that we might "overestimate our capacity to be imitators of Christ," particularly if we content ourselves to reducing Christ to the level of a "role model" and neglect to be "truly transformed by him."[13]

Not coincidentally, *In His Steps* espouses an Abelardian view of the Cross. Henry Maxwell, the fictional hero of the book, got things moving in his congregation after preaching a motivational sermon. As Sheldon tells it,

> He had emphasized in the first part of the sermon the Atonement as personal sacrifice, calling attention to the fact of Jesus' suffering in various ways, in His life as well as in His death. He had then gone on to emphasize the Atonement from the side of example, giving illustrations from the life and teachings of Jesus to show how faith in Christ helped to save men because of the pattern or character He displayed for their imitation. He [then moved to] the third and last point, the necessity of following Jesus in His sacrifice and example.[14]

The Moral influence model of the atonement, as Sheldon acknowledges, locates the salvific power of the Cross in its influencing sinners by a moving portrayal of self-sacrifice. They are then inspired to live the kind of life they ought. The element of truth here is expressed memorably by Isaac Watts: "love so amazing, so divine, demands my soul, my life, my all." But is that how Christ *saves us*—by a stirring object lesson? Sinners need more than fresh motivation or a vivid example. Those who are dead in trespasses and sin (Eph. 2:1) are unable to begin living the life God requires.

When we stand in the pulpit and ladle out "Steps to Success," "Five Ways to Make Your Marriage Better," or "How to Be a Better Father,"

Sheldon, but he mistakenly identifies the latter with the 'Christocentric evangelical tradition.' If 'evangelical' describes one committed to the 'evangel' of the incarnate Son of God crucified and risen to accomplish an objective atonement, then Sheldon requires a different label.

13 *When Christ Lives in Us* (Nashville: Abingdon, 1995), p. 7; cf. Todd Speidell, "Incarnational Social Ethics," *Incarnational Ministry: The Presence of Christ in Church, Society and Family*, ed. Christian D. Kettler and Todd H. Speidell (Colorado Springs, CO: Helmers and Howard, 1990), p. 146.

14 Charles M. Sheldon, *In His Steps* (New York: Smithmark, 1992), pp. 1-2.

without reference to the Living Christ, we're not giving people Good News at all. We're appealing to their fallenness. We're just repeating what society has been telling them all week: that life is a project for Do-It-Yourselfers, that living is all about the rugged individualist who through discipline, creativity, exertion, and following the right mottoes can justify his own existence.

The Finished Work of Christ

The trouble is that bootstraps theology collides with the Gospel of Jesus Christ. The Gospel is not an encouraging word about a God who comes to top off our good works with a little extra frosting. Nor is it a set of mottoes for better living. It is the announcement of a decisive change that has taken place in the history of the world and therefore in the history of every single person. It is news about a God who eternally has his being in love as a communion of Father, Son and Holy Spirit, who, out of the overflow of that love brought humankind into being; and when our first parents turned away from his love, the Creator became the Creature, the Doctor became the patient, and in his life, death and resurrection in our humanity, brought about reconciliation and transformation for the world.

We are put right with God by sheer grace. 2,000 years before we were born, Jesus lived our life and died our death. Just before he gave up his spirit he cried out, "It is finished" (Jn. 19:30). He did not say, "We're almost there. I've done my part, and if sinners will just do theirs, contribute their 50% or 30% or at least 5% (through sincerity and repentance), salvation will be accomplished."

"It is finished." The exegesis of that declaration is found in the story of the criminal crucified next to Jesus who said, "Jesus, remember me when you come into your kingdom." Please note that there was absolutely nothing that that sinner could contribute to his justification. He was bound hand and foot to a cross. There was no time for any attempts at turning over a new leaf, or doing some good deeds to compensate for his bad ones. In the words of an old Gaither gospel song, all he had to offer him was brokenness and strife. To him, Jesus said, "It is finished." To him, Jesus promised, "Truly I say to you, today you will be with me in paradise" (Lk. 23:42,43).

The work of Christ is finished. To quote Abraham Lincoln's *Gettysburg Address* out of context, it is "far beyond our poor power to add or detract." We can reject what Christ has done. We can deny him. We can turn away from so great a salvation and thereby lose out eternally. But we cannot contribute one thing to the saving work of Christ. It's all by grace. When we were still *powerless*, Christ died for us (Ro. 5:6). "Faith," as Professor James Torrance is fond of saying, "is the dawning awareness that God in Christ has done it all."

What *Is* Jesus Doing?

Life in Christ

Through faith, we are not only saved *from* sin, but also *for* sonship and daughterhood. This is the point profoundly made by John McLeod Campbell in his classic, *The Nature of the Atonement*.[15] Calvin describes our life with God as a "union with Christ." This union is not a primarily a legal relation, an association of tolerance by God with us for the sake of his Son's having satisfied certain legal conditions. There is certainly a judicial dimension to the atonement, but to construe it as the central meaning is to miss its heart, which is filial. Thus Galatians 4:4 indicates that God sent forth his Son, born of a woman, born under the law, to redeem those who were under the law, so that we might receive the adoption of sons. God's heart will not be satisfied if all the children of earth one day stand at attention, saying, "Yes sir" and obeying his commands.

The legal dimension is real, but it is grounded in the filial. " The law, as Campbell used to say, "is God's heart coming out in the shape of law."[16] Because he loves us, he gives us his laws as guidelines for living. But law is not the *first thing* in our life with God. It is the *second thing*. First, foremost, primary and determinative, is grace. God graciously unites himself to our humanity in order to restore us to sonship and daughterhood. Reconciled to God, united to him through faith by the Holy Spirit, we are enabled to live as sons and daughters, which is to say, obediently and lovingly.

We are brought into a living union with Christ. This relation is being-constituting. T. F. Torrance talks about "onto-relations" as a way of describing the kind of bond that Christians have with Christ. He shows how particle physics interprets particles, not as separated entities but as interrelated with other particles, "continuously connected together in dynamic fields of force where the interrelations between particles are part of what particles really are."[17] But this way of thinking originated, says Torrance, in the Christian doctrine of the Trinity as a Communion of Love between the Persons of Father, Son and Holy Spirit. Anderson likes to refer to our "co-humanity"[18] as a way of underscoring our "being-in-

---

15 John McLeod Campbell, *The Nature of the Atonement* (Grand Rapids: Eerdmans, 1996). Cf. James B. Torrance, "The Contribution of McLeod Campbell to Scottish Theology," *Scottish Journal of Theology*, vol. 31 (August, 1973), pp. 295-311.
16 McLeod Campbell, *Responsibility for the Gift of Eternal Life* (London: Macmillan and Co., 1873), p. 106.
17 *The Mediation of Christ* (Grand Rapids: Eerdmans, 1983), p. 58.
18 Anderson attributes the concept to Karl Barth, *Church Dogmatics*, III/1, pp. 208f, while proceeding to develop the theme much further in his *The Shape of Practical Theology* (Downers Grove, Ill: InterVarsity Press, 2001), pp. 135-38.

communion" (John Zizioulas),[19] our humanity being grounded in our relatedness to one another and to God through the humanity of Christ.

This relation is a union with *Christ*, in his Person and work. Who he is as the Second Person of the eternal Trinity, as the Creator and the Redeemer, and what he does in his life, death, resurrection and ascension, are inseparable. Who Christ is cannot be divided from what he does. His actions reflect his nature, and since his nature is consubstantial with the Father, to see Jesus is to see the Father.

This is so, not because of an identity among the Persons of the Trinity, for they are to be distinguished from one another. The doctrine of the Trinity means, among other things, that the Father is not the Son or the Spirit (no Person is to be confused with either of the other two) and yet all three persons share the same reality, power and eternity within the unity of the Godhead. This sharing of reality (or 'substance' as Chalcedon puts it) can be described as perichoresis. There is a perichoretic interpenetration among the Persons. Father, Son and Holy Spirit mutually indwell one another, while retaining their distinctiveness. Thus after telling Philip, "He who has seen me has seen the Father," Jesus goes on to explain that "I am in the Father and the Father [is] in me." He restates the point in the next verse: "the Father . . . dwells in me" (Jn. 14:8-11).

Christ as the Way of Knowing God's Nature

No mortal has seen God at any time, but Jesus, the eternal Son of God, comes straight from the bosom of the Father to make him known (Jn.1:18). In fact, the way of knowing God is *exclusively Christological*. "No one knows the Father except the Son and anyone to whom the Son chooses to reveal him" (Matthew 11:27; cf. Lk.10:22).

In Christ we see a God who is not content to remain in the safe immunity of heaven, but who condescends, stoops, and kneels to make common cause with our humanity, assuming our flesh into a saving union with himself. In Christ we are permitted to apprehend the true nature of God. That nature is love: gracious, merciful, unconditional love. God *is* love (I Jn. 4:8). Yet in biblical revelation, love is not left in the abstract, or as a word awaiting our definition. Love is defined by the Cross: "In this is love, not that we loved God, but that he loved us and sent his Son to be the expiation for our sins" (I Jn. 4:10). *The Godness of God lies in his love, not in some naked, absolute, self-determining will.*[20] To this, it may be protested, Is

---

19 John D. Zizioulas, *Being as Communion* (London: Darton, Longman and Todd, 1985).
20 *Contra* Paul Helm, who defends John Owen's assertion that there is "no natural affection and propensity in God to the good of his creatures," on the grounds that undeserved love or mercy bestowed by God can only be an act of *will* towards whomever he wishes. Helm argues that if undeserved love must be extended by God to all people, then it is no longer undeserved ("The Logic of Limited Atonement," *The Scottish Bulletin of Evangelical Theology*,

What *Is* Jesus Doing?

God not free? Does not God have an absolute will? To be sure, but as Karl Barth would say, his freedom is his love and his love is his freedom. God cannot will anything contrary to his nature, which is love.

This is a pivotal issue, because many posit another God, a God who is not truly love, but bare will. In the Middle Ages, an attempt was made to construct a doctrine of God based on a dialectic of two powers, the *potentia absoluta* (absolute power) and the *potentia ordinata* (ordained power). Absolutely speaking, it was asserted, God can do *anything*, for that is the Godness of God. Thus William of Ockham averred that for our salvation God could have become incarnate as a stone, a block of wood or an ass.[21] But in the plan of God, according to the arrangement he willed or ordained to have with humanity, some medieval theologians suggested, *facere quod in se est, deus not denegat gratiam*. To the one who does what is in him, God does not deny grace.

This was not a thoroughgoing Pelagianism, with its doctrine of salvation by works. Rather, it represented a middle way between salvation by merit and salvation by grace. We are sinners, and thus cannot save ourselves. But we can, by "doing what is in us," doing our best, cooperate with grace. God has ordained that he will respond by giving us more grace than we deserve.[22] Such may seem appealing, since it provides a place both for divine and for human responsibility. But the Gospel is not about humans doing their part and acting responsibly. It's about sinners who, while still powerless, were redeemed by the Son of God. Still today, there is a semi-Pelagianism in much of Christianity, whether in its Roman Catholic or Protestant (whether liberal, conservative or charismatic) forms. It comes in the form that says, "God has acted graciously in Christ to bring salvation, but if you want to receive it, you must do *your* part." Christ has died and risen again for your sins, and if you repent, if you desist in whatever your particular sins are, then forgiveness will come.

As a pastor, I have had countless persons tell me, after hearing that kind of semi-Pelagian Gospel presented down through years, "I'd like to become a Christian, but I don't believe I'm ready to give up *x* or *y* yet." I tell them, "The Gospel is not about your readiness. It's about what God has already done on your behalf and in your humanity in the Person of his

---

vol. 3, no. 2, Autumn, 1985, pp. 47-54). Cp. James B. Torrance, "The Incarnation and Limited Atonement," *Evangelical Quarterly*, vol. LV, no. 2, pp. 84-5. Thus, it would seem, God protects his mercy by ladling it out stintingly. This appears to be an instance of reasoning deductively from certain preconceived postulates regarding the divine nature, rather than thinking through the inner logic of Father and Son in the light of the incarnation, as I John 4:10 does.

21 Alister McGrath, *Intellectual Origins of the European Reformation* (Oxford: Blackwell, 1987), p. 21.

22 I have explored this theme in greater depth in *Grace, Law and the Doctrine of God in the Theologies of St. Thomas Aquinas, John Calvin, and John McLeod Campbell* (unpublished Ph.D. dissertation, University of Aberdeen, Scotland, 1993), pp. 129f.; 212ff.

Son. The barriers are already down. The way is open to come home to the Father's heart." In the Father's embrace, in a living union with God through Christ, one begins a lifelong repentance.

The Gospel is not merely a prerequisite of ministry, as if one is reconciled to God and then moves on to carry out "his" or "her" ministry. Christian ministry *is* a Gospel Ministry. By this, I do not mean that the Gospel is an important "tool" of ministry or even its major theme. Paul declared, "When I was among you, I resolved to know nothing but Jesus Christ and him crucified" (I Cor. 2:2). The atoning grace of God in Christ was the keynote in Paul's preaching and ministry, but that Gospel itself was grounded in the living Christ. *The Crucified One occupies the center of all true ministry.* He does not simply leave us the message of what he did in his life, Cross and Resurrection 2,000 years ago, and leave us to believe it and act upon it. *He is the message.* To put it in other terms, for the apostle Paul, and therefore for us, the *work* of Christ is grounded in the *person* of Christ. What he does must be understood with reference to who he is. Who he is not only shapes our understanding of the Gospel, but our understanding of ministry itself. As James Torrance puts it,

> Christ does not heal us by standing over against us, diagnosing our sickness, prescribing medicine for us to take, and then going away, as an ordinary doctor might. No, He becomes the patient! He assumes the very humanity which is in need of redemption, and by being anointed by the Spirit in our humanity, by a life of perfect obedience, by dying and rising again, for us, our humanity is healed *in him.*[23]

Christ's assumption of our humanity is not a temporary expedient, a brief episode during his saving actions in Palestine long ago. Not at all! "There *is* one God, and one mediator between God and man, the *man* Christ Jesus" (I Tim. 2:5, italics mine). In an ongoing condescension that staggers our comprehension, *he continues to share in our humanity, and goes on presenting us in himself in his mediatorial, priestly ministry before the Father, and he goes on living his life through those who are brought into a living union with himself*. The Christian life is *life in Christ*.

The Life of God in the Human Soul

Henry Scougal, a Professor of Divinity at King's College, Aberdeen, Scotland, who died in 1678 at the age of twenty-eight, wrote an influential

---

[23] James B. Torrance, "The Vicarious Humanity of Christ," *The Incarnation–Ecumenical Studies in the Nicene-Constantinopolitan Creed A. D. 381*, ed. Thomas F. Torrance (Edinburgh: Handsel Press Ltd., 1981).

little book entitled, *The Life of God in the Soul of Man*.[24] It is considered a spiritual classic and has been reprinted many times. In his book, Scougal laments that so few people seem to understand what true Christianity is. Some think, he wrote, that Christianity is mainly "orthodox notions and opinions." They imagine that all God wants is for us to have the correct mental understanding of him, as if we will have to pass a theology exam when we enter the pearly gates (thank God, we will not)!

Others think it is a matter of "external duties"–obeying the laws of the Bible, doing the right things. They think that God's salvation is won by our performance. If we obey his commands well enough, we will be sufficiently righteous to be entitled to heaven.

Still others believe that real Christianity is having the right "affections," "rapturous heats and ecstatic devotion."[25] In other words, they think it's mostly about our feelings–excitement and spiritual goose bumps. For them, Christianity is all about having exciting feelings and loving feelings and happy feelings. Some people go to endless conferences and church camps looking to recharge their feelings.

Yet the essence of Christianity is neither intellectual nor legal nor emotional but "quite another thing." Here, the young Scottish teacher is getting at the heart of what Jesus intended to accomplish when he came to earth, lived, died, and rose again on the third day. What, then, is real Christianity? Says Scougal, "True religion is a union of the soul with God, a real participation of the divine nature . . . or in the Apostle's phrase *it is Christ formed within us* [Gal. 4:19]." The root of this divine life is faith, and its "chief branches are love to God, charity to men, purity and humility."[26] These outward duties, however, do not make a person a Christian. They only matter when they manifest the actual Life of God within. *The Life of God in the human soul*: That's the Christian life. And it happens through Christ's uniting our humanity with his in all that he has done and is doing.

So it is with Christian service. True ministry is ministry in Christ. Jesus himself makes this point when he tells the disciples that he is the vine, they the branches, and that "apart from me you can do nothing" (Jn. 15:5). Effective ministry, fruit-bearing, comes as the life-giving power of the Vine flows through the branch. Again, he tells them in Matthew 28:20, immediately on the heels of the Great Commission, "I am with you always." The ongoing presence of the Living Christ empowers our going, our disciple-making, and our teaching. Better, it is in the going, the discipling, and the teaching *of Christ* that we are given to share.

William Barclay, who saw this area, at least, with real clarity, wrote:

---

24 Henry Scougal, *The Life of God in the Soul of Man* (London: Inter-Varsity Fellowship, 1961).
25 *Ibid.*, p. 15.
26 Ibid.

> For Paul, Christ had been the *beginning* of life, for on that day on the Damascus road it was as if he had begun life all over again. Christ had been the *continuing* of life; there had never been a day when Paul had not lived in his presence, and in the frightening moments Christ had been there to bid him be of good cheer (Acts 18:9, 10). Christ was the *end* of life, for it was towards his eternal presence that life ever led. Christ was the *inspiration* of life; he was the dynamic of life. To Paul, Christ had given the *task* of life, for it was he who made him an apostle and sent him out as an evangelist to the Gentiles. To him Christ had given the *strength* for life, for it was Christ's all-sufficient grace that was made perfect in Paul's weakness. For him Christ was the *reward* of life, for to Paul the only worthwhile reward was closer fellowship with his Lord. If Christ were taken out of life, for Paul there would be nothing left.[27]

When the living presence of Christ is understood as his solidarity with our humanity, the union of the Triune God with fallen humanity in the life, death, resurrection and ascension of Jesus Christ, this description of the Christian life and ministry is exactly right.

Leading Worship as Participating in the Priestly Ministry of Christ

James Torrance has shown that worship is not a human accomplishment but a divine gift, the gift of sharing through the Holy Spirit in the Son's communion with the Father. He comes as the One True Priest in solidarity with our humanity, to offer that love and obedience and worship that we cannot offer. In his Once-and-for all Self-Offering and in his ongoing intercession for us, he constitutes a living way for us to enter into the very presence of the Father. We are given to participate in the Priesthood of Jesus as a Royal Priesthood through the Holy Spirit.[28]

Worship is not "our" response to God, as if God did his part in Christ 2,000 years ago and now we do our part in worship. Often, it is suggested that in worship, God is the audience and we are the performers. If that were true, then our Christian life, at its deepest, most important point, is left to our piety, our strength of commitment, our intensity of feeling, our ability to focus our minds and pray with clarity and sing with sincerity. Tragically, in all too many churches today, the worship leader gives exactly that impression, exhorting the congregation to "sing louder," "really

---

27 William Barclay, *The Letters to the Philippians, Colossians, and Thessalonians*, rev. ed. (Philadelphia: The Westminster Press, 1975), p. 27.
28 James B. Torrance, *Worship, Community, and the Triune God of Grace* (Downers Grove, Ill: InterVarsity, 1997).

mean it," "put your heart into it," "offer a real sacrifice of praise." Worship is not the construction of some tower of Babel, a human attempt to reach the heavens by human endeavor (see Genesis 11). It's not a Pelagian offering of ourselves apart from the One Offering that is acceptable to God.

In worship, as in the rest of the Christian life, there is One Way into the presence of God, and that is the Living Way constituted by the vicarious humanity of Jesus. Therefore we can draw near in full assurance of faith and know that our prayers will be heard and our worship received (Heb. 10:19-22).

Too many of our songs are human-centered, preoccupied with *our* love for God, *our* obedience, *our* resolution. We even sing about "enthroning Jesus," as if he were standing around uncertainly and powerlessly, awaiting *our* coronation. Philip S. Watson, in his landmark study of Luther, suggests that there are in general two types of religion, classified according to whether God or humans predominate and become the center of gravity in the divine-human relationship. "If the religious relationship centers in man–if my relation to God depends essentially upon me–then it can be described as anthropocentric or egocentric; if it centers in the eternal and the divine, then it is theocentric." In the former type, "I offer my gift in order to win the Divine favour and so to obtain what I wish from the Divine power." He goes on to show how this is demonstrated in the attempt to perform in such a way that through meritorious works or personal holiness we guarantee our standing before God.[29] That is not Christianity.

The living God gives what he demands. Christianity is anchored in the Triune God of grace who condescends to don our broken flesh, heal us, and lift us back to himself in the life, death and resurrection of Jesus. Worship is the gift of sharing in all that Christ has done and is doing as our Great High Priest. In Christ, we can dare to come into God's presence in our unworthiness and half-heartedness and confess all that. We can say, "I believe–help my unbelief" (Mk. 9:24), and find that God in Christ graciously makes us worthy, heals our divided hearts, and strengthens our faith.

Pastoral Ministry as Participating in the Kingly, Shepherding Ministry of Christ

There is only One King, but sometimes we forget that. It is tempting, in this culture of self-realization, to seek to build our own kingdom, so that we can stand up in front of the people and say, "Look what I did!" and pretend to be glorifying God. Our language betrays us. Most assuredly,

---

[29] Philip S. Watson, *Let God Be God–An Interpretation of the Theology of Martin Luther* (London: The Epworth Press, 1947), pp. 34-35.

true ministry is never *my* ministry; this is not *my* church, and I could never hope to "win someone to Christ."

There is only One True Minister, and that is Jesus Christ. He exercises his kingly office as a Shepherd. Please note, however, that this shepherd is no meek pushover! The Lord who is "my shepherd" also keeps both his rod and his staff handy! But his discipline is exercised in love. Jesus is the Great Shepherd of the sheep and we are his under-shepherds (I Pet. 5:1-4). He's the Pastor, and we're Assistant Pastors, by his grace. Understanding this could release a lot of us from ministerial burnout. Guiding a church and engaging in pastoral counseling are not mere human possibilities. Anderson declares that the kind of caring required to address the estrangement and alienation and fragmentation of the human situation today "is not to be found in a human 'capacity' to bear the sufferings of others, or even prevent them, but the 'care' is the transcendence of God's love which man possesses only as 'incapacity.'" In God's transcendence, we are "delivered from the burden of being gods."[30]

In his ground-breaking doctoral thesis, Anderson showed that God's historical transcendence is not constituted by his distance from humanity but by his proximity, his solidarity with flesh. The otherness of God is not his remoteness but his closeness. Yet his closeness is a hiddenness which requires participation, an act of faith as the gift of the Spirit, in order for finite humans to know him.[31] This constitutes a telling critique of much traditional theology, with its assumption that the transcendence of God is "either his eternal aseity or his divine attributes." In such a theological framework, the *kenosis* passage in Philippians could only mean that God's self-emptying would require him to modify or conceal his transcendent nature. But *kenosis* is the transcendence of God: "Jesus is the God who is for man. He embodies the transcendent limit of the reality of God."[32] Anderson's eloquence and clarity at this point deserve extended quotation:

> This *kenosis* is the act of God as Subject who transcends his own immanent existence and *becomes* man, thereby placing him transcendently in relation to man at the most intimate and most absolute level. The form of the servant is thus, first of all, the God who is for man. When one comes up against the form of the servant in Christ, one is up against God himself. [33]

This means that Christ is present in our humanity in ministry to the world:

---

30 Ray S. Anderson, *Historical Transcendence and the Reality of God* (Grand Rapids: Eerdmans, 1975), p. 297.
31 This is offered as a stumbling attempt to summarize a key theme developed at great length far more articulately and compellingly in Professor Anderson's book.
32 *Ibid.*, pp. 164-65.
33 *Ibid.*, p. 167.

Thus, instead of pointing away from himself, from his own humanity, to Christ, the Christian must say: to become involved with me is to come up against Jesus Christ who is 'present' to our humanity through the reality of the Holy Spirit who completes my life in the personhood of divine communion. While it is true that one cannot speak as another (or the same) Incarnation of Christ, one should live and speak incarnation*ally* so that Christ has again hands to reach out into the world to give, feet to walk the roads of life with men, and arms to embrace the lonely and the estranged.[34]

The central theme of the Christian life and ministry is this: "I am crucified with Christ. Nevertheless I live. Yet not I, but Christ liveth in me, and the life I live in the flesh I live by the faith of the Son of God, who loved me and gave himself for me" (Gal. 2:20). That's the central dynamic of the Christian life: "I–yet not I, but Christ." Although I have often lost sight of this, I must say that many times I have found it to be the only way to engage in ministry. When the phone rang and the voice on the other end told me that a seven-year-old boy had just died in a farming accident; when a 27-year old woman took her life; when an elderly man who had been saying No to Christ all his adult life was about to undergo major surgery; when a wife made the heartbreaking decision to "pull the plug" on her husband whose vital signs were too low and then asked me to pray for his healing: in each of these situations, I said a quick prayer, "'Not I, but Christ.' Jesus, you'll have to minister, because I can't," *and he always came through.*

Ministry is not in the first instance a human act. Ministry is shaped and constituted by *Christ*. Outside of him there is no ministry but only shallow advice or therapeutic half-measures; ministry becomes administration and marketing and empire-building or even abusing and drawing people into a cultic attachment to oneself rather than to God. Yet Jesus Christ, crucified, risen and now ascended, goes on exercising his prophetic, priestly and kingly rule as Exalted Head and Lord.

The Christian life and ministry are not, in essence, a matter of considering, What Would Jesus Do? Rather, the central issue is, What *Is* Jesus Doing? If he already stands in solidarity with the humanity of the world, if he is exercising his prophetic ministry through the preaching of his Gospel, if he is interceding for us in worship as our Great High Priest, if he is carrying out his kingly shepherding ministry through those called to be pastors, if he is found in the least of the brothers and sisters (Matt. 25:40), then our agenda is clear: Joyfully participate!

---

34 *Ibid.*, p. 263.

F. LeRon Shults

Sharing in the Divine Nature: Transformation, *Koinonia* and the Doctrine of God

Introduction

Readers who are familiar with the writings of Ray Anderson will immediately recognize the first two concepts in my subtitle as common themes in his work. His scholarship is driven by a passion for facilitating the transformation of persons and communities by calling them into a fellowship (*koinonia*) with God that actively participates in God's ministry in and to the world.[1] Although he has not developed an explicit "systematic" presentation of the third idea in the subtitle, reflections on the "doctrine of God" permeate his theological writings. In his early books, Anderson focused intensely on the idea of the reality of God, especially as it was articulated in the theology of Karl Barth.[2] In his lectures, he seldom missed an opportunity to point out the relation between our concepts of God and our experience of redemption. For Anderson, conceptual exploration serves the deeper existential journey of spiritual transformation and the wider pastoral engagement in reconciling praxis. In the same way, my overarching goal in this chapter is to explore the conceptual meaning of and intrinsic relation between these themes in a way that discloses the transforming power of the biblical claim that believers are called to become *sharers in the divine nature* (2 Peter 1:4).

Part 1 outlines three of the most important developments in the doctrine of God in the 20th century: the retrieval of divine Infinity, the revival of Trinitarian doctrine and the renewal of eschatological reflection. First, in response to early modern attempts to secure God as a rational

---

[1] This is especially evident in works such as *The Shape of Practical Theology: Empowering Ministry with Theological Praxis* (Downer's Grove, IL: IVP, 2001) and *The Soul of Ministry* (Louisville, KY: Westminster John Knox, 1997). This aim also guides his interdisciplinary engagement with psychology in books such as *Christians Who Counsel* (Grand Rapids, MI: Zondervan, 1990). In addition to thanking Ray for the way he has shaped my theological thinking over the years, I also want to thank my own students, many of whom have indirectly shaped this chapter by their penetrating questions and honest feedback.

[2] See, e.g., his dissertation published as *Historical Transcendence and the Reality of God* (Grand Rapids, MI: Eerdmans, 1975). In the collection of texts he edited as *Theological Foundations for Ministry* (Grand Rapids, MI: Eerdmans, 1979), Anderson included more selections from Karl Barth than any other theologian.

object we find an increased emphasis in theology on divine *Infinity*. Second, in the return to a robust doctrine of *Trinity* we see a reaction against the depiction of God as a single subject, which was a common starting point in the Enlightenment. Finally, we observe a growing interest in the idea of divine *Futurity* as a way of describing God's relation to the world; this is in part an attempt to move beyond the inadequacies of the early modern focus on the divine as first cause. Each of these developments was driven in part by a desire to overcome early modern metaphysical assumptions, which had led in some cases to conceptions of God's Infinity and Eternity as defined merely over against the finitude and transience of the world, and to a strong dichotomy between God's unitary essence and the Trinitarian relations revealed in Scripture.

As I trace some of the theological forces behind these developments in the subsections of Part 1 (Infinity, Trinity and Futurity), I begin in each case by describing the impetus provided by Karl Barth, whose influence continues to be felt in each of these trajectories. Second, I draw attention to the broader streams of influence in which Barth was embedded; new exegetical insights based on biblical scholarship and the growth of ecumenical dialogue were particularly important. Fresh Protestant engagement with Roman Catholic and Eastern Orthodox theology has led to deeper mutual self-understanding, which may help to allay Western worries about the East's emphasis on *theosis* and becoming "sharers [*koinonoi*] of divine nature." Even if we remain critical of metaphysical presuppositions that underlie particular articulations of *theosis*, especially those that appear to suggest a "divinization" of the creature, we may find resources in the dialogue for retrieving this important biblical emphasis on being "united" with God. Finally, I point briefly in each subsection to the distinctive proposals of three Protestant thinkers who have appropriated Barth (more or less critically) as they attempt to press further in each trajectory: Jürgen Moltmann, Robert Jenson, and Wolfhart Pannenberg. My interest here is not so much to commend aspects of their theological models, but to suggest that the conceptual space they have helped to open provides new resources for articulating the Gospel in late modernity.

Part 2 explores this conceptual space in search of better ways to convey the Christian experience of *koinonia* and transformation in relation to the Infinite Trinitarian Futurity of the biblical God. If we weave together the insights of these three developments, we may be able to provide a more adequate understanding of the dynamics of our being called to share in the divine nature (2 Peter 1:3-4):

> His divine power has granted to us all things that pertain to life and godliness, through the knowledge of him who called us to his own glory and excellence, by which he has granted to us his precious and very great promises, that through these you may

> escape from the corruption that is in the world because of passion, and become partakers of the divine nature.

The last six words translate the Greek phrase, "*genesthe theias koinonoi physeos.*" We must remember that the way we understand our entry into a fellowship (*koinonia*) of relational unity with God will depend on how we conceptualize the divine nature (*physis*). The constellation of patterns that emerge as we reflect on (what I will call) perfect Infinity, robust Trinity and primal Futurity can clarify the meaning of life "in Christ." The subsections of Part 2 are my attempt to illuminate this nexus of interrelated themes by expositing the biblical claim that salvation involves "sharing" in the *knowledge, suffering* and *glory* of Jesus Christ. These ideas pervade the writings of several New Testament authors, but already in the Petrine corpus all three are present. James Starr argues that the whole message of 2 Peter is anchored by the phrase "in the knowledge" [*en epignosei*] of Jesus Christ, which serves as an *inclusio* for the letter (1:2, 8; 3:18).[3] 1 Peter also describes a sharing (*koinoneite*) in Christ's suffering (4:13) and glory (5:1). As we will see below, these three "partakings" are laced together throughout the New Testament, which links growing in the knowledge of God in Christ both to enduring all things with patience and to experiencing the hope of glory by the indwelling power of the Spirit.

As I explore this biblical promise of transforming fellowship in Part 2, I will suggest that intercalating the theological trajectories[4] of Part 1 may help us better articulate the intuitions behind the "attributes" of God that are traditionally referred to as omniscience, omnipotence and omnipresence. My goal is to correlate these predicates to our experience of faith, love and hope in the biblical God. If these three survive the eschatological consummation (1 Cor. 13:13), and yet we already experience them now, it makes sense to think that they have something to do with our sharing in the divine nature. We long for a relation to God in which we are neither absorbed nor abandoned. Theology has the task of articulating a doctrine of the biblical God as the origin, condition and goal of this creaturely longing, which is proleptically fulfilled through spiritual union with God in Christ. In the context of this limited space such an articulation can only be programmatic, but I will attempt to show how the three general developments of Part 1, which are part of a broader "turn to

---

3 Starr, *Sharers in Divine Nature: 2 Peter 1:4 in Its Hellenistic Context*, [*Coniectanea Biblica* New Testament Series 33] (Stockholm: Almqvist & Wiksell, 2000), p. 27.

4 Readers who are interested in further examining these theological trajectories will find a heavy dose of footnotes in Part 1. No footnotes appear in the subsections of Part 2, for these simply outline some of my own reflective explorations within this conceptual and existential space.

relationality,"⁵ may contribute to the fulfillment of this task in late modernity. My presentation of the biblical idea of becoming "sharers" in the divine nature through spiritual union with Christ will be guided by three desiderata: respecting the Infinite distinction between Creator and creature, emphasizing the Trinitarian structure of this fellowship, and accounting for the "not yet" and the "already" of human participation in divine life.

Part 1. Developments in the Doctrine of God

1.1. *Infinity*

Karl Barth's emphasis on divine Infinity is already evident in his early book on *The Epistle to the Romans*. In the preface to the 2nd edition, he announced: "If I have a system, it is limited to a recognition of what Kierkegaard called the 'infinite qualitative distinction' between time and eternity, and to my regarding this as possessing negative as well as positive significance: 'God is in heaven, and thou art on earth.'"⁶ This emphasis is linked to Barth's well-known insistence that God is "wholly other." Later in his career, Barth admitted that his early focus on the *diastasis* between God and humanity abstracted the "wholly other" and absolutized it over against humanity. He came to realize that insofar as the Word of God in Jesus Christ reveals that God is made known to creatures as "for" us and "with" us, and insofar as we experience life in the Spirit by whose power God is "in" and "among" us, we also need to speak of the "humanity of God."⁷ If God is "wholly other" without qualification, this might imply that God is defined as that which is over against creation. He recognized the need to avoid a naïve metaphysical dualism between God and the world that would imagine two "universes" that can be spanned by human language or thought. Theology must reject the Enlightenment's ideal of an autonomous human ego that rationally grasps all things (including the divine) from some inner epistemic Archimedean point.

In his *Church Dogmatics*, Barth provided a more detailed treatment of the idea of Infinity. He explicitly rejected the 17th century Protestant Scholastic view of Infinity as a comprehensive attribute that describes the

---

5 I have treated some of the philosophical and scientific forces that contributed to the turn to "relationality" as a dominant epistemological, ethical and ontological category in the first chapter of *Reforming Theological Anthropology* (Grand Rapids, MI: Eerdmans, in press). In the last three chapters, I demonstrate the demise of substance dualism and faculty psychology, and spell out the implications for the traditional loci of personal identity, sin and the image of God.

6 Barth, *The Epistle to the Romans*, translated by Edwyn C. Hoskyns (London: Oxford, 1933), p. 10. The first German edition had been published in 1919.

7 Barth, *The Humanity of God* (Richmond, VA: John Knox, 1960), pp. 44-45.

divine essence over against the world. Yes, God is Infinite, but "*He is also finite* – without destroying, but in his Infinity – in the fact that as love He is His own basis, goal, standard and law." Barth argued that properly predicating "Infinity" of God requires that we do so in a way that "does not involve any contradiction that it is *finitude as well.*"[8] Barth explained that God "is infinite in a manner in which the antithesis and mutual exclusiveness of the infinite and the finite . . . do not enclose and imprison Him . . . The infinity which as a concept stands in antithesis to finitude . . . is quite insufficient to describe what God is in relation to space and time" (CD, II/1, 467). He tried to avoid the tendency, which was all too common in early modernity, to depict God as one of the objects of human reason, even as that object that is on the other side of the finite/Infinite distinction. Barth insisted that God is known only through God, and only by God's gracious overcoming of the distinction between Creator and creation. God is "indissolubly Subject," and human knowing of God is first of all an acknowledgement of being addressed by the Word of God. God is not simply "the Infinite" as dialectically defined over against and so bound to the "the finite." God is "completely different,"[9] beyond and yet encompassing the distinction between Infinite and finite. If one conceptualizes the God-world relation in terms of two *kinds* of being ("infinite" and "finite") that together compose "All," then this "All" replaces God as the Absolute. Both "God" and "world" become parts of the "Whole." As Barth recognized, this way of speaking is not consistent with the idea of God as the Unlimited and Unconditioned, but marks "God" off as that part of the Whole that is limited (and so conditioned) by the finite.

By briefly observing the philosophical approach to "Infinity" in the work of 17th century philosopher René Descartes, we may begin to see how and why a focus on God as a conceptual object became important for some of his theological contemporaries. In his *Meditations* (1641), Descartes wanted to identify those objects in his consciousness that are "clear and distinct ideas," which as such cannot be doubted. Although Descartes is most famous for his idea of the indubitable existence of the doubting – and so thinking – self (*cogito ergo sum*), this idea depends upon a prior idea: namely, the Infinite (or God).[10] The idea that Descartes has of God "is the

---

[8] *Church Dogmatics*, ed. G.W. Bromiley and T.F. Torrance (T&T Clark, 1936-1977), II/1, pp. 467, 468 [emphasis added].
[9] In *The Mystery of God: Karl Barth and the Postmodern Foundations of Theology* (Louisville, KY: Westminster John Knox, 1997, p. 20), Stacey Johnson suggests this translation of *ganz anders* as better capturing Barth's intention. See also the comparison between Barth's theological method and Derrida's economy of différance in Graham Ward, *Barth, Derrida and the Language of Theology* (Cambridge University Press, 1995).
[10] For Descartes, the idea of a doubting self is intrinsically tied to the clear and distinct idea of an infinite and perfect being. "For how would I understand that I doubt and that I desire, that is, that something is lacking in me and that I am not completely perfect, if there were no idea of a more perfect being in me from whose comparison I might recognize my defects?"

maximally clear and distinct idea of all the ideas that are in me."[11] An inherent tension may be found at the heart of his proposal. On the one hand, Descartes believed that we *must* think of God as a clear and distinct idea, for the idea of the Infinite secures the self as an existing thinker. He was convinced that if he did not have this idea indubitably secured, then he could never be quite certain about anything else. On the other hand, we *cannot* think of God in this way because, as Descartes himself realized, the very idea of "Infinity" itself would be destroyed. He admits elsewhere that "the idea of the infinite, if it is to be a true idea, cannot be grasped at all, since the impossibility of being grasped is contained in the formal definition of the infinite."[12] Recent scholarship on Descartes has shown that he may in general have preferred an emphasis on reason's inability to grasp God's essence,[13] but the important point here is that the domestication of divine Infinity as an object of reason was buttressed by his language about the Infinite as a clear and distinct idea. This contributed to a basic dualism between the Infinite and the finite in Enlightenment theology.

In the early 19th century, the philosophical incoherence of this dualism became one of the most important themes for G.W.F. Hegel. He was ruthless in his critique of what he called the "spurious" infinite, i.e., any idea of the Infinite that defines it merely as that which is determined by its polarity to the finite. A contradiction thus occurs "as a direct result of the circumstance that the finite remains as a determinate being opposed to the infinite, so that there are *two* determinatenesses; *there are* two worlds, one infinite and one finite, and in their relationship the infinite is only the *limit* of the finite and is thus only a determinate infinite, an *infinite which is itself finite*."[14] In other words, when we think of the Infinite, we are naming something that we take to be distinct from the finite, i.e., *not* finite. But the problem with stopping there is that this makes the "Infinite" one thing among other things, an object set over against and opposed to the finite.

(*Meditations on First Philosophy*, edited and translated by George Heffernan, University of Notre Dame Press, 1990, p. 139). Presupposing that all causes contain the same (or more) substantive reality than their effects, Descartes argued that a finite thinking self could not be the cause of this idea, and so an Infinite being must exist as the cause of this idea and of the finite self.

11 Ibid.

12 Descartes, "Fifth Replies," *The Philosophical Writings of Descartes*, 3 vols, trans. John Cottingham, et al. (Cambridge University Press, 1991), 2:253. Already in the Third Meditation, he had accepted that he cannot "comprehend" the nature of the infinite, but argues that simply having the idea itself (as that which cannot be comprehended) clearly and distinctly is sufficient.

13 See, e.g., Anne Ashley Davenport, *Measure of a Different Greatness: The Intensive Infinite, 1250-1650* (Leiden: Brill, 1999), pp. 416ff. Cf. Karsten Harries, *Infinity and Perspective* (Cambridge, MA: The MIT Press, 2001), pp. 282-289.

14 *Hegel's Science of Logic*, trans. A.V. Miller (Amherst, NY: Humanity Books, 1999), pp. 139-140 [emphases in original].

Finite things, by definition, have limits; the fact that a thing is *not* something else is essential to its finitude. If we merely de-fine the In-finite in terms of what it is *not*, then we have just made it finite by marking its limits. The Infinite is then placed under the category of finitude. If we think of the finite as simply "outside of" or "next to" the Infinite, then our conception of the latter is not absolutely unlimited. An idea of "true Infinity" would both transcend and embrace the distinction between finite and Infinite.

Some 19th century liberal theologians took this in the direction of pantheism (or panentheism), emphasizing the immanence of the divine in human self-consciousness. In reaction, some conservative theologians rejected Hegel's philosophical analysis and attempted to defend divine transcendence by buttressing early modern dualism. For example, we can hear explicit Cartesian echoes in the work of Charles Hodge, whose theological influence on 19th and 20th century American theology can hardly be overestimated. Hodge insisted that we have a "perfectly *clear and distinct idea* of the infinity of God" and that "we know God in *the same sense* in which we know ourselves and things out of ourselves."[15] This response is understandable in light of the either/or dichotomy that forces a choice between pantheism and dualism. If humans are to know God, and if the only way to "know" is through the power of the human intellect that is able to grasp and define the substantive reality of things, then humans must know the Infinite (immaterial, etc.) substance of God by mentally grasping it and clearly distinguishing the qualities that mark it off from other substances. After the philosophical turn to relationality,[16] however, the old substance metaphysics that held up the horns of this dilemma is collapsing, and more dynamic categories and relational thought-forms are emerging that may help theologians move beyond this liberal/conservative dichotomy. Although Barth's emphasis alternated between transcendence and immanence during his career, his reflections on Infinity were part of a broader theological retrieval of pre-modern and Reformation emphases on the relationality intrinsic to Christian faith.

One of the most important forces behind the retrieval of divine Infinity in the 20th century has been the growth of ecumenical dialogue between West and East. The Eastern Orthodox theologian John D. Zizioulas offers this summary of one of the key intuitions of his tradition: *"God and the world cannot be ontologically placed side by side as self-defined entities."*[17] This intuition was evident already in the fourth century Greek-

---

15 Hodge, *Systematic Theology*, Vol. 1 (Grand Rapids, MI: Eerdmans, 1981), pp. 359, 365 [emphasis added].
16 For background on this philosophical shift, see my "The Philosophical Turn to Relationality" in Dana Wright (ed.), *Redemptive Transformation in Practical Theology* (Grand Rapids, MI: Eerdmans, 2002).
17 *Being as Communion* (Crestwood, NY: St. Vladimir's Press, 1997), p. 94 [his italics].

speaking Cappadocian theologian St. Gregory of Nyssa. During this period theologians were surrounded by the classical Greek distaste for *apeiron* (the limitless). For many Greek philosophers, the reality of a substance is known as the human mind marks its limits, grasping its genus and differentiae. For them the idea of "limitlessness" seemed to imply incomprehensible chaos. With good apologetic intentions, the Christian theologian Eunomios asserted that the divine essence *is* knowable by human reason. Gregory argued that this kind of apologetics rendered God finite. Long before Hegel, Nyssa was eager to avoid collapsing into a spurious concept of Infinity as applied to God:

> The divine by its very nature is infinite, enclosed by no boundary. If the divine be perceived as though bounded by something, one must by all means along with that boundary consider what is beyond it... In the same way, God, if he be conceived as bounded, would necessarily be surrounded by something different in nature.[18]

For Nyssa, divine Infinity is not something negative (as Greek metaphysics assumed) but rather a positive reality: it suggests an absolute perfection beyond the grasp of the human mind. God's Infinite Essence is not "side by side" with the world, limited by the reality of creatures. Only because God is perfectly Infinite, as unlimited superabundance, are humans (and all creation) able to participate in the goodness of God's life.[19] Later Eastern Orthodox theologians would spell out a distinction between the divine *essence* and the divine *energies*.[20] Human creaturely life participates in the latter though not the former; this distinction helped avoid the implication that *theosis* (sharing in the divine nature) involved the essential divinisation of creatures. It also protected against thinking of the divine essence as one rational object among many, as one part (even the greatest part) of a larger whole.

In Roman Catholic theology as well, we may trace a growing interest in the significance of divine Infinity during the last century. Often this took the form of retrieving the emphases of earlier Latin theologians such

---

18 *Vita Moysis*, II, 236. Trans. and quoted in Everett Ferguson, "God's Infinity and Man's Mutability: Perpetual Progress according to Gregory of Nyssa," *Greek Orthodox Theological Review* 18/2 (1973), p. 65.
19 For quotes and analysis see Patricia Wilson-Kastner, "God's Infinity and His Relationship to Creation" *Foundations* 21 (Oct-Dec, 1978), pp. 305-21.
20 As Vladimir Lossky explains, humans experience the divine energies by the gracious manifestation of divine light, but the divine essence (or, as St. Gregory of Palamas preferred, God's "superessence") is unknowable (cf. *In the Image and Likeness of God*, Crestwood, NY: St. Vladimir's Press, 1985, pp. 52ff). For a comparison of this model to the different kind of dualism that emerged in the West, see Duncan Reid, *Energies of the Spirit: Trinitarian Models in Eastern Orthodox and Western Theology* (Atlanta: Scholar's Press, 1997).

as St. Thomas Aquinas[21] and St. Anselm. The key to Anselm's so-called ontological argument in his *Proslogium* is the idea of "that than which nothing greater can be conceived."[22] Setting aside the issue of the fecundity of this argument as a "proof" for God's existence, the important point to notice is that Anselm was operating with an idea of God as the Creator of the world that does not place divine and human being under the same general category. Robert Sokolowski suggests that this understanding of God emerged only through reflection on the Incarnation; only if God is infinitely distinct from the world (and not one being among many) can we think of the Logos becoming flesh without squeezing out the particularity of the creature.[23] The idea "that than which nothing greater can be conceived" carries with it the implication that nothing "greater" is conceived when we add together God and the world. Because God cannot be "conceived" as a being in the world, not even the greatest being,[24] adding the world to God does not result in anything "greater" than God. If the idea of "the world added to God" was greater than the idea of God alone, then God would not be "that than which nothing greater can be conceived," for then something greater than God could indeed be conceived – namely, God and the world together.

Several other forces[25] were at work in this retrieval of divine Infinity, but I limit myself here to noting briefly the distinctive contributions of three leading Protestant theologians who have been influenced by Barth, and who share the desire to overcome the early modern idea of God as a rational object and the simplistic dualism that flowed from it. Arguing that the modern focus on the distinction between God and the world led to an exploitation of nature (and "others"), Jürgen

---

21 David Burrell, C.S.C., is among the foremost Catholic thinkers who have retrieved Thomas' emphasis on the Infinity of God. Cf. his *Knowing the Unknowable God* (Notre Dame, 1986) and *Freedom and Creation in Three Traditions* (Notre Dame, 1993). For Burrell (and Thomas) God *is* different from creation, but God differs differently.

22 "Proslogium" in *St. Anselm: Basic Writings*, trans. S.N. Deane (La Salle, IN: Open Court, 1962), p. 54.

23 Sokolowski, *The God of Faith and Reason: Foundations of Christian Theology* (Washington, DC: The Catholic University of America Press, 1982).

24 Unfortunately, many Protestant thinkers have misread Anselm on this crucial point and taken him to mean that God is "the greatest of all conceivable beings" (e.g., Millard Erickson, *Christian Theology*, 2nd ed., Grand Rapids, MI: Baker, 1998, p. 184). This is exactly what Anselm is trying to deny, as he says explicitly in Chapter XV of the Proslogium: "thou art a being greater than can be conceived." To argue that God is among all conceivable beings "the greatest" is to make God a rational object, side by side with the world.

25 Liberation and feminist theology have been particularly influential. In his *A Theology of Liberation* (Maryknoll, NY: Orbis, 1988), Gustavo Gutiérrez urged that we find a new way of approaching theology that overcomes the focus on rationalizing doctrine, and reflects on Christian praxis in the light of the Word of God. In *She Who Is* (New York: Crossroad, 1997), Elizabeth Johnson suggests that exclusively male symbols for God have obscured the classical Christian insistence that God's very nature is illimitable and unobjectifiable.

Moltmann places a "recognition of the presence of God in the world and the presence of the world in God" at the center of his doctrine of *God in Creation*. The Infinite God dwells in finite creation, and the finite creation finds space "in" God, who is the "dwelling place" of the world.[26] Robert Jenson also emphasizes the intimate connection between the Infinite and the finite rather than their distinction. He wants to think of God's "being" in radically temporal terms and so describes God's eternity as "*temporal infinity*." For Jenson, God's being cannot be separated from God's narrative: "God is what happens between Jesus and his Father in their Spirit."[27] He is aware of the criterion of the "true" Infinity, and clearly wants to maintain the intuition that Infinity embraces the finite; yet he explicitly uses language that is "designed to blur the boundary between God and creature."[28] While these emphases overcome the hard dichotomy between God and the world, some critics worry that the panentheistic tendencies of Jenson and Moltmann fail to uphold divine transcendence.

Wolfhart Pannenberg also treats the criterion of the "true Infinite," arguing that the Israelite experience of the holiness of God points to a resolution. "The Infinite is truly infinite only when it transcends its own antithesis to the finite. In this sense the holiness of God is truly infinite, for it is opposed to the profane, yet it also enters the profane world, penetrates it, and makes it holy."[29] The authors of the New Testament testify that this holiness is ultimately mediated in and to the world by Jesus Christ and the Holy Spirit. For Pannenberg, the philosophical categories of "part" and "whole" have special significance for theology. God is not simply a "part" of the whole nor simply the "whole" as the sum of the parts of finite reality. God is the "unifying unity" of the world, distinct but not absolutely distinct from the totality of the finite. "The infinity of the unifying unity (and so also its difference from that which as finite is *eo ipso* a part of the world as unified unity) can only be maintained if it is not only the source of the unity of the parts but also the source of the parts themselves."[30]

Although these three theologians disagree on *how* to uphold both divine immanence and transcendence when speaking of divine Infinity, they share with Barth the goal of developing an adequate articulation of

---

26 *God in Creation*, trans. Margaret Kohl (San Francisco: Harper and Row, 1985), p. 13, 148. Moltmann relates the idea of God's *Shekinah* presence to both the doctrine of Trinity and to his understanding of divine Futurity in *The Coming of God*, trans. Margaret Kohl (Minneapolis: Fortress, 1996).
27 *Systematic Theology*, Vol. I, (Oxford, 1997), p. 221.
28 Ibid., p. 225. Jenson says that God "makes room" for us in the divine being, which *is* a conversation. "The opening of that room is the act of creation" (p. 226).
29 Pannenberg, *Systematic Theology*, v. I, trans. G.W. Bromiley (Grand Rapids, MI: Eerdmans, 1991), p. 400.
30 Pannenberg, *Metaphysics and the Idea of God*, trans. Philip Clayton (Edinburgh: T&T Clark, 1990), p. 143.

what I will refer to here as "perfect Infinity."[31] As we will see they also hold in common a sense that the solution has something to do with the relational nature of God (robust Trinity) and the eschatological consummation of the world (primal Futurity).

1.2. *Trinity*

Robert Jenson described the Trinitarian turn in late 20th century systematic theology as characterized by "dependence on Karl Barth for inspiration though not much for matter; by adherence to Karl Rahner's axiom 'the immanent Trinity is the economic Trinity' in an ontological fashion that he himself would probably not have countenanced; and by a remarkable degree of renewed speculative freedom."[32] Let us once again begin with Barth in our brief review of this flow of ideas. In the first volume of his *Dogmatics* Barth self-consciously diverges from the custom of the Protestant Scholastics and their followers. Why, he asks, did they treat the "That" and "What" of God first, as though these could be separated from the "Who?" (CD, I/1, 301). This separation in the doctrine of God had been solidified when Thomas Aquinas tried to establish the Unity of God (in his *Summa Theologiae*) before turning to a treatment of the Persons of God revealed in Scripture. Although the Trinitarian dynamics of the Christian experience of justification by faith were central for the early Reformers, their 17th century "Scholastic" followers returned to the medieval model of Thomas, privileging abstract unity and simplicity over the dynamic relationality of the persons of the Trinity. During the 18th century, which saw the rise of modern atheism, the majority of Protestant theologians in the West tried to ground their systems on broadly "theistic" concepts of the divine as a single subject with an all-powerful will and an all-knowing intellect, rather than on an explicitly Christian (Trinitarian) idea of God.[33] Meanwhile, treatment of the Trinity was moved further and further from the center of the doctrine of God so that by the 19th century,

---

31 This phrase is intended to point materially beyond the formal philosophical criterion of "true" Infinity. *Perfect* Infinity suggests metaphysical fullness and leads more naturally to a discussion of the plenitude of the eternal being of the trinitarian relations. I agree with Philip Clayton's assessment of the inherent problems with the idea of "infinite perfection" (*The Problem of God in Modern Thought*, Grand Rapids, MI: Eerdmans, 2000), but this does not preclude an appropriately qualified use of the idea of perfect Infinity.

32 "Does God have Time?" in *Essays in Theology of Culture* (Grand Rapids, MI: Eerdmans, 1995), p. 192.

33 As Michael J. Buckley, S.J., notes, in early modernity Christianity "transmuted itself into theism" in order to protect its god from the challenges of mechanistic science; the Christian religion alienated itself from its own resources disclosed in the revelation of Christ long before "a-theists" arose. A-theists simply drew out the logical implications of a "theism" that had become detached from the trinitarian God. See *At the Origins of Modern Atheism* (New Haven: Yale, 1987), pp. 346ff. Orthodox Protestant Scholastic theologians *affirmed* the doctrine of the Trinity, as they had the idea of Infinity, but these affirmations were not always integral to their systematic presentations.

Schleiermacher had relegated it to a brief section at the end of *The Christian Faith* (1831).

Barth explicitly reversed this trend by making "The Triune God" his first material topic after the introductory chapter on the "Word of God as the Criterion of Dogmatics." It was precisely this criterion that led him to a reconsideration of the place of the doctrine in the structure of theological presentation. However, simply putting Trinity first in the order of treatment is not enough – its content must be "decisive and controlling for the whole of dogmatics" (CD, I/1, 303). Despite this formal revolution, materially Barth still imagines God as a single subject: "*God* reveals Himself. He reveals Himself *through Himself*. He reveals *Himself*" (I/2, 296). The statement "God reveals Himself as the Lord" is for Barth the root of the doctrine of the Trinity. When speaking about the Trinity, only to the *one* Lord does Barth believe the term "person" should be properly applied; here he defines a person as "an I existing in and for itself with its own thought and will" (I/1, 358). In later volumes he explains that the free differentiation and relationship between I and Thou in humanity takes place "between two different individuals, whereas in the case of God they are included in the one individual... the I-Thou relationship is the only genuine distinction in the one divine being" (III/1, 196). He qualifies the "one name" of God (which is the "threefold name" of Father, Son and Spirit), insisting that it refers to "the one 'personality' of God, the one active and speaking divine Ego" (IV/1, 205). Many theologians have argued that Barth's application of the self-reflection logic of German Idealism to the one divine Ego collapses into the same problems that Barth himself saw in Augustine's psychological analogies – the projection of our own experience as single subjects onto the divine nature. This is why Jenson noted that Barth has been a source for inspiration in the revival of Trinitarian doctrine, "though not much for matter."

As in the case of the retrieval of divine Infinity, here too we can also see that the flames of Trinitarian discussion have been fanned by the growth of ecumenical dialogue about the Holy Spirit between East and West. One of the major issues in the split between (what are now called) the Eastern Orthodox and the Roman Catholic churches in 1054 A. D. was the proper understanding of the relation of the Holy Spirit to the Father and Son. While the early ecumenical creeds affirmed that the Spirit "proceeds from the Father," the West had later inserted the phrase "and the Son" (*filioque*). After centuries of mutual condemnation, we find in recent decades several promising developments. The 1991 "Agreed Statement on the Holy Trinity," for example, was the result of dialogue between the Orthodox Church and the World Alliance of Reformed Churches.[34] In his

---

[34] For analysis, see T. F. Torrance, *Trinitarian Perspectives: Toward Doctrinal Agreement* (Edinburgh: T&T Clark, 1994).

Being as Communion, John Zizioulas sets out the rationale for the Eastern emphasis on God's relational being. He notes that Athanasius' efforts to secure the "consubstantiality" (*homoousios*) of the Son and the Father led to a transformation of the idea of "substance," which had in Greek philosophy been kept separate from the category of "relation." Zizioulas argues that "to say that the Son belongs to God's substance implies that substance *possesses almost by definition a relational character*."[35] If the Creator as origin of all Being is inherently relational, the ultimate character of being should be conceived as communion, not as abstract substance. For the Cappadocians, the being of God was not based in an abstract *ousia*, but in a Person, namely, the Father. This idea of the Father as the source (or "font") of deity led many in the West to worry about subordinationism, but the main point for our purposes here is to note that this model was intended to underscore the belief that the Incarnation had revealed that the very being of God is relational.

As Roman Catholic theologians have responded to the concerns of the East over the insertion of *filioque*, a renewed focus on Pneumatology has emerged. Ralph Del Colle traces an important stream in this renewal in his discussion of recent proposals for a "Spirit-Christology" in which Christology is informed "with an equally important and central pneumatology, while at the same time preserving the integrity of the doctrine of the trinity."[36] As part of the broader revival of Trinitarian doctrine, many Catholic theologians have attempted to retrieve thinkers like St. Augustine and Richard of St. Victor as resources for responding to the *filioque* debate. One example must suffice: after a careful assessment of various models of the Trinity over the centuries, David Coffey suggests the following resolution – "The Holy Spirit proceeds from the Father and receives from the Son."[37] Trinitarian reflection on the Spirit (and so on the Trinity) has been spurred by the exponential growth of the Pentecostal and charismatic movements of the last century (and not only in Roman Catholicism),[38] as well as by increased communication among the major religions.[39]

---

35 *Being as Communion*, p. 84. Emphasis in original.
36 Ralph del Colle, *Christ and the Spirit: Spirit-Christology in Trinitarian Perspective* (New York: Oxford, 1994), p. 4.
37 David Coffey, *Deus Trinitas: The Doctrine of the Triune God* (New York: Oxford, 1999), p. 155. By the 12th century, Richard of St. Victor had concluded that from the assertion that the divine includes some one person (who is good), then it follows of necessity that we acknowledge a fellowship of divine persons (*De Trinitate*, III.14).
38 See Richard Shaull & Waldo Cesar, *Pentecostalism and the Future of the Christian Churches* (Grand Rapids, MI: Eerdmans, 2000). For a nuanced theological and philosophical response to these developments, see Michael Welker, *God the Spirit*, Trans John F. Hoffmeyer (Minneapolis: Fortress, 1994).
39 The Trinity has emerged as a central theme not only in ecumenical, but also in inter-religious dialogue. See, e.g., Mark Heim, *The Depths of Riches: A Trinitarian Theology of*

The most influential Roman Catholic theologian in the 20th century revival of Trinitarian doctrine was Karl Rahner. His 1967 book *The Trinity* deeply affected the theological conversation by introducing the axiom: "The economic Trinity is the immanent Trinity, and the immanent Trinity is the economic Trinity."[40] The *economic* Trinity refers to how God is revealed in the outworking of the history of salvation; the *immanent* Trinity has to do with God's eternal being as distinct from creation. Rahner's point is that we should not think of these as two wholly *separate* things. The eternal God *is* the God is revealed in Christ by the Spirit. On the other hand, if the economic and immanent Trinity are absolutely identical, then God eternally depends on the world to be what or who God is. This axiom fueled the dialogue, but did not of itself answer the question of *how* to speak of the distinction *and* unity of the economic and immanent Trinity. Most Christian theologians who have dealt with Trinity after this point have interacted with Rahner's axiom, although they have interpreted it in different ways.[41] This is true among many Trinitarian thinkers in liberation and feminist thought[42] generally, and it also holds for the three Protestant theologians we discussed above in relation to the retrieval of divine Infinity.

Throughout Pannenberg's *Systematic Theology*, from §1 of volume I to the last sentence of volume III, the relation of the immanent and economic Trinity (their distinction and unity as a comprehensive explanation of the relation of all finite things to the infinite God) is the key to Christian theology's claim to truth. In chapter 5 Pannenberg referred to the Trinitarian persons as "separate centers of action [selbständige Aktzentren]

Religious Ends (Grand Rapids, MI: Eerdmans, 2001); Kevin J. Vanhoozer, ed., *The Trinity in a Pluralistic Age: Theological Essays on Culture and Religion* (Grand Rapids: Eerdmans, 1997); Gavin D'Costa, *The Meeting of Religions and the Trinity* (Maryknoll, NY: Orbis, 2000); Raimundo Pannikar, *The Trinity and the Religious Experience of Man* (Maryknoll, NY: Orbis, 1973).

40 Rahner, *The Trinity*, trans. J. Donceel, with an Introduction by C.M. LaCugna (New York: Crossroad, 1997), p. 22. Originally published in 1967.

41 For a review of such interpretations, see Ted Peters' *God as Trinity* (Louisville, KY: Westminster John Knox, 1993). Barth had his own rule that "statements about the divine modes of being antecedently in themselves cannot be different in content from those that are to be made about their reality in revelation. All our statements concerning what is called the immanent Trinity have been reached simply as confirmations or underlinings or, materially, as the indispensable premises of the economic Trinity" (CD, I/1, 479).

42 Many liberation thinkers see a close connection between a concept of God as a single absolute ruler and the oppression of the poor. For this reason, they argue for an emphasis on God as trinitarian communion as the basis for human relations with each other and God. See, e.g., Leonardo Boff, *Holy Trinity, Perfect Community*, trans. Phillip Berryman (Maryknoll: Orbis, 2000). For feminists, a similar move is made in reaction to the domination of women. In *God for Us: The Trinity & Christian Life* (San Francisco: HarperCollins, 1991), Catherine Mowry LaCugna attempts to revive the inherent link between the doctrine of the Trinity and the practical experience of salvation in order to provide a relational ontology that grounds our shared life together.

and not just modes of being of the one divine subject,"[43] and in chapter 6, he explicitly connected the Trinity to the criterion of the true Infinite. As he explained in an earlier work, the Trinitarian idea of God "without blotting out the difference between creator and creature, transcends while preserving this opposition by means of the idea of the reconciliation of the world."[44] Robert Jenson recognizes that the theological reason for distinguishing between the "immanent" and the "economic" trinity is the freedom of God; God "could have" been the same God without creation.[45] *How* this could be, however, "we can know or guess nothing whatsoever."[46] Instead of engaging in such speculation, Jenson simply identifies God by and with the triune narrative of history; he depicts the "persons" of God's identity as *dramatis dei personae*, "characters of the drama of God."[47] The unity of the immanent and economic Trinity, argues Jenson, is based on the power of futurity and freedom *in* the Trinitarian God: "The freedom *in* and *to* which the Son is begotten of the Father is the Spirit."[48] God's temporal Infinity, which makes space and time for creatures, is also Trinitarian: "The Son mediates the Father's originating and the Spirit's liberating, thereby to *hold open* the creatures' space in being."[49]

Jürgen Moltmann's interest in the Trinity has been shaped by his passion for responding to the concerns of those who have experienced social oppression, whether due to racism, sexism or classism.[50] In all cases, the Trinity is key for overcoming conceptions of God that have been used to condone or support such domination. Moltmann notes that when the reflection logic of an Absolute Subject is applied to the Father and the Son, "the Son is nothing other than the self of the divine 'I,' the counterpart, the other, in whom God contemplates himself..."[51] Unlike Barth, for whom the one divine Lordship controlled interpretation of the Trinity, Moltmann wants to privilege Trinity over "monarchy" as he describes the unity of God. He stresses that the three are not all "persons" in exactly the same sense; in unique ways the personality of each in their relations to the others secures the unity of the one God. The persons and the relations are reciprocal or "genetically" connected: "The unity of the Trinity is

---

43 Pannenberg, *Systematic Theology*, I, 336.
44 Pannenberg, "Problems of a Trinitarian Doctrine of God" *Dialog* 26/4 (1987): 256.
45 Jenson, *The Triune Identity* (Philadelphia: Fortress, 1982), pp. 139ff.
46 *Systematic Theology*, I, p. 143.
47 Ibid., I, pp. 75, 110ff.
48 Ibid., p. 144.
49 *Systematic Theology*, II, pp. 25, 27.
50 See, e.g., "I Believe in God the Father: Patriarchical or Non-Patriarchical Talk of God?" in *History and the Triune God*, trans. John Bowden, (New York: Crossroad, 1992), 1-18; *God for a Secular Society: The Public Relevance of Theology*, trans. M. Kohl (Minneapolis: Fortress, 1999); *Experiences in Theology*, trans. M. Kohl (Minneapolis: Fortress, 2000).
51 *Trinity and the Kingdom*, p. 143.

constituted by the Father, concentrated around the Son, and illumined through the Holy Spirit."[52]

Although these three theologians articulate the relations of the persons differently, they are all interested in developing a robust doctrine of the Trinity that sees the conditions for creaturely differentiation and fellowship with God as already provided in the eternal relationality of the divine nature. They also share the belief that presenting an adequate doctrine of the Infinite Trinitarian God will require careful attention to the ontological implications of Christian eschatology.

1.3. Futurity

Because the concepts in this subsection may be less familiar to many readers than the ideas discussed in the retrieval of divine Infinity and the revival of the doctrine of Trinity, I will dedicate more space to outlining them. Like the terms Infinity and Trinity, the word "Futurity" brings with it an implicit danger. Just as we must avoid the collapse into a "spurious" understanding of Infinity or into a naïve tritheism, so too we must not think of divine Futurity merely as one of the modes of time. Predicating the term "Futurity" of the divine nature should not be taken to mean that God is necessarily placed "in" the future or posited "as" the future *over against* the past and the present. Recognizing the inherent limitations of all religious language, in Part 2 I will use the term "Futurity" doxologically, as a witness to the Eternity of the Infinite Trinitarian God as the origin, condition and goal of all the modes of creaturely temporality.

Karl Barth provided a fresh impetus for the renewal of theological discourse on this topic as well. In *The Epistle to the Romans*, he explicitly rejected the idea that human conduct could be traced to the will of God as its efficient cause; who would dare, he asks, speak of God and humanity as "links in a chain of causality?"[53] Barth insisted that God confronts humanity not as first cause, but as Primal Origin. "If Christianity be not altogether thoroughgoing eschatology, there remains in it no relationship whatever with Christ."[54] This connection between eschatology and Christology is spelled out further in the *Church Dogmatics*. They are inherently linked because the incarnation of the divine Word in Jesus Christ leads us to speak of divine Eternity as a true Eternity that "includes this possibility, the potentiality of time . . . [that] has the power to take time to itself" (CD, II/1, 617). For Barth, God's Eternity embraces time in three

---

52 Ibid., p. 178.
53 *Romans*, p. 356.
54 Ibid., p. 314. Bruce McCormack has shown how Barth exchanged one model of eschatology for another between the two editions of *Romans*. In the 2nd edition Barth "abandoned the process eschatology of *Romans I* in favor of a radically futurist 'consistent' eschatology." *Karl Barth's Critically Realistic Dialectical Theology* (Oxford: Clarendon, 1995), p. 208.

"forms," which he calls pre-temporality, supra-temporality and post-temporality. He argues that the Reformers (and many theologians before them) showed a dangerous one-sided interest in *pre*-temporality that led to the problems of determinism in the doctrines of election and providence.[55] Barth also criticized much of the theology of the 18th and 19th centuries (especially Schleiermacher's) as too focused on God's *supra*-temporality – their emphasis was on the present moment of human consciousness and its dependence on the divine.

In the second volume of the *Dogmatics*, Barth recognized that in his early writings his enthusiasm for thinking "with new seriousness about God's futurity" (II/1, 636) had led him into the danger of collapsing into an equally reductionistic obsession with *post*-temporality. The idea that human history does not finally share in the wholly other Futurity of God, however, is not consonant with the biblical message that history moves toward a "real end." To avoid post-temporal reductionism, Barth argues that the three forms of Eternity are equally God's eternity and "therefore the living God Himself."[56] In the last completed volume of the *Dogmatics*, he returns to the intimate connection between Christology and eschatology; the expectation of the *parousia* of Jesus Christ as the "end, and therefore the dawn of eternal light" permeates the Christian life in hope (IV/3.2, 934). Barth's argument for a positive "embracing" relation between Eternity and time led to a radical reconsideration of both the ideas of God as first cause and "Eternal Now." Those who followed in his wake realized that God and temporality must be thought together, and Futurity must somehow be included.[57]

Once again we should recognize the currents in which Barth was swimming, the broader forces that made his accomplishment possible and that continue to call for more adequate articulations in the doctrine of God. The beginning of the renewal of eschatological reflection in the 20th century may be traced to insights from biblical research. Among Old Testament

---

[55] Colin Gunton suggests that the Reformers began the process of replacing abstract concepts of causality with concepts that connote more personal and loving agency. Cf. his "The End of Causality? The Reformers and their Predecessors" in Gunton (ed.) *The Doctrine of Creation* (Edinburgh: T&T Clark, 1997), pp. 63-82.

[56] CD, II/1, 638. For a discussion of Barth's view of Eternity and time, see George Hunsinger, *Disruptive Grace: Studies in the Theology of Karl Barth* (Grand Rapids, MI: Eerdmans, 2000), pp. 186-209, and Ingolf Dalferth, "Karl Barth's Eschatological Realism" in S.W. Sykes (ed.) *Karl Barth: Centenary Essays* (Cambridge, 1989), pp. 14-45.

[57] Although Barth does not quote him in this context, it may be that here too he is dependent on Kierkegaard. In *Works of Love*, Kierkegaard speaks of Eternity as "taking upon itself the form of the future, the possible [and] with the help of hope it brings up temporality's child [the human being]" (Princeton, 1995), p. 252. In *The Concept of Anxiety*, he suggests "that the future in a certain sense signifies more than the present and the past, because . . . the future can in a certain sense signify the whole. This is because the eternal first signifies the future or because the future is the incognito in which the eternal . . . preserves its association with time" (Princeton, 1980), p. 89.

scholars, we find an increasing recognition that the religion of Israel was based on an eschatological hope in the coming of God's kingdom.[58] The ancient Jews lived in anticipation of the promised "day of the Lord," which would bring not only judgment (Amos 5:18-20) but also peace (Zech. 2:10-11). The upright person lived in expectation of the fulfillment of the divine promise, trusting that the Lord will bring to pass a new reality in which justice and peace are secured. This attitude is in contrast to the philosophical fatalism of Israel's neighbors.[59] In New Testament scholarship, the renewal of eschatological reflection emerged out of the various quests for the historical Jesus. Albert Schweitzer's emphasis in 1906 on the distinction between "realized" and "consistent" eschatology shaped the debates about the relation of the kingdom of God to the present throughout the first half of the 20th century.[60] The question about the relation between the "already" and the "not yet" of the kingdom in the message of Jesus was the topic of books with titles such as *Christ and Time* and *The Presence of the Future*.[61] The importance of this surprising, in-breaking power of the kingdom had not been emphasized in early modern theology; most 17th century treatments of eschatology were limited to the "four last things," which were already determined by the divine decrees.[62]

The renewed focus on the New Testament witness to the coming Christ was crucial for those systematic theologians who initiated the theological turn toward divine Futurity. They tried to draw out the ontological implications of belief in the resurrection of Jesus and anticipation of his eschatological consummation of the world, implications that seemed to give metaphysical primacy to the future. As Carl Braaten argued, the Christian understanding of creation is primarily oriented not to the genesis of the world in the past, but to its "neogenesis in the arrival of God's creative future in the resurrection of Jesus – the prolepsis of the new creation." Christian faith is not grounded in the ability to trace the

---

[58] See, e.g., Gerhard von Rad, *Old Testament Theology*, 2 vols., trans. D.M.G. Stalker (Louisville, KY: Westminster John Knox, 2001). Original German published in 1957.

[59] Cf. Luther H. Martin, "Fate, Futurity and Historical Consciousness in Western Antiquity," *Historical Reflections/Réflexions Historiques* 17/2 (1991)151-169.

[60] Schweitzer, *The Quest of the Historical Jesus*, trans. W. Montgomery (New York: Macmillan, 1961). German, 1906. For a thorough survey see Gerhard Sauter, *What Dare We Hope? Reconsidering Eschatology* (Harrisburg, PA: Trinity Press International, 1999). Already in 1892 Johannes Weiss had pointed to the centrality of the arriving and future kingdom in the message of Jesus; *Jesus' Proclamation of the Kingdom of God*, trans. Richard Hyde Hiers and David Larrimore Holland (Philadelphia, 1971). Original German published in 1892.

[61] Oscar Cullmann, rev. ed., trans. Floyd V. Filson, *Christ and Time: The Primitive Christian Conception of Time and History* (London: SCM, 1962). George Eldon Ladd, *The Presence of the Future: The Eschatology of Biblical Realism* (Grand Rapids: Eerdmans, 1974).

[62] The four last "things" were (with some variation) the end of the world, the resurrection of the dead, the final judgment, and eternal life. The term "eschatology" was introduced in 17th century theological systems to refer to these things, which will occur "last" on the timeline of history.

world back to a "first cause" using inferential reasoning, but in the anticipation of the future of the world and "its orientation to God as its goal."[63] As we will see in Part 2, this Christological focus is important for all three trajectories, for reflection on the primal Futurity of the Coming One must be connected both to a robust doctrine of the Trinity (which links Jesus to the Father by the Spirit) and to a conception of God as perfectly Infinite (which allows for a relational unity between Logos and flesh, as well as between Holy Spirit and human spirit).

The increased interaction of Western theology with the East through ecumenical dialogue was also an important force in the renewal of eschatological reflection. The early Eastern focus on the Father as the "font" of deity who begets the Son and breathes the Spirit was part of a broader cosmological understanding of all things "from the Father to the Father." This introduced a temporal focus on the future as an anticipated participation in God (*theosis*). Here too John Zizioulas was one of the most influential interlocutors with the West as he articulated the Eastern Orthodox emphasis on the ontological importance of the future. He described the ecclesial identity of the church as a "hypostasis which has its roots in the future and its branches in the past."[64] This applies not only to the church but also to all of creation. For Zizioulas, "the truth of history lies in the future, and this is to be understood in an ontological sense: history is true, despite change and decay, not just because it is a movement *towards* an end, but mainly because it is a movement *from* the end, since it is the end that gives it meaning."[65] This sense of the future as the source of being in relation to God is reflected in the Eastern Orthodox eucharistic liturgy, which emphasizes not only *anamnesis* (remembering), but also an *epiclesis* – a calling upon the Spirit that creates the community by mediating the presence of the eschatological kingdom of God.[66]

Many Roman Catholic theologians have also contributed to the renewal of eschatological reflection. Karl Rahner attempted to hold anthropology and eschatology together by speaking of God as the "absolute future." For Rahner, the nature of human "transcendentality" *is*

---

[63] *The Future of God* (New York: Harper and Row, 1969), p. 104. Elsewhere, Braaten argued that prioritizing the future is implied by biblical belief that in Jesus of Nazareth the end of history has appeared, yet without ceasing to be future. "In his very being God is the future of the world. He is the common future and unifying force of all contingent events in nature and history . . . If God is not his own future, there would be some other future beyond him, and this would have to be thought of as God. The very idea of God requires that we think of him as the ultimate future." *The Futurist Option* (New York: Newman Press, 1970), pp. 28-29.

[64] Zizioulas, *Being as Communion*, p. 59. The church "does not draw its being from what is now but is rooted ontologically in the future, the pledge and earnest of which is the resurrection of Christ" (64).

[65] Ibid., 96.

[66] Alexander Schmemann describes the eschatological nature of the sacrament in *The Eucharist*, trans. Paul Kachur (Crestwood, NY: St. Vladimir's, 2000), pp. 34ff.

its openness to the future – not just any future, but to "the absolute future of God himself."[67] Human freedom has its basis in an openness to the Infinite, which is made possible by God's transcendent presence as the absolute future; this is "God himself or the act of his absolute self-bestowal which has to be posited by him alone."[68] Similarly, Edward Schillebeeckx urges that we speak of God not as "wholly Other" but as the "wholly New One," who is present to us here and now but as the power of the future.[69] In the broader theology and science dialogue several Catholic thinkers have also found Futurity to be a helpful metaphysical concept for clarifying the relation of divine eternity to the temporality of an evolving universe.[70] In addition we may point to reflection on social and historical issues among Catholics in response to the concerns of liberation theology.[71] Johann-Baptist Metz argues that "we must bring together that which has been so long disastrously separated: namely Transcendence (God) and Future, because this orientation toward the future is demanded by the biblical faith and message itself."[72]

We point finally to the proposals of the same three Protestant thinkers whose critical appropriation of Barth we have already observed in relation to Infinity and Trinity. Pannenberg makes the connection between

---

[67] Karl Rahner, *Foundations of Christian Faith*, trans. William Dych (New York: Crossroad, 1978), pp. 431, 457.

[68] Rahner, "The Question of the Future" *Theological Investigations*, Vol. 12 (New York: Seabury, 1969), p. 185. For discussion of Rahner's views, see Peter C. Phan, *Eternity in Time: A Study of Karl Rahner's Eschatology* (Selinsgrove: Susquehanna University Press, 1988).

[69] *God the Future of Man*, trans. N.D. Smith (New York: Sheed and Ward, 1968), p. 186.

[70] Pierre Teilhard de Chardin's concept of the "Omega Point" was an attempt to hold together the Future, the Universal and the Personal. This Omega is supremely present, but as "Prime Mover ahead" (*The Phenomena of Man*, trans. Bernard Wall, New York: Harper & Row, 1959, pp. 260-272). In *God After Darwin: A Theology of Evolution* (Boulder, CO: Westview, 2000), John Haught asserts that evolution "seems to require a divine source of being that resides not in a timeless present located somewhere 'up above,' but in the future, essentially 'up ahead,' as the goal of a world still in the making" (p. 84). He suggests that we may explain the novel informational possibilities that evolution has made available to it as arising "from the always dawning future" (p. 87). He makes the theological claim that "all things receive their being from out of an inexhaustibly resourceful 'future' that we may call 'God'" (pp. 87, 90).

[71] For Gustavo Gutierrez, Christian hope is not like Marxist hope that relies on human effort; rather, it opens us up "to the gift of the future promised by God." The hopeful relation to the gift, however, "makes us radically free to commit ourselves to social praxis" (*A Theology of Liberation*, p. 139). A similar dynamic is evident in some feminist theology. Anne Carr, for example, notes that "to envision God as future, as ahead, rather than above and over against the human and natural world, is a reorientation that helps women to see the feminist dilemmas in the church as a temporary one" (*Transforming Grace: Christian Tradition and Women's Experience*, San Francisco: Harper & Row, 1988, p. 153).

[72] Metz, "The Church and the World" in *The Word in History*, Ed T. Patrick Burke (New York: Sheed and Ward, 1966), p. 73. Translating Exodus 3:14 as "I will be who I will be," Metz suggests that "God revealed Himself to Moses more as a power of the future than as a being dwelling beyond all history and experience" (*Theology of the World*, London: Burns & Oates, 1969, p. 88).

causality and Futurity explicit: the traditional formulations of the divine essence and attributes are dead ends because their "basis in every form is the idea of God as the first cause of the world."[73] Building on ideas he finds in Clement of Alexandria, Pannenberg wants to think of the *eschaton* as the creative beginning of the cosmic process. He argues that we can only resolve the conceptual problem of thinking of an "end" of time (after which we still have "life") if we assert "that *God and not nothing is the end of time.*"[74] This requires the idea that God's Eternity is the condition and not merely the antithesis of time. These themes were already evident in Pannenberg's earlier work where he attempted to clarify the relation between human freedom and its basis in an infinite reality "which reveals to freedom its future, the coming God."[75] His assertion that God is the "power of the future" was based on his understanding of Jesus' message about the Father and its confirmation by his resurrection through the Spirit; he describes "the coming God as the God of love whose future has already arrived and who integrates the past and present world, accepting it to share in his own life forever."[76]

For Robert Jenson the "futurist option" in theology must be rooted in an appeal to the Person of the future, who is risen and coming.[77] The eschatological existence of the Christian is opened only by a word that poses a decision, which calls forth reliance on a promised future. Here "future" is not simply some future thing that will come in the course of time "but 'futurity,' the futurity of human life to itself, the freedom of authentic decision."[78] He notes that the Futurity of God must be discussed not only in connection with the category of word, which opens the future, but also with the word of promise, which "gives that future."[79] For Jenson, Barth's treatment of the Holy Spirit was not as compelling as his depiction of the Father-Son relation; he attempts to fill this lacuna by giving Pneumatology a higher priority. Jenson radicalizes what Barth called post-temporality by linking it to the Spirit, who now sounds like the "first" person of the Trinity.

> The Spirit is the hypostasis of God's futurity and so of God's relatedness. The Spirit is therefore the determination of the

---

[73] *Systematic Theology,* I, p. 364.
[74] *Systematic Theology,* III, p. 595.
[75] *The Idea of God and Human Freedom,* trans. R.A. Wilson (Philadelphia: Westminster, 1973), p. 93.
[76] *Theology and the Kingdom of God* (Philadelphia: Westminster, 1969), p. 71.
[77] "Appeal to the Person of the Future" in Braaten and Jenson, *The Futurist Option* (New York: Newman Press, 1970), pp. 147-158.
[78] *The Knowledge of Things Hoped For* (Oxford, 1969), p. 168.
[79] *God After God,* p. 189. This is a basic theme in his *Story and Promise* (Philadelphia: Westminster, 193).

nature of the triune – that is, future and related – God. We therefore replace the formula that in the Trinity there is an Origin and two Originateds with the formula that in God there is a Goal and two Anticipations, an anticipated Anticipation and a pure Anticipation.[80]

Sensitive to Barth's worry about reducing the divine being to the post-temporal, however, Jenson explicitly calls God the God of the Future, the Past and the Present. Nevertheless, in his *Systematic Theology* he is willing to say that God is "primally future to himself and only thereupon past and present for himself" – God is *temporally* infinite "because 'source' and 'goal' are present *and* asymmetrical in him."[81] Jenson believes that God does have a real future, but it is a future in which God confronts "himself" as or in the person of the Holy Spirit."[82]

The Futurity of God has been a dominant motif in Jürgen Moltmann's writings, emerging already in his early call for a hermeneutics of "hope seeking understanding" in the book that gave a name to a growing movement – *Theology of Hope*. The coming consummation of God's kingdom through the Spirit is already present in the promises of Jesus; the gospel "proclaims the present breaking in of this future, and thus *vice versa* this future announces itself in the promises of the gospel."[83] In *The Crucified God* Moltmann sees the future of God in the sign of the Crucified Christ; God is revealed as the One who raises the dead.[84] This future is mediated pneumatologically; the Spirit is "the power of futurity," and it is through the power of the Spirit that the creatures are "opened up and urged on by the future of the thing that is entirely new."[85] In several

---

80 *God After God*, p. 174.
81 *Systematic Theology*, I, p. 217.
82 "The Spirit is God as the Power of his own and our future; and it is that the Spirit is God as the Power of his own future, as the Power of a future that is truly 'unexpected' and yet connected, also for him, that the Spirit is a distinct identity of and in God" ("What is the Point of Trinitarian Theology" in *Trinitarian Theology Today*, ed. C. Schwöbel, Edinburgh: T&T Clark, 1995, p. 41).
83 *Theology of Hope*, trans. James Leitch (Minneapolis: Fortress, 1993), p. 139 [original German, 1965]. Moltmann describes those who follow Jesus as interpreting the world in light of God's future for the world; they are "placed in the midst of a history which is instituted and determined by the mission of Jesus and by his future as revealed and made an object of hope in the fore-glow of Easter" (p. 202).
84 *The Crucified God*, trans. R.A. Wilson and John Bowden (New York: Harper & Row, 1974), pp. 187ff.
85 *The Church in the Power of the Spirit*, trans. M. Kohl (New York: Harper & Row, 1977), p. 34. Moltmann does not intend to imply that the past is unimportant, but rather that the history of Christ must be understood in terms of both its origin and its future (pp. 56ff). Cf. his statement that "for the Christian faith, the two things – history and the future – come together in the Christ in whom that qualitatively new future is present under the conditions of history"

places, Moltmann stresses the difference between the Latin terms *futurum* and *adventus*; the former is the "future" that develops out of the past and present, but the latter is "what is coming."[86] Theology is primarily concerned then not with the "end" of the world but with the "goal" of the world, with the Advent of the Future that has already begun.[87]

Like Pannenberg and Jenson, Moltmann is explicitly responding to worries about the implications of older theological ideas of divine causality for the experience of human freedom. He does not see how the early modern view in which God pre-programs a "redemptive plan" may finally be distinguished from historical Deism.[88] The cosmological arguments of theism, which move backward from effect to cause, do not answer the atheistic protest about suffering and evil, but in fact *provoked* them. He asks: "If metaphysical theism disappears, can protest atheism still remain alive?"[89] Moltmann also points to the changes in natural scientific descriptions of causality away from the idea of a transition from *causa* to *effectus* toward a transition from possibility to reality.[90] He argues elsewhere that these theories of time justify taking "future" as the "transcendental condition for the possibility of time in general."[91] Alongside a concern for perfect Infinity and robust Trinity, then, we also find a growing interest in exploring the potential of what I will call "primal Futurity"[92] as a way of speaking about God that opens up conceptual space for understanding how human existence may be transformed through fellowship with the biblical God.

("The Future as a New Paradigm of Transcendence" in *The Future of Creation*, Philadelphia: Fortress, 1979, p. 16).

86 *Adventus* translates the Greek *parousia*, which the New Testament applies to the One who is coming. The German term *Zukunft* translates these latter terms, and is important for Moltmann's understanding of a conception of time in which the future as God's power in time is the "source" of time as God's coming to the world by making all things new (*The Coming of God*, pp. 22-29). Cf. Moltmann's essay "Theology as Eschatology" in Moltmann and F. Herzog (eds) *The Future of Hope* (New York: Herder and Herder, 1970).

87 Cf. his "Is the World Coming to an End or has its Future already Begun?" in Fergusson and Sarot (eds.), *The Future as God's Gift* (Edinburgh: T&T Clark, 2000), pp. 129-138.

88 *The Coming of God*, p. 13.

89 *Crucified God*, p. 221.

90 *Theology of Hope*, p. 243.

91 "The Bible, the Exegete, and the Theologian" in *God Will be All in All: The Eschatology of Jürgen Moltmann*, ed. R. Bauckham (Edinburgh: T&T Clark, 1999), p. 228. See the other essays in this book for exposition and analysis of Moltmann's eschatology.

92 The adjective "primal" is intended to protect against the popular misunderstanding of "Futurity" noted at the beginning of section 1.3; namely, defining it as one mode of time over against others. This mistake is more easily avoided, I believe, if we link primal Futurity to perfect Infinity and robust Trinity, which is the goal of Part 2.

Part 2. Sharing in the Divine Nature

The reason so many of us in the West are resistant to the idea expressed in 2 Peter 1:4 – that believers are called to become sharers in (or of) the divine nature – may lie deep in the presuppositions that shape our doctrine of God. Often we imagine "all that is" as divided into two "kinds," divine and non-divine. This way of construing the distinction between Creator and creation succeeds in protecting against *pantheism*, but it easily leads us into the opposite problem: conceptualizing the relation between Infinity and finitude (or Eternity and time) in terms of a simple *dualism* in which God and the world are two parts of a broader whole. This in turn leads to the difficulty of understanding the distinction and unity of the immanent and economic Trinity. When pantheism and dualism are perceived as the only options, Western theology has most often leaned toward dualism in order to protect the transcendence of God. The early modern ways of speaking about God as a rational object, a single subject, and first cause buttressed this dualism, creating a worldview in which any talk of the participation of humanity in the Creator's *nature* seemed to entail that the non-divine creature *becomes* divine.

After the turn to relationality, the metaphysics of substance that forced this choice between pantheism (one substance) and dualism (two substances) has been severely challenged. If we are willing to respond reconstructively[93] to the late modern trajectories outlined in Part 1, our prospects for rendering intelligible the Christian experience of spiritual union with God in Christ are more promising. A renewed emphasis on the Infinite Trinitarian Futurity of God opens up conceptual space for making sense of our sharing in the divine nature, and provides resources for speaking of this *koinonia* as knowing, acting and being "in Christ." Even in early Eastern patristic theology, the real meaning of "deification" was "Christification," as Panayiotis Nellas has shown.[94] In what follows I reserve the term *sharing*[95] for the intensification of the religious relation to

---

[93] In *The Postfoundationalist Task of Theology* (Grand Rapids, MI: Eerdmans, 1999), I outline the epistemological and hermeneutical contours of this way of responding theologically to culture.

[94] *Deification in Christ*, trans. Norman Russell (Crestwood, NY: St. Vladimir's, 1997); see especially Chapter 1. For additional background and examples of ecumenical dialogue on this issue, see Paul R. Hinlicky, "Theological Anthropology: Toward Integrating *Theosis* and Justification by Faith," *Journal of Ecumenical Studies* 34/1 (Winter 1997), pp. 38-73, and Robert Rakestraw, "Becoming Like God: An Evangelical Doctrine of Theosis," *Journal of the Evangelical Theological Society* 40 (June 1997), pp. 257-269.

[95] For the purposes of this chapter, I make a terminological distinction between existing, participating and sharing in the divine nature. Romans 11:36 tells us that *all things* are from, through and to God. This means that to be creaturely is to *exist* in this dynamic movement in

God, which Christians experience as the indwelling and transforming presence of the Spirit of the One who raised Christ from the dead (Rom. 8:11). In the subsections that follow, I spell out this "sharing" in terms of what the Bible calls fellowship in the knowledge, suffering and glory of Jesus Christ. This *koinonia* is the power of the Gospel of the biblical God who transforms our epistemic, ethical and ontological anxiety into faith, love and hope.

2.1. Sharing in the Knowledge of Jesus Christ
"No one knows the Son except the Father, and no one knows the Father except the Son" (Matt. 11:27). "No one comprehends what is truly God's except the Spirit of God" (1 Cor. 2:11). If *only* the Son knows the Father, and *only* the Spirit comprehends what is truly God's, then how do believers come to know God? By sharing through the Spirit in Jesus' fellowship with the Father, whom he has made known. In his first epistle, John explains that it is through the Spirit, who "is the truth" (5:6), and through the Son of God, who "has given us understanding," that we "know him who is true" (5:20). This is not merely cognitive assent, however, but a radical intimacy of being known: "we are *in him* who is true, in his Son Jesus Christ" (5:20). The gift of the Spirit is what makes possible our abiding *in God* and God's abiding *in us* (3:24). The Gospel of John portrays Jesus as making God known by inviting others to be born anew of the Spirit, who mediates the mutual knowledge of the Son and the Father (e.g., John 1:18, 3:5, 4:23, 14:20, 17:26). Entry into this fellowship of Trinitarian knowing is made possible by sharing in Jesus Christ's knowledge of the Father in the Spirit.

The New Testament authors are not primarily interested in securing God as an object of reason that is grasped by the mind, but in witnessing to the One by whom and through whom and in whom we know and *are known*. Paul rejoices that the Galatians "have come to know God," but immediately clarifies himself – "or rather to be *known by* God" (Gal. 4:9). While "knowledge puffs up," Paul observes that "anyone who loves God is *known by* him" (1 Cor. 8:3). In Romans, he insists on the inscrutability of the divine; God is not just one of the things that we intellectually fix in our

---

relation to God. Like the rest of creation, humans are created in and for the Logos, and our existence is upheld by the Spirit of life; God is the one *in* whom "we live and move and have our being" (Acts 17:28). What makes the human experience of creaturely existence "in God" unique, however, is the possibility of thematizing this relation as a searching and groping for the divine (Acts 17:27). Human persons *participate* in a way that is qualitatively different than the experience of other creatures; self-conscious creatures experience a personal knowing, acting and being as a *becoming*. The Christian doctrine of creation implies that this participation (which is made possible by the ordering differentiation of the divine Logos and the dynamic unifying power of the divine Spirit) is real regardless of the extent to which persons explicitly reflect on their relation to the Creator.

minds, but the One from whom, through whom and to whom are all things (11:36). "All things" includes human knowing. When Paul corrects the Athenians' view of the "unknown God," he does not provide them with a new object for them to idolize along with their other concepts of the divine. Instead he urges them to remember that God is the one "*in whom* we live and move and have our being" (Acts 17:28). While the Ephesians are encouraged to know the love of Christ, at the same time they are reminded that this love "surpasses knowledge" (3:18-19). The mystery of God that has been "made known" (1:9) is not an abstract or enigmatic idea, but the presence of the Spirit of Christ who renews and reorients the mind itself (4:23) so that "in him" believers share in the mutual knowing of the Trinitarian persons. Christians find their new identity through a dynamic knowing and being known, a conscious *becoming* from, through and to God, who "fills all in all" (1:23). In this transformed existence that grants new life, "Christ is all and in all" (Col. 3:11). The Philippians (4:7) are told that the peace of God surpasses "all understanding" [*panta noun*]. Divine peace is not simply a concept that the human *nous* categorizes as it does other concepts; it is an infinite spiritual presence that grasps and guards the "hearts" and "thoughts" of believers.

This existential connection in the New Testament between faithful knowing and being grasped even finds expression etymologically. The root of the Greek word for *faith* (*pistis*) means "to bind" and the term covers a wide semantic range that includes binding oneself intimately to others, to God, and even to one's self. The word "epistemology" shares the same Greek root as *pistis*, pointing to a deep connection between knowing and faith in the "bindings" of human experience. We are dealing here with personal and social fields of in-tentionality. This is beautifully illustrated in John 2:23-24, where Jesus refused to "entrust" (*episteuen*) himself to the crowds of people who "believed" (*episteusan*) in him, because their faith was an attempt to bind him to their own preconceived notions of Messiah. Derivatives of the term *epignosis* (which connotes a fuller, more intimate knowing "with" or "upon" than plain *gnosis*) are commonly used in the New Testament to emphasize the relationally binding character of knowing in Christ. Faith and knowledge, then, primarily have to do with relationships, with "bindings," and not with the abstract power of the soul's intellectual faculty to secure the truth.

This attitude toward "knowing" was rooted in the experience of the ancient Israelites. In the Hebrew Bible, truth (*emet*) is that which is disclosed in history as dependable, reliable and faithful. "Knowing" (*yada*) is not the contemplation of abstract eternal forms, but a faithful moving into relation. It involves a commitment that encompasses but transcends the Western focus on intellectual assent. Knowledge is oriented toward gaining wisdom, and wise persons orient themselves in upright and faithful relations to God and their neighbors. The semantic range of the word for "knowing" even covers sexual intercourse, a connection that is carried over into English in the King James Version: "Now the man knew (*yada*) his wife Eve, and she conceived" (Gen. 4:1). Human knowing implicates the whole person within the relational dynamics of life with God and neighbors. The Hebrew Bible does not have an abstract noun that correlates precisely to the English term "faith." The word *emunah* means faithfulness (or faithful), and is typically applied to a person who is known and trusted. Here too we may trace an etymological connection between faithfulness (*emunah*), and truth (*emet*). The thought world of the ancient Israelites was not bound by modernist theories about abstract and neutral knowledge – for them, knowing is oriented toward faithful relations.

Linking *omniscience* to the biblical idea of divine *faithfulness* may help us understand how human knowing can share in divine knowing. Speaking of God's knowledge as a *scientia* that bears on all (*omni*) things makes more sense if we weave together the insights of Infinity, Trinity and Futurity. An emphasis on perfect Infinity helps us remember that this "sharing" is not like other finite "sharings" in which my sharing with you leaves less for me. God does not know less or more when creatures share in divine knowledge, because God's knowing is perfectly Infinite. In the Bible *God's* knowing is generally related to God's faithfulness – an intimate knowing and providential care in relation to creatures. The emphasis in Scripture is not on the power of a divine intellectual "faculty" that believes all and only true propositions, but on the faithful presence of One who hears and is heard. Throughout the Psalms, the Lord is praised for his steadfast faithfulness to his people, i.e., for binding himself to them. The psalmist's prayer for the Lord to "know" his thoughts (Ps. 139:23) is grounded in his experience of the One who has knit him together (v. 13) and holds him fast (v. 10). There is no place to flee from this presence, from this being known and searched (v. 1, 7). The knowledge and faithfulness of Yahweh are intertwined. Because God is faithful, nothing escapes God's knowing. The *Trinitarian* dynamics of divine knowledge are disclosed in the New Testament through God's faithful action in Christ by the Spirit.

Besides failing to uphold the early church's insistence that the biblical God is *three* persons in one essence, the idea that the divine essence is a *single* subject also faces serious philosophical objections. Although the concept of the divine as a Mind (*Nous*) was dominant in middle Platonism (e.g., Philo), already in the third century A. D. Neoplatonic philosophers (e.g., Plotinus) had achieved the insight that the Absolute cannot be conceived as "mind." This follows from the meaning of the terms Absolute (Unconditioned) and mind (knower). The unequivocal use of the predicate *nous* implies a basic distinction between the subject itself as knower (*nous*) and that which is known (*noeton*); further, if knowing occurs (which is presupposed in calling the subject a knower), this requires positing a principle of unification that makes knowledge (*noesis*) possible. In other words, the existence of a *noeton* and a principle of *noesis* are conditions for the existence of a *nous*. Therefore, if one desires to maintain the idea that the eternal divine essence is Unconditioned or Absolute, one cannot define it as "a Mind." To do so would lead to a spurious view of Infinity. To respond that God eternally knows God's *self* and that God *is* this eternal knowing does not solve the problem, but denies the initial claim: that God's *eternal essence* may be defined as a single Mind. This response implies the existence of three eternal divine essences, which then requires a fourth essence "behind" them as the Absolute. It also fails to recognize that all of a mind's knowledge (even knowledge of "its" "self") involves differentiation at the most basic dialectical level (negation and categorization). Rather than let go of the idea that God is a single *Nous*, many theologians have instead given up on the coherence of the doctrine of the Trinity.

Things look more promising, however, if we begin by thinking of the essential life of the three persons of the Trinity as an eternally shared mutual knowing. The Trinitarian persons are related faithfully; the Trinitarian God *is* this faithfulness of the persons to and for and in one another. This does not mean that each person of the Trinity is Infinite separately, for that too would fall into a spurious concept of Infinity. Rather, their triunely structured dynamic life *is* perfect Infinity. The theological revival of the doctrine of Trinity allows us to think of the divine essence as omniscient eternally (and not only in relation to creation), as the perfect faithfulness of the three persons in their eternal relations to each other. The roots of the idea that the Christian God is essentially a single subject can be traced to a tendency in some of the early church fathers to conflate *pneuma* (spirit) and *nous* (mind). However, while the Bible does say "God is Spirit" (John 4:24), it does not say "God is Mind." The idea of Spirit can be rendered consistent with the criterion of true Infinity, while Mind cannot. God is not a *single* subject who "knows" using the power of a divine intellectual "faculty." Unlike finite creaturely knowing, the knowledge of the triune God is not determined by external objects of knowledge. God's Infinite Trinitarian knowing graciously grants creatures their own knowing, as they are held in being by the wisdom and faithfulness of the divine essence. "In Christ" believers share in this intensely peaceful fellowship of knowing and being known.

Yes, God knows everything – God knows all creaturely being. But God's knowing of all is *God's* knowing, a *Trinitarian* "knowing" of creatures as an intimate faithful grasping, a holding all things close while granting all things space and time to become what they are called to be. I suggest that we intercalate the three trajectories of Part 1 by speaking of God's knowing in relation to the world as *constitutive, incursive* and *evocative*. These three concepts must be thought into each other to avoid misunderstanding. God's knowing in relation to the world is constitutive – it grants creatures their existence. This granting of existence, however, is not merely a setting apart of creation over against God. God's faithful creativity is both incursive and evocative. God's knowing constitutes *as* it moves incursively in faithfulness toward and addresses creatures. This constitutive incursion is also evocative, for as it grants existence and moves toward creatures it calls them toward fellowship in the divine life. For Jesus, no other future could threaten the promise of God's creative upholding of the world by the power of the Spirit. As we share in the knowledge of Jesus, we experience God's faithfulness as an intimate knowing that holds us, loves us, grants us hope through promise, and draws us toward true being and glory. *Omniscient faithfulness* is the very "knowing" of the Trinitarian life that holds together the plurality of finite creatures and calls them into Eternity.

Precisely here the primal Futurity of the divine nature helps explain the human experience of not-knowing, the human inability to grasp that which is essentially beyond finite comprehension. The knowing, and so the *believing* (faith), of human persons is dependent on the evocative faithfulness of the Trinitarian persons, whose eternal shared life is essentially future for creatures. Human knowing is made possible by the Futurity of God that calls creatures toward a share in the fullness of Trinitarian knowing, which is manifested in creation as divine wisdom. God's wisdom is not merely quantitatively higher than human wisdom; it is the origin, condition and goal of human wisdom. "For wisdom is more mobile than any motion; because of her pureness she pervades and penetrates all things. For she is a breath of the power of God, and a pure emanation of the glory of the Almighty . . . Although she is but one, she can do all things, and while remaining in herself, she renews all things . . ." (Wisdom of Solomon 7:24-27). Our knowing gropes after God but it cannot grasp or capture the divine faithfulness, which is always ahead of us. The Christian responds to this inability, this not-knowing, with humble delight as she worships the One whose knowing of her makes possible and answers her longings for wisdom, and yet calls her ever forward into a deeper intimacy of knowing and being known.

Through faith in Christ, believers find themselves in the embrace of the Trinitarian God, which alleviates their "epistemic" anxiety. The believer's worry about knowing God is eased not by her ability to objectify (secure) a concept of the divine but by her experience of being "filled with all the fullness of God" (Eph. 3:18-19). The Christian knows God as she is known by God, and so experiences already this promising presence that is eternal life. "And this is eternal life, that they know thee the only true God and Jesus Christ whom thou hast sent" (John 17:3). On the other hand, the believer's knowing of God is not static or "finished" – Paul recognizes that now he knows "in part" but he anticipates knowing fully "even as I have been fully *known*" (1 Cor. 13:12). This future is experienced now as a sharing in the relation of the Son to the Father, a relation that was manifested in the history of Jesus through his reliance on the life-giving power of the Holy Spirit. God's faithfulness is now the source of the believer's hope in the coming of Christ (1 Thess. 5:23-24). Omniscience is the perfectly Infinite faithfulness of the promising Trinitarian God. Jesus' identity was constituted by this knowing and being known: by entrusting himself to the Father (1 Peter 2:23), and offering himself through the Eternal Spirit (Heb. 9:14), he was made perfect through suffering (Heb. 2:10; 5:8, 9) and so became the pioneer and source of our salvation.

2.2. *Sharing in the Suffering of Jesus Christ*

One aspect of the Gospel that does not always get sufficient attention in North American Christianity is the good news that we are called to suffer with Christ. 1 Peter urges its readers to "rejoice insofar as you are sharing [koinoneite] Christ's sufferings" because whoever has suffered in the flesh (in the way Christ did) "has finished with sin" (4:1, 13). This initially does not appear to be good news – until we realize that it opens us up to an intimate fellowship with and in the infinite goodness and love of the Trinitarian God. As Paul announces to the Philippians that the righteousness of God is available to them as they are bound to Christ, he prays that he "may know him and the power of his resurrection, and may share his sufferings, becoming like him in his death, that if possible I may attain the resurrection from the dead" (Phil. 3:10-11). Suffering for Christ is graciously granted by God to believers as a privilege (Phil. 1:29). The Thessalonians are commended for suffering for the kingdom of God (2 Thess. 1:5), for they suffer the "same things" that Jesus suffered (1 Thess. 2:14). Koinonia in Christ's suffering is also a koinonia in one another's suffering (2 Cor. 1:4-7), because Christ suffered (and was raised) for the sake of others. "And he died for all, that those who live might live no longer for themselves but for him who died for their sake and was raised" (2 Cor. 5:15). Timothy is encouraged to join "in suffering for the gospel, relying on the power of God" (2 Tim. 1:8) and he is expected to "share in suffering" as a soldier of Christ (2:3, 9), for "all who want to live a godly life in Christ Jesus will be persecuted" (3:12).

Becoming sharers in the divine nature, then, takes shape "in Christ" as a life of cruciformity. All three of the synoptic Gospels (Matt. 10:38-39; Mark 8:34-35; Luke 9:23-24; cf. John 12:25) report Jesus' saying that those who would follow him must deny themselves and "take up the cross" – only the one who loses her life for Jesus' sake will find (or save) it. Jesus Christ was made perfect through suffering (Heb. 2:10, 5:8-9) and our becoming like him is a cruciform process. When we are "crucified with Christ," it is no longer we who live but Christ who lives in us (Gal. 2:19-20); yet, we live as we are united to him in faith that is "made effective through love" (5:6). "Those who belong to Christ have crucified the flesh with its passions and desires" (5:24). We are fellow heirs with Christ "provided we suffer with him in order that we may also be glorified with him" (Rom. 8:17). To the Philippians, Paul describes his own activity in Christ as being "poured out as a libation upon the sacrificial offering of your faith" (2:17). He urges the Romans to "present your bodies as a living sacrifice" (12:1). Loving and being loved by God is not merely an abstract inner feeling, but a radical experience of fellowship that intensifies as we actively share in the suffering of Jesus Christ. This is how we become ministers of reconciliation (2 Cor. 5:18), drawing others into fellowship with God's infinite goodness.

The concepts of goodness and suffering inevitably lead us to the ideas of God's love and God's power—i.e., to the issues of divine agency and the so-called "problem of evil." It is important to note that Scripture is not obsessed with developing a theodicy. Romans 8:20 does not attempt to exculpate God from responsibility for the ordering of the world, but exclaims that "the creation was subjected to futility not of its own will but by the will of the one who subjected it in hope." Jesus does not try to justify God to the poor and the oppressed; rather, he says, "Blessed are those who mourn, for they will be comforted . . . Blessed are those who are persecuted for righteousness' sake, for theirs is the kingdom of heaven" (Matt. 5:4, 10; cf. Luke 6:20ff). The classical prophets of Israel are not afraid to say that God's power holds for all things, including "weal" and "woe" (Is. 45:7; cf. Jer. 18:6; 45:4, 5; Amos 3:6; Job 9:12; Eccl.7:13). This lack of defensiveness is bothersome on the assumptions of early modern theology; for if God is a single subject whose intellect knows ahead of time what will happen, and whose will is the efficient first cause of all events, then God is obviously that rational object in the world to which all evil is culpably traced.

The claim that "God is love" (1 John 4:8) is essential to the Christian Gospel. God's love for the world as the power of salvation is central to our faith (John 3:16; Rom. 5:5, 8:35,39). The concept of "love" is inherently relational and dynamic, and applying it to God in any meaningful sense brings us to the question of divine action - the power of God in relation to goodness. If God is both all-powerful and all-loving, then why does evil exist? As they try to explain evil, many "theists" fall somewhere on a continuum between divine determinism (God causes everything including evil) to human libertarianism (evil is explained wholly in reference to free will). The very construction of the continuum, however, presupposes the idea of God as an all-knowing single subject, as a person of a certain sort: one who is wholly good and who acts with ultimate power in the world. How can both this kind of a person and evil exist? It seems that either God's power or God's love must be limited. The tension between these poles, which frames much of the contemporary debate, is forced upon us by a particular way of conceptualizing God's power and goodness. As long as God is conceived as a single subject who stands over against the world as the efficient first cause of all creaturely effects, holding together absolute divine love and absolute divine power will appear impossible.

Instead we might attempt to link *omnipotence* and *love* by exploring the renewed emphases on Infinity, Trinity, and Futurity. This may enable us to understand our longing for goodness by depicting the power of the biblical God of love as the origin, condition and goal of human agency. God's love is manifested in the life of Jesus in relation to the Father and the Spirit. Moreover, the way in which we are to share in that love is also disclosed: "We know love by this, that he laid down his life for us; and we ought to lay down our lives for one another" (1 John 3:16). The doctrine of the Trinity can help us talk about God's "acting" in a way that does not collapse into finite subjectivity. God *is* love. The infinite divine being *is* the mutually shared love of the three persons. This shared love is the power of the Trinitarian persons in their relational unity. The perfectly Infinite Trinitarian divine essence transcends while embracing the distinction between relation-to-other and absolute self-identity. This means that the conditions for the plurality of differentiated creatures, for the emergence of personal finite agents, and for their fellowship in the divine love, are already found in the Eternity of the biblical God.

Jesus insisted that God alone is good (Luke 18:19, Matt. 19:17). *God's* goodness, however, makes others righteous by granting a share in divine holiness. This is ultimately disclosed in the life of Jesus Christ, who refused to exploit or grasp equality with God and was obedient even to death on a cross (Phil. 2:6-8). He was "declared to be the Son of God with power according to the Spirit of holiness by resurrection from the dead" (Rom. 1:4), and so through him "the righteousness of God has been disclosed" (3:21-22). God's goodness is manifested in the sending of the Son and God's love is "poured into our hearts through the Holy Spirit" (5:5), so that it transforms our human agency as it shares in a righteousness that is not its own. The righteousness of God has been revealed so that in Christ "we might become the righteousness of God" (2 Cor. 5:21). The Christian belief in atonement and regeneration presupposes robust relations among the persons of the Trinity, for it is through Christ that we "have access in one Spirit to the Father" (Eph. 2:18). Our whole experience of salvation is Trinitarian: "If the Spirit of him who raised Jesus from the dead dwells in you, he who raised Christ from the dead will give life to your mortal bodies also through his Spirit that dwells in you" (Rom. 8:11). As "moral" creatures, human persons seek a way of living that will secure "the good life." Suffering is linked to the fact that our agency is insufficiently powerful to relate us to the goods that we desire. The "ethical" anxiety of the Christian is alleviated by sharing in the self-giving goodness of the Trinitarian God. Her longing to be securely related to goodness is fulfilled as she experiences the atonement effected through Jesus Christ in the life of the Spirit.

The problems that arise when we predicate "action" of God in the same way we predicate "action" of finite agents might be avoided with the help of the idea of primal Futurity. When a finite agent acts (intentionally) to fulfill a desire, she imagines a goal that is ahead of her in *time*. Her movement toward that goal is driven by her desire to secure a (perceived) good that she does *not* currently possess. In other words, she acts in time moving toward a "better" future. If we place God's "acting" under these same conditions, we are in danger of making temporality a broader category than divine agency and of implying that God is not (yet) perfectly good. But does God attempt to secure goods that God does not possess and that are "ahead" of God in time? How could this be if God alone is good and if God's eternity is the origin and goal of time? Further, if God were a single subject, then unequivocally attributing "good agency" (or even "best conceivable agency") to the eternal divine essence would require the eternal existence of other objects in relation to which God could act with goodness, and of other subjects in comparison to whom God could be defined as "better" or "best." On the other hand, if divine goodness is the primal Futurity of the shared eternal life of the Father, Son and Holy Spirit, then we may speak of omnipotent love as the constitutive incursion of Eternity in(to) time that calls all things toward redemption. God determines all things with all of *God's* determining. Nothing escapes God's power, but this is the power of love that holds the other in being and calls the other to being.

Drawing on resources from the renewal of eschatological reflection, we might speak of the biblical deity as the Trinitarian God whose eschatological coming to, in and for the world does not *compete* with human acting but grants it space and time to be, evoking and addressing the creaturely longing for loving fellowship. This would allow us to think of divine action as the promising omnipotent love of divine Futurity that calls us toward a share in the Trinitarian goodness. The truly good news is that the Futurity of the Infinite Trinitarian God graciously gives to us that which we most deeply desire: a peaceful share in an eternal goodness that saves us from the push and pull of finite evils and goods. God's life is perfectly Infinite goodness, so that *no* evil and *no* good is worth comparing to the glory (Rom. 8:18) that is promised and in which we are already being transformed. This transformation involves a struggling, a "groping" after God (Acts 17:27), but "finding" God is first of all a being-found that evokes gratitude for the grace that gives us "life and breath and everything" (17:25). Creaturely sharing in God's perfectly Infinite goodness does not make God more or less good. For St. Anselm, God is not only that than which nothing greater (*maius*) can be conceived but also that than which nothing better (*melius*) can be conceived. The Bible does not have an "answer" for the logical or evidential problem of evil; rather, it witnesses to the promised consummation of God's eschatological kingdom that is overcoming evil, so that "God may be All in All" (1 Cor. 15:28).

Earlier I referred to the "so-called" problem of evil; my intention was to cast suspicion on this early modern way of framing the question. Even in the story of the Garden of Eden, it is not merely "the problem of evil" – the forbidden flora is called the tree of "the knowledge of good *and* evil" (Gen. 2:17). When we look at Jesus' ministry, the problem is not simply the evils of physical suffering and social oppression, but also the "goods" of this life that have seduced the healthy into thinking they do not need a doctor and the rich into believing that they do not need a deliverer. In response to the finite evils of sickness and oppression, Jesus heals and sets free, but salvation is more difficult for those who are defining their lives by their own attempts to maintain control over finite goods. The rich young ruler (Matt. 19:16f, Mark 10:17f, Luke 18:18f) was unable to respond to the Gospel because of the problem of good – the "goods" of this world had seduced him into relying on his own moral agency. We cannot fulfill our longing for goodness no matter how deeply we drink from the goods of the finite world. As we struggle between the repulsion of finite evils and the seduction of finite goods, we are torn apart. God's love transcends this pushing and pulling, yet in such a way that it is immanently present to us through them as we are called us to share in the Infinite goodness of the Trinitarian life.

Sharing in the suffering of Jesus Christ is not an impotent acceptance of victimization, but an active *koinonia* in the omnipotent vulnerability of the Trinitarian God. This infinite power of love absorbs all wounds, transforming the wounded and the wounders. Christian praxis responds to suffering with faith, love and hope, because evil is finite and cannot ultimately separate us from God's goodness. Similarly, Christian agency is not seduced by finite goods because these do not provide that for which we are truly longing: righteous relations within loving community. Sin and death no longer bind and terrify, and wealth no longer deceives the Christian. Believers can count it all joy (James 1:2) when they suffer and can be content in any and all circumstances (Phil. 4:11-12). This is impossible if we try to hold together our lives through our own agency; only insofar as our lives are "hid with Christ in God" (Col. 3:3) are we able to experience this deep joyful contentment. The Christian community does not simply accept the suffering of the poor and the abused as a necessary part of the world. Christian suffering works against generic suffering by sharing in the reconciling praxis of divine love, which gives itself up for the other. As we die to our obsession with acting in ways that secure our own finite goodness, we are called to live in the redemptive fellowship of divine goodness, which moves (in)to the world with the infinite power of love. Suffering and death do not have the final word. "For if we have been united with him in a death like his, we shall certainly be united with him in a resurrection like his" (Rom. 6:5).

2.3. Sharing in the Glory of Jesus Christ

Scripture also makes it clear that knowledge of and fellowship with God involves sharing in the glory of Christ. The author of 1 Peter describes himself as "one who shares in the glory [*doxes koinonos*] to be revealed" (5:1). This is why he can encourage his readers to "rejoice insofar as you share Christ's sufferings, that you may also rejoice and be glad when his glory is revealed" (4:13). If someone suffers as a Christian, she should glorify God (4:16). Why? Because this is how Christ suffered, entrusting himself to God (2:23). We too have been called "to God's eternal glory in Christ" (5:10), and our sharing in God's gracious movement toward others is "so that God may be glorified in all things through Jesus Christ" (4:11). In 2 Peter, the phrase "sharers of the divine nature" is preceded by the announcement that God has "called us to his own glory and excellence" (1:3).

The biblical emphasis on the human relation to God's glory through Jesus Christ is not limited to the Petrine corpus. The author of Hebrews describes the Son as the "reflection of God's glory" (1:3) who is "now crowned with glory" (2:9) and through whom God brings "many children to glory" (2:10). Here too we see that the glory of God is shared with human creatures. The Christian does not simply "have" or become God's glory; rather, her whole being is oriented toward the arriving kingdom of glory. "We wait for the blessed hope and the manifestation of the glory of our great God" (Titus 2:13). Believers are urged to trust God, who is able to "make you stand without blemish in the presence of his glory with rejoicing" (Jude 1:24). God calls us "into his own kingdom and glory" (1 Thess. 2:12). Paul explicitly links the idea that believers share in the glory of Jesus Christ to the claim that he is the image of God. The good news is "the gospel of the glory of Christ, who is the image of God" (2 Cor. 4:4). God "has shone in our hearts to give the light of the knowledge of the glory of God in the face of Jesus Christ" (4:6). For "all of us . . . are being transformed into the same image from one degree of glory to another; for this is from the Lord, the Spirit" (3:18). Believers are sanctified by the Spirit so that we "may obtain the glory of our Lord Jesus Christ" (2 Thess. 2:14). It is by God's grace that we are made worthy of the call, so that "the name of our Lord Jesus may be glorified in you, and you in him" (2 Thess. 1:12). Already here and now the believer shares in the divine glory through life in the Spirit of Christ. This sharing does not occur all at once; rather, it is a dynamic process of becoming: "momentary affliction is preparing us for an eternal weight of glory beyond all measure" (2 Cor. 4:17).

The Trinitarian structure of divine glory is especially evident in John's Gospel. "We have beheld his glory, glory as of the only Son from the Father" (John 1:14). This glory is both the Father's and the Son's. The glory of Jesus is manifested in his signs (2:11), and the disciples believe in him. But Jesus does not seek his own glory (8:50); he recognizes that it is "my Father who glorifies me" (8:54). Jesus tells the disciples: "Now is the Son of man glorified, and in him God is glorified; if God is glorified in him, God will also glorify him in himself, and glorify him at once" (13:31-32). Further, it is the coming "Spirit of truth" who "will glorify" Christ "*because* he will take what is mine and declare it to you" (16:14). What does the Spirit take and declare in this act of glorifying? "All that the Father has" (16:15), which he has given to the Son. Notice that we are not dealing here with a single subject obsessed with *self*-glorification, but with a mutual glorification among the Trinitarian persons. Immediately before his betrayal, Jesus speaks to the Father: "Glorify your Son so that the Son may glorify you . . . I glorified you on earth by finishing the work that you gave me to do" (17:4). The disciples are being drawn by the Spirit into this mutual glorifying of the Father and the Son; they too are called to do the same works "that the Father may be glorified in the Son" (14:12-13). The fellowship (or "abiding" – 15:4-10) of the disciples in the Son's relation to the Father also redounds to the glory of Jesus who prays: "I am glorified in them" (17:10). The glorious relation between the Father and the Son is mediated by the Holy Spirit, who is sent to dwell with and in believers and to call them into relational unity. Creaturely sharing in the Trinitarian glory of God is made possible by the unifying work of the Spirit (as "Paraclete" – 14:16) who mediates the promise of Jesus: "The glory you have given me *I have given them*, so that they may be one, as we are one" (17:22).

Linking the three developments in the doctrine of God we observed in Part 1 may help us conceptualize human being as a real creaturely becoming that is already oriented in its very existence to the call of the biblical God to share in divine glory. If God is present to all things as their determinative first cause, how can humans really be free? If humans are really free, then how can God be the power that determines all things? The debate over the relation of God to human freedom, which typically results in this well-known theological impasse, has often been construed in terms of the faculty psychology of "free will" (ours vs. God's). Instead of focusing on the competition between human and divine "voluntaristic" powers, however, I suggest that we may be able to escape the horns of this dilemma by defining human *freedom* in *ontological* terms. That is, we can speak of human freedom as the real and actual *being* of personal creatures. This being is a becoming that finds its origin, condition and goal in the call of the triune Creator to an ever-intensifying share in the relation of the Son to the Father in the Spirit. Personal being is experienced as a relation to reality that is both free and not-free. The feeling that we do not have the power to determine the reality of our own future is an existential threat.

We want to belong in the future, to find our place in an ultimate reality in which the dissolution of our being no longer hangs over us. The existence of human beings in community is characterized by a desire for harmony, for patterns of reality that will hold personal life together without crushing it – for a metaphysical matrix in which joy and peace flourish. To be a person is to be-coming in openness to a future outside the self, and to hope for being in relation to that future.

The Hebrew word for glory (*kabod*) has the root meaning of "heaviness." Our own free being is not heavy enough to hold down reality and to secure our place within it, and this ontic weightlessness terrifies us. We long for a share in the *free* being of God, to be secured in the weighty presence of divine glory. This longing is what is most real about us as personal creatures. The Gospel is the good news about life in the Spirit of Christ, a new life that provides ultimate ontological peace because nothing, not even death, can separate us from the freedom of divine love (Rom. 8:38-39). Paul tells the Galatians that he has freedom "in Christ Jesus" (2:4) and that they were "called to freedom" (5:13). It is "for freedom that Christ has set us free (5:1). This freedom is tied both to glory and to the future: "creation itself will be set free from its bondage to decay and *will obtain* the freedom of the *glory* of the children of God" (Rom. 8:21). This true freedom is an anticipatory sharing of the promising presence of divine glory. This *hopeful* being emerges in relation to the divine presence, for "where the Spirit of the Lord is, there is freedom" (2 Cor. 3:17). Christians must not forget the past or ignore the present, but they are called to an active hope that shares in the incursive Futurity of the peaceful presence of God, which transforms all temporality. The eternal future of God's glory has been manifested in the face of Jesus Christ, and Christian life is a gracious experience of the divine Spirit whose charismatic presence is already conforming us into his image. This divine determination that orients us toward the beauty of holiness does not compete with human freedom, but calls it into being.

If thought in conjunction with the Futurity of the Infinite Trinitarian God, we may link the concept of divine *omnipresence* to the *hope* of the biblical God. *This* presence grants the possibility and actuality of human freedom as it is called to share in the divine nature. Christian hope is a way of becoming in redemptive relation to God. Human life is transformed by hope into a charismatic becoming in the Spirit, a being oriented toward the infinitely beautiful presence of the God of hope. God's presence in the world is not like the presence of a pagan god who causes things in the world in the same way that finite human agents do, moving through time and competing with creatures for worldly space. God's causative presence is not limited to a primordial past. God grants contingent being to creaturely reality, holding all things in being and calling all things toward a new creation. God's (omni)presence is not simply the presence of one "other" being (not even the "greatest" conceivable being) in the world. God's presence to creatures is primally Future, and as such the presence that holds past and present in being. As we confront the future, we may arrogantly fight or cower in fear but we cannot hold off or control the future because it "outweighs" us. This temporal asymmetry is held in being by God's presence.

God's incursive being-there for us is the evocative hopeful presence of Futurity that constitutes creaturely becoming. If God is "that than which nothing greater (or better) can be conceived," then the idea of primal Futurity better expresses the relation of divine eternity to time than any idea of the past, the present, or an unrelated abstract time-lessness. We can always conceive of a temporal reality that is greater (or better) than the past or the present; in fact, hope for such a reality keeps persons moving forward. We can also conceive of various "futures," some of which are better and greater than others. But we cannot conceive of anything greater or better than the Absolute Future as the totality of infinitely shared life. The all-encompassing real presence of eternal Futurity is closer to us than we are to ourselves, but precisely as an infinitely transcendent presence that opens us up to being in hope. We long to be truly free — to find ourselves existing harmoniously within a pattern of being in which we are free from the pain of self-determination and free for the joy of relating to others without fear that they will smother or abandon us. As God's infinite trinitarian glory that calls creatures into being, the Futurity of God is the promising presence that fulfills this desire for belonging in eternal peaceful *koinonia*.

The ontological anxiety of early Christian believers was dissolved as they focused wholly upon the risen Lord, whose *parousia* was at the same time both anticipated as a final fulfillment in which God will be "all in all" (1 Cor. 15:28) and also already experienced proleptically through the indwelling Holy Spirit who is its "pledge" (Eph. 1:14). All of their attention was on the Future that is breaking into the present, on the presence of the Promising One who is coming so that they may be glorified with him along with all of creation (Rom. 8:10-25). This focus on the future was in continuity with the Jewish anticipation of the Messiah, whose coming would bring peace to the community of God. The ancient Israelite experience of God was mediated by a hope for a coming future in which *shalom* and justice reign. They lived in the presence of this promise, as they anticipated a "day" in which the glory of God would dwell with them forever. Time and again, the prophets called them to turn toward Yahweh as the only source of their determination, because their existence was rooted in the future that God brings. "Do not remember the former things, or consider the things of old. I am about to do a new thing; now it springs forth, do you not perceive it?" (Isa. 43:18-19a).

Protestant theology has often been resistant to the Eastern idea of *theosis* because in some of its historical formulations it appears to make creatures divine and so to erase the distinction between divine and human glory. An emphasis on the human relation to God's glory as mediated through the glory of Jesus Christ may help us articulate this biblical intuition without either deifying human nature or denying human freedom. The claim that God's glory is "beyond all measure" (2 Cor. 4:17) is crucial. Here again we have the idea of perfect Infinity. God's glory is not like the glory of creatures that can be measured quantitatively. God's glory is perfectly Infinite, and so does not replace that which it glorifies but gives it a share in its being. The infinite glory of the shared trinitarian life is eternally full and so can be shared with creatures without being limited or diminished. The "riches in glory in Christ Jesus" (Phil. 4:19) satisfy *every* need, because these "riches of his glory" are mediated by the indwelling presence of Christ through the Spirit (Eph. 3:16-17). Salvation is a dynamic being-called into an ever intensifying share of the divine glory, which *is* eternal life. Because God's glory is perfectly Infinite, it may be shared without loss or fading. The "riches of the glory" are made known to believers as they share in this mystery, "which is Christ in you, the hope of glory" (Col. 1:27).

As the shared being-in-relation of the eternal Trinitarian persons, God's presence it is not like the presence of finite things that displace or crush other presences. It is the infinite presence of God that gives, holds and calls finite creatures into being. We should also be careful to speak of primal Futurity as perfectly Infinite in order to avoid the implication that God's eternity is merely over against the temporality of creatures. The presence of divine Futurity is the condition of the creaturely experience of temporality. This "calling" to share in glory, this constitutive hoping that is ours and makes us what we are, is inherently linked to the creation of human beings as *imago Dei* – this *is* our freedom. We *are* becoming free as Christ is formed in us. God's glory is the gracious presence that draws all things toward reconciliation; God's grace is the glorious presence of the divine promise of reconciliation. It is this gracious offer of a share in the divine life of freedom that *constitutes* the creaturely freedom of human persons. While human freedom cannot and should not be separated from ethics and epistemology, it is ultimately an ontological category. This being-gifted-as-called, this gift of living as called-to-be with others, *is* personal freedom. This dynamic of free openness to the other, experienced as the longing for peaceful belonging, which as a creaturely reality is always upheld by divine grace, *is* personal be-ing. The God of hope (Rom. 15:13) calls human freedom into being as a hopeful becoming.

The apostle Paul interprets reality in light of the experience of the resurrected Christ, in whom the Christian now lives through the Holy Spirit. A "new creation" has begun, and believers already participate in it as they anticipate its consummation. Paul urges the early Christians to set their eyes on the future, on the *parousia* of the eschatological man (*ho eschatos adam*, 1 Cor. 15:45). The Gospels also lead the reader to focus her attention on the coming of Jesus. "Keep awake therefore, for you know neither the day nor the hour" (Matt. 25:13). "Beware, keep alert; for you do not know when the time will come" (Mark 13:33). " . . .stand up and raise your heads, because your redemption is drawing near" (Luke 21:28). In John's account, Jesus repeats to his disciples that "the hour is coming" (5:25-29) and promises to draw all people to himself (12:32). This hour which is "coming" is also in some sense "now here" (John 4:17). It is this radical placing of one's metaphysical hope in the eschatological arrival of the kingdom that marked off the Christian from her religious neighbors. Jude "looks forward" to the mercy of Jesus Christ that leads to eternal life (1:21). The early church was not obsessed with proving God's existence as the first cause of the world; it was pointing all people to the One who is the source of future (eternal) life and who calls us to share in that future. This "hope of sharing the glory of God" (Rom. 5:2) secures our being "through the Holy Spirit who has been given to us" (5:5) and is leading us "to eternal life through Jesus Christ our Lord" (5:21).

The gift and call of free personal being is created by God's presence; human freedom is given (originates) with the call of God to share in divine glory. God's gracious *evocative* presence calls creatures to share in the trinitarian life. This evocation is the *constitutive* presence of the perfectly Infinite Trinitarian God – the presence of Eternity that grants to creatures a longing for fellowship with the divine. This presence is *incursive* – it confronts, addresses and holds the human creature in relation to God. The faithful addressing of creatures by the God of hope takes the form of the divine promise, and as such calls creatures into being. As 2 Peter says, this call to God's "own glory and excellence," this sharing in the divine nature is made possible through God's "precious and very great *promises*" (1:3-4). If God's presence as Futurity was simply defined over against created temporal modalities, then we would be in danger of collapsing into a kind of post-temporal determinism. However, if the perfectly infinite Futurity of the trinitarian life of God creates the modes of time and all creaturely becoming by upholding and calling it into a share in that life, then we may speak of *omnipresence* as the *hope* of God that grants human freedom its ontological reality. In the intensification of the religious experience of salvation, creatures do not become God, for the finite cannot grasp the infinite Future. But as personal creatures, we can joyfully accept the gracious gift of our finitude in freedom, which is a real relation to the reality of God whose eternal Futurity upholds and intensifies our relational being as becoming. The glory of the Trinitarian God is manifested in Jesus Christ's life of hope in the power of the Spirit to grant eternal life in relation to the Father. Sharing in Jesus' relation to that glorious eschatological Future is the *telos* of creaturely existence – the chief end of human persons and communities is to glorify and enjoy God forever.

Conclusion

I have suggested that weaving together the insights of perfect Infinity, robust Trinity and primal Futurity may open up conceptual space for better understanding the biblical call to become sharers in the divine nature. Christians intuitively "think" of God as somehow "subjective" and as the "cause" of all creaturely reality. I explored some theological ways of buttressing these intuitions that do not collapse into the problems associated with the early modern emphases on God as rational object, single subject and first cause. I offered a programmatic outline of an approach that would set out the illuminative power of the Infinite Trinitarian Futurity of the biblical God as the origin, condition and goal of human knowing, acting and being by correlating the traditional attributes of omniscience, omnipotence and omnipresence with faith, love and hope. I attempted to braid the theological trajectories of Part 1 by reflecting in Part 2 on the biblical witness and the Christian experience of salvation, always guided by the desiderata set out at the end of the Introduction. This conceptual exploration is offered in the service of the ongoing theological task of conserving the intuitions of the lived biblical tradition by liberating them for dialogue with contemporary culture, which in turn serves the evangelical task of calling others into a transforming fellowship in the knowledge, suffering, and glory of Jesus Christ.

Susan Buckles

Life in the Spirit and the Spirit of Life

In the church bulletin on a recent Sunday appeared a koan, a classical Oriental puzzle in paradox meant to silence a chattering Western mind. Admittedly, the intent of that Sunday lesson was soon forgotten--evidently there was no paradigm shift for me that morning.

Such was not the case for those of us privileged to be a part of Ray Anderson's classes. "Paradigm" having been defined, we were ushered into an opportunity for re-thinking and re-discovery from which few emerged without a greatly expanded re-ordering of our picture of God's grace, sovereignty, trustworthiness and, above all, presence. Whether welcomed or resisted, few could walk out of a series of Ray Anderson classes without carrying with them a revolutionary conception of the God who walks beside us as divine Advocate, with human voice and hands, calling and equipping us to be human beings in the divine image.

It is on this foundation that the following essay will attempt to build, highlighting two aspects of the inner logic of how "God is with us," pushing them to the point of seeming paradox in an attempt to appreciate the radical nature of each. One of these is the oneness of the divine presence, activity and reality with authentic humanity, creating and maturing human freedom and personhood. This is a testimony to the value and purpose of God's creation of human being. The second aspect is the complete inability, incapacity, and above all unwillingness of the human to be "with God." This is the sickness for which there is no conceivable remedy, canceling out all that was meant for human life. In this context that "the Chosen One must suffer and die"[1] while discarded barrenness is granted life becomes the inconceivable revelation of the glory of a God who does not leave us alone in judgment but makes it the place of his dwelling. It is this that draws us near: Who is this God who does not fulfill our expectations, but dismantles our categories and explanations to replace them with the richness of divine Presence? And who are we, created "male and female" in the divine image but falling short of God's glory, made a "little lower than the heavenly beings" (Psalm 8), yet living with deceived and deceiving hearts (Jeremiah 17:9)?

---

[1] Ray S. Anderson, "Expanded Course Syllabus: Reconciliation and the Healing of Persons," Winter 2000, p. 5.

Such questions are particularly timely in a period of increasing interest in personal spirituality, often guided more by subjective effect or personal meaningfulness than by objective content. Popularized New Age forms of naturalistic spirituality and neo-pagan romanticism tend to substitute transcendence through enlightened understanding, or by various types of otherworldly or creation-centered experience and ritual, for relation with a personal God. In such a context, self-realization and self-actualization are thought to be found by transcending individual limitations through merging with the "All" of reality in a vaguely defined sense of peaceful acceptance--seemingly with the assumption that evils and tragedy are not part of this whole.

Postmodern skepticism concerning the very concept of "truth" also plays a role in creating a climate in which questions of spiritual reality appear nonsensical, except from a personal, experiential perspective. Moreover, although couched in alternative terminology, even the most radical proposals ironically may reflect an undercurrent of the same body-spirit dualism which has influenced the nature and practice of Christian spiritual life over the centuries. On the one hand, this has encouraged the development of a materialistic secularism that confines "spiritual life" to a quality of this-worldly existence while, on the other, fostering approaches to spirituality that seek the (divine) "spirit" within for deliverance from the ambiguities of individual particularity and human "flesh."

Many contemporary approaches to Christian spiritual formation are also strongly influenced by developmental and psychological studies that explain spiritual growth almost exclusively in light of stages of human development. Others are dominated by Jungian methodologies which find the apex of human life to be "individuation" through the reconciliation of polarities in the self, in conformity to "Christ" as more an archetypal model than the Jewish messiah. While the greater psychological sophistication and desire to relate "spirit" to human life displayed in such approaches can be helpful, too often they reflect a worldview in which human life and value are defined in terms of maximization of individual potential, while core relationships and productive activity are placed within this context. Even for those that do maintain the centrality of Christ, at least for the most mature levels of growth, the question that arises is whether new life in Christ is to be seen as a dimension "added to" human growth and development, as a part of the "real nature" of this process--or as the defining issue.

In light of these varied cultural influences, it is worthwhile to ask how a God who steps into history in human form in order to recreate human being "from the inside out" may relate to such points of view. The following is an exploration of how the revelation of God in Christ by the Spirit confronts all our ways of seeking a "spiritual dimension" with a God who is present to bring a new heart and new Spirit into our this-worldly reality in a way that involves our whole being as human persons. This takes place in a manner which makes participatory relationship with God and other persons central to its essence, disclosing loving communion to be the heart of reality and of the formation of human persons. Specifically, what follows will address the ministry of the Spirit for recreation in light of how (1) God in Christ is one with human life for the purpose of its recreation in a way that necessitates death and new birth; (2) God is present in and through human persons in the Body of Christ to create an arena for encountering the presence of God in a humanly formative way; and (3) God is present giving life to the creature for the renewal of all creation.

The Spirit in the Life of Christ

The first step in addressing these questions will be to consider the character of God's presence in the human person of Jesus of Nazareth and the activity of the divine Spirit in his life, not only as "God incarnate" but also as the fully human Anointed One. The reality of *incarnation*--God "becoming flesh"--indicates the arena in which encounter with the divine takes place, in a way that both affirms humanity and testifies to its inability to maintain itself in life-giving relation.

In recent decades the role of the Holy Spirit in relation to the human life of Christ has received increased attention, particularly in light of the contention that some traditional presentations of the incarnation too easily lead to a diminished appreciation for the full dimensions of Jesus' humanity, "like ours in every respect, yet without sin" (Hebrews 4:15). Although the New Testament clearly presents Jesus of Nazareth as anointed by the Spirit for his messianic ministry and acting in the Spirit's empowerment, this perspective on his humanity gradually diminished during the early centuries of the church as the divinity of Christ came to the fore. The affirmation of Jesus' oneness in being with the Father (the famous *homoousion* of the Nicene creed) was vital for the establishment of Christian orthodoxy, but in time this stress on the divine Christ came to overshadow his role as human mediator. Similarly, while the concept of the hypostatic union of two natures in Christ was intended to uphold the full reality of his humanity as well as his divinity, by interpreting this largely in a static manner, little room was left for understanding the maturation of Jesus of Nazareth as a human person in relation to God or in other emotional and intellectual ways. In this climate it was natural to conceptualize Christian spiritual formation more as a progressive "purification" for the vision of God, which Jesus unceasingly enjoyed as the incarnate Son, than as a participation in his holiness, life and ministry, a perspective which continues to affect assumptions about Christian spirituality today.

For the same reason the corresponding portrayal of the role of the Spirit in Jesus' human life was minimized. While his unique identity as the incarnate Son was rightly stressed, the significance of Jesus' anointing by the Spirit in relation to his mission tended to be pushed to the background. The unfortunate result is a diminished conception of how God is with us in Christ, which hinders our ability to discern the activity of God in and through human life, or allows the life of Christ to become simply a template for a generalized conception of the divinity in all persons.

In considering the role of the Holy Spirit in the life of the incarnate Christ, therefore, the chief difficulty has appeared to be the coordination of a real experience of the Spirit equipping and guiding Jesus in his human life, with the concept of the Divine Logos "assuming" human nature.[2] Yet it is more appropriate to consider these two perspectives not as being at odds but as complementary, reflecting the "double movement" of Incarnation.[3] This includes two inseparable yet distinguishable elements. The first of these is the movement from God to humanity. In the human life of Jesus of Nazareth, we have the full presence of God "in person" and a true revelation of the Father. The other pole of the double movement of incarnation is human response to God. This has to do not only with a *revelation* of God but also Jesus' *enactment* of "true human being," which, because of Jesus' identity, takes place not for himself alone but as a vicarious act that changes the possibilities for all persons. Herein lies a key to understanding the coincidence of the amazing affirmation of human life implied in incarnation, and the necessity of its complete remaking as a creative act of God in the person of Christ. The God who encounters us in Christ is not a passive force but an active personal Presence, moving into the created arena "to seek and to save the lost" (Luke 11:10).

Likewise the presence and activity of the Spirit in the life of Christ can be understood from a double perspective. As the unique, Only-Begotten Son, Jesus' life and death take place in that oneness of heart and will with the Father that characterizes the Trinitarian life of God. It is this that makes the reality of *incarnation* possible and is reflected in the unique involvement of the Spirit in the life of Jesus from the beginning. From the perspective of Jesus' humanity, however, the Spirit also can be seen to play a special role in sustaining Jesus in the unity of life and heart he shares with the Father, amidst the ambiguities of human life and its formative relationships. This perspective highlights Jesus' reliance upon the Spirit in an on-going way to equip and empower him in his ministry and guide him

---

[2] Such an approach also seems inevitably subordinationist in regard to the Spirit, which is the classic Eastern critique of the Western *filioque*.

[3] See for instance Ray S. Anderson, *The Soul of Ministry* (Louisville, Kentucky: Westminster John Knox Press, 1997), 87f; and Thomas F. Torrance, *The Mediation of Christ*, Expanded Edition (Colorado Springs: Helmers & Howard, 1992) for extended discussions of this concept, which occupies a central position in the incarnational theologies of both.

in recognizing "what the Father is doing" (John 5:19f)--an experience which also is open to those who receive the Spirit of Christ.[4] It also better allows Jesus' life and mission to be seen in continuity with the Old Testament, essentially related to the activity of the Spirit of God in Israel and the fulfillment of the Kingdom of God.[5]

From this perspective it is apparent that the revelation of God in the life of Christ takes place not in static terms but in the dynamism of relationship, that of Jesus with the Father, in the anointing of the Spirit upon his ministry and in the human receptivity of his person. As the "only begotten of the Father," Jesus is also the "first among many brothers and sisters" for whom this sonship is realized in a history of obedience and service to the Father.[6] Born into our situation, Jesus "[took] hold of humanity in its estrangement from God and [bound] it back into relation with God through his own love as the Son of the Father."[7] In the course of life he "beat his way forward,"[8] bending the human will into submission to God, accepting judgment and offering perfect obedience to the Father. Hebrews 5:8 expresses this clearly, "Although he was a son, he learned obedience, and being perfected, becomes the source of eternal salvation for all who trust in him." As paradoxical as it may seem for the Son of God to "learn" human obedience, this concept is vital for an understanding of Jesus' humanity, deepening our conception of the role of the Holy Spirit in relationship to Jesus' sonship and ministry and providing a foundation for perceiving the manner in which the Spirit of the Risen Christ is now active in the lives of his people. His life of active love and receptivity toward the Father and in orientation toward his mission is not one of static perfection (which would call the reality of his humanity into question and be of no help to us) but entails a "normal" human process of maturation and growth.

From this perspective it is evident that the vicarious quality of Jesus' life was enacted in the unfolding of his personal pilgrimage as a human being. As he pursued his mission in a unique oneness with the Father, He encountered the ambiguity, growth and challenge which is inherently part

---

[4] Jürgen Moltmann, *The Way of Jesus Christ*, trans. Margaret Kohl (New York: HarperCollins, 1990), 139f.

[5] Anderson stresses the importance of this continuity in light of God's faithfulness and Jesus' role as the "True Israelite," who fulfills God's purposes for Israel and opens the way for the inclusion of Jew and Gentile in one Body. See for instance the discussion in *Historical Transcendence and the Reality of God* (London: Geoffrey Chapman Publishers and Grand Rapids, Michigan: William B. Eerdmans Publishing Company, 1975), 124ff. This also forms a central theme in Moltmann, *The Way of Jesus Christ*.

[6] See discussion of Jesus as the Servant of the Father in Anderson, *The Soul of Ministry*, 78ff.

[7] Ray S. Anderson, *Soul of Ministry*, 75.

[8] T. F. Torrance, *Theology in Reconstruction* (Grand Rapids. MI: William B. Eerdmans, 1965), 132. Torrance concludes not only that this is true of Jesus, but also that this is a way of humiliation we must make our own, "whether in knowledge or activity."

of human life, as well as the unbelief and resistance or indifference to God's gifts which characterize the human community under the power of sin. In this his uniqueness is not something that removed him from this world or from exhibiting his own personality and character as a human being;[9] instead, it allowed him to play a unique role within and on behalf of all God's people.

The key to Christ's life was his identity as the Son of the Father. The central task of Jesus' life, therefore, may be envisioned as cultivating and maintaining a "face to face" relation with God, while vicariously sharing our humanity that has turned from God in sin and unbelief.[10] In orienting his human life to the Father in the Spirit, Jesus' remaking of human being in his own person involves bringing sinful, broken, unbelieving humanity into the presence of God's life, in vicarious repentance and for vicarious renewal and recreation. This is a very different thought from that of realizing a "divine potential" in his soul's identity with a universal spirit of peace and wisdom. Nor is it a primarily private, inward experience. Both growth as a human person and the work of redeeming the humanity he has taken to himself were active and demanding processes in which Jesus appears to have rejoiced in the grace, activity and presence of God.

It may be further suggested that as part of this relationship Jesus also bore the cost of submitting to discipline, accepting the inevitable absence of a fully loving human environment not by disconnecting from relationship but by bearing this pain in himself. The ongoing tension thus indicated between the life of Christ in union with the Father and the human life he shares with us is well expressed by Isaiah's description of the "man of sorrows, acquainted with grief" (Isaiah 53:3). Jesus himself is the one who must mourn the ultimate absence of the face of God from the center of human existence, corporately as well as individually, which confronts him at every turn. The only way to continue in his incarnate life is by suffering this pain we cannot bear through upholding by the divine

---

9 Ray Anderson discusses this dismissal of the ultimate importance and reality of human personality and character as a central inadequacy of New Age thought in *The New Age of Soul: Spiritual Wisdom for a New Millennium* (Eugene, OR: Wipf and Stock Publishers, 2001), 30ff., 115ff.

10 For God's face to be turned toward human beings is a biblical expression for God's openness toward them in divine favor and pleasure and openness of relation. In contrast, for God to turn his face away implies judgment and the absence of blessing, while humans correspondingly hide their faces in shame and unbelief. This image is discussed by Jürgen Moltmann, *The Crucified God*, trans. R. A. Wilson and John Bowden (New York: Harper & Row, 1974), 242, who relates it to the godforsakenness of those who have turned from God (Romans 1); and by James E. Loder, *The Transforming Moment* (Colorado Springs, CO: Helmers & Howard, 1989) 101ff., who gives it particular importance in relation to the development of human personhood and recreation in Christ.

Spirit, who leads him to the cross.[11] Such a choice to remain aware of the power of sin and brokenness over against his own experiential knowledge of God's gifts and merciful kingdom allowed Jesus to live a true human life, in contrast to a "normality" or spirituality that functions to distract from the reality of the human condition. In fact, it may be suggested that, humanly speaking, this played a large part in Jesus' motivation and empowerment for ministry.

In this way, upheld by the Spirit, Jesus' core personhood took form in his complete receptivity to the Father's love in obedience and oneness of heart and will. Here the "double movement" again is apparent, now in relation to the question of how the union of divine Logos and human being in the one person of Jesus of Nazareth can be conceived and lived out in concreteness.[12] "Inasmuch as Jesus lives wholly and entirely from this love of the Father and wills to be nothing of himself, Jesus is nothing but the incarnate love of the Father and the incarnate response of obedience," the perfected human response to God's Gift in whom God is fully present.[13] This is reflected in Jesus' own self-testimony that his empowerment and authority were not something he possessed in himself but the gift of the Father in him (cf. John 14:16f and 12:49 as two examples). This complete receptivity to the Father as the Source of his life, the lived acknowledgment that he does not possess life in himself, is the positive reality of human life. Where we encounter barrenness in ourselves, in his life offered to the Father there is fullness of life and good fruit as the gift of God.

This indicates the thoroughly relational nature of God's work that makes us more human, not less, more able to enter into life-giving relation, not more isolated. Because we have alienated ourselves from the life-giving presence of God, Jesus actually enters the human situation so that God can meet us in our estranged humanity. Jesus is the human being who hears, who responds, and who fulfills and restores the divine image from out of our estranged position and life.

This reality is nowhere more powerfully expressed than in the cross, where the tragic quality of God's encounter with humanity is clearly disclosed. As becomes evident in the responses to Jesus' life and preaching, God's self-gift to humanity is met by increasing resistance. This is especially seen in the hardening opposition against Christ's table

---

[11] Anderson's imagery of Jesus "yoking himself" with humanity (cf. Matt. 11:38) in bearing human weakness and sin (*Historical Transcendence and the Reality of God*, 173) is informative in this context. The character of this aspect of Jesus' ministry is particularly brought out in the portrayal of his agony in Gethsemane.
[12] Gary Badcock, *Light of Truth, Fire of Love* (Grand Rapids, Michigan: William B. Eerdmans Publishing Company, 1997), 154.
[13] Gary Badcock, "The Anointing of Christ and the *Filioque* Doctrine," *Irish Theological Quarterly* 60 (1994): 233.

fellowship with sinners and "Sabbath breaking" for the sake of the liberating work of God. The preference for religious structures over the work of God represents the same sort of impulse to fulfill God's promises by humanly generated means as did Abraham's choice to seek a younger mother for the child of the promise. Despite the intention of securing God's ways, our human judgments can become hindrances to accepting the activity of God when it appears in its re-creative character, resulting in slavery to a counterfeit of God's ways.[14] The promise of the Spirit as the beginning of the new creation through resurrection from death is presented as the only way to overcome this hardness of heart. New life in the Spirit of Christ's resurrection is nothing short of a new birth and complete recreation.

If there is any point at which we see the futility of the human ego's attempt to hold the power of mortality at bay, it is in the godforsaken death of the one who lived continually before the face of God. In his chosen oneness with humanity our lifelessness is disclosed, as is the Spirit's sustaining anointing upon him for this task. Jesus suffered death in "the power of indestructible life" (Hebrews 7:16), "through the power of the eternal Spirit"(Hebrews 9:14), upheld in oneness of life and will with the Father as he gave himself over to the divine purpose to save. As it was *in the Spirit* that he healed and taught, it was above all *by the Spirit* that he offered himself to the Father and was maintained in a oneness of life and will in the midst of the power of death.

It is in this context that the paradox that "the Chosen One must suffer and die" is to be placed. The ongoing life of choosing oneness with the Father **and** with human being results in the hiddenness of the divine presence in Christ. God's redemptive power, which is opposed by the self-protective religious system, is concentrated increasingly within the life of Jesus the Servant.[15] Thus he carries the human resistance that has become a prison for both those who enact it and those who are affected by it.

It is his oneness with God's heart of compassion that leads Jesus in this way. Here is the union of lavish love and abandonment--not at odds but united in one act. In Christ, God acts to reconcile the world by taking to himself human godforsakenness. What is shocking is the depth of our predicament and of God's powerfully saving presence. In Christ, God is redemptively present and active, not overcoming mortality as though it were ultimately unimportant but entering into its depths with us, following us into our forsakenness in order to reach us with life that overcomes death and allows a return to the face of God in the Christ who meets us here.

---

[14] See the nuanced discussion of Ishmael and Isaac in light of God's promise to Abraham in Anderson, *The Soul of Ministry*, 46f.
[15] Anderson, *Historical Transcendence and the Reality of God*, 129ff.

Thus the union of the Chosen One with the Spirit of God is not a statement of God's power directed *against* his human creature, establishing us in our barrenness and lostness, nor is it simply a living out of what has always been true. Christ comes as the Source and Gift of new life itself, which does not cling to its own advantages or even its own being, but "empties [itself,] taking the form of a Servant" (Philippians 2:4f). This is confirmed by Jesus' resurrection, which, like his death, is not enacted for himself alone but "for many."

With Jesus' resurrection and the outpouring of the Holy Spirit upon the disciples at Pentecost, the Spirit that anointed Jesus for ministry and sustained him in relation to the Father comes to be identified specifically in relation to the Risen Lord. This is the Spirit of Servanthood and Sonship as defined and enacted in Jesus' human life, bearing the human character and personality of Jesus of Nazareth. As Jesus is the human person in whom there is no resistance to the Spirit's presence and activity, so this is the "shape" the Spirit bears in coming to us.[16] The Holy Spirit now is called the Spirit of Christ (Romans 8:9), the Spirit of God's Son (Galatians 4:6), the Spirit of Jesus Christ (Philippians 1:19),[17] and is recognized by likeness to Christ, making him present in the midst of his people and witnessing to him, disclosing the crucified Jesus to be the Risen Lord. While in his earthly life the Spirit was seemingly "concentrated upon" Jesus, now the Spirit of God comes to Christ's followers through his intercession to allow them to share his ministry and relation to the Father. In this there is a double mediation, in that the Spirit poured out by the Risen Christ makes Christ present in the midst of his people.

In this context Jesus' unique reception of the Spirit can be understood as a vicarious gift, allowing us to share in his life and anointing. As T. F. Torrance has written, through union with Christ in his humanity the Spirit comes to us profoundly humanized, having "composed himself, as it were, to dwell with human nature, and human nature [having] been adapted and become accustomed to receive and hear the same Holy Spirit."[18] This amazing statement indicates the condescension of God's accommodation to humanity in the very process of redemption and new creation, so that something qualitatively new takes place. In our "closedness" to God a space has been made for the Spirit of God fully to indwell human life, bringing the transforming presence of the risen Christ.

This full union of the Spirit of God with the human person of Jesus of Nazareth likewise becomes the key for discerning the presence and

---

16 Cf. Dunn, *Jesus and the Spirit*, 320.
17 James G. D. Dunn, *Jesus and the Spirit* (Philadelphia: The Westminster Press, 1975), 318.
18 T. F. Torrance, *Theology in Reconstruction* (Grand Rapids. MI: William B. Eerdmans, 1965), 246.

activity of the Holy Spirit. For example, does the "spirit" being nurtured individually and corporately in the name of Christ and presented through the ministry of the Body of Christ bear the character of the person of Jesus? Does it open the way for others to be drawn in love and faith to the same Jesus who came as a Physician to those sick in heart, soul and body and rejoiced in God's work of deliverance?

The resurrection of Christ and the coming of the Spirit also is the basis for the concept of Christ's "humanizing humanity." As the Firstborn of the new creation and the Logos in whom and for whom all has been brought into being, Jesus' humanity is inclusive. Life in the Spirit is not so much an otherworldly experience as a renewal of humanity in the image of Christ, who has assumed, healed and restored our humanity to us. Our relation with God and commissioning from God is given as a share in that of Christ by the Holy Spirit.

Thus, the restoration of God's life to us does not come by immersion in a universal world soul or the attainment of a transcendent consciousness, but through God seeking us out in Christ to restore us to a humanizing, life-renewing personal communion with God and others. This gift comes from a context completely other than our own, yet brings life and enablement that disclose human beings as God's creatures and children in Christ. To find one's life in Christ by losing it expresses a different kind of paradox than does the attempt to gain life through conformity to a naturalistic world soul or by a passive spiritual encounter. Christian spirituality is not a quest to discover one's true nature in metaphysical *unity* with an impersonal force of life, but to find one's place in the mission of Christ as part of his *community*. Christian formation is thus a matter of participation in Christ and his humanity by the Spirit in a relational sense that encompasses the whole person, in all aspects of our life and relationships. It is this that allows the offering of our lives and ministries to be God's gift.

The Spirit in the Life of the Body of Christ

Having looked at the Spirit in the life, death and resurrection of Jesus, the focus now will shift to the new context for human life brought into being by the Spirit of Christ. While the identity of the church is many-faceted, this section will concentrate on the nature of this setting in regard to the building up and equipping of the members of the Body through humanizing relationships, rather than upon the broader character of the church's life and mission.

While Jesus' own resurrection is the decisive act for the in-breaking of the new creation and the outpouring of the Holy Spirit, the new birth of the church as the Body of Christ also demonstrates the incapacity of human being as the arena in which God bestows the Spirit. The Apostle

Paul understands the inclusion of the Gentiles in judgment upon God's own unbelieving people as especially significant. "You Gentiles," he suggests on more than one occasion (cf. Ephesians 2:4ff., Colossians 1:2) were dead, cut off from the life-giving root and cast aside. Now not only has God rejuvenated these withering twigs but also has revealed the condition of all humanity. As the word of forgiveness contains both condemnation and mercy and correspondingly calls for repentance and faith, so the universal condition of the barrenness of human spirit distant from the life of God is a word of judgment that opens the way to the reception of grace by all.

To be raised with Christ includes incorporation into this new community as an integral part of the Spirit's distinctive activity. The Spirit unites the members of the Body with Christ in the double movement of his human life as Servant and Son and into a fellowship of worship, proclamation and mission. The existence of such a renewed community can be seen as a form of "co-humanity." It is not the individual alone who is the basic picture of what it means to be a human being in the image of God, but persons-in-relation to God and one another whose common life is to mirror God's relation to creation and the divine life. Integral to how human persons are constituted is relationship to others by and through which our experiences of the world and our own place in relation to this outer "reality" are interpreted and defined. Not only our own identity in relation to others, but the very categories by which we interpret life experiences and our implicit beliefs about what is "real" are formed from infancy in such a relational context.

Into this setting the Spirit of God breaks with the judgment of death and the miracle of new life, ushering us into a context in which the rules for life have been rearranged and renewed empowerment and hope come from unexpected sources. The one crucified in weakness is disclosed to be the Son of God in power by his resurrection; the last are called first and the Lord is the Servant of all. This is a new reality by which to interpret the basic self-world matrix. It is not surprising, therefore, that a humanizing rebirth in Christ places us in a new family context in which reality can be redefined.[19] The key to this is the indwelling presence of Christ, who makes possible a new human community that will continue his message, as the beginning of God's purposes for all creation.

Union with Jesus in his humanity by the Spirit is thus a way of enabling us to be more fully human in accord with the basic structure of human being. Freedom for new life is not to be confused with an arbitrary liberty--freedom "from" the other in an individualistic sense--but is the freedom to live creatively in the grace of God "because personal being is

---

19 For a detailed discussion of this aspect of the life of the Christian community, see Anderson, *Historical Transcendence and the Reality of God*, 237f.

constituted by relatedness."[20] This mirrors Jesus' freedom and fullness of life in receiving his message and personhood in receptivity and obedience to the Father and his will. As the Body of Christ the church may be understood as the context in which believers are invited to work out together the actual lived renewal of the image of God in a way that bears fruit in the world. This is not just a formal change but, by the *kouninia* of the Spirit, it is so deeply anchored in the nature of human being as to constitute a recreation of human personhood through the transformation of the relational structures by which it is formed and exists.

The *charismata* in particular bear witness to the corporate character of the presence of Christ in the church through the person-forming and re-forming relationships of the members to one another and toward God in Christ. This should not be misunderstood as a one-sided focus upon the miraculous or "other-worldly;" while the Spirit's gifts may exhibit this character, fundamentally these are gifts of grace. More specifically, the *charismata* can be characterized as vehicles by which the grace of God is active in a specific form "in the life of individuals for the sake of others [as] gifts of God which are effectively brought into the life of the community by the Spirit."[21] Equipping comes through experiencing oneself as a subject and recipient of God's grace, in the midst of a community of worship and mission in which this grace is made known, recognized and received as the essence of new life. In this context, as persons are taught, healed and empowered in relation to their own areas of pain, sin and weakness they receive a special enablement of the Spirit that bears a "death-defying" gracious character, for participation in the mission of Christ. The awareness of the power of sin and death in one's own life and that of the community is God's gift, disrupting settled resistances to God's life and providing the opportunity for change. In this way new life comes with an empowerment that is not of ourselves, and yet works with and through persons in continuity with their life history, taking up both the truth of human fallenness and of God's redeeming purposes.

This is the Spirit reflected in the life of the Body and its ministry in the world, if it is acting in the Spirit of Christ. In this way the Spirit forms the new community into a context for the growth of persons who can function as priests to one another, witnesses of God's grace and equippers for the ministry of the Kingdom of God. This corresponds to the fundamental character of the *charismata*, which draw attention to the gracious activity of God in "earthen vessels." Even under the best of circumstances, lived communion with God as well as human communion

---

20 Colin Gunton, *The Promise of Trinitarian Theology*, 2nd edition (Edinburgh: T&T Clark, 1991), 131.
21 Gordon Fee, *God's Empowering Presence* (Peabody, Mass: Hendrickson Publishers, Inc, 1994), 607.

is constantly ruptured and renewed. To view one another in a merely utilitarian way[22] or as only fellow travelers on parallel spiritual paths is destructive of communion, the community equivalent of living only on the basis of motives for individual survival and self-satisfaction. In such a situation the community settles down in its barrenness, wondering at its lifelessness. This is in contrast to a life in which our humanity is accepted as the context for discovering God's grace. Apart from such practice in sharing and extending God's grace to one another, the community will remain distant from Christ and fail to flourish.

As gifts of grace, however, the *charismata* can be understood as a manifestation of the redeeming presence of the Holy One. On this basis people receive one another as gifted "in keeping with `the gift of Christ that has been apportioned' to them" as part of a formative, equipping process.[23] However, even empowerment for mission is not sufficient in itself, for persons must also be *equipped* for service.[24] This calls for a nurturing, teaching, enabling ministry of personal formation as part of the fundamentally familial character of Christian community, an arena for "growing up" in faith and life. Here the new identity that is established is not based in social roles, but is received as a gift through the shared life formed by the Spirit. Therefore the context for the gifts includes all facets of the church's life through which the active working of God meets its members in their humanity, re-creating structures for the interrelated formation of persons. [25] In this way the gifts of grace, though not originating in our humanity, are restorative of it.

Thus in the Body of Christ, as in Jesus' human life, we see God deeply invested in the human context, working through human persons and relationships, bringing the grace of Christ to bear in such a way that the Spirit's power "is made perfect in [our] weakness." This is the same quality of life that allows the church to act as an incarnational community, in solidarity with the world.[26]

---

22 Dietrich Bonhoeffer, *Communio Sanctorum* [*The Communion of Saints*]: A Dogmatic Inquiry into the Sociology of the Church, trans. R. Gregor Smith (New York: Harper & Row, 1960), 146.

23 Fee, 707, cf. Anderson, *Historical Transcendence and the Reality of God*, 236f.

24 See discussion in Anderson, *Historical Transcendence and the Reality of God*, 257f.

25 This is related to a renewal of the "love of life" and energy for living sacrificially, as presented in Jürgen Moltmann's overall discussion in *The Spirit of Life*, translated by Margaret Kohl (Minneapolis, Minn.: Fortress Press, 1992).

26 This is a major topic in itself, to which there is not room to do justice here. For an excellent treatment see Anderson, *The Soul of Ministry*, 137ff, and *Historical Transcendence and the Reality of God*, 252ff.

The Spirit as the Life of Creation

This kind of participatory life, sharing in Jesus' humanizing humanity by the Spirit and participating as a "living member" of the Body of Christ, is not only in accord with the nature of human persons but also reflects the triune life of God. In this section a brief description of the divine Being as loving communion, expressed specifically through the concept of Trinitarian *perichoresis*, will be followed by a summary of the character of the Spirit's ministry in relation to creation, according to three of its central aspects.

Developed in the early church as a way of expressing the fundamentally relational nature of reality in its dynamic, creative character, the concept of Trinitarian *perichoresis* is being rediscovered in contemporary theological thinking as a way to present the dynamic quality of the life of God, characterized by reciprocity of self-gift to and for the other.[27] It expresses a conception in which the divine persons are fully united through mutual indwelling, while maintaining a fundamental integrity that is enhanced by and grounded in this union. Ultimately this Trinitarian conception is rooted in the character of the threefold experience of God--Father, Son and Spirit--evident in the life of Jesus, which becomes the basis not only for a triune conception of God's life as Holy Love, but for its expression in these particular terms. Any true picture of what it means for the personal God to be "one" as well as "three" in a personal, dynamic sense is developed primarily on the basis of the nature of the reality of God in Christ's life. This in turn is the basis for the shared life of the church as the Body of Christ, which exists through the personalizing *koinonia* the Spirit brings.

Although there cannot be a one-to-one correspondence between the divine *perichoresis* and the nature of human personhood, implications of the perichoretic triune Being of God for human formation and spirituality are rich and varied. Above all, the matrix for personal being is seen to be a fundamentally relational one. This is not static in nature, existing fundamentally either as a natural "oneness" with the divine or according to rigid patterns or systems of hierarchy or behavior, nor are its outward signs necessarily clear-cut. It may exhibit a miraculous character; it may be hidden in the brokenness and commonality of life. More importantly, it is a relationality made up of life given and received in such a way that the particularity of each person is honored and the intimacy of relationships within the Body thereby deepened. It is thus creative and dynamic in nature. Giving of and out of one's personal being, sowing an abundance of

---

27 This description is drawn from Colin Gunton, *The One, the Three and the Many: God, Creation and the Culture of Modernity*, The 1992 Bampton Lectures (Cambridge: University Press, 1993), 164.

seeds and lavishly offering grace seems to carry with it a particular empowerment for newness, creation and healing that goes beyond restoration of a lost good to the birth of something of multiplied worth. Therefore it is expressed in images of birth and fruit, not work and product: the grain of wheat that bears fruit in dying, the mysterious seed planted that is "reborn" into a whole plant--the shameful death of Christ that overcomes death and ushers in a new creation. Such results are neither predictable nor probable, but disclose the dynamic, creative character of God whose intimate presence births "more than we can ask or think" (Eph. 3:20).

As the life of Christ in relation to the Father and that of the church in relation to the Lord are participatory in nature, creation as a whole reflects the oneness of divine love and creaturely freedom as well. The characteristic sign of the Spirit's presence has been identified as a growing oneness of life and heart that does not subvert but establishes the other in its own reality.[28] This is the basis for human freedom, mirroring the Spirit's unique anointing upon and unity with the person of Jesus. It is the *presence* of God in Christ by the Spirit--not the absence of God that leaves us to ourselves--that makes us free. The human growth and maturation we seek is the gift of oneness with God in Christ. This is the paradox from a perspective that understands freedom to be self-generated. Here freedom comes as a gift of relationship that enhances all the members of it.

In bringing the gifts of life and freedom, the Spirit's distinctive ministry is to complete God's purposes for human persons and all creation. Although a pattern of growth and development is familiar in all areas of life, this expected pattern must be placed within a life-out-of-death context in relation to the one who drives Jesus into the wilderness to be tempered for his vocation, and leads him in the way of the cross throughout his life as he confronts the powers of darkness and evil in humanity in order to drive them out. It should be no surprise, therefore, that the perfecting activity of the Spirit in creation bears a similar character. James Loder has described this as a fourfold pattern characterizing all human formation and transformation, in which the life we naturally construct for ourselves in relation to others is met by the power of death (including in its proximate forms of loneliness and meaningless)--but a death which has been overcome by Christ, allowing this to become the arena in which Christ has become present to meet us through faith.[29] It is here that the grace of God destroys the power of death itself, not as a natural outcome, but as the gift of the Spirit of the Risen Christ.

In considering the activity of the Holy Spirit for the perfection of creation, therefore, this movement must be kept in mind. The same going-

---

28 Gunton, *The One, the Three and the Many*, 164.
29 A detailed elaboration of this theme is the subject of Loder, *The Transforming Moment*.

down-into-death in order to fill it with God's life and presence that is fulfilled in Christ *for* us is received *in* our lost humanity by the Spirit. There is an integral link between the communion of persons created by the Spirit and this perfecting work. As the Spirit acts to restore the relations upon which human life depends through forgiveness and reconciliation, so the Spirit upholds and perfects human life from within the creaturely dimension in this same manner, in accordance with the rhythm of death and resurrection. To give ourselves in our own particular identity in relation with others in a way that results in generativity and meaning is a picture of the fruit of just such a way of life out of nothingness, offered in God's grace. This shared life reflects that of the triune God and is the only form that does not eventually close back in upon itself and become a prison of death and limitation. In this way, to live by the Spirit of Christ is to be caught up in a movement toward the fulfillment of our creaturely purpose.

Thus in contrast to an a-personal conception of spirituality, at the heart of the Spirit's perfecting activity is the formation and maturing of personhood. The Spirit does not overwhelm creaturely reality but initiates an interaction which enhances the distinctively relational, personal quality of life, in accord with God's own Being, even as the Spirit empowers and upholds Jesus in his distinctive identity as Son of the Father and Messiah.

In this portrayal, God and the human person (or community) are presented not simply as two entities placed over against each other but as intimately interrelated. In the Spirit, God becomes present to the human "not just externally, not just from above, but also from within, from below, subjectively."[30]

> What is of importance here is the unlimited freedom of God, not only to become man in Jesus Christ without ceasing to be God, but really to impart himself to us in the Spirit while remaining the transcendent Lord over all our creaturely being and knowing.[31]

As Christ fulfills both sides of the double movement between God and humanity, so in the Spirit God acts on both sides of the relation, opening to humans in revelation and opening human persons for reception and understanding, activating a two-way relation. Here is an echo of the humility of God seen in the Incarnation, God with and in the creature to

---

30 Karl Barth, *Church Dogmatics*, I/1, edited by G. W. Bromiley and T. F. Torrance, translated by G. W. Bromiley, etc. al (Edinburgh: T & T Clark, 1936-69; 2nd ed. of I/1, 1975), 451.

31 T. F. Torrance, *The Christian Doctrine of God, One Being, Three Persons*, 152. Barth similarly identifies the Holy Spirit as God himself, able "not only to come to man, but also be in man, and thus open up man and make him capable and ready for himself, and thus to complete his revelation in him" (CD I/1, 450).

reconstruct human persons from the same depths of estrangement into which Christ has entered. This allows "real life" to be reborn, recreating human being neither as divine puppet nor as divine energy, but as the covenant partner with God. In this way God acts from the human side and within in a way appropriate to the Spirit's distinctive personhood, even as Jesus takes up our humanity.

This reestablishment of created life is also a clue to its value. From this perspective the time-embeddedness of our lives, set between the boundaries of birth and death, can be understood as the gift of space for growth in love. This is in contrast to views that would characterize finiteness as irrelevant or a hindrance to spiritual life. Instead the finiteness and particularity that allows relationship with others can be seen as an integral part of the "goodness" of created human being, allowing persons to enact their unique identity in relation to God's grace.

It is especially significant that within a biblical conception of the utter moral and personal distinction between God and humans, God's gracious, outgoing love is willing to take up residence in the sphere of creation, not only to grant an existence to that which is other than God but also to be the life of the creature. In this way, a dynamic, creative, personal union of relationship is possible between the Creator and creature. From this perspective, to speak of God "in" creation in the person of the Spirit is not pantheism, but precisely the opposite, a reality that enables relation between human persons and God. It is the perichoretic life of God that makes this possible, the intimacy of mutual indwelling that does not absorb but grants life to the other in love.

Life in the Spirit

As in the incarnate life of Christ, in the Spirit God gives us God's very Self. In this sense the Holy Spirit can be understood as expressing the innermost nature of God--God as self-communicating love.[32] This is a gift that not only inspires our awe and reverence but invites and empowers our response in faith, allowing us actually to live in the love of God, acting as the foundation of our worship and as the reality that creates formation in Christ. This final section is a brief reflection on the quality and character of this life "in the Spirit."

The nature of human life is such that although human persons receive new creation wholly as a gift, it is impossible to conceive this as an automatic process--response of faith and obedience is necessary. This comes not as a demand from outside but as part of *receiving* God's intimate presence. There need be no separation between growth in human maturity

---

[32] Walter Kasper, *The God of Jesus Christ*, 226. See also extended discussion in John J. O'Donnell, "God the Holy Spirit" in *The Mystery of the Triune God*, 99.

as a relational, creative existence and growth in relation to God. Instead, "in upholding living, rational creatures from below and within them" the Holy Spirit matures and perfects our humanity through participation "in the very life and holiness of God himself."[33] This process is not characterized by harsh discipline but by creation of an orientation that enhances openness toward God, freeing the human creature for his or her own life, offered in love.

> Thus in establishing his relations with us in the Spirit, God upholds us from below and sustains us within, and brings us as people whom he has made for himself to our true end in communion with himself, and thereby makes us participate in his own eternal life.[34]

"Spirituality" is thus grounded in God's life in our lives and ourselves in God. To return to the analogy of new birth, it may be recalled that to live "in" another and draw life from another is the primary experience of life. This is not an absorption meant to eliminate individual distinctives but a foundation that provides nourishment for the birth of identity and giftedness.

The womb itself is a powerful symbol of life and the power of life, of the ability of persons to participate in this power yet not control it. There is a mystery about this emptiness that can nurture life as a gift but cannot create it. This can be received from out of the context of co-humanity as a unique, vital gift for the community or it can be de-humanized and brought under oppressive control. In contrast, the biblical stories portray barrenness as being without earthly security and cut off from the promise of God. The life of the one without offspring has no means of continuing on, and the barren woman lives with a sense of shame under the judgment of God, of isolation and fundamental failure as a woman and a person that is akin to the curse of godforsakenness in the absence of the divine presence.[35]

To this barrenness as a representation of the human "capacity" for spirituality there are various responses. There is that of Herod and the religious authorities who see God as Adversary to the construction of human life, amassing tokens of wealth, power and spiritual authority to defend against the life of God. Conversely, there is the response of those without resources or hope, who settle down to dwell in a barren landscape until the Word of Life comes. And then there is that granted by the Spirit

---

33 T. F. Torrance, *The Trinitarian Faith* (Edinburgh: T & T Clark, 1988) 229.
34 T. F. Torrance, *The Christian Doctrine of God, One Being, Three Persons* (Edinburgh: T & T Clark, 1996) 153.
35 Cf. Anderson, *Soul of Ministry*, 43ff.

of Christ, as reflected in as reflected in the wise men, who, in response to God's promise, offer gifts to the One of surpassing authority; in Mary, who echoes her coming Son with her acceptance: "Let it be to me according to your Word," the Word which intersects our barrenness and summons to life; and in Elizabeth, who hides herself in amazement yet responds in faith to new life already at hand, blessing Mary and her Child. In these responses we see the Spirit present as Advocate, foreshadowing the stance of Christ himself.

And so the barren womb leads us to the virgin womb, made fruitful as the unique dwelling of God, while the fruitful womb as God's gift becomes symbolic for our empty life before God and our response of faith in Christ by the Spirit. The willingness of the handmaid is similar in character to the giving over required by the process of birthing itself. This allows a movement of life to take over that is not our own, that is facilitated not by control but by receptivity in faith, empowerment and thanksgiving.

In a similar way, at the core of human being in the Spirit of Christ is an active relationality of gift and reception rooted in the triune God as "a dynamic personal order of giving and receiving."[36] The quality of life meant to exist in the church as the Body of Christ is likewise rooted in the divine life, the character of which is not a monistic "oneness" that erases the distinctiveness of particular personhood and giftedness, nor an otherworldliness that separates spiritual wholeness from common life in this world. Instead it is a life of intimacy that enhances personal distinction and freedom for relation through shared being and giftedness. To live in this Spirit teaches us a new language of praise, appreciation, thanksgiving and wonder, of affirmation and gifting, which renews human relationships and allows us to rejoice in God.

Thus through Christ our spirituality is grounded in the perichoretic Triune life of mutual glorification in love. At the heart of renewed humanity in relationship to God we discover a recreation of the capacity for adoration and worship that makes us distinctively human, enabling movement beyond enclosure in the self toward a communion that fosters freedom, creativity and love. Life in the Spirit thus anticipates the consummation of God's purposes for creation, the time of seeing face to face in the renewed creation in which God will be all in all.[37] In this context human persons discover their own uniqueness and giftedness "to the praise of his glorious grace" (Ephesians 1:6).

---

[36] Gunton, *The One, the Three and the Many*, 225.
[37] Jürgen Moltmann, *The Spirit of Life*, 212.

Michael Jinkins

CrossRoads: A Christian Understanding of Vocation

"Experience itself is not the criterion for what is the truth of the Word of God. But the truth of the Word of God must be discerned in terms of its effect when applied to humans in their life situation."
Ray Anderson, *The Soul of Ministry*[1]

Of Roads Diverging and Miles to Go

The words have been used so often that the phrases threaten to break down into mere clichés, but to those who face the question of how they should answer God's call, the following lines from two poems by Robert Frost still speak. The first poem evokes dark woods, lovely, snow covered and deep, that invite us to linger, to stay put, as the poet says:

> But I have promises to keep,
> And miles to go before I sleep,
> And miles to go before I sleep.
>   (Robert Frost, "Stopping by
>   Woods on a Snowy Evening")[2]

The second poem, even more familiar, places us at a kind of crossroad; again we have stopped, this time in a leafy yellow wood where roads diverge. Frost, of course, speaks to us from his own crossroad, his own struggle with vocation, the choice he made to become a poet, the agony of that choice and the consequences of that choice, in the awareness that he was saying no to some things, perhaps forever, when he said yes to the poet's calling. In the end, he steps back and tries imaginatively to look out over the whole course of his life. He writes:

> I shall be telling this with a sigh
> Somewhere ages and ages hence:
> Two roads diverged in a wood, and I —

---

[1] Ray S. Anderson, *The Soul of Ministry: Forming Leaders for God's People* (Louisville: Westminster/John Knox Press, 1997), 15.
[2] Robert Frost, *The Poetry of Robert Frost*, ed. Edward Connery Lathem (New York: Holt, Rinehart and Winston, 1969), 224-225.

> I took the one less traveled by,
> And that has made all the difference.
> (Robert Frost, "The Road Not Taken")[3]

How appropriate that we should think of miles to go and crossroads diverging when we think of God's call. For Christians all the roads we traverse lead from one cross to another, from the cross of Jesus through our own baptisms, by which we participate in his baptism and resurrection and through which we are called to follow him, toward the crosses we are compelled to share with Christ in the promise that we may be raised in him to new life as though risen from watery graves. All our roads are cross-littered roads. All our roads become crossroads, including those roads that emerge from dark woods beckoning us to linger and roads diverging drawing us to respond to the call of Christ, to embrace Christ's vocation.

There is simply no way to properly articulate a theology of vocation without getting personal about the roads we travel and the roads we choose, because God's call is the most personal, the most intimate, yet also, ironically, the most public, thing we face as human beings. Over the next few pages, I shall explore what it means for us as Christians to speak of vocation as God's call; but as I do so, I do not want us to lose sight of the very personal and the very public dimensions of this call.

Ray Anderson is right when he says that our experience does not function as "the criterion for what is the truth of the Word of God." He registers here a timely protest against making an idol of our experience. We must respect the image-shattering work of the Word of God, the divine iconoclast who resists all human attempts to be manipulated and held captive even by our most profound religious experiences. However, as Anderson also understands, "the truth of the Word of God must be discerned in terms of its effects when applied to humans in their life situation."[4] Experience matters, as John Calvin also knew, because God condescends to know us, to meet us, to reconcile us, in this world, amid the things of this world. Calvin assures us that it is none other than God with whom we have our dealings in all of life.[5]

---

[3] *Ibid.*, 105.
[4] Anderson, *op cit.*
[5] The passage in Calvin to which I allude is one which John T. McNeill uses to such extraordinary effect in his introduction to Calvin's political thought: *"in tota vita negotium cum Deo."* John T. McNeill, editor, *Calvin: On God and Political Duty* (Indianapolis/ New York: The Bobbs-Merrill Company, Inc., second revised edition, 1956), vii.

Michael Jinkins

CrossRoads in Biblical Perspective

The life story of Albert Schweitzer is familiar. One of the greatest minds, one of the greatest talents, of the twentieth century, Schweitzer walked away from the comfortable fame and relative fortune he knew in Europe to become a medical missionary in French Equatorial Africa. By the age of thirty, Schweitzer had earned four doctorates, in philosophy, theology, music and medicine. His doctoral dissertation in music, a two-volume study of Johann Sebastian Bach, became a classic in the field; his dissertation in theology, *The Quest of the Historical Jesus*, redefined biblical studies for the twentieth century. At the height of his fame, with Western Europe lying at his feet, and his whole professional career among the cultural elite ahead of him, Schweitzer made the decision to become a medical missionary. Again, the story is familiar, though it is worth recounting, how on the day he stood at the train station, waiting to leave behind everything that was familiar, everything that was secure, a friend is said to have asked him, "Albert, why are you doing this?" And he answered simply, "My master bids me go."

I am reminded by Schweitzer's story of the simplicity and the comprehensiveness of Jesus' call which we observe in the synoptic gospels. "As Jesus passed along the Sea of Galilee," Mark's Gospel tells us, "he saw Simon and his brother Andrew casting a net into the sea — for they were fishermen. 'Follow me [Jesus said to them] and I will make you fish for people.' Immediately they left their nets and followed him. As he went a little farther, he saw James son of Zebedee and his brother John, who were in their boat mending their nets. Immediately he called them; and they left their father Zebedee in the boat with the hired men, and followed him" (Mark 1:16-20). And, of course, the hauntingly simple story in the next chapter of Mark's Gospel, the story which takes our breath away in its abruptness, by both how little and how much it tells us: "As [Jesus] was walking along, he saw Levi son of Alphaeus sitting at the tax booth, and he said to him, 'Follow me.' And he got up and followed him" (Mark 2:14). Life and death hang in the balance on these texts. Bonhoeffer comments:

> Things used to be different. Then [prior to the call of Jesus] they could live quietly in the country, unnoticed in their work, keep the law, and wait for the Messiah. But now he was there; now his call came. Now faith no longer meant keeping quiet and waiting, but going in discipleship with him. Now his call to discipleship dissolved all ties for the sake of the unique commitment to Jesus Christ. Now all bridges had to be burned and the step taken to enter into endless insecurity, in order to know what Jesus demands and what Jesus gives. Levi at his taxes could have had Jesus as a helper for all kinds of needs, but

he would not have recognized him as the one Lord, into whose hand he should entrust his whole life. He would not have learned to have faith . . . . This is the impossible situation, in which everything is based on only one thing, the word of Jesus.[6]

The subject matter and content of Christian vocation is the word of Jesus himself. This is, of course, a scandal to reasonable and respectable ears. No strategies are laid out, no plans that might convince the faint-hearted of the rationality for following this person in this direction at this time. "Follow me," Jesus says. Everything else is footnote, news below the fold of the front page, fine print on a contract left unread. The "experience" of the person addressed by the word of Jesus is swallowed up in the one making the address, swallowed up with no promise, except the promise of death in the following. The one who would cling to his life, we are reminded, loses his life. Only the one who loses his life for the sake of Jesus – lost in the word of Jesus, lost in the word of the address, in the invitation to follow – only that one is given life. The sacramental richness of the rite of initiation, Christian baptism, is prefigured and ultimately fulfilled in Christ's call to follow in that everything the one addressed receives, hears, experiences, washes away in the water of the call itself. All that remains is Christ, the one who calls.

Bonhoeffer tells us that belief in God through Jesus Christ is inseparable from our hearing and responding to the call: "As long as Levi sits in the tax collector's booth and Peter at his nets, they would do their work honestly and loyally, they would have old and new knowledge about God. But if they want to learn to believe in God, they have to follow the Son of God incarnate and walk with him."[7] However, it is not the experience of their call that sustains them, it is the one they follow; it is not the quality of the faith they learn that transforms them, it is the one in whom they trust.

Not every story in the gospels has a joyful ending ("joyful," that is, as participation in the cross of Christ). Mark also tells us (Mark 10: 17-31) of a man traditionally called the Rich Young Ruler. Jesus loved him, we are told. Jesus called him to follow. But, we are also told that this wealthy young leader went away from Jesus in sorrow, because "he had many possessions." Rather, we might say, his many possessions had him. We have here not demon possession, but *possession* possession. A tragic story. However, the Rich Young Ruler, despite his ultimate failure, at least understood something that so many "casual" followers of Jesus seem not to understand: Whoever hears the call of Jesus and whoever decides to follow

---

6 Dietrich Bonhoeffer, *Discipleship*, ed. Geffrey B. Kelly and John D. Godsey, tr. Barbara Green and Reinhard Krauss (Minneapolis: Fortress Press, 2001), 62-63.
7 *Ibid.*, 62.

him must be prepared to share in his life and fate.[8] The cost of following Jesus is total. Christ's vocation requires us to relinquish ultimate control over our ends and our means.

"My master bids me go," Schweitzer is said to have said. And, as Bonhoeffer knew, those who do not follow remain behind. In the first instance, when we speak theologically of vocation, it is of this radical, comprehensive and unconditional call to follow Jesus that we must speak. Perhaps the most striking aspect of the call of Jesus Christ, a feature which emerges throughout the New Testament, is the fact that we have all been called to follow him. The call is not an "experience" limited to a clerical minority. Wherever Christ's word reaches, there the call speaks. Sometimes when we talk of "the call to ministry" we miss this fact, but every one of us is called by Jesus to follow him, whatever we may do in life, however we may earn our livings. For the follower of Jesus Christ, every profession is at its most fundamental level shaped, enriched and judged in light of this profession of faith in Christ that is the irreducible expression and consequence of our following Christ. Baptism bears witness to this underlying reality: we are baptized into the Christ who has faith for us, our response to Christ's initiative for us is itself a participation by the power of the Spirit in Christ's trust in the Father on our behalf. This is the "experience" of vocation – the vocation of Jesus Christ on behalf of the world of humanity – that makes our vocation possible. However our vocation is lived out professionally, we engage in whatever we do as followers of Jesus.

Some persons are called to the ministry of Word and sacrament, to a preaching ministry, or a teaching ministry in service to the church. And these particular ordained offices are recognized by the community of faith by the laying on of hands, by the taking of vows, and by commissioning to use particular gifts God has given to accomplish particular tasks required by God in the church and the world. But these are not the only professions to (and in and through) which Christians are called: some are called to follow Jesus as classroom teachers, and others as attorneys, some as physicians, nurses and other kinds of health care providers, others as contractors and business leaders, administrative secretaries and laborers, scholars and bus drivers. In each and every case, we are addressed by the words of Jesus that drew Peter from his nets and Levi from his counting table, remembering that they had to leave behind these nets, these counting tables, in order to follow Christ as Christ intended. But we must remember that even a pulpit can become a net that snares us, even the pastor's study can become a mere counting house, if our exercise of these "holy offices" is not also and at the same time a response to the call to follow Christ alone. It is possible, in other words, to remain behind, to

---

8 Eduard Schweizer, *Lordship and Discipleship* (London: SCM Press, 1960), 17.

deny the cross, to refuse to live the baptism with which Christ was baptized for us, while serving as a pastor, or an evangelist, or a seminary professor. As Eugene Peterson reminds us, "Many a Christian has lost his or her soul in the act of being ordained."[9] Conversely, it is altogether possible to follow Christ in costly discipleship while pursuing what we commonly, and inaccurately, describe as a "secular career."

Whatever else we may say about the call of Jesus Christ we must be very clear: vocation, in a Christian sense, is the call to follow Jesus as baptized persons, as disciples, as members of the Church which is the Body of Christ. The call of Jesus is specifically addressed to each of us and corporately to all of us. As Calvin said, "The Lord bids each one of us in all life's actions to look to his calling." The call of Jesus delivers us from what Calvin described as the "great restlessness" that is inflamed by "human nature."[10] Our salvation is inseparable from Christ's call. Indeed, in some sense, our salvation consists in Christ's vocation. So St. Augustine famously observed, we never shall find peace for our restless hearts until we rest in God.[11]

Most of us believe that Calvin and Augustine speak the truth when they tell us that the call to follow Jesus Christ brings peace to our restless hearts. But why are they right? What is it about God's call that brings peace? The answer lies in the biblical usage of the term call. In the Bible the word "call" refers both to God's naming of us and to God's summoning us.

1. God calls us to name us. According to scripture, God tells us who we are in calling us. God calls us by name. Biblical theology, at this point, ties together God's creation of humanity and our baptism into the name of the triune God who creates us out of nothing. God creates all things. God calls all that is into being. The only thing that stands between us and non-existence is the Word of God.

God alone gives identity to all that God has created. And when God created humanity in the image of God, God called *us* by name. Yet, the names of our creation, Adam and Eve, became also the names of our fall, and God chooses not to call us by these names alone.

The names of our fallen humanity, the names of our failure, never cease to be our names. Like scars they mark us. Nevertheless, God judges, calls into question, and ultimately relativizes the power of those names over us, because God has chosen to name us again and anew in and through the waters of baptism. This is what we are saying, in effect, when

---

[9] Eugene Peterson and Marva Dawn, *The Unnecessary Pastor: Rediscovering the Call* (Grand Rapids: William B. Eerdmans, 2000), 14.
[10] John Calvin, *Institutes of the Christian Religion*, ed. John T. McNeill, tr. Ford Lewis Battles (Philadelphia: The Westminster Press, 1960), III.10.6.
[11] St. Augustine, *Confessions*, tr. Henry Chadwick (Oxford/New York: Oxford University Press, 1991), 3.

we name a child at the baptismal font. "Adam, Eve, you were formerly called. Receive in Christ the new name by the power of grace."

Karl Barth wrote that while chronologically Adam comes first, and therefore we are in a sense named in Adam before we are given our name in Christ, theologically, "[o]ur relationship to Christ has an essential priority and superiority over our relationship to Adam. . . . Adam's humanity is a *provisional* copy of the real humanity that is in Christ."[12] However, "*Jesus Christ is the secret truth about the essential nature of* [humanity], *and even sinful* [humanity] *is still essentially related to Him.*"[13] Like a tidal wave sweeping all before it, God's reality of grace in Jesus Christ folds over our historical existence in baptism, and washes us in the life, death and resurrection of Christ. Whether we are infants, mere weeks old, held in a parent's arms at the baptismal font, or have forty years behind us, with a resume of sins to make Cain blush, it is God who acts in baptism, naming us in Christ by the power of the Spirit and without any assistance on our part. It is through the watery breath of baptism that we are called to follow Christ.[14]

God calls us by and through the name of Jesus Christ, and so we know who we are. Our theological identity is inseparable from our calling, and our theological identity, given to us in Christ, becomes the substance of our calling and the promise of our transformation. God's calling has always carried with it this potential for transformation: Abram was called by God, and Abram became Abraham; Sara was called by God, and Sara became Sarah; Jacob was called by God, and Jacob became Israel; Simon was called by God, and Simon became Peter; Saul was called by God, and Saul became Paul. God's call identifies us, telling us who we are, bearing witness to the unprecedented possibility in our becoming we never imagined.

Several years ago, Don McCaig wrote an extraordinary book on the training of border collies. He said that the most important command any dog learns is its name.[15] This has theological significance. We know who we are because Jesus calls us by the name God gives us in baptism. Call/follow and faith; call/command and obedience: each is bound up with the other. Knowing who we are in Christ, we know who we are called to be; knowing who we are called to be, we know what we are called to do. Our becoming is named in Jesus Christ.

---

12 Karl Barth, *Christ and Adam: Man and Humanity in Romans 5*, tr. T. A. Smail, intro. Wilhelm Pauck (New York: MacMillan, 1956, 1957), 46-47.
13 *Ibid.*, 107-108.
14 These themes are powerfully explored in Oscar Cullmann's classic monograph, "Baptism in the New Testament," No. 1 in the series: Studies in Biblical Theology, tr. J. K. S. Reid (London: S C M. Press, 1950), 9-22.
15 Donald McCaig, *Eminent Dogs Dangerous Men* (New York: HarperPerennial, 1992), 39.

A Christian Understanding of Vocation

2. When God calls us, God summons us. God calls Moses by name from the burning bush, "Moses, Moses!" Moses answers the Lord, "Here I am" (Exodus 3:4). God calls Isaiah in the temple, as smoke fills the air and the foundations shake, "Whom shall I send, and who will go for me?" Isaiah answers, "Here am I; send me!" "Jesus calls us o'er the tumult," as the familiar hymn says; and the call is a summons. God's call never leaves us where God's call finds us.

Thornton-Duesbery traced the usage of the verbal form "to call," the noun "calling," and the verbal adjective "called," through the New Testament, and his statement provides a wonderful summary of what it means to be summoned by God.

> The verb 'to call.' The 'caller' is God (Rom. 9:11, Gal. 5:8, etc.), and the divine purpose in which 'calling' is one stage is set out in Roman. 8:28-30. The calling is into God's kingdom and glory (I Thess. 2:12); to salvation (II Thess. 2:13-14); to eternal life (I Tim. 6:12); to God's marvelous light (I Peter. 2:9). It has a moral content and purpose; 'not for uncleanness, but in sanctification' (I Thess. 4:7); for patience in suffering (I Pet. 2:21); for freedom (Gal. 5:13); for peace (I Cor. 7:15, Col. 3:15). The basis of the calling if the free grace of God and of his Christ (Gal. 1:6, 15). It reaches [humanity] through the Gospel (II Thess. 2:14). It sets before them a glorious hope (Eph. 4:4).
>
> The noun 'calling' is similarly used. It is of God, who will not go back upon it (Rom. 11:29); 'a high (lit. upward) and heavenly calling' (Phil. 3:14, Heb. 3:1). It is filled with hope (Eph. 1:18, 4:4). It must be held sure (Eph. 4:1, II Pet. 1:10; and cf. the whole passage Heb. 3:1-4:13, where the fact of the believer's calling is made the basis of exhortation to steadfastness).
>
> The verbal adjective 'called' is sometimes used absolutely of the call to salvation (Rom. 1:6,7, I Cor. 1:2,24, Jude 1, Rev. 17:14), but also of calling to a particular office (Rom. 1:1, I Cor. 1:1; cf. Heb. 5:4, and see also Acts 13: 2 and 16:10).[16]

According to the biblical witness, when we are called by God, when we are named by God, when God seeks us by name and beckons us to follow into that way which is both the way of death and life, the way of the cross which is alone salvation, we are inevitably summoned to another

---

16 J. P. Thornton-Duesbery, "Call, Called, Calling," in ed. Alan Richardson, *A Theological Word Book of the Bible* (New York: Macmillan, 1950), 40.

place, to move beyond where we are settled, to live out the implications of the name we have been given, to become toward who we are in Christ.

This must take a specific and particular form in each person's life. And it demands that we examine every aspect of the lives we live in light of God's call: including marriage, family and employment. How does the call to follow Jesus shape the various decisions we face? A marriage partner? Our relationships to parents, siblings, children? The way in which we earn a living, plan a career, set personal and professional goals? It is altogether possible and sensible to restrict the "religious" concerns of life to a separate zone, to avoid confusing religious issues with romantic ones, or professional, or political ones. Again, this is sensible. It is, however, impossible for the Christian to restrict the implications of the call to follow Jesus Christ in this manner. If Christ is Lord of our lives, then Christ is Lord of our whole lives. Nothing in life is too profane or mundane for the scrutiny of the Lord who calls us.

The call of Christ as Lord also represents a challenge to our assumption that we can control the ultimate shape of God's call. There is in virtually every Christian tradition a tendency to believe that there are a very limited number of ways God's call can be lived out professionally, especially as this is understood in term of "Church offices." There is not one of us who has not been called by God; but no two of us have the same identical calling. Though the ultimate goal of God's calling, to be transformed into the image our Lord Jesus Christ, is the same for us all, our journeys will lead in a variety of directions. Therefore, it is essential for the Church to remain open to the movement of the Spirit, to the ways in which God seems to be working among those people God calls, to take seriously the possibility that God's call of persons can be significantly out ahead of the Church's interpretation of its faith and tradition.

Ecclesiological CrossRoads

Annie Dillard, in a wonderful essay, "Living Like Weasels," presents her understanding of vocation. She says that we all have choices to make with regard to our calling. "We can live any way we want," she says. "People take vows of poverty, chastity, and obedience — even silence — by choice." However, she continues:

> The thing is to stalk your calling in a certain skilled and supple way, to locate the most tender and live spot and plug into that pulse. This is yielding, not fighting. A weasel doesn't 'attack' anything; a weasel lives as he's meant to, yielding at every moment to the perfect freedom of single necessity.
>
> I think it would be well, and proper, and obedient, and pure, to grasp your one necessity and not let it go, to dangle from it

limp wherever it takes you. Then even death, where you're going no matter how you live, cannot you part. Seize it and let it seize you up aloft even, till your eyes burn out and drop; let your musky flesh fall off in shreds, and let your very bones unhinge and scatter, loosened over fields, over fields and woods, lightly, thoughtless, from any height at all, from as high as eagles.[17]

Maybe this is what the Bible means by "the high calling," just hanging on and flying wherever God's call carries us. This is, admittedly, a pretty daunting assignment for those of us who are acrophobic. But what surrender this is, this "yielding" as Dillard calls it. To speak of this aspect of God's call I must speak personally.

I was seventeen years old when I was called to what the tradition I grew up in called the "preaching ministry," seventeen years old and, up till that point, on my way to university to prepare for the legal profession. We called it "surrendering to preach" then. I think we lost something very crucial when we stopped talking about answering God's call as a kind of surrender, a letting go of our agenda for our future. There is something ultimately very peaceful in surrendering, in running up the white flag of truce to God's call, whatever shape that call takes and however intrusive it may feel at the time. There's something wonderfully weasel-like in yielding to the summons of God.

Dillard's analogy brings to mind Parker Palmer's life-long struggle with his vocation, and his awareness that God's call of us corresponds to God's creation of us. "One dwells with God by being faithful to one's nature. One crosses God by trying to be something one is not."[18] God has made us with gifts that God intends us to employ. God has fit us for certain things and not for others. In some sense, exploration of God's vocation for us is a process of "coming to ourselves," to use the phrase that emerges in that paradigmatic parable of vocation: the parable of the prodigal son. Sometimes it is only while we are dining on husks with the pigs (and not all "husks" are tasteless, and not all "pigs" are unpleasant) that we "come to ourselves" and realize that we were intended for something else altogether. But, just because the process of discernment brings us close to our own true selves does not mean that it is easy to do. The self is a very slippery thing. The medieval Christian mystic, Lady Julian of Norwich, observed that we are hidden from ourselves. Indeed,

---

17 Annie Dillard, "Living Like Weasels," in *Teaching a Stone to Talk: Expeditions and Encounters* (New York: Harper & Row, 1982), 16.
18 Parker Palmer, *Let Your Life Speak: Listening for the Voice of Vocation* (San Francisco: Jossey-Bass, 2000), 51.

according to Julian, we are unable to know ourselves, who we are and for what we are intended, until we find ourselves hidden in Christ.[19]

This is why the Church, over the past two thousand years or so, has searched for ways of testing our discernment of God's call. In his excellent study titled, "The Call to the Ministry," H. Richard Niebuhr distinguished four distinct elements in the particular call to ordained ministry, the ministry of Word and sacrament. While his comments speak primarily to this specific ordained calling, the categories in which he works apply to our broader understanding of the Christian vocation of all the baptized.[20]

1. The first element in what Niebuhr describes as the four-fold call to ministry is **the call to be a Christian**. We have already rehearsed this element of vocation at some length, but I want to reiterate that this is the very heart of what it means to speak of God's calling. This is the call addressed to us all. Bonhoeffer speaks of this element of the call in his *Discipleship*, when he says: When Christ calls a person, Christ bids him come and die. We are all called to follow Christ, to know that grace that costs everything else in life.

2. The second element of the call to ministry is what Niebuhr describes as **the secret call**. This is the most difficult element of the call to describe. Niebuhr calls it a "secret." It is an odd secret, though, never meant to be kept. Others have called it "private," but it could not be both Christian and private. To be Christian is to live publicly, and no purely private calling could be a Christian calling. For a similar reason, this aspect of vocation is poorly called individual, because the individual, in the modern sense at least, is an anomaly to faith in Christ. To be Christian is to be in communion, even as to be human is to live in relationship with others in the image of the triune God, who has his very being in communion. Even the idea of an "inward call" is problematic because what we call "inwardness" is simply a metaphor expressing the way we reflect on concerns and ideas, and is ineluctably "between" us as persons in relation (all inwardness is after all mediated by the most communal and social reality of human life, language).[21] God works quietly in our lives: in

---

19 Julian of Norwich, *Revelations of Divine Love,* tr. Clifton Wolters (London: Penguin, 1966), 161.

20 This four-fold outline comes from H. Richard Niebuhr, *The Purpose of the Church and Its Ministry* (New York: Harper & Row, 1977), 63-66.

21 I deal with these ideas at greater length and depth in *The Church Faces Death: Ecclesiology in a Post- Modern Context* (New York: Oxford University Press, 1999), and *Invitation to Theology: A Guide to Study, Conversation and Practice* (Downers Grove: InterVarsity Press, 2001), especially in chapter nine. Obviously I have in mind aspects of Ludwig Wittgenstein's thought, but also of John Macmurray, specifically his *Persons in Relation: Volume II* of *The Form of the Personal* (London: Faber and Faber, 1961), especially chapter one, and of John D. Zizioulas's influential study, *Being as Communion: Studies in Personhood and the Church* (Crestwood, NY: St. Vladimir's Seminary Press, 1985). I would also recommend Paul Fiddes, *Participating in God: A Pastoral Doctrine of the Trinity* (Louisville: Westminster/John Knox,

our consciousness of who we are, in the midst of our experiences of God in the life of faith, and in the hearing of the Word under the guidance of the Spirit, who persuades us to follow Christ in a particular manner and summons us to take up the way and ministry of Jesus Christ.

This aspect of God's call, however, is especially subject to distortion. The individual experience of vocation is subjective, and frequently may be mistaken because of our changing emotions and affections. Many are those who "feel" they are called to a specific ministry who are not well-suited or appropriately gifted for that ministry. Thus Niebuhr reminds us that the "secret call" is in need of confirmation, of more objective testing, and God tests and confirms one's sense of call.

3. God tests and confirms the secret call by what Niebuhr describes as **the providential call**, the discernment of a person's giftedness for a particular task of ministry, a person's being given by God those requisite talents for the exercise of that specific ministry. I would like to illustrate by speaking specifically about the ministry of Word and sacrament, though what I am going to say is as true of any calling to which God calls persons.

The old saying in seminary is "we can't put *in* what God has left *out*." There are many people who have a real interest in ordained ministry, who may possess strong, rich and powerful experiences of Christian grace, but who are not called to the ordained ministry of Word and sacrament, who simply do not have the specific personal qualities needed by pastors, such as resilience, resources of critical self-reflection, willingness to open themselves up to continuing growth (and criticism) that is required of those who lead in the Church, who do not possess the raw material to be good preachers, good teachers, or good administrators in a congregation. Charles Haddon Spurgeon, the popular nineteenth-century English preacher, counseled young people that if they did not have a strong enough voice to fill up an auditorium, then they were simply not called to preach. While the advent of public address systems have dated his advice, his sense of providential call remains valid. God gives us gifts appropriate to the ministries to which God calls us. It is incumbent upon the Church herself to counsel those who seek to discern God's call in such a way that they can gain a deeper sense of what ministries God has gifted them to undertake.

Some people discover that they are not called to the ministry of Word and sacrament only after (sometimes years after) they have been ordained. The consequences can be painful, even tragic. One who goes into this form of ministry to find a permanent retreat from the harsh realities of the world is going to be disappointed. The calling to ordained ministry is not the same as the calling to a life of prayerful seclusion and monastic

---

2000), and Miroslav Volf, *After Our Likeness: The Church as the Image of the Trinity* (Grand Rapids: William B. Eerdmans, 1998) for excellent treatments.

retreat. The calling to the ministry of Word and sacrament is a calling to secular or pastoral ministry; it is a calling to leadership in and through the lives of human organizations and institutions, a constant public engagement in the name of Christ and Christ's Church. Not everyone has the gifts for this particular ministry. The gifts needed for this kind of ministry are given by God and are only improved upon in seminary training. If God has not supplied the gifts for this ministry, this is not one's ministry.

Again, much the same can be said of other callings as well. God fits us providentially for the ministry to which God calls us. There is no need to assume that this fitness is permanent. God's summons is lifelong, but we may find God summoning us in different directions over a lifetime, and we may find that God continues over a lifetime to fit us anew to serve in new ways.

4. God also tests the secret call by **the ecclesiastical call**, as Niebuhr describes it, "the summons and invitation extended to a person by some community or institution of the Church to engage in the work of the ministry." We say this theologically when we say that God calls us to ministry through the voice of the Church. The Church is the Body of Christ, and it is through Christ's Body and for the sake of the ministry of Christ's Body in the world, that Christ calls us. There are, in other words, two objective tests, two objective confirmations for the relatively subjective inward call of God. Again, as Niebuhr writes:

> The Church everywhere and always has expected its ministers to have a personal sense of vocation, forged in the solitariness of the encounter with ultimate claims made upon them. It has also generally required that they show evidence of the fact that they have been chosen for the task by the divine bestowal upon them, through birth and experience, of the intellectual, moral, physical and psychological gifts necessary for the work of ministry. Finally, in one form or another, it has required that they be summoned or invited or at least accepted by that part of the Church in which they undertake to serve. . . . Whatever the variations, it seems true that when a clear idea of the ministry prevailed there was also a clear idea of what constituted a call to the ministry and for the most part such a clear idea took into account the necessity of all four calls and ordered their relations.[22]

---

[22] H. Richard Niebuhr, *The Purpose of the Church and Its Ministry*.

A Christian Understanding of Vocation

As each of us seeks to discern the call of God that God speaks to our own hearts, we have this promise: God is speaking to the hearts of others about us too. God gifts and equips those whom God calls; and while God's call may be whispered in the secrecy of our own hearts, God shares this secret with others in the community of faith. God has given us the gift of the Church to confirm and question, to test and challenge and support our sense of calling and our giftedness, so that we can determine whether the voice we heard calling us came from God or if the ministry to which we believe ourselves called is one that resonates within the life of the Church. There is no calling that is higher or lower than any other as long as the calling is from God, but there are callings that are true and callings that are mistaken.

Conversely, the Church may be the bearer of the news that the call we heard to a particular ministry was perhaps misheard. However difficult it may be to accept, the Church from the time of the Apostles has had the responsibility to assume this role, a role sometimes derisively called "gate keeping," sometimes abused by those who see ordained ministry as a kind of fraternal order whose membership is limited to "the right sort of people." Despite abuses, the Church's role in the discernment of vocation is clear: to test and confirm the call of all persons to the various ministries of the Church. When this role is abused, it tragically cuts off from ministry gifts which the Church needs in its common life (usually insulating the Church from more disturbing voices and risky ministries), but when this role is exercised properly it represents a far-reaching empowerment of persons to serve the Word of God in the Spirit of Christ.

Church and Seminary at the CrossRoads

Many of the conversations we have in Church and seminary these days revolve around the topic of formation: Christian formation, spiritual formation and pastoral formation in particular. I am persuaded that it is in the Church that we are primarily formed as Christians, as persons of the Spirit, and as pastors. This is, in part, simply an extension of the Christian understanding of call.

We are, as human beings, formed in our concrete relationships to one another as we live out God's call of us, as we move from moment to moment, from decision to decision, from one situation to another, along life's journey of vocation, through the process of being named and renamed, formed and reformed and transformed, of being summoned by God in Christ.

This is why Dietrich Bonhoeffer writes: "The person does not exist timelessly; a person is not static but dynamic. The person exists always and only in ethical responsibility; the person is re-created again and again in the perpetual flux of life. Any other concept of person fragments the *fullness of life* of the concrete person."[23] Bonhoeffer counters any idea that persons spring into being out of a social and historical vacuum. "It is," he continues, "a Christian insight that the person as conscious being is created in the moment of being moved . . . thus, the real person grows out of the concrete situation."[24] Again, Bonhoeffer wants us to understand that a proper social conception of human formation is an essentially Christian view of the person, that we become persons in concrete social, cultural, historical, and political contexts, in specific moments, in particular settings and circumstances. We are who we are because of a multitude of diverse situation-specific factors. We are who we are because of the presence of others in these contexts. We become in Christ in relationship to one another.

The belief, then, that we are historically shaped and social beings is a theological, and not merely a sociological, affirmation. We believe we are historically shaped because we are created, sustained in being and redeemed by the God whose very being is in becoming, as both Karl Barth and Eberhard Jüngel observe.[25] We believe we are social beings because we are created, sustained in being and redeemed by the God the holy Trinity, as, again, Karl Barth, and also Alan J. Torrance, and Catherine Mowry LaCugna observe.[26] Our understanding of Christian, spiritual and pastoral formation naturally grows from our theological understanding of human formation. We are who we are by virtue of our nurture as Christians in the context of specific communities of faith.[27]

All of this is to say that God's call to follow Jesus Christ which arises out of concrete communities of faith draws us ever more deeply into these communities of faith. God's call to follow Christ leads us along a road that is churchly. We learn of Jesus Christ through these Gospels and letters that the Church has gathered and protected and treasured for centuries. We learn how to follow Jesus Christ both from the Church and in the Church. While the Word and Spirit of God must never be equated with the Church, and may radically call into question and even judge the Church at any given moment, the Word and Spirit work (as Irenaeus long ago affirmed)

---

[23] Dietrich Bonhoeffer, *Sanctorum Communio: A Theological Study of the Sociology of the Church*, tr. Reinhard Krauss and Nancy Lukens, ed. Clifford J. Green (Minneapolis: Fortress Press, 1998), 48.

[24] *Ibid.*, 49.

[25] Jüngel, *Gottes Sein Ist Im Werden* (Tübingen: J. C. B. Mohr, 1986), in which Jüngel reflects on Barth's *Church Dogmatics*, principally volume I.1.

[26] I suggest that if one wishes to trace this theme in Barth's *Dogmatics*, that they examine first Alan Torrance's treatment of the subject in *Persons in Communion: Trinitarian Description and Human Participation* (Edinburgh: T. & T. Clark, 1996). Catherine Mowry LaCugna's discussion of "Living Trinitarian Faith," is a stunning study of the ecclesial shape of trinitarian thought, *God For Us: The Trinity & Christian Life* (San Francisco: Harper, 1991), 377-411.

[27] See Kathryn Tanner, *Theories of Culture: A New Agenda for Theology* (Minneapolis: Fortress Press, 1997), chapters 5-7.

as the left and right hand of God in and through and for the sake of the Church's faithful service to God in God's world.

The Church shapes us all for the calling to which God calls us. Thus, it is the Church that makes pastors of those of us called to pastoral ministry. What role, then, does seminary play? Seminary provides a crucial, though subordinate, role in the process of pastoral formation. Seminary provides opportunities to learn critical, disciplined theological study, to gather the tools and models necessary to do theological reflection, to engage in the analysis and careful study of the sacred texts and practices of the Christian faith. Seminary provides deeper access to the wealth of the Church's witness, the skills to understand more clearly the confessions and doctrinal statements of the Christian faith, better insight into our complex and long history as people of God, and a more incisive perspective on the moral and ethical life we share. Seminary provides the theological education which the Church values and sees as indispensable for our practice of ministry.

Sometimes the better a seminary does its work (especially its critical work in relation to the Bible and the theological legacies of the Church), the less comfortable some in the Church will be with it. Sometimes the seminary will neglect certain tasks in favor of others, and the Church and seminary are periodically compelled to renegotiate their boundaries and their understandings of which tasks are essential and which are not, which tasks belong primarily or exclusively to whom and which tasks are inappropriate to either Church or seminary. Complementarity, mutuality, even countervalation, mark the complex relationship between Church and seminary, but the relationship is crucial, and if either partner fails to participate in good faith, both inevitably suffer.[28] What is at stake in the relationship between the Church and the seminary is nothing less than the support of the vocations of ministry to which God calls God's people. While much is negotiable, this, at least, is not.

---

[28] One of the most fascinating documents touching on the relationship between the Church and what we would now designate as the seminary is John Calvin's "Ecclesiastical Ordinances" (October 1541) in which Calvin writes: "The office proper to doctors is the instruction of the faithful in true doctrine, in order that the purity of the Gospel be not corrupted either by ignorance or by evil opinions. As things are disposed today, we always include under this title aids and instructions for maintaining the doctrine of God and defending the Church from injury by the fault of pastors and ministers. So to use a more intelligible word, we will call this the order of the schools."J.K.S. Reid, ed. *Calvin: Theological Treatises* (Philadelphia: Westminster Press, 1954), 62-63. Also see: E. Harris Harbison, *The Christian Scholar in the Age of the Reformation* (New York: Charles Scribner's Sons, 1956), 137-164.

Michael Jinkins

Warning Signs at the CrossRoads of Pastoral Ministry

Ray Anderson places the particular calling to pastoral ministry within the context of the ministry of the baptized, observing that the "office of ministry . . . is subordinate to the function of ministry and receives its authority from Christ's ministry as the ministry of the whole body."[29] The pastor is not the sole possessor of the call of God in a congregation. All are called to a variety of ministries. And this variety of ministries is itself authentically Christian, authentically churchly, inasmuch as it participates in that ministry which is Christ's own. Yet there is a peculiar expectation (different, if not higher) placed on the pastor that is not groundless. Reinhold Niebuhr, when he was still the young pastor of the Bethel Evangelical Church in Detroit, Michigan, before he went to New York City as a professor at Union Seminary, said of the pastoral calling: "Here is a task which requires the knowledge of a social scientist and the insight and imagination of a poet, the executive talents of a business [leader] and the mental discipline of a philosopher."[30]

Niebuhr's observation is true. There is no greater challenge, nor greater privilege, than living with people through the most intimate, personal, painful and joyful moments of human existence. The pastor is there for it all, from cradle to grave. The pastor is there for the specific purpose of persistently reminding us of the priority of the reign of God in all of life.[31] Pastoral ministry does place one at the fulcrum point of the life of a community, in a visible manner, and this makes the pastor accountable in a way that other members of the community are not. Those who cannot stand public scrutiny will find ministry well-nigh intolerable, but those who long to be the center of attention may be even more disastrous for the Church.

One should not consider entering pastoral ministry merely because of its joys, whatever we conceive them to be, as real and as enduring as those joys undoubtedly are. One should not consider entering ordained ministry merely because of its challenges, as real and as stimulating as those challenges may be especially for those of us who enjoy problem-solving. The only reason to enter the pastoral ministry is that God compels us to do so, that God calls us to live out the call to follow Jesus Christ, the call of the cross, in this specific way.

The late Alan Lewis, once my colleague in Constructive Theology here at Austin Seminary, said in his contribution to an earlier *Festschrift*

---

29 Anderson, *op cit*, 84.
30 Reinhold Niebuhr, *Leaves from the Notebook of a Tamed Cynic* (San Francisco: Harper, reprint 1980), 173-174.
31 Eugene H. Peterson, *Working the Angles: The Shape of Pastoral Integrity* (Grand Rapids: William Eerdmans, 1987), 15-29.

honoring Ray Anderson: "There is no imperative more urgent for the renewal of ministry today than recognition of the synonymity of vocation and the cross . . . . God's call and Christ's cross are not only mutually conditioned: they are the same reality."[32] Of course, this was Bonhoeffer's point in saying that Christ bids us come and die.

The call of Christ, and particularly the call of Christ lived out in pastoral ministry, imperils the lives of those who answer it; it threatens all that we are and all that we do. This must be said and this must be heard clearly. When Luther prayed that God not forsake him lest everything in his life, his ministry, and his church would be brought to destruction, he was not taking a flight into rhetorical fancy. He was stating the simple truth. In the early Church, repeatedly we meet similar warnings. John Chrysostom, the most celebrated preacher of the early Church, gave this advice to a young person considering the call to ordained ministry: "The right course, I think, is to have so reverent an estimation of the office as to avoid its responsibility from the start."[33] Gregory the Great said to Augustine of Canterbury, the missionary he sent to England: "It is better never to undertake any high enterprise than to abandon it when once begun," reminding us of Jesus' caution that those who lay their hand to the plow, but then look back, are not worthy of the kingdom of heaven.[34]

If a "shepherd of souls," again Chrysostom says, must be a person of wisdom, grace, character and cleanliness, possessing a quality even higher than any human goodness, then who can blame the person who refuses to become a pastor. Why should anyone want to risk his soul if he can avoid doing so?[35]

Gregory the Great, in his classic study on pastoral discipline, calls into question the rashness with which some people enter upon ordained ministry. He says that the pastoral way of life is so dangerous, and so painful, and so disciplined, that anyone who is free from its perils and strictures should not imprudently seek this way, and those who are so imprudent as to seek the pastoral calling should feel apprehension in doing so. "No one ventures to teach any art unless he has learned it after deep thought. With what rashness, then, would the pastoral office be undertaken by the unfit, seeing that the government of souls is the art of arts! For who does not realize that the wounds of the mind are more hidden than the internal wounds of the body? Yet, although those who have no knowledge of the powers of drugs shrink from giving themselves

---

32 Alan E. Lewis, "Vocation in the Ecclesia Crucis," in Christian D. Kettler and Todd H. Speidell, *Incarnational Ministry* (Colorado Springs: Helmers & Howard, 1990), 113.
33 St. John Chrysostom, *On the Priesthood*, tr. Graham Neville, On the Priesthood (Crestwood, New York: St. Vladimir's Seminary Press, 1984), 80.
34 The Venerable Bede, *A History of the English Church and People*, tr. Leo Sherley-Price, revision, R. E. Latham (London: Penguin, revised edition, 1968), 67.
35 Chrysostom, 76.

out as physicians of the flesh, people who are utterly ignorant of spiritual precepts are often not afraid of professing themselves to be physicians of the heart."[36]

Indeed, one of the greatest pastors and theologians of the early Church, Gregory of Nazianzus, literally ran for the hills immediately after being ordained by his aging father. When Gregory returned to his congregation he wrote them a moving sermon explaining why he had fled. "I did not, nor do I now, think myself qualified to rule a flock . . . , or to have authority over the souls of people . . . . , for the guiding of human beings, the most variable and manifold of creatures, seems to me in very deed to be the art of arts and science of sciences . . . . [T]he scope of our art is to provide the soul with wings, to rescue it from the world and give it to God, and to watch over that which is in God's image; if it abides, to take it by the hand, if it is in danger, to restore it, if ruined, to make Christ to dwell in the heart by the Spirit."[37] A person would be foolish to take on such responsibilities over the hearts and souls of persons unless compelled by God to do so, but as fearful a thing as it is to enter the ordained ministry without God's calling, it is, if anything, even more perilous to deny God's call even if it is to the ministry of the Word.

I began by reflecting on the words of the poet Robert Frost. I shall close by reflecting briefly on lines from another poet, Dante Alighieri. In the opening of his "Divine Comedy," Dante places himself in his poem, revealing himself with the opening lines: "Midway in our life's journey, I went astray from the straight road and woke to find myself alone in a dark wood."[38] Commenting on Dante's world, Dorothy Sayers says that if we wish to read the Tuscan poet, "We must try to believe that man's will is free, that he can consciously exercise choice, and that his choice can be decisive to all eternity."[39]

A Christian understanding of God's call assumes as much as well. When Christ comes to us and summons us to follow him, we may remain where we are, or we may respond. Theologically speaking, I recognize that our response is impossible unless the Spirit of God strives within our hearts, but the freedom to say "no" to God's call is assumed. And the consequences are understood as real.

---

36 St Gregory the Great, *Pastoral Care*, tr. Henry David (New York: Newman Press, 1950), 21. Gregory's thought on the pastoral office are explored especially well by Andrew Purvis in his recent book, *Pastoral Theology in the Classical Tradition* (Louisville: Westminster/John Knox, 2001), 63-75.
37 St Gregory of Nazianzus, "In Defence of his Flight to Pontus," in *The Nicene and Post Nicene Fathers* (Grand Rapids: Eerdmans, reprint 1983), Second Series, Volume VII. 207, 208, 209. See John McGuckin's study, *Saint Gregory of Nazianzus: An Intellectual Biography* (Crestwood, NY: St. Vladimir's Press, 2001), 100-110.
38 Dante, *The Inferno*, tr. John Ciardi (New York: Mentor/Penguin, 1954), Canto I.
39 Dorothy Sayers, from the introduction to her translation of *The Divine Comedy I: Hell* (Harmondsworth, Middlesex: Penguin, 1949), 11.

A Christian Understanding of Vocation

Recently in the course I teach on the theology of Christian vocation, I asked students to tell their personal experiences of God's call. Many told stories of years spent running from God, hiding from God, vainly trying to convince God that God was mistaken in calling them. They seemed to know intuitively, if not explicitly, that the costs of following Christ are high, but they also learned along the way that the costs of denying Christ's call to follow are higher still. Each person in the class, without exception, bore witness in his or her own way to the uniqueness of their various experiences, but running through all of their testimonies there remained a singular witness to the truth of the Word of God. Certainly they could have chosen to follow or not to follow. But they could not have remained behind and known Christ as Lord.[40]

---

[40] My closing, of course, deliberately reflects both Bonhoeffer's challenge in *Discipleship*, to which I have already referred, and the closing of Anderson's chapter on "Jesus as Servant of the Father," in *The Soul of Ministry*, 86, which reads: "Perhaps it is time we think not so much of where we are called to minister, but where we are sent to be servants. Then we will know who the master is!"[1] Karl Barth, *Church Dogmatics*, III/2, p. 136 and III/4, p. 625.

Part Three

✷

On Being Human and Becoming Christian

Gary W. Deddo

*

Resisting Reductionism:
Why We Need Theological Anthropology

In 1982, Eerdmans published Ray Anderson's groundbreaking book, *On Being Human: Essays in Theological Anthropology*. The rich veins of reflection opened up in that work are deep and continue to yield fruitful theological insight and inform the practice of ministry. The wealth of that work has not yet been exhausted. This essay is meant to assist in further exploration of it.

Of course the significance of Anderson's work in theological anthropology lies not just in the nature of what he published in 1982 (and subsequently) but also in the trajectory which US society, and indeed Western culture, has traversed during these past two decades. If the twentieth century chronicles Western culture's loss of God, it seems likely that the twenty-first century may very well be characterized as the subsequent loss of humanity. While there were those in the previous century who valiantly claimed that a humanism without God in the way was all that was needed for human thriving, this present century may indeed expose the impossibility of that possibility. As Karl Barth said, and Anderson's work reflects, there is no such thing as a godless humanity.[1]

As consensus about the nature of humanity seems to grow ever more remote, the escalating public debates on issues such as abortion, euthanasia, reproductive technologies, genetic engineering and homosexuality look intractable. Even the lingering discussions of decades past concerning contraception, the death penalty, mental health, racism and the nature of gender, marriage and family have eluded final resolution. Not only do these unresolved issues disturb the societal peace outside the church, but they also perturb the fellowship of the church itself. At the vortex of these controversies lies the mystery of human being.

The present context desperately calls for a profound and robust anthropology. Without a firm grasp on the nature of humanity, we face the prospects of what C.S. Lewis called "the abolition of man," in a book of the same title. If the church as the church of Jesus Christ is to address its own internal challenges and to offer the surrounding culture its best, it cannot afford to provide anything less than a truly theological anthropology. In this brief essay I would like to highlight several crucial aspects of Ray Anderson's legacy of a theological anthropology that we must build upon if we are to address the powerful dehumanizing trends of thought and action growing around and among us. For that foundation seems to me to hold great promise for responding to the ever-growing challenge of discerning the true outlines of humanity in this present twilight.

A Truly Theological Anthropology

Unfortunately it is still not unusual to hear even from pastors the warning: "Now let's not get too theological!" Theology has a bad name. And perhaps it deserves it, for the sheer volume of divergent forms of what has passed for theology is mind numbing. Adding to the confusion is the fact that there seems to be considerable disagreement as to what constitutes good theology, which can lead to skepticism about all theology. In response to this challenge, the church and its leaders will not fare well by offering anything less than a thoroughly and truly Christian theology. What Ray Anderson offers is a serious contender for a theology worthy of that title. But what are the distinctives of such an essentially Christian theology of human personhood? In what follows I offer my own interpretation of lessons gleaned from Ray Anderson's work. It will become obvious that I, along with Ray, am also indebted to the profound thought of Karl Barth on these matters.

Revelational and Christological

A *theological* anthropology must first of all be essentially oriented to its proper subject: God. Ludwig Feuerbach, in the nineteenth century, scoffed at such a human possibility. He prophesied that the only possibility was for human beings to project themselves onto a cosmic screen and call it God. Indeed, a theological anthropology must acknowledge the human propensity to justify itself by creating gods after its own image. It must also admit that if there is to be any true knowledge of God, such knowledge will first be a divine possibility, not a human potential. As Karl Barth wrote in his foreword to Feuerbach's *The Essence of Christianity*, God is the great iconoclast who knocks over our idols by setting up his own divine image in their place.

Awareness of this propensity is not the result of postmodern insight. It was announced in no uncertain terms in ancient Israel's strict prohibition and continual warnings about idolatry, setting up false images. Enshrined in those negative commands God reserved, for himself only, the right to provide a true image of him. The Gospel acknowledges this human bent while announcing that in Jesus Christ God has indeed accomplished a *self*-revelation that brings us to repentance and so brings an end to our self-justifying ways. Jesus Christ has given us access to a true knowledge of God which calls into question all other images of God. If there is to be a truly theological anthropology, we must begin with Christology. God's self-revelation in Jesus Christ is our only hope of being rescued from idolatry and so from exchanging the glory of the divine for the self-justifying image of the creature.[2]

But there is a crucial second reason that a theological anthropology must be Christologically oriented. If humanity is to escape its own propensity for self-justification, it must also have access to an image of *humanity* that is not merely a reflection of itself. This is especially true if there is something seriously amiss with humanity as a whole and in its particulars. If there is no North Star to orient the ship of humanity, then we are condemned to navigate ourselves by some dim light perched atop our own mast. The Gospel comes to us yet again as good news that in Jesus Christ we have not only the revelation of God but also of true humanity. Jesus is the new Adam, both the origin and destiny given to us by the grace of God.[3] He is our only hope of being rescued from the gravitational force of human self-centeredness, being curved back in upon ourselves (*incurvatus in se*), as Martin Luther put it. In Jesus Christ we have the revelation of true God *and* true humanity. Our theological anthropology must bear no uncertain witness to this reality.

We must clarify this point to avoid misunderstanding. The Incarnation does not essentially establish the grounds for declaring that Jesus is human just like us. Rather, the direction of comparison is the reverse: in Jesus Christ we see who we really are. It is not that he is like us, but that we are to be like Jesus Christ. Any *imitatio Christi* will be the fruit of *participatio Christi* and not the other way around. And the direction of comparison cannot be subsequently reversed. The church cannot make the mistake of assuming that we know what humanity is and then placing Jesus Christ under cross-examination to see if he measures up. Nor can we look to Jesus for mere empathic identification with us as we are and presently understand ourselves. Doing so would only lead us once again into the temptation of self-justification and would propel us towards crucifying him again. Jesus Christ is the revelation of a humanity that we are not entirely familiar with. Although Jesus comes to be with us and accept us as we are, he comes not to leave us there but to take us to where he is going, where we have never been. The Incarnation is not God's permission for us to wallow in self-pity and make excuses for our sorry condition and ourselves because we have been "only human." The truth is that we have been less than human. Human existence has been corrupted

---

[2] See Ray S. Anderson, *On Being Human: Essays in Theological Anthropology*, Eerdmans, Grand Rapids, 1982, Chapter 1.

[3] See Philips E. Hughes, *The True Image: The Origin and Destiny of Man in Christ*, Eerdmans, Grand Rapids and InterVarisity Press, Leicester, England, 1989, for a well done exposition of the two themes of origin and destiny in Christ.

by the evil of sin, which is alien to humanity. The only escape from our fallen and unnatural condition and so from absolute servitude to such pitiful self-justification is submission to the self-revelation of God and humanity in Jesus Christ. For he alone is the one both consubstantial with God and us, as we hear announced at Chalcedon. Jesus Christ calls us not only to repent of our images of God but also of our self-made images of humanity. For in him we see true God and true humanity.

Incarnational and Relational

What this means is that a truly theological anthropology, along the lines forged by Ray Anderson, will resist all manner of reductionisms. It first of all resists being reduced to mere cultural or philosophical anthropology. What follows is an exploration of how a truly theological anthropology will expose those reductionisms and uncover the true nature of humanity.

The first and most devastating reductionism tempts humanity to know itself autonomously, that is, apart from the self-revelation of and relationship with the triune God. Such approaches may or may not be atheistic. But the question of God in connection with humanity becomes secondary, ancillary, optional. They assume that humanity can at least be sufficiently understood for all practical purposes in terms of the disciplines of physics, biology, psychology, sociology, cultural anthropology, etc. Religion need not be denied, but only subsumed under the category of one or another of these disciplines controlling the investigation of the religious "phenomenon" of the human. Such approaches exhibit total confidence in a "bottom-up" approach to investigating humanity.

Methodological Naturalism

A word on the danger of a methodological naturalism in anthropology should be added at this point. One's methodological approach will color, constrain and most likely control what one says and understands "at the top," for the latter will be built on a foundation already laid. A methodological naturalism can only warrant a metaphysical naturalism even if one affirms, on other non-scientific (subjective? esoteric? speculative? non-cognitive? irrational?) grounds, a transcendent reality.

There are many who claim that a methodological naturalism is metaphysically neutral and perfectly adequate for Christians to use since the purported objects of knowledge are parts of creation, not the Creator. Now it is of course quite proper, in fact essential, to distinguish between the Creator and creation. Yet application of a methodological or even epistemological naturalism towards creation really assumes an autonomy and separation of creation from God which is quite different from affirming its distinction. At most the only affirmation of a transcendent reality compatible with this frame of mind would be a deistic metaphysic, in which claims of an ultimate origin and destiny of creation would play no functional role in the knowledge of creation. They would only serve as fideistic assertions bracketed out of the scientific enterprise. Indeed the present discussions among Christian academics are bearing this tendency out. Those defending a methodological naturalism are more and more explaining that God's perfection is best manifested in a creation that has built into it everything it would ever need to evolve, develop and perfect itself (autonomously!) from the beginning. This view is being upheld as consistently Christian despite the biblical and theological doctrines of providence and redemption, the history of which culminates in the radical in-breaking of God in Jesus Christ. The relationship and interaction of God with creation at every level is essential to the biblical narrative. The interaction becomes more significant as one moves towards the more human or personal and redemptive aspects of that relationship. Perfection in this theological frame is the perfection of interaction and relationship, that is, a perfection of becoming through covenantal loving.

But, if creation cannot be truly grasped except in terms of its ultimate origin and destiny, which lie in the mind and purposes of God and issue forth in God's interaction with creation throughout its history, then creation cannot be truly grasped autonomously. Creation must be approached as God's creation at every point. The distorting impact that a methodological naturalism will have will be magnified as the focus of investigation moves from lower and impersonal aspects (physics, chemistry) to higher and more personal aspects of creation (plants, animals, persons, persons in relation to others and persons in relation to God and God's ultimate purposes). The greatest distortions will take place when human nature is investigated. Perhaps this is why the success of science has been so much greater at the level of physics and chemistry than say at the level of psychology, sociology and ethics. However, if everything ultimately is what it is by virtue of intentional relation with God, then a methodology that makes irrelevant this essential connection will have a distorting affect to some degree on the knowledge of all things.

Finally, if we follow Michael Polanyi and biblical models of knowing, things must be known, and so the methods constructed for knowing them, according to their highest natures and ultimate purposes. That is, method must be conformed to metaphysics not vice versa. For Christians knowledge of creation must include acknowledgment of a vital connection with God the Creator and Redeemer of all things in the past, fallen present and future. Christians should be the first to acknowledge that all knowing is personal knowing and that no method for knowing can legitimately be reduced to merely impersonal, naturalistic proportions even when the natural dimensions of creaturely things are given their due regard. Methodology necessarily reflects metaphysical assumptions and has implications that to one degree or another impact all of our knowing.

A theological anthropology will not dismiss or deny such naturalistic investigations, but it will build from the top down, that is, on the basis of the full revelation of humanity which shows that the essence of humanity is determined in relation to God. Other investigations will indeed have their own contributions to make, even if pursued from the bottom up. However, such explorations cannot be given autonomous explanatory power. A theological anthropology will critically incorporate them from the top down.

Furthermore, as opposed to bottom up naturalistic explanations, assuming the truth of divine revelation will not be regarded as a subjective bias that threatens the integrity of the investigation. Rather, revelation will be regarded as providing both the proper objective and subjective starting points for approaching the knowledge of humanity. The knowledge of humanity embodied in Jesus Christ as the central object and norm of investigation will provide the objective starting point. Given this starting point outside of us, it should be clear that humility and receptivity will be the only proper subjective orientation before that revelation. Objective knowledge of God's humanity requires a certain subjective posture of humility, trust, and commitment to the content of the revelation given.[4] An impersonal or neutral approach to the knowledge of humanity in Jesus Christ, its Savior and Lord, can only set up obstacles to recognize the truth about humanity.

Calvin is often misunderstood in this connection. Yes, he rightly saw that the knowledge of God and humanity are intimately connected. But he did not believe that one who started with either object would end up in the same place. The knowledge of God in Christ was primary for Calvin. Humanity could only be truly grasped in terms of the knowledge of God. Furthermore, Calvin never consented to approaching humanity in a way that was autonomous from knowledge of God.[5] Calvin cannot be used to justify such inversions or reductionisms.

Now our language about knowing humanity from "above" and "below" can be misleading. By "from above" we do not mean apart from our creaturely existence. We mean, on the basis of God's self-revelation. But that revelation came from above to meet us below. In Jesus Christ "above" came into view "below," giving us access to God's own knowledge of humanity within our human sphere. We know humanity in the humanity of Jesus Christ.

---

[4] See Michael Polanyi, *Personal Knowledge: Towards a Post-Critical Philosophy*, University of Chicago Press, Chicago, 1974, for the discussion behind this affirmation.

[5] See T.F. Torrance, *Calvin's Doctrine of Man*. Eerdmans, Grand Rapids, new edition, 1957.

A Christological Orientation

What do we discover about humanity in Jesus Christ? That in essence humanity has no origin, existence, meaning, or destiny except in deepest connection with God through Jesus Christ in the power of the Spirit.[6] Jesus Christ is who he is by being completely one with God and one with humanity. Jesus has no being except by being entirely from, with and for God and humanity in all that he is, says, and does.[7] In Jesus Christ we see true human being as one who is completely oriented to intimate and involved communion with the Father in the Spirit. The Gospel of John, especially chapters 13-16 and culminating in 17, provide profound insight into how Jesus' identity in act and being was constituted by his relation to the Father in the Spirit. He was one with the Father and the Spirit and desired no life outside of that sphere of communion. Quite the contrary, his humanity was entirely oriented to being in relationship with his heavenly Father.

Jesus is the incarnate Son of God united to the Father by the Spirit. He is entirely caught up in this being-in-communion, so that we could say that his whole ministry towards others was to take them to the Father and send them the Spirit so that they would be included in that very fellowship he had with the Father in the Spirit. In Jesus we see that humanity has its being by being in communion with God, Father, Son and Holy Spirit. The very shape of that communion is revealed in Jesus Christ. The Apostle Paul noted that when the Spirit of Jesus comes upon us we call out in a way which echoes Jesus' own prayer, "Abba, dearest Father." Consequently, when we are baptized, we are baptized in the one name: Father, Son and Spirit for that name marks our new identity as those united to Jesus Christ. Salvation itself is sharing in the Son's own communion with the Father in the Spirit.

The Humanism of God

Such a revelation calls into question every attempt to ascertain the true nature and destiny of humanity apart from its essential connection to God. For there is no humanity apart from or outside of that reality and relationship established in the Incarnate One. Humanity is essentially shaped and determined by the election of humanity to be the humanity of God through the gracious hypostatic union of God and man in Jesus Christ. Autonomous humanity is a fiction, a lie, a deception. There exists

---

[6] See Anderson, *On Being Human*, Chapter 3.

[7] See Karl Barth, *Church Dogmatics*, III/2, pp. 140-198, 209, for an exposition of these simply profound prepositions.

now, through the new and true Adam, no other humanity than God's own humanity. That's what Barth called the humanism of God![8]

A determination that reaches to such ontological depths and eschatological horizons poses no threat to a personal independence or differentiation. Being the Son of the Father was no threat to the personal identity and life of the Son. Rather, that relation establishes and secures the proper distinction between Father and Son. This relational reality carries with it its own logic--the logic of God's own covenant love. Human being is essentially a being-in-relationship, a being-in-loving. Relationship with God is essential to human being, not ancillary or optional. God and humanity are not ontological opposites incapable of communion. Rather, as C.S. Lewis says, humanity was made to "run on God" in a way analogous to an automobile and gasoline.

Those educated in the tradition of western philosophy have a difficult time grasping at the deepest level of being the nature of this union in a way that does not obliterate the personal difference. To locate this problem philosophically we could say that within an Aristotelian substantival ontology (reinforced by Newtonian physics, Cartesian metaphysics and modern Deism, naturalism, and solipsism) relations can only be regarded as accidental, optional, or non-essential to human being. In this framework, the ontological significance of relations necessarily reduce in either of two directions. Either the two essentially differentiated things, no matter how closely related, cannot have real union and so remain essentially separate (the relation between them remaining accidental and extrinsic). Or, upon union, the essential union obliterates the differences. A theological anthropology radically calls into question such an atomistic anthropology.

Considered psychologically, we often perceive only two options within relations: either fleeing or fusing. We feel we either must have personal autonomy and remain essentially untouched by another and so stay in self-control (and maintain control over others) or we must lose ourselves and become submerged in the other.[9] Of course neither of these options seems entirely satisfactory, so that much of fallen human life can be seen as a wild and even destructive oscillation between these two alternatives.

The self-revelation of God and humanity in communion shows a different way forward, the way of covenantal love, of union and communion. This is the theo-logic of *agape*. We are who we are essentially first by being in relation with God. The shape of our participation in that

---

[8] See Karl Barth, "The New Humanism and the Humanism of God," *Theology Today*, Vol. 8 (May 1951) pp. 157-166, translated by Friedrich L. Herzog.

[9] Some of this thinking is reflected in the terminology of "disengagement" and "enmeshment" in family systems theory.

relation foundationally and eternally conditions the quality of our life. And right relation is no threat to our true individuality, for we are created to be and become in and through covenantal relationship.

Nothing is more crucial than to grasp and re-grasp the essential and particular relational shape of humanity given in Jesus Christ.[10] Bad habits of the Western mind (the Eastern mind has its own problems, but let's deal with the log in our own eyes first) must be overcome if we are to work out a theological anthropology. It is a relentlessly uphill battle, for our default position is that relationships, yes, even with God, are optional, non-essential rather than constitutive of our being. Metanoia (repentance of mind) is required to affirm joyfully that being itself is a constantly given gift that we cannot give ourselves. We are not Energizer bunnies with our own built-in being-providing batteries. God alone is self-existing. All else exists by virtue of the gift of being--freely given by God for the sake of communion with God and with others.

Trinitarian Shape

The relational shape of all humanity revealed in the Son of God incarnate is grounded ultimately in the very triune being of God.[11] For in Jesus Christ we find that the very being of God is not a monad, an unvariegated mass of divine substance but a unity, namely a unity of Father, Son, and Spirit. The oneness of God is a communion, not undifferentiated and monolithic stuff. Relationship of holy love is essential, internal, and eternal to the Triune God. In the inner life of the Trinity, there is ontological room for loving long before there is a creation. There is holy space for a real exchange of glory, life and covenant love in the Triune life. The Father eternally gives out of his being the Son's Sonship and the Son gives back out of his being the Father's Fatherhood all in and through the Spirit who both gives and receives from the Father through the Son. God is in this way a living and loving God from all eternity.

Commensurate with who this God is, it should be no surprise (in hindsight!) that creation was created for a union and communion which reflects the very triune character of God. It should make perfect sense, then, that the whole of human responsibility can be captured in the two dimensions of love commanded towards God and neighbor in Scripture. What else would a Triune God like this essentially command? What else would essentially glorify such a God? What else would image and bear witness to this God?

---

[10] See Anderson, *On Being Human*, Chapter 4, for this theme.

[11] This concern can be found throughout the opening chapters of Anderson, *On Being Human*, pp. 36, 49, 76, 85, 114, 118, 121, 175 and 182.

Gary W. Deddo

A Communion with Others

Our Christology already indicated that Jesus Christ was essentially the One from God who was from, with, and for God *and* humanity. Jesus Christ is who he is also in relationship to others. In Christ, God extended himself to others in self-giving love. So, as we live out our communion with the Triune God, we too, in imitation of God's own free and loving acts of creation, Incarnation, and redemption, should extend our communion to include others. Humanity has its being by being in relationship with God and with others.

It is no wonder, and yet a profound mystery, that the church itself, then, must first of all be regarded as a communion of persons. The early church grasped its Trinitarian nature when it regarded itself as being an icon of the Trinity. The divine pattern of love was to be imaged in the church as a witness to its divine constitution.[12] Humanity was created for union and communion in a holy love through sharing in the very Triune life: partially and imperfectly now, but entirely and eternally in its consummation. For salvation in Jesus Christ is nothing other than sharing by grace in his perfect union and communion with the Father and the Spirit. By sharing in the Son's very own Sonship, we thereby really become the children of God. In the words of Scottish preacher and novelist George MacDonald, God in Jesus Christ "brothers us."[13] When we as the people of God extend communion to others, it reflects the very communion of our Triune God.

Human and Creaturely

So on the one hand we should guard against reducing the divine to the human and on the other hand isolating humanity within its own created sphere with no relationship to God. However, there is another way that humanity faces a reductionism. That is when no distinction is made between its essential humanity and its creaturely aspects.[14] So much theological discussion about the nature of humanity created in the image of God has made foundational a comparison between humans and other creatures. The capacity for reasoning and self-awareness has most often been identified as the distinguishing marks of the human being.[15] While a theological anthropology will certainly distinguish between animals, even

---

[12] See Timothy Ware [Bishop Kallistos], *The Orthodox Church*. Penguin Books, London, revised ed., 1993, p. 239.

[13] See George MacDonald, *Unspoken Sermons*, Series 2, "Abba Father," p. 129.

[14] See Anderson, *On Being Human*, Chapter 2.

[15] See Karl Barth's important discussion in *Church Dogmatics*, III/2, "The Phenomena of the Human," pp. 71-132.

the higher ones, and humans, does this comparison really identify the *humanum*, that which truly distinguishes the human creature from all others? Anderson, following the lead of Karl Barth, thinks not, for two negative reasons and one positive reason.

First, concentration on the differences focuses on creaturely capacities and potentialities. However, these attributes do not seem unambiguously to identify qualitative differences but quantitative differences along a continuum. Certain animals do seem to have at least some limited capacity for reasoning, communicating, forming societies, and having a certain self-awareness. There is a growing conviction within the biological and behavioral sciences that these differences are a matter of development; creatures more highly evolved have more developed capacities than those less evolved. Some explain that human capacities operate at higher levels because, as the parts of human physiology have reached the highest levels of development, the whole that emerges is greater than the parts. Personhood is then construed as the result of higher levels of physiological development. Such an approach does not eliminate difference altogether, but it does eliminate a difference of kind while emphasizing continuity. Capacities don't essentially differentiate. Some following this route claim to be able to avoid reductionism, but I do not believe that it can resist collapse into naturalism/materialism or deism. Why not? The answer lies in the second disconfirming reason.

The most important question that arises is not whether or not human capacities are the result of a unique history of physiological development, although that is where much of the present debate is tending to go. The real question is whether these capacities, no matter how developed, can be regarded as that which make persons truly persons, whether they constitute the *imago Dei*. For Anderson, like Barth, the response is decidedly no. The biblical account clearly acknowledges a continuity between animal and human creatures. They are both taken from the ground. Apparently there is no need to deny this connection. But more importantly the explication of the *imago Dei*, both in the biblical narrative of Genesis and more particularly in the New Testament, does not build upon either the connection or distinction from the animals. Biblical teaching on the *imago* emphasizes the uniqueness of humanity, not in terms of capacities but of original relationship and destiny with God. The in-breathing of the Spirit into the nostrils of humanity is what constitutes this difference in Genesis. God dynamically shares something of his very spirit with humanity that sets it apart. The primary problem with an inter-creaturely analysis for identifying the *imago* is that, unlike the Genesis narrative, it requires no essential reference to relationship with God. The *imago* as a creaturely potential can exist by itself as the private possession of an individual. The result is an essential anthropocentrism that then collapses further into an undifferentiated and general creatureliness--even if developmentally understood. God in the end becomes irrelevant, especially in any personal and relational way.

The inadequacies of the current debate between those who hold to a substantival dualism and those who affirm an emergent view of personhood should now be apparent. In this debate the question is whether or not possession of a non-empirical soul is what makes humans truly human in a Christian frame. Note that for neither side is relationship with God essential to humanity. Beyond an initial moment of creation, God may or may not be required either for humans to have souls or to exist without souls. In either case, humanity is analyzed autonomously to see whether or not it can phenomenologically be accounted for with or without a soul. This is strictly analogous to the analysis of humanity on the basis of creaturely capacities. Like that investigation, the soul stands for a neutral, even if higher, and unique capacity (compared to animals?) with an indeterminate destiny and which perhaps involves, but requires, nothing more than a deistic origin. The question then is whether the relatively autonomous human being can be accounted for adequately with or without reference to a soulish capacity. It seems to me that, framed in this way, the debate is stillborn and sub-Christian. I would predict that its outcome will be indeterminate and interminable. But more serious, it leaves out of the discussion what makes human beings human; God's relationship with them originated, mediated, and culminating in Jesus Christ. In this discussion Jesus Christ is entirely peripheral to the discernment of the true outlines of humanity. Certainly such a debate must be regarded as less than profoundly Christian even if minimally theistic.

Image of the Image

Admittedly, the Old Testament accounts of humanity created in the image of God are not exhaustive. But what we find in the New Testament is the startling fact that Jesus Christ himself is identified as the true image of God and that we are being renewed according to that image. Looking back to Genesis, then, the Hebrew is best rendered as human beings being created "according to the image of God" not "as" or "to be" the image of God. That is, humanity is created according to the Son of God, the Image of the Father, who became incarnate. We were created to be Christ-like. This, then, is the positive reason that humanity cannot be reduced to its merely creaturely dimensions, or even to having a soul.

Can this notion be filled out anymore? Anderson, again advancing along the same pathway as Barth, says yes. We were created to be addressed by the Word of God and to respond to that Word.[16] Humanity

---

[16] See Anderson, *On Being Human*, Chapter 3.

stands in relation to the Word, which determines its origin and destiny. Being created according to the image points to the purpose God established that there should be creaturely beings that would become the children of God by sharing in the Son of God's own Sonship. We have been designed to live in a particular relationship of union and communion through the Son with the Father in the Spirit. The Godward aspect of the *imago Dei* is essential in this framework. It is also essentially relational.

What then of human creaturely capacities? Whatever capacities we have and however developed, they are certainly caught up and participate in the realization of that purpose and destiny to become those Christ-like children of God who partake of the divine nature (2 Pet. 1:4). We are not the children of God without these creaturely capacities but with them. But what constitutes our humanity, with or without a soul, is not a human possession or possibility at all. Rather, the purpose, act and decision of God through Christ graciously establish our humanity. The *imago Dei* is a divinely given designation and gift from the Father through the Son in the Spirit. Humanity is what it is by virtue of this connection, this relationship.

The *Telos* of Humanity Transcending Human Capacity

This sets a Christian notion of persons and purpose apart from most Western habits of mind. For Aristotle the *telos* of things, their ultimate destiny or purpose, is intrinsic to that thing. Each distinct thing has its own *entelechy* (in-built *telos*) that would come to be realized or actualized in each particular thing. The great oak is in the acorn. Although not always apparent, the acorn contains within it the seeds of its own perfection. In the Christian frame, however, the perfection of the creature lies outside of and external to the creature. Humanity fulfills its purpose/*telos* only through the personal gift and act of God. Thus, through Christ and the indwelling of his Spirit, human beings become what they could never become on their own, namely the eternal children of God. Indeed, we become sharers in the divine eternal life. This is made possible only by the act and decision of God to create and redeem people through the incarnate Son of God, our Lord and Savior. Such a destiny occurs through the history of a relationship of God with humanity. That relation to God mediated to us in Jesus Christ is what makes us human.

So we return again to our starting point--humanity is what it is and will be what it will be in and through relationship to God. We cannot grasp the *humanum* of humanity apart from this history of relationship no matter what creaturely capacities (including the possession of a spiritual substance such as a soul) we may exhibit. How should we understand those capacities? It seems to me that they are best regarded as aspects of our creatureliness. They are the creaturely channels through which we may manifest our true personhood in our creaturely sphere. Even the soul, then, must be regarded as a creaturely soul, even if it provides for certain unique creaturely potentials.

Barth regarded capacities and potentialities as merely "the symptoms" of humanity, not its essence, and emphasized that the human subject, the who of humanity, could not be identified with them.[17] The human subject could not be reduced to those capacities but identifies the one who uses those potentialities--the agent. That creaturely capacities could be used for good *or* evil was decisive for Barth. Our capacities are morally and spiritually neutral. With our tongues we may bless or curse God and fellow humans. However, the biblical narrative does not depict humanity disconnected from a divine purpose, standing neutrally before a disinterested God who waits to see just how those various capacities will be used. God did not wait to be addressed by a decisive word from humanity, but addressed them with a particular Word which willed the right and good use of those capacities for right relationship with God and neighbor. Creation, according to the Image, placed humanity under a certain blessing, obligation, and destiny. And the *telos* of that very positive relationship constitutes the essence of humanity.

Human Being and Becoming

Human being is constituted through the gift of participating in a history of relationship with God through Christ, which results in its becoming far more than what it ever could become apart from that dynamic of personal union and communion. It follows then that a merely physical or biological analysis of human beings could never begin to apprehend the essence of humanity. This limitation is especially binding if such a "scientific" investigation was committed from the start to a bottom up explanation. Such approaches by definition must exclude reference to (even if not metaphysically deny) anything not empirically and (at least in principle) universally verifiable. The only purpose discoverable via this naturalistic route would be one that must inhere in the creature itself and be a potential possessed by all in general. Its *telos* could never refer to more than a self-delimited self-actualization. It could only mark out an autonomous, that is, self-given and self-established purpose.

Such a "discovery" from the position of a *theological* anthropology could only serve to point towards the fallenness of humanity, its being curved back in upon itself. We would have to regard any self-designated purpose as its anti-*telos*, for it could only affirm what humanity had become post-fall: namely, humanity considered autonomously, apart from God and its origin and destiny. Such a materialistic project would lead at

---

[17] See Barth, *Church Dogmatics*, III/2, p. 198.

best to the discovery of a creature autonomously possessing and arbitrarily using its neutral capacities. Such descriptions certainly could be of use to those committed to a theological anthropology, but they could never supply the foundation for a theological anthropology.[18]

We could conjecture that the social sciences might fare better than the physical sciences in approaching the true nature of humanity. But again this proves not to be the case. To the degree that psychology, social psychology, sociology, and cultural anthropology are not speculative (and therefore not a species of philosophy), these disciplines, too, can only illuminate the creaturely dimensions of human existence. The results of such investigations, Anderson points out, can only lead to a deterministic or a perfectionistic view of humanity.[19]

Let's briefly trace out that necessarily reductionistic line of argument. The social sciences have as their proper field of investigation the history of humanity from the moment which has just passed to as far back as we have information about the human creature in its self-understanding and action as individuals or as groups, societies, aggregates. Within that history they take into account the living dynamics of relationship and a broad range of human capacities not pertinent to the physical sciences. Nevertheless, such disciplines do severely restrict our grasp of the origin and destiny, the purpose and place of humanity. Like the physical sciences, this is especially so if from the beginning reference to the domain of divine agency and intentionality is excluded from serious consideration. No advantage is gained even if certain human practices (such as religion in general and Christianity in particular) that make such references are studied. Although some kind of *telos* might be discerned within human relationships, nevertheless, it could only represent a corporate form of anthropocentrism. Humanity would still begin and end alone with itself apart from God, unable to become anything more than what its own ambivalent capacities allow.

Anthropology and Eschatology

When we utilize the social sciences as if they were autonomous disciplines, they necessarily suffer another serve restriction, namely the exclusion of the future from its domain of investigation. The social sciences certainly

---

[18] Indeed Ray Anderson's work demonstrates this very asymmetrical integration of theology and other disciplines. A marvelous model of such integration with sociology is the book Anderson co-authored with Dennis Guernsey, *On Being Family*, Eerdmans, Grand Rapids, 1985. For a testimony to the fruitfulness of a truly theological anthropology for other disciplines and for ministry, see the essays in *Incarnational Ministry: The Presence of Christ in Church, Society, and Family*, edited by Christian D. Kettler and Todd H. Speidell. Helmers and Howard, Colorado Springs, 1990.

[19] Anderson, *On Being Human*, p. 35.

can project out of the past into the future, but the past will always have a determinative say in the possibilities contemplated of the future. The only viable prophetic voice heard in this sphere is the bell-shaped curve.[20] The social sciences can provide no eschatology, especially one that reaches beyond the extinction of creaturely potentials at the death of individuals, societies, or, indeed, the death of all humanity. Explorations limited to the creaturely sphere at best proffer an extension of the past projected into the future.

Now what is clear in Anderson's view is that a theological anthropology is essentially conditioned eschatologically.[21] Humanity is essentially what it will be according to the possibility created by Jesus Christ who gives humanity a future that it could never give itself. We cannot grasp true humanity by looking back to its past, either to its fallen past or even to its ultimate origin. Within a theological anthropology the essence of humanity is revealed in the destiny secured for it by its Lord and Savior, the one who has come and will come again. We cannot ascertain the nature of humanity apart from the truth and reality of this hope of an eternal union and communion with the Triune God. This hope breaks apart the determinism inherent in every scientific investigation that necessarily is restricted to the creaturely past.

While we cannot subject this hope to evaluation according to what is currently accepted scientific/empirical criteria, it is nevertheless based on an object located within the creaturely sphere. That object is the subject Jesus Christ, the Son of God incarnate. For there in time and space we came in contact with the proclamation, determination, and vision of the future of humanity. How is this so? A clarifying point must be made here: So often, even in Christian theological circles, we mistakenly identify Jesus' creatureliness with his humanity.[22] We mistakenly begin with our own pre-understanding of our humanity, which, as mentioned above, most often is identified with our creatureliness, and then compare Jesus to ourselves to see if he too is human just like we are. This is a colossal error. We do not see the essence of Jesus' humanity when we see how he, like us, has an earthly body, eats, sleeps, wears clothing, enjoys bread and wine, and he gets dirty, tired, hungry and angry like we do. What these things do indicate is Jesus' assumption of our creatureliness. While this assumption of our creatureliness certainly ought not to be denied or

---

[20] Jacques Ellul is especially illuminating in this connection. See his *Ethics of Freedom*, Eerdmans, Grand Rapids, 1976.

[21] See Anderson, *On Being Human*, chapter 11, especially pp. 175ff.

[22] Apparently the Apostle Paul at one time made a similar error. He says in II Cor. 5:16 "even though we once regarded Christ from a [merely] human point of view, we regard him thus no longer."

neglected, it cannot be regarded as the deepest truth about his humanity or ours.

So, where and when do we truly see the full humanity of Jesus? Is it at the wedding at Cana? Asleep in the boat? Turning over tables in the temple? Struggling with temptation in the wilderness or in the Garden? No. We see the essential humanity of Jesus Christ held out for us in promise in his ascension. True humanity is exalted humanity, our humanity raised up to be with our Lord in the very presence of the Father. While we will still be very much creatures, we will not be left in our fallen state, and apparently much of what we assume is intrinsic to our limited existence will fall away as it did for our ascended Lord. We will have immortal and incorruptible bodies that will apparently allow us to interact with time and space in new ways. We will see that it is not and never was human to sin, but rather that holiness is natural, not alien, to humanity. We will find that humanity can by grace very well exist in the holy presence of God. Humanity and divinity were destined to be together in Jesus Christ. Indeed humanity, as true exalted humanity, can share in the divine eternal life when it is mediated to us through the God-man Jesus Christ in the power of the indwelling Holy Spirit. A theological anthropology must be essentially eschatological, for in Christ we see what we will become: namely, like him through union with him in his resurrection and ascension. True transfigured humanity has only appeared on the earth once, but there we saw the promise of our destiny revealed to us.

In the light of the ascension, we cannot take our present experience of our creatureliness, with its fallenness, potentials and limitations as the criteria for the full truth of our humanity or Christ's. The social sciences autonomously can never proffer such a hopeful vision of humanity as we have revealed to us in Christ.[23] Solely on the basis of their own resources they can only promise us a deterministic future eternally tied to the past or alternatively condemn us to a perfectionism which, despite that past, denies the past. On their own they can only set forth the sheer possibility of an imaginary future which might possibly be realized--if only humanity would strive continually and heroically to set itself free from its past, indeed, from itself. Humanity, then, is condemned to perfect itself, by itself, to become something (super-creaturely? quasi-divine?) other than itself. A theological anthropology can never allow itself to be reduced to such deterministic or idealistic slavery. To do so would be to give up the good news of the true hope of humanity promised and fulfilled in Jesus Christ. By grace we may indeed compare our humanity to the ascended

---

[23] The point being, of course, that any human science need not and should not function alone anymore than we can fully grasp the function of a machine, much less a person, except in connection with its purpose.

and exalted humanity of Jesus Christ, which will include our redeemed creatureliness.

Election and Humanization

A Christological and therefore Incarnational and Trinitarian theological anthropology will also be founded upon several other distinctives if it is to be true to the humanity in right relationship with God revealed in Jesus Christ. The eschatological nature of humanity makes it clear that human being is essentially a becoming, a becoming whose trajectory was established in Jesus Christ. We now must add that such becoming involves a personalization of human agency.[24]

John Macmurray has argued that Enlightenment rationalism, materialism, and Deism not only made the agency of God irrelevant but also destroyed in the process the significance of human agency.[25] The modern search for human autonomy called for the elimination of divine activity within the universe and relocating divine purpose immanently within the structures of the universe discoverable by empirical investigation and transmuted into mechanistic natural laws. However, the Christian Kierkegaard and the atheistic existentialists who, even if not consistently, followed him in this discernment sensed the impending loss of human agency in this scheme. The so-called existentialists acknowledged the futility of human action yet proclaimed that human beings must somehow strive to grant themselves their own fleeting significance in that world, despite the closed natural system of cause and effect and the inevitability and finality of death itself. Ironically, in the attempt to secure autonomy from divine purpose, humanity lost the vitality of its own agency. For the very reductionistic methods of scientific explanation spawned by the philosophical commitments of the Enlightenment, which seemed to grant humanity its autonomy, enslaved him in a mechanistic and solipsistic world. Consequently, modern and postmodern thought are entirely satisfied with explanations, even explanations of humanity, which make no reference to an ultimate purpose either given by God or enacted by persons. Purposeful human agency, along with divine agency, has disappeared.

Persons were thereby not only cut off from God, but also cut off in any positive sense from each other (Sartre: "Others are hell"!). It should be apparent that a social, political, or for that matter even a personal, ethic is impossible within that framework. Despite Kant's heroic attempt to put

---

[24] See Anderson, *On Being Human*, chapter 5.
[25] Macmurray, John. *The Self as Agent*. Faber and Faber Limited, London, 1953. The Gifford Lectures, Vol. 1, 1953-54. Reprinted by Humanities Press International, New Jersey and London, 1991.

forth an ethic of duty that would allow for human autonomy, such a project has collapsed under its own weight. Ironically, all that remains of his pragmatic ethic in our so-called postmodern mind is a purely externally applied heteronomous legal power over individuals constructed and arbitrarily enforced by others. Given the trajectory of the West in its reaction to throw off Christianity, is it any wonder that the result is the moral anarchy evidenced in Stalin, Hitler, Mao, Ho Chi Min, Pol Pot, Idi Amin, Ceausescu and Milosevic? And in the context of our liberal democracy we are presently observing the collapse of humanism and the rise of a radical hedonistic utilitarianism with Peter Singer as one of its foremost prophets.[26] In his view all essential differences between humans and animals must be eliminated. The creaturely capacity of sentience, the ability to experience pain or pleasure, is held up as the central distinctive of higher life. The moral aim is reduced to maximize pleasure and minimize suffering for those whose capacities are developed sufficiently to appreciate those benefits. In Peter Singer's reckoning those who are very young, very old or too impaired do not qualify to be the beneficiaries of these aims but rather are subject to at least benign neglect if not active elimination. These are the wonders conceived of a humanity and human obligation in a post-Christian and secularized world.

The True Self and Freedom

A theological anthropology should never surrender its apprehension of the human self-determined and set free under the purposes of God for union and communion with God through reconciliation to God in Jesus Christ. Human selfhood can never be identified with a creaturely autonomy that has no essential relation to God as God and to others as created in the image of Jesus Christ. Jesus Christ constitutes selfhood through the gift of a truly human agency that freely chooses to conform itself to its purposeful election to belong to the people of God. As the purposely chosen people of God, such persons live in the hope of their becoming who God intends them to be in and through their union and communion with God. We are all created to become who we are destined to be by participating in the covenant reality made actual and real by Jesus Christ. The freedom and sovereign purpose of God, then, does not threaten or eliminate the free and so personal agency of humanity but rather secures and assures it.

Indeed this freedom is unidirectional; it runs only from death to life, from abandonment to belonging, from darkness to light, from injustice to

---

[26] See Peter Singer, *Rethinking Life and Death: the Collapse of Our Traditional Ethics*, St. Martins Press, 1996 and *Practical Ethics*, Cambridge University Press, Cambridge, second edition, 1993. For a critique see *Rethinking Peter Singer: A Christian Critique*, ed. Gordon Preece, InterVarsity Press, Downers Grove, Illinois, 2002.

righteousness, from hell to heaven. But there is no other alternative, for autonomy is a lie and evil has no future. God has determined it to be so. The only future for humanity is the future held out for us in Jesus Christ. He humanizes humanity by bringing it (and all its creaturely capacities) into perfect harmony with the divine purpose and design to be holy as God is holy. Holiness is not a threat to humanity; it is only a threat to inhumanity. Relationship with God in Christ is no threat to human freedom and selfhood, but rather is its only hope for becoming truly human by being essentially shaped by the communion designed and deployed in Jesus Christ, the true Adam. In him we see true personhood, and in him we too will become human persons. As for now we are merely on our way. But we see where we are being taken.

Participation in Covenantal Freedom

The relationship of divine and human agency has always posed a philosophical dilemma. But that mystery can never be adequately resolved through speculative reflection. Rather, we can see the perfect harmonization of divine and human will realized in time and space in Jesus Christ himself. That is where we can become convinced that neither divine nor human willing need cancel each other out or be delicately balanced against competing needs. Divine freedom and human freedom were perfectly actualized under creaturely conditions in Jesus Christ, crucified, risen and ascended. What term shall we use to speak of this interaction of human and divine agency?

In this connection we would do well to recover the biblical and theological notion of participation (Gr. *koinonia*). In this Christologically illuminated framework, the purpose, agency, and act of God establishes the arena of actuality and reality in which humans participate and thereby have a share in their own becoming by the grace of God. The sovereign election of us in Jesus Christ makes room for our unidirectional acts of freedom. We are made free for one thing and one thing only, free to choose, affirm, and embrace our election and therefore our destiny in Jesus Christ. This is the sense in which Ray Anderson wants to reorder our thinking so that it now moves from actuality to possibility.[27] Because humanity has been put on a whole new foundation of reconciliation with God, that actuality provides the possibility of life in union and communion with God.

To deny this truth and reality, that Jesus is the Lord of humanity, is to attempt to live in unreality. Undoubtedly, such misuse of our divinely given freedom will have consequences for the quality of our interaction

---

[27] See Anderson, *On Being Human*, the chapters in Part 3, which carries this very title.

with God. However, one of those consequences will not be the undoing of what God has done in our place and on our behalf. Such denial has no power to establish an alternative and counter reality in which we may live where Jesus is not Lord and Savior, the new Adam. A theological anthropology can never concede a cosmic dualism. Eternal death is not an equal and opposite form of eternal life. The grace of God upholds human agency that we might make use of our agency to affirm and participate in the truth and reality of our election to become the children of God. Union with Christ means participation in the life he gives us. The more God acts on our behalf, the more room there is for us to participate. True freedom leads in one direction, to share in the freedom of Christ-likeness. That human freedom requires the arbitrary selection of moral opposites is a lie that comes straight from the serpent in the Garden. It must be banished from the Christian frame of mind.

Freedom in Fellowship

Those who in the power of the Spirit of Christ affirm their election will, in and through participation in their becoming, live in relation with others on the basis of the same hope for them that they have for themselves. The actuality of our reconciliation to God in Christ has at the same time founded a reality horizontally extended among human creatures. On that plane we also essentially live in relations, relations of freedom for fellowship, to borrow Karl Barth's categories. Humanity exists, as Barth traces it out horizontally, in three spheres of relationship: as children of parents, as male and female, and as neighbors.[28] Right relationship means we will treat persons according to God's humanizing purposes for them. Barth provides a wonderful fourfold identification of the humanizing qualities of such relationships: seeing eye to eye, mutually speaking and hearing one another, serving one another, and doing all this gladly and in freedom.[29] We are called to be human by responding in these ways to the humanity of those others whom we will necessarily encounter in these relationships essential to human existence.

Of course these very relationships of parents and children, men and women, and among the various ethnic/cultural/racial groups are those we find so troubling. The good news is that the dividing wall of hostility within these very relationships has been broken down among God's human creatures so that there is one new humanity (Eph. 2:15). In the framework of a theological anthropology, reconciliation among persons is founded upon the reconciling work of God. The actuality of God creates

---

[28] See these sections under the heading, "Freedom for Fellowship," in *Church Dogmatics*, III/4.

[29] See Karl Barth, *Church Dogmatics*, III/2, p. 249 ff.

the possibility of its manifestation among humans. If we were to investigate humanity autonomously, solely with the tools of physics, chemistry, biology, psychology, sociology and philosophy, would we conclude that all humanity has in actuality, in principle, been reconciled? No. But when Jesus Christ put all humanity on a whole new foundation of relationship with God, all inter-human relations were also put on a whole new foundation. That gracious work provides the basis for a transformed sociology and social ethic.

We were created to be in a covenant love relationship with God and humanity by the same Spirit of love that from all eternity unites the Father and Son. Human existence is essentially a being-in-relationship with God and with others. The essence of our being-in-relation along these two axes is fully revealed in Jesus Christ: conceived by the Holy Spirit and born of woman. It is revealed in his perfect love for God and perfect love for humanity resulting in his perfect self-giving, which reconciled humanity to God and gave them a share in his perfected and ascended humanity.[30] On that basis, we can also then see more deeply into the creaturely structure of our being. We have our being by being children of parents. For without parents we would not be. We have our being by being male and female in all we do. We have our being by being neighbors to those near us and like us and to those distant and less culturally, socially, economically like us. To be united to Christ is to have brothers and sisters of every nation, tongue, and tribe. It's a Pentecost reality! To belong to Christ is to belong to the Body of Christ. We are members of that great congregation.

The All-Inclusive Humanity of Jesus Christ

Here we must stop to point out that election for participation in covenant love does not mean (even though some might argue that it may logically imply) rejection. But rather, it means just the opposite. The election of God in the new Adam has universal intention. Those who presently recognize their election participate in it by extending that election to include others. In the words of J. B. Torrance, Jesus' humanity is an all-inclusive humanity. Christians announce the news that only in Jesus Christ can all others be included. He alone is the new Adam. He is the One for the many. That is the inclusive exclusive claim of Christianity.

---

[30] For an explication of Karl Barth's theological understanding of these intertwining relationships, see Gary Deddo, *Karl Barth's Theology of Relations: Trinitarian, Christological and Human*, Peter Lang Publishers, New York, 1999.

Why We Need Theological Anthropology

Seeing Humanity in the Dark

In fact, human agency, human freedom, and human becoming in Christ have everything to do with becoming more and more a channel of God's own gracious election and covenantal love towards all, even one's enemies. Jesus Christ redeems our humanity and leads us to more and more recognize, hope in and act towards others on the basis of their true humanity held out for them in him. I come to see that Jesus is their Brother as well as mine. To be fully human is to see in the most distorted situation the humanity of the other and to participate with God in having their humanity restored. That is, we are to love our "opposites" with God's own love, whether they be parents, members of the other sex, or foreigners. For our *own* humanity depends upon it.

The Test of True Humanity

To be human is to recognize the humanity of the other, especially when it is hidden within a broken creaturely existence. The debates over abortion and euthanasia often assume that it is only the status of others that is in question. Is the fetus yet human? Is someone with Alzheimer's disease still human? But the real question is not whether they are human, but whether we are! Our own being and becoming human will be manifest only as we recognize their humanity and love them in a way that affirms and upholds their humanity, that is, pursues God's intentions for them to share in Christ's own union and communion. Humanity alive to God desires to see others included in the blessing of the living God who brings life out of death no matter now distorted or undeveloped a condition we find them in. This recognition of true humanity is intrinsic to Christian faith. The Christian is one who has been given the gift of discerning the true humanity of God in the womb of the unmarried teenager Mary as well as in the suffering and death of the fruit of her womb on the cross. Those who have thus begun the journey with Jesus towards humanization will also be those willing to bear the burden of hope for the as yet unborn and extending comfort to those for whom the potentialities of life are all but extinguished.

Two clarifying matters may be helpful here. In the frame of a theological anthropology the aim of love for others cannot be reduced either to the mere maximization of the actualization of creaturely capacities or to the mere avoidance of pain and maximization of pleasure. Humanity is surely expressed through the medium of creaturely potentiality and powers. But one's humanity itself is a gift that can be upheld by God even under the most severely constricted and distorted conditions where that humanity hardly, if at all, shines through. Essentially love sees far beyond the barriers which prevent the realization of human potential to affirm in hope God's own love and electing purposes. Of course, wherever possible, the people of God welcome and promote the joyful expression of our true humanity and will not hinder or prevent such expression. Such manifestation of the glory of humanity bears witness to the goodness of God's humanity. But neither will it forget the gift of humanity in the purposes and intentions of God when that humanity is hidden or distorted. Our own humanization is at stake when we do or do not love the unborn, the incapacitated, the neighbor or the enemy. Jesus teaches us to recognize humanity and to participate with him in its humanization.

Humanity and Suffering

We must also say that suffering in and of itself is not destructive of humanity, even though it hides its manifestation and puts it under tremendous burden and constraint. Suffering also may indeed be a channel for exploitation by temptation. But a theological anthropology can never concede that suffering itself can separate us from the love of God. This in no way condones our making anyone suffer. Love alleviates suffering to the extent it can but only in ways that continually acknowledge the abiding humanity of the sufferer. It is indeed possible to inhumanely relieve or avoid suffering. Withholding the truth, over-medicating, providing inadequate palliative care, indulging, or making the person feel they are a burden can all be dehumanizing. Withholding medical care solely on the basis of a cost-benefit analysis and finally, actively promoting the premature death of someone will often if not always be dehumanizing. There are limits as to how we may alleviate suffering, for there are things worse than suffering or even death--namely the repudiation of our own humanity or that of others. The rejection of the humanity of the others will have a dehumanizing affect on us. If unchecked by repentance it will inevitably lead to the repudiation of the true humanity (in perfect relation with divinity) of Jesus Christ. This, we are warned in the New Testament, leads to the second and eternal death beyond our earthly demise.

This is why, it seems to me, that Mother Theresa always sent the novices of her order to minister to the dying who had no hope of recovery in this life. To recognize the true humanity of persons in this condition calls first for the recognition of the humanity of the Crucified One. Those who love Jesus Christ crucified are those who are learning to love others who seem less than human. They can do so because of their hope for a transformed humanity founded upon the One raised and ascended for us on behalf of all.

Humanity under the Gracious Judgment and Exaltation of God

The final distinctive of a theological anthropology is that it will always remember that humanity lives by the grace of God. That is, humanity exists within an essentially fallen condition, yet with hope for redemption only because God's future has already broken into that desperate situation. This in-breaking signals a consummation yet to come.[31] In Jesus Christ crucified we not only see our humanity in union and communion with God but also fallen and under judgment. What might seem a normal state for humanity is revealed to be abnormal, broken and twisted to its very root. In the cross of Christ the depth of our need, guilt and shame is exposed--not in order to condemn us but to rescue us from ourselves. In the cross we see that humanity does not just need to be freed from its creaturely limits of finite strength and knowledge or merely be given correct or higher ideals. We see that humanity cannot rescue itself by some incremental self-advancement. Death seems to have the last word over humanity. In Christ we see that humanity is enslaved to malevolent corrupting powers greater than itself for evil itself as a conspiratorial power (Satan and his angels) seems to overcome good--the morally and spiritually perfect humanity of Jesus Christ. Apart from the gracious deliverance of God through death itself, his humanity, and so ours, has no hope and no future. In Christ we see that humanity is so threatened and polluted that it must be done away with, suffer a terrible judgment, and then be re-made from the inside out if it is to reach its God-given destiny. A theological anthropology, then, will resist reduction of the hope of humanity to a moralism or idealism of human self-improvement just as much as it rejects the hopelessness of a fatalism and determinism of human abandonment by or autonomy from God.

    No autonomous human investigation can discover humanity under grace, although it may identify among other complicating factors symptoms of this truth. Grace alone shows us the true nature of our need and of God's adequacy. Humanity to be free of its evil corruption needs to be judged, condemned to death, and then made alive again. How can this be? It is possible because in Jesus Christ our fallen, rebellious and broken humanity was judged. Dying in him now changes the very nature and meaning of death, because in him we are also raised again to new life as renewed creatures set free from the power of sin and its devastating consequences. On the cross of Christ we see the true condition of humanity in its alienation from God. But only in the resurrection and ascension of Christ do we see the radical transformation of humanity so that it may reach its destiny as the people of God.

---

[31] See Anderson, *On Being Human*, chapter 7.

In the end, a theological anthropology can be nothing less than a theology of grace. As Karl Barth has said, "We are prohibited [by the gospel] to take sin more seriously than grace, or even as seriously as grace."[32] For it is by grace alone through faith alone in the glorified humanity of Jesus Christ that these distinctives will be preserved at this moment in the life of the church as it faces enormous reductionistic pressures, which threaten not only the loss of God and God's grace in Jesus Christ but also the loss of our humanity--our ability to recognize the truly human in ourselves, in our neighbors, and in Jesus Christ.

---

[32] Karl Barth, *Church Dogmatics*, III/2, p. 41.

"FACES"

"God left my stained glass windows
He disappeared into the street
Now I look in every lonely face
Hoping we will meet

but all I ever see
are empty faces
looking back at me

God became a man, I'm told
Has anyone seen him since?
I cry out in every known tongue
Risking my defense

but all I ever see
are empty faces
laughing back at me

People wearing masks are strangers
Hiding God from my embrace
Sometimes I tear away their disguise
Hoping to touch His face

but all I ever see
are empty faces
turning back from me

I was touched by another's love
My mask became a useless game
And now I know that in my face
God's love becomes a name

and all I ever see
are open faces
showing love to me"

                Ray S. Anderson, *Soulprints*

Todd H. Speidell

*

The Humanity of God and the Healing of Humanity: The Trinity, Community, and Society

"Social justice is not an abstract principle, nor is it an ideal to be pursued. Social justice is the core of human experience. It is bread and water; it is blood and bones; it is brothers and sisters who unlearn the knowledge of how to hurt and how to kill and who learn to live in the power, the freedom and the hope with which God intended that we should live. If there is any theological basis for social justice, it lies between us, within our humanity; it is anthropological. Social justice is a divinely ordained order of human existence . . . Social justice flows not from the justice of God as an abstract principle but from his humanity as an historical and continuing power of reconciliation. It is not God's justice but his humanity that is our hope."

Ray S. Anderson, The Shape of Practical Theology

The Church's service often presupposes a theology of mission that is "secular" or "spiritual" but too rarely Christian. When Christians dualistically divorce the sacred and the secular, the theological and the ethical, the Gospel announces that the Word assumed and healed our humanity. All people received the dignity of their humanity in Christ, who forms communities in society based on the love of the Father for humanity and the presence of the Spirit in the world.

The Church, T. F. Torrance asserts, confronts a twofold temptation when facing the stark reality of human need. On the one hand, the institutionalization of worldly power poses a utilitarian temptation to secure success via political lobbying, which of course requires that one develop social, political, and economic clout of one's own. On the other hand, the authorization of a spiritual retreat poses an otherworldly temptation to abdicate meeting social needs by yielding social concerns to the power structures of the state, while restricting itself to the service of forgiveness. In either case, Torrance warns, "Christ clothed with His Gospel has been kept apart from Christ clothed with the need and plight of men."[1]

---

[1] Thomas F. Torrance, "Service in Jesus Christ," in *Theological Foundations for Ministry*, ed. Ray S. Anderson (Grand Rapids, MI: Eerdmans, 1979), p. 730.

The Christian Church must heal within itself this division of "Christ clothed with His Gospel" and "Christ clothed" with desperate human need. Being in Christ means following the One sent by the Father in the Spirit by participating in his life of worship, mission, and service. The One whom we follow, James Torrance notes, "is a whole Christ," not "a *nudus Christus*." Jesus comes to us, Torrance proclaims, "as our Brother Man, to be our great High Priest, that He might carry on His loving heart the joys, the sorrows, the prayers, the conflicts of all His creatures, that He might intercede for all nations as our eternal Mediator and Advocate . . ."[2] Jesus comes from God as "the True Priest, bone of our bone, flesh of our flesh"—healing us by assuming "that very humanity which is in need of redemption," so that "our humanity is healed *in him*." [3]

Ray Anderson tells the story of a Roman Catholic woman who went into a Christian bookstore and desperately asked for a cross. As a good Protestant bookstore, it only carried naked, barren crosses. "Yes, I'm looking for a cross," the woman commented, "but do you have one with the little man on it?" Anderson adds, "And a cross without its humanity is a cross without its power of reconciliation." He continues,

> But the truth of the gospel is not that humanity has been put on the cross; it is rather that the cross has been sunk deep into humanity. The incarnation has the cross on it before the incarnate One hangs on the cross. More stupendous than the thought of a crucified God is the self-giving and suffering love of the humanity of God. More powerful and more effective than an instrument of death is the instrumental means of reconciliation through incarnational presence in life. More significant than the cross as a religious symbol is the power released through the bearing of the cross under the already inspired witness of resurrection and healing.[4]

The novelist Walker Percy portrays a hospital chaplain Percival, who took the "religious" name Fr. John when he became a priest but who is unsure of the power and presence of God. He visits his old friend Lancelot, who is in a psychiatric prison for murdering his adulterous wife. It is Lancelot who summons and questions this pastoral counselor:

---

2 James B. Torrance, "The Place of Jesus Christ in Worship," in *ibid.*, pp. 348, 367.
3 Idem, "The Vicarious Humanity of Christ," in *The Incarnation: Ecumenical Studies in the Nicene-Constantinopolitan Creed*, ed. T. F. Torrance (Edinburgh: Handsel, 1981), pp. 138, 141.
4 Ray S. Anderson, *The Shape of Practical Theology: Empowering Ministry with Theological Praxis* (Downers Grove, IL: InterVarsity, 2001), pp. 315f.

Yes, I asked you to come. Are you a psychiatrist or a priest or a priest-psychiatrist? Frankly, you remind me of something in between, one of those failed priests who go into social work or 'counseling,' or one of those doctors who suddenly decides to go to the seminary. Neither fish nor fowl . . . So something went wrong with you too. Or you wouldn't be here serving as assistant chaplain or substitute psychiatrist or whatever it is you're doing. A non-job.[5]

My older brother, David, attempted suicide over ten years ago. Tormented by paranoid delusions that his loved ones were against him and by schizophrenic withdrawal and hallucinations, he was psychologically debilitated to the point of utter despair. My mother, of non-expressive Scandinavian heritage, trained at Moody Bible Institute, and married to an ordained Baptist minister, confessed after this terrible incident that she could no longer pray. (Consider the two false options in the prologue of Job—to praise God for suffering or to "[c]urse God and die!" [Job 1:21; 2:10 in *The New English Bible*]). As a seminary student at the time studying with Ray Anderson, and reflecting upon the years of coping with the despair of schizophrenia, I could only think to share with her Dietrich Bonhoeffer's powerful line from prison, "Only a suffering God can help."[6]

The Church must develop theological instincts and not simply good intentions, for its service is to God, not to the world. It is God who sends his Son into the world, and it is he who has graciously given to the Church a distinctive service to God: namely, to be human with others before God. Because God has restored to us our true humanity in Christ, the Spirit leads the Church to re-*present* the One Christ in whose face we may see the loving heart of the Father for the world.

"The incarnation did not 'Christianize' humanity," Anderson observes; "it 'humanized' humanity." By implication, he infers,

---

[5] Walker Percy, *Lancelot* (N.Y.: Ivy, 1977), pp., 3ff. Fr. John does convert from being a comfortable Catholic and half-baked psychologist by the end of the novel. Lancelot and Fr. John represent a Kierkegaardian "either-or": Lancelot advocates an ethical utopia without faith to combat the malaise that underlies purely aesthetic existence and Fr. John represents the mystery of faith in a godless world. Lancelot challenges the priest's newly found faith: "So you plan to take a little church in Alabama, Father, preach the gospel, turn bread into flesh, forgive the sins of Buick dealers, administer communion to suburban housewives? . . . Very well. But you know this! One of us is wrong. It will be your way *or* it will be my way" (pp. 239f.; emphasis added to underscore the Kierkegaardian "either-or").

[6] Dietrich Bonhoeffer, *Letters and Papers from Prison* (N.Y.: Collier, 1971), ed. Eberhard Bethge, p. 361. Also, Walker Percy's protagonist in *The Thanatos Syndrome*, Dr. Thomas More, who practiced psychiatry before he went to prison, perceptively comments, "Sometimes I think that is the best thing we shrinks do, render the unspeakable speakable" (N.Y.: Ivy, 1987), p. 17.

No longer can sexual status, economic status or racial distinctives be used as criteria for relationship with God or for seeking advantage over others. The incarnation was not for the purpose of putting the humanity of God on the cross but for the purpose of sinking the cross deeply into human life. When God 'dies' on the cross, what is put to death is all that is inhuman in humanity.[7]

Humans may now freely respond not only to God as Father but also to others as brothers and sisters. The many social, political, and liberationist theologies of our day would do well to heed Anderson's admonition that what both the Church and world desperately need is nothing less than the humanity of God as the basis and reality of our own created and restored common humanity.[8]

The Church's social mission should not reduce needy people to sociological abstractions, such as "the poor," "the disadvantaged," or other labels that enable us to evade personal relations with our neighbors in need. Anderson perceives in Karl Barth's concept of neighbor a radical solidarity of cohumanity in Christ, in whom both "near and distant neighbors" confront us with "the concrete existence of the other" as the context for ethical reflection.[9] "Christian ethics," then, should not baptize the abstract duties or principles of deontological ethics nor the calculations and consequences of utilitarian ethics nor even the emphasis on character in virtue ethics. Instead, God commands us to live in concrete

---

[7] *Shape of Practical Theology*, pp. 139, 157.

[8] Cf. the "progressive Marxist" and "revolutionary Christian" posture of Cornel West, who advocates the alliance of "black theological reflection and action . . . rooted in the progressive Marxist tradition . . ." (*Prophesy Deliverance: An Afro-American Revolutionary Christianity* [Phila.: Westminster, 1982], p. 106) — though any kind of theological reflection recedes into the background of his later *Race Matters* (N.Y.: Vintage, 1983). In his *Prophetic Fragments*, West advocates "interpreting the Christian faith *in light of* our present circumstances" (emphasis added), set against the caricatured alternatives that he perceives and poses: "transcendental reflection on the nature of morality" or "historical mimicking of the liberal tradition." The Christian faith, for this ideologue, "must lead to some form of democratic and libertarian socialism" (Grand Rapids, MI: Eerdmans, & Trenton, NJ: Africa World, 1988), pp. 130, 134. Also cf. J. Moltmann, who more theologically upholds a Trinitarian theology over and against what he calls a mere "moral monotheism," but he too resorts to socialist abstractions when he advocates, for example, the "unity of everything" and the "abolition of property" (*The Trinity and the Kingdom: The Doctrine of God* [San Fran.: Harper & Row], 1981), pp. 216f. For a powerful and penetrating critique of such "anthropocentric theologies," see Christian D. Kettler, *The Vicarious Humanity of Christ and the Reality of Salvation* (Lanham, MD: Univ. Press of America, 1991), especially ch. 5, "The Humanity of God as Critique of Anthropocentric Theologies."

[9] *Shape of Practical Theology*, pp. 146ff.; also see pp. 161ff. for a discussion of the "Sociocultural Implications of a Christian Perception of Humanity."

responsibility to one's neighbors as fellow human beings created, loved, and redeemed by God.[10]

God lives and reveals himself as a union and communion of Father, Son, and Spirit. The Father sends the Son in the Spirit both to reveal God's heart for the world and to reconcile the world unto God. The Spirit of the incarnate, crucified, risen, ascended, and coming Christ leads us into worship, communion, mission, and service.[11] Churches that neglect this trinitarian basis for human life are left bereft of a message, of any hope of witness, mission, or service, and of a reality of human community and reconciliation that is rooted in God himself.

The Scottish philosopher John Macmurray, who began his personal pilgrimage in the Church of Scotland and later supplanted traditional religious practice with a quasi-Marxist faith, always believed that Christianity was superior to Marxism in its understanding of community. The state can at best coerce, and at worst depersonalize, its citizens without producing the personal relations that characterize Christian community. Modern western philosophy, too, lacks a proper commitment to personal communion and agency, focusing instead on isolated individuals contemplating the world. The Cartesian thinking self withdraws from others to contemplate ideas, thus separating reflection from action and persons from communion. Despite Macmurray's central emphasis on personal communion, he ironically lived his religious life as an isolated individual, and only later in life did he find a real sense of Christian community among the Society of Friends that his earlier Marxist faith could never realize.[12]

Macmurray's philosophy of community—namely, that persons are who they are in relationship to others, and that these relationships are necessarily and preeminently personal[13]—sorely needed a real basis and

---

[10] I have surveyed these four ethical traditions, based on duty (deontological ethics), consequences (utilitarian, egoistic, and altruistic ethics), character (virtue theory), and God's commands (Divine Command Theory), in my *From Conduct to Character: A Primer in Ethical Theory*, rev. ed. (Eugene, OR: Wipf and Stock, 2000).

[11] I have pursued the theme of "Incarnational Social Ethics" in *Incarnational Ministry: The Presence of Christ in Church, Society and Family* (Essays in Honor of Ray S. Anderson), ed. C. D. Kettler & T. H. Speidell (Colo. Springs, CO: Helmers & Howard, 1990), pp. 140-52.

[12] See especially his two volume *The Form of the Personal: The Self as Agent* (London: Faber, 1957) and *Persons in Relation* (London: Faber, 1961), and his *Search for Reality in Religion* (London: Allen & Unwin, 1965).

[13] Harry Guntrip cites his philosophy training with John Macmurray's "personal relations" school of thought as a deep influence on him and of great significance to the "object relations" school of psychotherapy, which modified the drive theory of classical psychoanalysis in a way remarkably similar to Macmurray's emphasis on persons in relation. See Guntrip's *Personality Structure and Human Interaction: The Developing Synthesis of Psycho-Dynamic Therapy* (N.Y.: International Universities, 1961), pp. 19, 124.

ontological antecedent for personal relations. Abandonment of the Trinity can merely lead to moral and political imperatives detached from the indicatives of the triune God's being of love, grace, and freedom. The state cannot produce community, as Macmurray rightly perceived, but the Church must not arrogate to itself a Christ-like role "to save the world," in Macmurray's unfortunate words, by its own loving existence.[14] Because of our serious situation as sinners, Karl Barth warns, we must be wary of the pride of self-help and all attempts to regain our freedom and responsibility; our only hope is the grace of God.[15]

Christians who base their hope for humanity on a paternalistic state or on a politicized Church, on the one hand, or on abstract, schizoid intellectualizing about doctrine,[16] on the other hand, neglect the foundation of their faith and the reason of their existence *qua* the body of Christ. The triune God upholds persons in community or fellowship (such as church, family, or friendship), for the personal relations of humanity reflect the very being of God as a communion of persons in free, mutual, loving, and giving relations. The Christian Church must witness to the personal relations of God's own being known to us in Jesus Christ as a theological basis for contemporary social and political discussions. "The church finds its true ministry," as Anderson puts it well, "in the upholding, healing and transformation of the humanity of others as already grasped and reconciled to God through the humanity and ministry of Jesus Christ."[17]

What are some concrete implications of this trinitarian-incarnational theology of Christian community in society? Current discussions of "diversity," first of all, tend to run amok of a trinitarian theology of differentiation within unity by emphasizing otherness over oneness. Instead of dynamically balancing the unity and plurality of various

---

[14] *Search for Reality*, pp. 76f. Also, see my "A Trinitarian Ontology of Persons in Society," *Scottish Journal of Theology*, Vol. 47.3 (1994), pp. 283-300.

[15] Karl Barth, *Church Dogmatics* (Edinburgh: T. & T. Clark, 1956), eds. G. W. Bromiley & T. F. Torrance, tr. G. W. Bromiley, IV/1, pp. 458, 463ff.

[16] Cf. Walker Percy, *The Moviegoer* (N.Y.: Ivy, 1960): "The proofs of God's existence may have been true for all I know, but it didn't make the slightest difference. . . . REMEMBER TOMORROW: Starting point for search: It no longer avails to start with creatures and prove God. Yet it is impossible to rule God out. The only possible starting point: the strange fact of one's own invincible apathy—that if the proofs were proved and God presented himself, nothing would be changed. Here is the strangest fact of all. Abraham saw signs and believed. Now the only sign is that all the signs in the world make no difference. Is this God's ironic revenge? But I am onto him" (pp. 128f.).

[17] Ray S. Anderson, "Christopraxis: the Ministry and the Humanity of Christ for the World," in *Christ in our Place: The Humanity of God in Christ for the Reconciliation of the World* (Essays presented to Professor James Torrance), ed. Trevor Hart & Daniel Thimell, pp. 19f.

peoples in a way that indirectly mirrors the mutual relations of the Trinity, slogans of diversity in schools and society often foster a balkanized society of competing victim groups. Rights replace responsibility; diversity degenerates into divisiveness.

The current emphasis on "diversity" also tends to betray the original civil rights vision of treating all people with individual respect and dignity and not merely as members of a group, or of not discriminating against individuals based on their race, sex, etc. "Affirmative action" programs today treat individuals in precisely the opposite way: as members of groups and not as individuals; some "diversity" programs even attempt to achieve proportional representation of races based on the assumption that "numerical imbalances" indicate a pattern of "institutional racism." This return to a pre-civil rights posture of treating people differently based on race, sex, etc., both patronizes already well-to-do minorities, so that the advantaged benefit in the name of the disadvantaged, and prevents society from moving beyond "white guilt" and "black victimization."[18]

A one-sided emphasis on diversity, often conceived as the color of one's skin (not the content of one's character!), tends to promote self-segregating patterns of intolerance and, ironically, uniformity.[19] The superficiality of assuming that *racial* "diversity" ensures *intellectual* diversity resorts to the rebuilding of stereotypes, not breaking down the walls of racial divisiveness. Treating people as means to an end and not as ends in themselves (a word on behalf of Kant from the school of Karl Barth and T. F. Torrance!) elevates social engineering schemes over truly affirming one's fellow humanity.

Learning and scholarship, as another example, should be envisioned and practiced for the sake of the formation of persons-in-community and not merely as an impersonal process of accumulating and disseminating information. Analogous to parents passing on wisdom for daily living to their children, teachers also form relationships with students that should impart learning and wisdom, so that students are equipped for life and not

---

18 See Shelby Steele, *The Content of Our Character: A New Vision of Race in America* (N.Y.: HarperPerennial, 1990), pp. 77ff., 144; Stephen L. Carter, *Reflections of an Affirmative Action Baby* (N.Y.: BasicBooks, 1991), p. 80.
19 Cf. Percy, *Thanatos Syndrome*: "One of life's little mysteries: an old-style Southern white and an old-style Southern black are more at ease talking to each other, even though one may be unjust to the other, than Ted Kennedy talking to Jesse Jackson—who are overly cordial, nervous as cats in their cordiality, and glad to be rid of each other. In the first case the old-style white and the old-style black—each knows exactly where he stands with the other. Each can handle the other, the first because he is in control, the second because he uses his wits. They both know this and can even enjoy each other. In the second case—Ted Kennedy and Jesse Jackson—each is walking on eggshells. What to say next in this rarified atmosphere of perfect liberal agreement?" (pp. 37f.).

merely for tests![20] The novelist Walker Percy's *Love in the Ruins* portrays a character Dr. Thomas More (ironically named for the author of *Utopia*), who is a psychiatrist that uses an "ontological lapsometer," or a machine to evaluate patients' emotional disturbances.[21] This "utopian" (Gk.: *ou* + *topos* = "no place") doctor, who does not like to deal with actual people and their problems, reminds one of professors who prefer isolating themselves in their offices for research and writing over relating to students.

Schools may thus become sanctuaries instead of factories of learning, engaging the passions of one's heart, mind, and soul—worshipping God with one's whole being in the context of formal courses and informal mentoring relationships. For example (and I follow the lead here of my own mentor, Ray Anderson), I meet with small groups of students during lunch time to discuss great works of theology, philosophy, literature, psychology, and so on, which we read prior to such meetings. Our goals are the same as for my formal courses:

(1) to read consistently and well as a basis for sharing one's ideas[22];
(2) to learn to listen to others as well as to speak[23]; and
(3) to test out one's ideas in relationship with others, for one does not need to know everything to say something.[24]

Teaching is a personal, social, and spiritual activity, not simply a matter of technique, for it occurs within a context of whole persons in relationship to other whole persons and before the God of Jesus Christ.

---

20 Will Barrett, the protagonist of Walker Percy's *The Last Gentleman*, is a drifter and searcher, whose education did not prepare him for the reality of life: "The old spurious hope and elegance of school days came back to him. How strange it was that school had nothing whatever to do with life. The old talk of school as a preparation for life—what a bad joke. There was no relation at all. School made matters worse. The elegance and order of school had disarmed him for what came later" (p. 157).
21 "Only in man does the self miss itself, *fall* from itself (hence *lapsometer!*)"—*Love in the Ruins* (N.Y.: Ivy, 1971), p. 31.
22 "Perhaps the secret of talking was to have something to say," as Walker Percy puts it in *The Second Coming* (N.Y.: Washington Square, 1980), p. 48.
23 As Karl Barth comments in his *Church Dogmatics*, "Two monologues do not constitute a dialogue" (Edinburgh: T. & T. Clark, 1960), tr. Harold Knight et al., III/2, p. 259.
24 As Lessing remarks, "If God held all truth in his right hand, and in his left hand the lifelong pursuit of it, he would choose the left hand" (quoted in *A Kierkegaard Anthology* [Princeton: Princeton Univ., 1973], ed. Robert Bretall, p. 195). A more accurate but less quotable version appears in *Concluding Unscientific Postscript to Philosophical Fragments* (Princeton: Princeton Univ., 1992), ed. & tr. Howard & Edna Hong: "If God held all truth enclosed in his right hand, and in his left hand the one and only ever-striving drive for truth, even with the corollary of erring forever and ever, and if he were to say to me: Choose!—I would humbly fall down to him at his left hand and say: Father, give! Pure truth is indeed only for you alone!" (Vol. I, p. 106).

Todd H. Speidell

Abortion, as a further example, concerns persons in relation: the mother and father, medical personnel, relatives or friends who assist or encourage abortion, and society, whose attitudes and laws may permit abortion, and of course the unborn child, who in Karl Barth's words, "is a man and not a thing, nor a mere part of the mother's body . . . a fellow-man whose life is given by God . . . ." Barth continues by developing a distinctively Protestant theology regarding abortion based on the Gospel: not by underbidding "the severity of the Roman Catholic No" but by replacing its "abstract and negative 'Thou shalt not'" with its own "Thou mayest" — a gracious permission to live life that includes a corresponding obligation to uphold it, and a profound sense of the mystery and awe of life that lives by the freedom of "may" instead of the burden of "must." Barth concludes by noting the need for exceptions, based on the *ultima ratio* of a pregnant mother's life in jeopardy, done with a clear conscience "before God and in responsibility to Him," and assured "in faith that God will forgive the elements of sin involved."[25]

To engage in abstract, hypothetical, and technical questions about whether the fetus is human, declares Dietrich Bonhoeffer, merely confuses the issue. "The simple fact," continues Bonhoeffer, "is that God certainly intended to create human life and that this nascent human being has been deliberately deprived of his life."[26] T. F. Torrance also understands the unborn child as "not a potential, but an incipient person"; "an integrated whole"; "genetically complete in the embryo from the moment of conception"; and open "beyond mere empirical observation" to "a *regulative force*" beyond itself. Such a "dynamic and ontological" relation, an "onto-relational and interrelational way of thinking," understands the unborn child in relation to God himself. God "is the Creative Source of all personal being and inter-personal relations — he is the personalising Person, who brings us into personal life and being through the inter-personal activity of a father and mother" from conception through birth, childhood, and the love of personal family life.[27]

With this theology of abortion on the back of my mind, my wife, Gail, and I faced a life-and-death decision regarding the impending birth of our daughter when Gail's water broke at twenty-two weeks of gestation. The doctor gravely informed us that our baby would have a ten percent chance of living, and on the slim chance that she lived, severe abnormalities were likely. Perhaps such a situation granted us the

---

[25] *Church Dogmatics* (Edinburgh: T. & T. Clark, 1961), tr. A. T. Mackay et al., III/4, pp. 415ff.
[26] Dietrich Bonhoeffer, *Ethics* (N.Y.: Macmillan, 1955), pp. 175f. Also cf. Walker Percy's *Thanatos Syndrome*, which discusses "*Doe v. Dade*, the landmark case decided by the U.S. Supreme Court which decreed, with solid scientific evidence, that the human does not achieve personhood until eighteen months" (p. 361)!
[27] Thomas F. Torrance, *The Soul and Person of the Unborn Child* (Edinburgh: Handsel, 1999), pp. 8ff.

freedom to abort with a clear conscience, at least based on consequentialist calculations and certainly with the announced blessing of our doctor. Perhaps Barth, Torrance, and especially Bonhoeffer (who permits no exceptions) were too severe in not showing openness to God's concrete command in borderline medical situations. Life, after all, is not an absolute right, and our daughter was appearing on the very margins of life.

The fact that our daughter, Jessa, was born alive—albeit at one pound and requiring critical care for five months and multiple surgeries before gaining relatively normal health—does not justify in retrospect our decision not to abort; this case could have turned out much grimmer. Our experience does illustrate, however, the profound and wrenching human decisions that humans must make in response to God, the author of life, and in community with others of good character and sound judgment.[28] Life is a gift for which we are responsible to uphold before God with a sense of gratitude and awe for the mystery of life.

The celebration of Holy Communion provides a final example of human relations before the God of Jesus Christ. This Sacrament should proclaim week after week the reality and presence of Christ's one body broken for us as a call to the reconciliation of the divisions that continue to plague the Church (denominational, racial, economic, sexual, and so on). Can the Church in good conscience confess belief in "one holy catholic and apostolic Church" (as in The Nicene Creed) and practice "closed communion"—barring fellow Christians and non-Christians alike because they do not share one's creedal or denominational affiliation? Can the Church truly be and become a place of belonging and community for sinners as a haven in a heartless world?

Christ's community, Barth proclaims,

> "points beyond itself. At bottom it can never consider its own security, let alone its appearance. As His community it is always free from itself. In its deepest and most proper tendency it is not churchly, but worldly—the Church with open doors and great windows, behind which it does better not to close itself in upon itself again by putting in pious stained-glass windows. It is holy in its openness to the street and even the alley, in its turning to the profanity of all human life—the holiness which, according to Rom. 12:5, does not scorn to rejoice with them that do rejoice and

---

[28] Whereas one physician recommended an abortion based on calculations and odds, another physician simply and helpfully announced, "This baby has a real chance!" "The Case of Gail and Her Baby" is published in my *From Conduct to Character*, pp. 21ff. Our story also appeared in *The Knoxville News-Sentinel* in the "Health & Science" section on March 14, 1994.

to weep with them that weep. Its ministry is not additional to its being. It is, as it is sent and active in its mission."29

Ray Anderson proclaims in quintessential fashion, "Only the church that is willing to repent of being the church can truly be the church of Jesus Christ."30 Consider the many individuals, for example, who are lonely and depressed and anxious and aimless, going to church week after week in search of community and purpose. Churches can at times exacerbate their plight through pointless, non-theological sermons, which fail to proclaim week after week that God comes to us in our greatest point of need to affirm, to uphold, and to redeem us for participation in community with God himself in our midst.31

The Church must lead the way in society as a place for belonging and believing, submitting to one Christ, practicing the communion of saints and sinners in true incarnational fashion, confessing a catholic creed of essential theology, and proclaiming the apostolic faith. The Church must practice the unity of its existence in Christ, tolerate the diversity of nonessential dogmas, and participate in the very love of God himself as Father, Son, and Spirit, who graciously permits the Christian community a role to witness in society to the union and communion of God.

---

29 Barth, *Church Dogmatics*, tr. G. W. Bromiley, IV/3, p. 725.

30 Anderson, *Shape of Practical Theology*, p. 180. Perhaps Ray would appreciate Walker Percy's characterization of the non-repentant Christian: "I stopped eating Christ in communion, stopped going to mass, and have since fallen into a disorderly life. I believe in God and the whole business but I love women best, music and science next, whiskey next, God fourth, and my fellowman hardly at all. Generally I do as I please. A man, wrote John, who says he believes in God and does not keep his commandments is a liar. If John is right, then I am a liar. Nevertheless, I still believe" (*Love in the Ruins*, p. 6).

Percy also writes, "Christ should leave us. He is too much with us and I don't like his friends. We have no hope of recovering Christ until Christ leaves us. There is after all something worse than being God-forsaken. It is when God overstays his welcome and takes up with the wrong people" (*Last Gentleman*, p. 293).

31 See the forthcoming work by Chris Kettler, *The Vicarious Humanity of Christ and the Cry of the Heart*. I am indebted to Dr. Kettler, as well as to Drs. John Cox, Kevin Dodd, and Gail Gnade for their constructive criticisms of my essay.

Trevor M. Dobbs

The Influence of John Macmurray:
A Philosophical Foundation of Object Relations Psychology

In the work of psychoanalysis links are formed with numbers of other mental sciences, the investigation of which promises results of the greatest value: links with mythology and philology, with folklore, with social psychology and the theory of religion.

                     Sigmund Freud, *Introductory Lectures on Psychoanalysis*

In *Christians Who Counsel: The Vocation of Wholistic Therapy,* Ray Anderson engages the reader in a unique approach to the task of bringing together psychology and theology in the service of Christian ministry. Ray develops the *hermeneutical task* of the development of the self through focusing his lens on the theology of therapy in the following way: "The capacity to be open to bad luck as well as good fortune is evidence of a 'hermeneutical' approach to life whereby the self possesses a core of positive values that transcend sheer facts such as disease or even death. The self actually interprets facts and experiences according to its core values."[1] He illustrates this concept with the AIDS patient who at one point responded to another person's interpretation of his plight by protesting that "he was not dying with AIDS, but living with AIDS."[2]

    The development of the capacity for such *therapeutic redefinition* of circumstance, such as where the apostle Paul applied this in his relationship to his own "thorn in the flesh," is one of the central tasks Ray takes up in his work. Ray cites the contribution of object relations psychology as a therapeutic approach as reflected in the work of Charles Gerkin and Frank Lake, noting the latter's "monumental work attempting to integrate object relations theory with Christian theology."[3]

    In subsequent chapters on the topics of *The Healing Praxis of Prayer* and *Counseling as a Christian Calling,* Ray makes use of the work of John Macmurray in applying his development of the concept of the self as a relational paradigm. The purpose of the following chapter is to identify

---

[1] Ray S. Anderson, *Christians Who Counsel: The Vocation of Wholistic Therapy* (Pasadena: Fuller Seminary Press, 1990), 45.
[2] Ibid.
[3] Ibid., 54.

Macmurray's specific influence on the development of the British school of object relations through his mentorship of one of its principle proponents: Harry S. Guntrip, the protégé of Ronald Fairbairn and Donald Winnicott.

The following chapter has the fingerprints of Ray Anderson all over it, as Ray was my own theological mentor in its writing. The chapter is a revised chapter of my doctoral dissertation, *The Psychoanalytic Psychology and Theological Philosophy of Harry Guntrip* (1998),[4] of which Ray was a dissertation committee member. I have had the special privilege of Ray's mentorship that spans two decades back to my days sitting under his teaching in my courses at Fuller Theological Seminary in the early 1980s. It was there that I first had my "heart burn within me" as he spoke about *hermeneutical horizons*, of which I understood very little at the time, but had the inner sense that Ray's core values reflected a theology that touched the depth of human experience. I carried these core theological values that I took in from him into my clinical training in marriage and family therapy, as well as into my training as a psychoanalyst. The following work is an attempt to show the depth of Ray's influence in my development and growth.

The Place of the Personal in Psychoanalysis

The stereotype of psychoanalysis in America is probably best represented by the images courtesy of Woody Allen: the detached doctor who silently listened to Allen pontificate about his childhood as he lay on the couch. Perhaps most unfortunate is that this picture of psychoanalysis *has* been characteristic of the American tradition.

A significant development within the Independent Tradition of British Object Relations theory in psychoanalysis has been a derivative of the "personal object relations" between Harry S. Guntrip and his mentors.[5] Guntrip's elaboration of this tradition in psychology reflects his respective relationships with his psychoanalytic mentors, Ronald Fairbairn and Donald Winnicott, along with the "Persons in Relation" theological philosophy of John Macmurray as his unifying point of reference.

Guntrip was a champion of the *Personal* in psychoanalysis. His legacy is seen in the naming of his collected papers by his protégé, Hazell, as *Personal Relations Therapy*, [6]a more humanized version of the traditional "object relations" language. Guntrip himself was a protégé of John Macmurray, professor of Moral Philosophy at London University and later

---

[4] Trevor M. Dobbs, *The Psychoanalytic Psychology and Philosophical Theology of Harry S. Guntrip* (Dissertation: Newport Psychoanalytic Institute, 1998).
[5] Dobbs, 1998.
[6] Jeremy Hazel, ed., *Personal Relations Therapy: The Collected Papers of H. S. Guntrip*, (Northvale, NJ: Aronson, 1994).

at Edinburgh University. Volume II of Macmurray's Gifford lectures of 1954, *Persons in Relation,* is the capstone of three decades of writing and is the principal influence on Guntrip's theological-philosophical thinking. Guntrip traces his own development in stating,

> I found my earlier studies in religion and philosophy were by no means irrelevant. I had been thoroughly trained in a "personal relations" school of thought, not only in theology but in the philosophy of Professor J. Macmurray. Such books as J. Oman's *Grace and Personality,* Martin Buber's *I and Thou* and J. Macmurray's *Interpreting the Universe, The Boundaries of Science* and *Reason and Emotion* had left too deep a mark for me to be able to approach the study of man in any other way than as a "Person."[7]

Guntrip did not approach integration of these influences in his life as a harmonizing of disciplines, which he would have called "an artificial attempt to 'fit them together.'" His *personal* journey led him to his consulting room with patients, where for many years he was in the process of working out this blending of his theology, philosophy, and psychology of the person. Within the intimacy of the encounters with his patients, and in the form of "the natural emergence of a fully psychodynamic theory of personality within psychoanalysis," he digested and metabolized these various aspects of the human person.[8]

Macmurray's Influence on Guntrip's Thinking

Guntrip, in his doctoral dissertation, (later published as *Personality Structure and Human Interaction*), traces the development of psycho-analytical theory as "an unconscious pattern of development of a dialectical type." [9] "The original *European psychobiology* of Freud" is presented as this Hegelian *Thesis*: the classic psycho-analytical teaching. He then presents the *psychosociology* in America, including Horney, Fromm, and H. S. Sullivan as the *Antithesis* to the classical stance. Guntrip's *Synthesis* is his British object relational orientation that "comes to correlate the internal and the external object-relationships in which the personality is involved" (*emphasis* in the original).[10] This approach is a way to

---

7 Harry S. Guntrip, *Personality Structure And Human Interaction* (New York: International Universities Press, 1961), 19.
8 Ibid.
9 Ibid., 50.
10 Ibid., 51.

interrelate the internal, intrapsychic Freudian emphasis with the external, interpersonal one of the American schools.

Guntrip's first mentor in his journey down the path of his theoretical development was John Macmurray, Professor of Moral Philosophy during Guntrip's days at University College at London University. The object relational themes within Macmurray's philosophical teaching were to have a profound influence on Guntrip.

Harry Guntrip cited John Macmurray as the philosopher who had "thoroughly" trained him in the "personal relations" school of thought. Professor of Moral Philosophy at University College in London in the 1930s, and eventually at the University of Edinburgh in Scotland by the 1950s, Macmurray's teaching and writings in the 1930s came to provide Guntrip with a transitional space between what he referred to as his traditional, conservative Salvation Army heritage, and the liberal modern theology of the twentieth century, both of which Guntrip found wanting. Macmurray was addressing the philosophical development of the twentieth century western mind, with a particular focus on the respective characters of science and religion, and the relationship between the two. This he set out in a rather technical way in his *Interpreting the Universe* (1933) [11] and in a much more compelling fashion in his book published in 1935, *Reason and Emotion*.[12] A summary of his basic arguments from this latter work will lay out his principal philosophical viewpoint that shaped Guntrip's own thought and worldview.

In a series of what were originally lectures, Macmurray lays out his philosophical metapsychology under the rubric of "Reason in the Emotional Life, I, II, and III," followed by what would be considered his theory of technique, "Education of the Emotions." In the latter part of the book, he takes up directly the topic of what we might call "religion and its vicissitudes," as he develops his theological philosophy that would so strongly influenced Guntrip. He explores the nature and meaning of religion through its various comparisons with science, reason, reality, and his view of its maturity in contrast to the religious "superstition" so commonly practiced.

Reason in the Emotional Life

Macmurray begins with a critique of the individualism and egocentrism of the dominant intellectualized culture, positing that "we are all enmeshed in that network of relation that binds us together to make up human society," like it or not.[13] He goes on to develop this theme that Winnicott

---

11 John Macmurray, *Interpreting the Universe* (New York: Humanities Press, 1933).
12 John Macmurray, *Reason and Emotion* (London: Faber and Faber, 1935).
13 Ibid., 14.

would echo in his musing that "there is no such thing as a baby without a mother." Macmurray's version is that "we have no existence and no significance merely in ourselves."[14]

"What is emotional reason?" Macmurray asks. It is that which has been dissociated from the popular notion of reason as "thinking and planning, scheming and calculating," losing its connection to "music and laughter and love."[15]

> We associate reason with *a state of mind which is cold, detached and unemotional*. When our emotions are stirred we feel that reason is left behind and we enter another world - more colourful, more full of warmth and delight, but also more *dangerous*. If we become *ego-centric*, if we forget that we are parts of one small part of the development of human life, *we shall be apt to imagine* that this has always been so and always must be so; that reason is just thinking; that emotion is just feeling; and that these two aspects of our life are in the eternal nature of things distinct and opposite; *very apt to come into conflict and requiring to be kept sternly apart*. We shall be in danger of slipping back into a way of thinking from which we had begun to emerge; of thinking that emotion belongs to the animal nature in us, and reason to the divine; that our emotions are unruly and fleshly, the source of evil and disaster, while reason belongs to the divine essence of the thinking mind which raises us above the level of the brutes into communion with the eternal.[16]

What was it that so captured Guntrip's interest that he would identify Macmurray as playing such a central role in the development of his own thinking? Macmurray's style of writing is one which Guntrip himself would eventually emulate: a colorful and engaging prose that artfully communicates concepts that are normally discussed with abstract and mind-numbing technical language in their respective fields, philosophy and psychoanalysis. Yet I would offer that the stronger appeal was very personal as Macmurray essentially describes the schizoid landscape of western culture that Guntrip wrestled with as his own psychological self-experience. Guntrip, I believe, found in Macmurray the hope of transcending the qualities of *the cold, detached and unemotional* schizoid adaptation: the *egocentrism* of the withdrawn ego that engages in the use of the splitting of the ego to manage the internal conflict between good and bad objects by *keeping them sternly apart*. What Guntrip would

---

14 Ibid., 15.
15 Ibid.
16 Ibid., 16; emphasis added.

later jointly pursue with Fairbairn in the remaking of Freudian metapsychology was the redemption of the emotional "id" experience as *unruly* and portending *disaster* to that of a hungering after attachment to the object which was the experience of meaningful aliveness.

Macmurray continues his own treatise that would foreshadow Guntrip. He describes reason "in general" (both the intellectual and emotional dynamics), as that which differentiates humans from the rest of organic life, as reflected in the common notions of speech, the invention and use of tools, and the organization of social life. "Behind all these there lies the capacity to make a choice of purposes and to discover and apply the means of realizing our chosen ends."[17] Here he foreshadows his volume I of the Gifford Lectures in *The Self as Agent*,[18] which challenges the Cartesian "thinking 'I'" as intellectualized and narcissistic. "Against the assumption that the Self is an isolated individual, I have set the view that the Self is a *person*, and that personal existence is *constituted* by the relation of persons."[19] The "capacity to make a choice" has the ring of existentialism to it, yet Macmurray will hold out for the language of the "practical." He sums up this enterprise of the 1950s, read by Guntrip, in his introduction: "All meaningful knowledge is for the sake of action, and all meaningful action for the sake of friendship."[20] This line, penned two decades after *Reason and Emotion*, is a distillation of his earlier writings. Yet, let us continue with our exposition of the latter as it coincides with Guntrip's seminal development.

In his complementary fashion, Macmurray cites science, art, and religion as the central expressions of reason in man, with science reflecting its intellectual nature and art and religion reflecting its emotional one. Here he develops what is essentially his philosophical basis for object relations. "Reason is the capacity to behave in terms of the nature of the object, that is to say, objectively. Reason is thus our capacity for objectivity."[21] Macmurray critiques the one-person psychology that looks for "something in the inner constitution of the human being to explain the peculiar nature of his behavior."[22] He defines reason as the capacity to behave in terms of knowledge of the outside world, rather than merely as a reflex of one's own. Science, as that which gathers data about the object, reflects the intellectual side of the coin of reason. Yet science itself has its own form of countertransference, the "desire to retain beliefs to which we are emotionally attached to for some reason or other. It is the tendency to

---

17 Ibid., 18.
18 John Macmurrary, *The Self as Agent* (New York: Harper & Brothers, 1953).
19 Ibid., 12.
20 Ibid., 15.
21 John Macmurray, *Reason and Emotion* (London: Faber and Faber, 1935), 19.
22 Ibid., 20.

make the wish father to the thought. Science itself, therefore, is emotionally conditioned."[23] Macmurray essentially describes the projective process "where we colour the world with our own illusions," to which the intellectual enterprise is as susceptible as the emotional.[24] Thinking is as subjective as feeling. In gaining knowledge of the outside world, of the nature of the object, the painful process of *disillusionment* applies to thinking as well as feeling. The central problem is that of the tendency toward egocentrism which prefers the illusion of self-sufficiency over the painful awareness of one's need for connectedness to the outside world. Again, this echoes the schizoid dilemma of a desire for connection and the fear of engaging in it. Fairbairn would later take the dependency of the infantile state, and rather than make it something to be outgrown, dependency becomes that which one matures into, an echo of Macmurray's basic premise.

Macmurray goes on to develop this parallelism that both thought and feeling strive toward an objectivity that allows one to behave in light of the nature of the object. It is interesting that during this same decade Heinz Hartmann was developing his own version of this theme of *adaptation to the environment* yet in the rationalistic manner to which Guntrip would take such exception for many years. What would be the difference? Macmurray makes the process of observation of the outside world, the external object, one based on action, whose motives are ultimately emotional. He cites that he follows Plato in his *Republic* and *Philebus*, that not only thoughts but also feelings could be true or false. It is a false dichotomy that thoughts are *rational* and that feelings are *irrational*, secondary and subordinate to cognitions. Macmurray ultimately takes a stance of embodiment toward the nature of reason. "For if reason is the capacity to *act* in terms of the nature of the object, it is emotion which stands directly behind activity determining its substance and direction, while thought is related to action indirectly and through emotion, determining only its form, and that only partially."[25] Thought ultimately becomes a form of reflection on the existential act that arises from one's (e)motives.

Macmurray turns to the issue of psychoanalysis directly, citing its contribution in revealing the extent to which our emotional life is unconscious. He takes a rather Winnicottian tack at this point, noting that "psychoanalysis has only extended and developed a knowledge which we all possess."[26] In the same way that Winnicott saw that all mothers knew

---

23 Ibid., 21.
24 Ibid., 22.
25 Ibid., 26.
26 Ibid., 27.

intuitively what it meant to hold and care for their child,[27] Macmurray presents this same sort of intuitive approach toward the functioning of the emotional life. Bringing this intuitive, emotional world into awareness is the daunting task undertaken by psychoanalysis but common to all for emotional development to occur. He draws out his thread of *egocentrism* as the confounding variable to development, which affects both thinking and feeling. This essentially is the narcissism of the *paranoid-schizoid* position of British Object Relations, where one *assimilates* one's experience of the outside world and reshapes it to fit one's internal world. Here the nature of the outside object is distorted to spare one the pain of the *disillusionment* of realizing where it is different from one's internal object representation. "The real problem of the development of emotional reason is to shift the center of feeling from the self to the world outside. We can only begin to grow up into rationality when we begin to see our own emotional life not as the center of things but as part of the development of humanity."[28] The process of emotional development is that of *accommodating* our current model of the world to the nature of the outside object in order to act toward it based upon its actual nature, rather than our projection upon it. Macmurray is essentially describing the development of the capacity for empathy, which he illustrates as learning to "appreciate" art as expressions of the artist's essential being, rather than evoking some form of aesthetic "pleasure" that narcissistically leaves us in an isolated state. He concludes with making a differentiation between notions of "love" that are essentially experiencing a pleasurable emotion that is stimulated by the other person, and that of "appreciating" the person for who he or she is in their own right. "Is he an instrument for keeping me pleased with myself, or do I feel his existence and his reality to be important in themselves? The difference between these two kinds of love is the ultimate difference between organic and personal life. It is the difference between rational and irrational emotion. The capacity to love objectively is the capacity which makes us persons."[29]

Education of the Emotional Life

Macmurray addresses what is essentially the clinical application of his thesis in the context of education. He seems to take a page from what Bion would later call in his book *Learning from Experience*,[30] as he uses the organic senses as his schoolhouse for the education of the emotional life. He takes pains to develop the idea of *sensuality* as the perceptual gathering

---

[27] D.W. Winnicott, *Babies and Their Mothers*, (Reading, PA: Addison-Wesley, 1987).
[28] John Macmurray, *Reason and Emotion* (London: Faber and Faber, 1935), 30.
[29] Ibid., 32.
[30] Wilfred Bion, *Learning From Experience* (London: Heinemann, 1962; Karnac, 1984).

of data from the outside world, much in the same way that Carl Jung described it in his *Psychological Types*.[31] Jung's category of *perception* entails the dominant use of one or the other side of a psychological polarity, apprehending the (external) object world with either *Intuition* or *Sensing*. Intuition is the perceptual process of apprehending the "bigger picture" through mental mapping, while Sensing is the perceptual process of ascertaining "facts" through sensory input.[32] Ironically, Macmurray earlier described a rather intuitive process of apprehending the emotional life in general, yet his methodology is patently empirical. On the one hand, he substitutes the word *sensibility* for *sensuality* in order specifically to avoid the popular shameful connotations of the latter, but on the other hand, his choice of *sensibility* seems to me to reflect his integrative style of thinking where *sensing* takes on a rather *intuitive* character. Here again I see the appeal to a Guntrip whose interest in integration of polarities would resonate with Macmurray.

Macmurray notes that the normal sensibility of Europeans is "underdeveloped and irrational because of the way we have treated it," that is, the egocentric focus on satisfaction of the senses, rather than using the senses as "the avenues along which we move into contact with the world around us."[33] He champions sense-life as the fundamental source to fullness and richness in life, providing "the material out of which the inner life is built."[34] Here the object relations theme of Guntrip's use of both Fairbairn and Winnicott stand out in bold relief. Guntrip's basic stance that all psychological roads lead to schizoid phenomena and the earliest oral experiences of "swallowing" up life can be seen in Macmurray's version of the introjection process. That the human is primarily object-seeking rather than pleasure-seeking is central to Macmurray's whole enterprise. The sensual experience of the infant with the mother was even better illustrated through Winnicott's descriptions as his development of the idea of "body ego" echoes Macmurray's sensibilities. Indeed, Macmurray waxes very "Winnicottian" in his own language as he develops this theme. Rather than employing utilitarian motives of applying "awareness" of the world for purposeful striving, Macmurray argues for sense awareness "for the sake of awareness itself," in order to "use them in a different and fuller way."

> We look at things not because we want to use them but because we want to see them. We touch things because we want to feel

---

[31] C. G. Jung, C. G., Psychological Types. In R.F.C. Hull (Trans.), *The Collected Works of C.G. Jung* (Vol. 6). (Princeton: Princeton University Press, 1971). (Original work published 1921).
[32] Kiersey & Bates, *Please Understand Me* (Corona Del Mar: Prometheus Nemesis Books,1978).
[33] John Macmurray, *Reason and Emotion* (London: Faber and Faber, 1935), 39.
[34] Ibid., 40.

them. Sensitive awareness becomes then a life in itself with an intrinsic value of its own which we maintain and develop for its own sake, because it is a way of living, perhaps the essence of all living. When we use our senses in this way, we come alive in them, as it were, and this opens up a whole new world of possibility. We see and hear and feel things that we never noticed before, and find ourselves taking delight in their existence. We find ourselves living in our senses for love's sake, because the essence of love lies in this. . . . You don't want merely to know about the object; often you don't want to know about it at all. What you do want is to know *it*. Intellectual knowledge tells us about the world. It gives us knowledge *about* things, not knowledge *of* them. It does not reveal the world as it is. Only emotional knowledge can do that.[35]

The complement to the immediacy of sensuous perception is that of spontaneous expression, "activities which are spontaneities of emotion, activities which are performed for their own sake, and not for any end beyond them."[36] These are words which Winnicott could have written himself. In his own turn of phrase, Winnicott coins the term "spontaneous gesture" of the infant and essentially of the person as that which expressed one's "true self." This seems very reminiscent of Macmurray's view of emotional life and the sensual apparatus through which such aliveness emanates.

Macmurray also offers a theological illustration of his treatise on the "sense-life" in a New Testament quote. "'I am come', said Jesus, 'that they might have life, and that they might have it more abundantly.' The abundance of our life depends primarily on the abundance of our sensuous experience of the world around us. If we are to be full of life and fully alive, it is the increase in our capacity to be aware of the world through our senses which has first to be achieved."[37] This sounds rather similar to the words that Fairbairn wrote in his diary entry during his college days, his own lobbying for a "full blooded Christianity." We shall now turn to Macmurray's specific description of "religion" and how it reflects the emotional rationality of humans.

Science and Religion

"For centuries, until relatively recent time, the pride and prejudice of religion tyrannized over the minds and consciences and even the bodies of

---

35 Ibid., 42-43.
36 Ibid., 73.
37 Ibid., 40.

men." So begins Macmurray's treatment of religion. He goes on to chronicle essentially the development of what he calls "religious imperialism, under the pseudonym of Christianity."[38] He describes the tradition of Jesus as having flowed into the vast organization of the Roman empire, mixed with Stoicism, and ultimately adopting the Roman tradition of empire in pursuing "universal domination over the spirit of civilized humanity."[39] The medieval spirit was the culmination of suppression of personal freedom, whose limits were reached in the Renaissance and Reformation. "The rediscovery of the art of Greece awakened the medieval spirit to the artistic spontaneity of the Renaissance, which in turn led to the rediscovery of the religious spontaneity of Jesus in the Reformation."[40] The "vast tissue of prejudice" that was Christianity was set on a course of disintegration, with the "continuous disruption of Protestantism into sectarian fragments" burning up like a meteor on reentry to the atmosphere of the earth. Macmurray cites science as the one creative achievement of the Reformation, "the one proper, positive expression of Christianity that the world has yet seen. The rest of modern culture--its art, morality, and religion--is simply the disrupted remnants of the pseudo-Christianity of the Medieval world. That is why the newly awakened pagan world clutches at our science while scorning our culture."[41] He describes an ongoing competition between the Roman and Protestant camps as the aftermath of the disruptive force of the Reformation, each competing for the re-establishment of the old autocracy. Control over the "inner springs of human life" was the "nut" over which the two sides have battled, with science, as the Reformation's child, being neglected by both. ". . . [W]hen science, come of age, entered upon the stage as arbiter of the dispute, it was only to crack the nut, give either party half of the shell and keep the kernel for himself."[42] Macmurray further illustrates his disgust for authoritarian structures in describing the religious system's attempt at rigid control over philosophy and science, and describes its ultimate demise and arrival at a form of impotence, the turning point being the loss of the battle over evolution, religion's "Waterloo" as it were. By the end of the nineteenth century, science was supreme, triumphing over the jealousy, fear, and superstition bred by medieval religion. "But it is difficult to fight an enemy who uses such underground methods without learning to use them oneself." [43] In the same way that Anna Freud was to describe the child who is abused as one who will "identify with the aggressor" as

---

38 Ibid., 171.
39 Ibid.
40 Ibid., 172.
41 Ibid.
42 Ibid., 173.
43 Ibid., 174.

part of its survival, the same is said to have happened to this child of the Reformation.

> In the hour of its triumph science has become as full of pride and prejudice as ever religion was. . . . There is nothing like pride for blinding us to our own limitations, driving us to assert as truth what is only our own speculative opinion, . . . Modern science is very liable to superstition, and tends to breed superstition in its devotees. The visionary dream of the medieval church of a universal empire over the hearts of mankind, purified by obedience and submission, was not so madly irrational as the modern dream of a world made peaceful and happy by obedience to the dictates of scientific thought."[44]

Macmurray gives a number of examples of this parallelism between science and religion, citing "pride and prejudice" as the ultimate culprits and the "parents of superstition." Macmurray's theme of *narcissism* seems to be the unifying one here, differentiating both science and religion in essence from their popular manifestations as authoritarian institutions. Macmurray fits so very well with the spirit of the *Independent* tradition in England.

His discussion echoes the one between Sigmund Freud and his friend the pastor, Oscar Pfister, where Freud critiqued "religion" as simple obsessional neurosis in *The Future of An Illusion*.[45] Pfister's friendly rejoinder in *The Illusion of the Future* presented essentially the same counterpoint as Macmurray, that faith in technology and science, even psychoanalytic science, as promising a brighter future was a neurotic illusion about the nature of being human. Macmurray's ultimate goal is to root out the superstition that he has already defined as irrational egocentrism. "Superstition is not religion because it masquerades in the cloak of religion; neither is it science because it masks itself in scientific terminology."[46]

Macmurray rejects a harmonization between science and religion by assigning them to separate spheres. "Science and religion are not logical definitions. They are forces in the world of men, and in the minds of men. The struggle between science and religion goes on in us, and it is a real struggle, a dramatic struggle, often a tragic struggle. . . . It is a deep seated *schism* in the personal life of every intelligent modern man who

---

44 Ibid., 174-175.
45 In W. W.Meissner, *Psychoanalysis and Religious Experience* (New Haven: Yale University Press, 1984).
46 John Macmurray, *Reason and Emotion* (London: Faber and Faber, 1935), 176.

wishes to be honest and sincere with himself."[47] He goes on at length in describing the tension between the two, where choosing one over the other is another example of "pride and prejudice," and to want to look at problems from both sides merely restates the problem and does not solve it. "It is as difficult a problem as the combination of the Wave theory of light with the Quantum theory of energy."[48] Here Macmurray cites the classic paradox of the twentieth century where two "truths" of a common phenomenon cannot be reduced down to a common denominator or synthesis, an irreconcilable polarity of the modern world. Ironically as one who has philosophically championed Plato to a degree, Macmurray opposes the common neo-Platonist dualism so characteristic of western culture that separates the "spiritual" and the "material." "Both meet in the mind of man, and demand to be related. . . . Science and religion are not concerned with two different worlds but with one and the same world--the only world there is."[49] His ultimate common denominator for the two is to see them both as truth-seekers. "All honest religion necessarily involves a strenuous effort to know the supreme reality, and the knowledge of God must involve all knowledge in its scope."[50]

Macmurray applies a form of analysis, breaking down condensations into elemental parts, a form of theological form criticism: finding the "nut" within the "shell." His goal is to compare "essential religion" with "essential science." On the one hand, he sees science ultimately as "fragmentary," a collection of specializations whose methodology is to "analyze and classify" in abstract terms in order to identify general laws. On the other hand, religion is unitary (like philosophy), seeking an at-one-ment with one God, through a methodology of the "concrete" that examines the wholeness of the individual, and is meant to be "always personal."[51] Of particular note is the relationship to reality itself.

> Science, though it may know everything in general, can know nothing in particular, and reality is always something in particular. It follows that science is not knowledge of reality. Is that startling? It is a commonplace of much philosophy, from Plato to the present day. . . . Science is descriptive, not explanatory. . . . Knowledge is by definition the apprehension of the real--not the description of it. . . . I do not say that it is not cognition, but simply that it is not knowledge in the full sense.

---

47 Ibid., 177-178.
48 Ibid., 179.
49 Ibid., 180.
50 Ibid., 183.
51 Ibid., 185-186.

For example, you cannot know anybody, your father or your friend, by science.[52]

For Macmurray, knowledge is ultimately *personal* and must apprehend far more than the data of organic existence, but must embrace all that goes into making up a *person*, which ultimately involves that which is *unseen*, that which technically speaking is *spiritual* (the Greek word for spirit, *pneuma*, literally means "wind" or "air"). The classic theological illustration of this personal knowledge is the Hebrew rendering from Genesis that "Adam *knew* (*yada*) his wife," and she conceived. Macmurray's concept of *knowing* is intimate and personal, and therefore requires the *religious viewpoint* as he defines it.

Reason and Religion

Macmurray continues his development of his object relations philosophy. Religion is one of the three general expressions of rationality, along with art and science, where rationality is defined as "objective consciousness" through the perceptive methodology of sensory apprehension as delineated above. This is only possible, he writes, "in beings who stand in conscious relationship to objects which they know and which are not themselves."[53] Macmurray essentially presupposes a developmental level that reflects at least a basic self-other differentiation, what Winnicott would later call "the first Not-Me possession" of the external object. He describes three general fields or types of external objects: "material objects, living creatures, or persons like ourselves."[54] These correspond to his threefold expression of rationality. "Science grows out of our rationality in relation to material things. Art grows out of our relation to living beings. Religion grows out of our relation to persons."[55] Religious institutions and beliefs in themselves may be required to be swept away in the interest of religion itself which is inherent in the human situation. He sees religion as the fuller expression of rationality as it subsumes all three of the fields. The relation of a person to a person also includes the relation of a body to a body and of living creature to living creature. This position would follow in light of Macmurray's use of the sensual (body) as the apprehension of the object, and his focus on wholeness requiring a living creature rather than a dissected one. He is careful to point out that he does not mean "more rational," just more inclusive or a "fuller" expression of rationality.

---

52 Ibid., 187-188.
53 Ibid., 195.
54 Ibid.
55 Ibid., 196.

He describes the appropriate use of science: to relate ourselves "properly to matter, and use it as our material and our instrument. Science is the sign that we have learned not to pretend that matter is what we would like it to be, . . . that we have learned that a patient effort to discover its real nature and to deal with it in terms of its real nature will give us power to use it as our instrument. Through science we relate ourselves *really*, as material bodies, to the material world."[56] Art is the medium through which we would relate ourselves to the organic world with "a pressure toward balance and rhythm and harmony, toward functional relationship," a rationality of the instinctual and emotional life.[57]

The religious field of personal relationships has the drive "to achieve equality and fellowship in the relations of persons."[58] Macmurray purposely defines religion without any reference to God. "The idea of God can have no fixed meaning of its own which is not related to our experience of human relationships; and it is the significance of the term to the persons who use it that matters."[59] Macmurray essentially goes on to critique the "God-talk" of society who "has crystallized a conception of God which is false, [where] the professed atheist may be more truly religious than the theist." [60] He invokes Kant as an ally in this endeavor to differentiate "false self" representations of religion from its essential enactment in genuine human interaction. "Kant is a milestone in the development of rational thought, and a giant among the intellectuals; yet he announced his great work as '*destroying reason to make room for faith*,' and dubbed the process of reason '*a dialectic of illusion.*'"[61] Macmurray here summons support for his own attack on "the arid speculations of the rationalists" in favor of the "experimental empiricism" of science which he touts as "the secret of its own superb rationality."[62] In short, Macmurray ends up with a form of natural religion, where one finds God on the planet rather than looking to the heavens, yet he does not appear to don the apparel of the more popular natural religion of the Enlightenment which saw God's fingerprints on the structure and design of the natural order. He seems to relegate that to the scientific and aesthetic realms without disputing their forms of rationality. Macmurray ultimately comes down on the side of a form of *incarnational* thinking, where it is within the particularly human sphere of interactions between persons that God shows his face. "In particular the really religious man will define the nature

---

56 Ibid., 202-203.
57 Ibid., 204.
58 Ibid., 205.
59 Ibid., 207.
60 Ibid.
61 Ibid., 208.
62 Ibid.

of God, not in terms of analysis of ideas or of transcendental beliefs, but in terms of his empirical knowledge of human relationships. So Jesus is reported to have said: 'He that hath seen me hath seen the Father, and how sayest thou, then, show us the Father.'"[63]

The Maturity of Religion

The "Maturity of Religion" was a theme of Macmurray's that was to make a significant impact on another member of the British school of psychoanalysis: Neville Symington. In his *Emotion and Spirit: Questioning the Claims of Psychoanalysis and Religion*, (1994), Symington gives his own account of the movement of religion from *primitive* to *mature*, taking a rather eastern slant in championing the detachment model of the *Upanishads* as his organizing principle. He describes Macmurray's "natural religion" as a "Socratic religion in the context of our contemporary world."[64] He essentially is referring to the Socrates "we meet in the dialogues of Plato."[65] He sees Socrates as a co-confrontor along with the Buddha and Jesus as challengers of primitive religion, which Symington describes as the "projection of the self as agent--the representational self--into the natural world or the imagined natural world."[66] Driven by the Darwinian survival instinct and paralleled by the Kleinian vision of the *paranoid position* as defined by the same process, he contrasts this with *mature religion*, the anthropological change which is marked by "burying ones dead," characterizing "the birth of the *representational self*, . . . [where] a being in its own right has died, not just a fragment of the tribe."[67] Symington reflects the Kleinian-Winnicottian developmental shift from the *paranoid position* to the *depressive position*, or in Winnicott's turn of phrase, developing the *capacity for concern*, where one becomes aware of one's own agency, the power to make an impact on the world, and the capacity to mourn loss rather than fear attack as coming always from the outside. Symington joins Macmurray in criticizing "rites, sacrifices and votive offerings," whether Buddhist or Christian, as essentially a primitive religion of placating the gods "out there" from a paranoid developmental stance.[68] Symington's version of mature religion parts company to a degree with Macmurray, however, as his emphasis is on a much more mystical detachment from narcissism, citing that the Christian mystics were "more spiritual men than Jesus," in contrast to Macmurray's patently

---

63 Ibid., 210.
64 Neville Symington, *Emotion and Spirit: Questioning the Claims of Psychoanalysis and Religion*, (New York: Harpers, 1994), 43.
65 Ibid., 37.
66 Ibid., 7.
67 Ibid., 10.
68 Ibid., 12.

interpersonal view.[69] Symington sees Macmurray as Socratic in that the "religion of Socrates differs from that of the Buddha and Jesus in that it resulted from a process of reasoning."[70] This would reflect Macmurray's organizing principle of rationality. Symington makes the greatest use of Macmurray in the movement from use of the object for self-gratification, to that of valuing the other to the point of recognizing that the human world has a claim upon us because each of us has a value which demands recognition. Macmurray (1936) says,

> The primary fact is that part of the world of common experience for each of us is the rest of us. We are forced to value one another, and the valuation is reciprocal. The recognition that the 'other' has a claim on me is the religious attitude of mind, and the inner signal of this claim is conscience.[71]

"Socrates said this claim is exerted upon me by the good. Macmurray puts this into a modern perspective by stating that the good is in the other, or that the good is immanent in other human beings, and that this has a claim upon my actions," with God symbolizing this claim. Symington prefers the notion of "Ultimate Reality as comprehended in the Upanishads, which is in me as well as the other."[72] This would appear to fit better with the dual intrapsychic *and* interpersonal view of object relations. He then makes his application to psychoanalysis as the field of concern with "that emotional activity of which we are unaware," that which occurs between people as well as "within the frontiers of the self." Psychoanalysis' aim is to "transform activity which is invisible and destructive into that which is constructive."[73]

In sum, Macmurray facilitated in Guntrip the articulation of a new direction in his pursuit of freedom from the imprisonment within his intellectualized-schizoid, personal world, one that was given theological structure and reinforcement during his days in the Salvation Army. The promise of "aliveness" spoken of by Macmurray was one that he also did not find within the modernist theology of his Congregational ministry training per se, as it also suffered from a different form of Hegelian "imprisonment in the 'I'." Macmurray's passionate philosophy of personal relations freed up Guntrip "intellectually" to continue his quest of apprehending this aliveness in his own person, which he pursued in his personal therapy with Ronald Fairbairn, and later with Donald Winnicott.

---

69 Ibid., 14.
70 Ibid., 37.
71 Ibid., 43.
72 Ibid., 44.
73 Ibid.

Ray Anderson cites Macmurray in illustrating his incarnational approach to ministry as one that requires our emotions being "directed toward the objective reality of other persons. Even the emotions and feelings that are most closely related to my self are given objective and rational status when integrated into my shared life with others."[74] Ray's mentorship of my dissertation has been my own "shared life" with him that helped give "aliveness" to the scholarly, intellectual work of doctoral study. Thank you, Ray, for sharing this with me.

---

74 Ray S. Anderson, *Christians Who Counsel: The Vocation of Wholistic Therapy* (Pasadena: Fuller Seminary Press, 1990), 148.

Willie James Jennings

Speaking in Tongues: Language, Nationalism, and the Formation of Church Life

What, in the face of the proliferating chronicles of human barbarity, would it mean to seek to contrive a pastoral and permanently innocent ethnic or racial identity? What is at stake in the desire to find an entirely pure mode of particularized being, and to make it the anchor for a unique culture that is not just historically or contingently divorced from the practice of evil but permanently fortified against that very possibility by its essential constitution?

Paul Gilroy[1]

[T]o be biracial – a cognitive and physical process of *being* in the world – in, and as a result of, a race conscious society, is *to be* an interruption, to *represent* a contestation, and *to undermine* the authority of classification.

Katya Gibel Azoulay[2]

They were amazed and in astonishment exclaimed, "Surely these people who are speaking are all Galileans! How is it that each of us can hear them in his own native language? [A]ll of us hear them speaking in our own tongues the great things God has done." They were all amazed and perplexed, saying to one another, "What can this mean?"

Acts 2:7, 11 (REB)

The Spirit that comes to the church comes out of the future, not the past.

Ray S. Anderson[3]

"Good theology is always on the verge of preaching," I recall Ray S. Anderson saying in class one day. But Dr. Anderson never needed to say that because his lectures always embodied gospel. Such embodiment marks a scholar as a

---

[1] *Against Race: Imagining Political Culture Beyond the Color Line* (Cambridge, Mass.: Belknap Press, 2000), 230.
[2] *Black, Jewish and Interracial: Its Not the Color of Your Skin but the Race of Your Kin, and Other Myths of Identity* (Durham, NC: Duke University Press, 1997), 188.
[3] "The Praxis of the Spirit & A Theology of Liberation," in *The Shape of Practical Theology: Empowering Ministry with Theological Praxis* (Downers Grove, IIL.: InterVarsity Press, 2001), 105.

theologian, and Ray S. Anderson is a theologian of the first order and a teacher of the church par excellence. The fundamental difference between Dr. Anderson and most scholars who teach and write theology is that Ray understands what it means to think theologically and knows how to bring people into the ancient practice of Christian theological reflection. This is why Ray S. Anderson is one of the most significant theologians ever born in America. I learned from Ray that theology is meant for the streets. True Christian theology orientates us toward God's work in the world through Jesus Christ. Good theology takes the world seriously because it takes Jesus Christ seriously as God's enfleshment in the world. I have taken to heart this advice of a master theologian. So I offer my reflections on a serious matter of the world--nationalism, national conflict, and the life of the church. If indeed good theology is on the verge of preaching, then I may be on solid ground in this essay because it grows out of a sermon preached in York Chapel at the Divinity School of Duke University. It is altogether fitting that I offer this reflection based on a sermon to one who is a fine preacher himself and who taught so many theologians to preach!

A good portion of my teenage years was spent in a Pentecostal church that believed strongly in the importance of speaking in tongues. The one great and constant refrain of the pastor and members of that church was that speaking in tongues was the evidence of the Holy Spirit. Although I respectfully disagreed with my Pentecostal pastor that it was the *only* evidence, I have come to believe that that pastor and church were onto something very important. Speaking in tongues is important for us! It is important for us for reasons that I don't think we often realize.

In this essay I would like to suggest that speaking in tongues is a far more important symbolic bodily practice than has been indicated within intra-Pentecostal or extra-Pentecostal discussions. By bodily practice I am not referring primarily to an individual Christian who speaks in tongues. Bodily practice in this sense refers to an ecclesial (communal) practice that is a crucial signature of life together as a church. Speaking in tongues is a crucial symbolic bodily practice in a way that is rarely recognized by those involved in or familiar with Pentecostalism. In no way do I wish to seem dismissive or disrespectful of those Christian communities that understand speaking in tongues as crucial to their worship life, individually or corporately. My suggestion in this essay is that speaking in tongues offers up a crucial definition of Christian community that speaks to some of the most important issues of culture, race, and belonging that we face today.

Those issues have to do with (1) how we envision our deepest commitments to people, to causes, to needs; (2) how we imagine the claims our people(s) ethnic, political, social, familial make on us; and (3) how we understand God to make claim on our lives. I contend that Acts, chapter 2 offers us an outline for addressing these questions. This passage of Scripture does this in a way that we contemporary readers of Scripture profoundly resist. The reason for our resistance is straightforward. The kind of politic Acts 2 announces would put us as the church at risk in any nation-state and make us potential traitors to our own peoples.

The Day of Pentecost and The Great Reversal

The Day of Pentecost narrated in Acts 2 is the great reversal of the demise of the Tower of Babel (a demise registered in Genesis 11:1-9). Walter Brueggemann, in his comments on this passage in his *Genesis* commentary, echoes a fairly common Christian refrain in interpretation.

> The Pentecost text is, of course, placed at the beginning of Acts. The history of the church begins in a new language community where human speech is possible. On the one hand, the new community in Acts 2 regarded its differences of language as no threat or danger, in contrast to the fear of Gen. 11:4. On the other hand, it sought no phony, autonomous unity. It was content with the unity willed by God without overcoming all the marks of scatteredness. And so a new eon begins.[4]

Brueggeman suggests that the emphasis in reading Acts 2 should fall on the act of hearing rather than speaking. Indeed, he surmises that the newness announced in Acts 2 might be "a fresh capacity to listen" that creates a "new language-situation of the faithful community" (104). Brueggeman builds on a long exegetical tradition in the church in giving deep theological substance to this Babel-Pentecost reversal. However I wish to suggest the point of reversal also has a more immediate locus, Acts 1 and the wishes and words of Jesus' disciples.

What takes place in Acts 2 is a direct response to a question that the disciples put to Jesus in chapter one. Jesus had risen from the horrific death administered through Roman techniques of torture. As he prepared to ascend to heaven, the disciples asked him, "Is now the time that you will restore [political and military] sovereignty to Israel?" Is it now that we will determine our own destiny, a destiny freed from these Roman oppressors? The disciples sought a restoration [Gk. *apokathistano*] for the nation of Israel that would be bound to Jesus' resurrection [Gk. *anastasis*]. The question of the disciples is paradigmatic of the religious hope of every people that experience violence at the hands of an oppressing nation. Can bodily resurrection be useful for national self-determination? Can resurrection be useful for a nation-state? The disciples' question was simply and quite symbolically powerful—*Risen* Jesus, is it now *our* time to rule?

---

4 (Atlanta: John Knox Press, 1982), 104.

The irony of this question often escapes us. This was the question of the disciples of Jesus. Jesus' disciples had seen him heal the sick and cast out demons. These sick and demon-possessed people were both within Israel as well as outsiders to Israel, that is, the *Goyim*, Gentiles. The disciples witnessed part of the conversation between Jesus and the Samaritan woman at the well. The disciples were there as Jesus worked among Israel's traitors and outcasts. Yet this question remained in their hearts and neither Jesus' death nor resurrection life could dislodge the question of national or ethnic power. But so as not to miss the point with these disciples, their question is vicarious. This is also the question of every people, every nation, and every ethnic group. When will our sovereignty as a nation, an ethnic group, as a people be established or re-established? When will it be our time to rule?

The disciples of Jesus show us the desire of the nations rooted in the claim of belonging to any people group. Israel is critically important in grasping the nature of this desire. Indeed, as T.F. Torrance suggested many years ago, the story of biblical Israel is one of struggle to live into its laic destiny.[5] That is to say, while Israel exists in this world as just any other ethnic group (from the eyes of other nations) Israel is called to live as the people [Gk. *laos*] of God, a people elected to a destiny in God. That destiny was and is to witness the claim of God on all people. In Scripture, God is working in this world through Israel to enable the people(s) of the world to acknowledge him as the one true Creator who has claimed all people. Israel's ethnic drama reaches a climax in the disciples' question to Jesus. The question rehearses a history of pain at the hand of oppressor-nations and a desire to be like other nations. We wish to rule ourselves! If the disciples throughout Jesus' ministry re-presented Israel in bodily form, then this question suggests that the resurrection had a limited impact on Israel. This is not to say the resurrection is unimportant. Nor am I trivializing the resurrection. The bodily resurrection of Jesus only intensifies the burning question—When will we rule? This question was asked of a Risen Jesus. I would suggest that the question is powerful and ubiquitous, because it comes out of the desire of the nations. We have always lived in the midst of the desires of nations and peoples for power, power to control their own destiny. This desire is all around us. It is inescapable for us and it was thrown into the face of Jesus. Jesus, when will you restore *your people* to power?

Jesus responds to this question by inserting the divine prerogative between the disciples and their proto-nationalism.

> It is not for you to know times or seasons which the Father has fixed by his own authority. But you shall receive power when

---

5 *Theology in Reconstruction* (Grand Rapids, Mich.: Eerdmans, 1965), 196.

the Holy Spirit has come upon you; and you shall be my witnesses in Jerusalem and in all Judea and Samaria and to the end of the earth (Acts 1:7-8).

The divine prerogative has God's own life as its source. Jesus yields to the authority of the Father and announces a new order of power located in the coming of the Holy Spirit. Jesus' response was simple; "Wait until the Spirit comes upon you, comes upon your bodies." Wait (Tarry!). The disciples wanted power and Jesus told them, "When the Spirit comes on you, you will receive power." This waiting disrupts nationalistic or ethnic desire. The waiting repositions the disciples within the action of the triune God presented by the risen Jesus. The waiting inaugurates the reversal of the desire of the nations, a desire lodged deeply in the heart of Jesus' disciples.

If these words noted in Acts 1 inaugurated the reversal, then Acts 2 narrates the reversal of the desire of the nations. The Spirit did indeed come and the disciples did indeed receive power. But the power they received was strange power. The power of the Spirit works in the opposite way to the power of nations or peoples or cultic and ethnic groups. When the Holy Spirit came upon their bodies they spoke in tongues. And all those gathered in Jerusalem, from everywhere in the known world, heard them speak in their native language. Each person heard his or her own language. The great reversal is one of desire. The desire of a nation or people for power and self-determination becomes transformed into a desire for the nations. It becomes a desire for becoming one with the nations. That desire must be registered in language.

Language and The Desire for the Nations

Language is the first and foremost signature of empire.[6] The colonialists understood this too well. Wherever they extended their hand the first task was to demand the natives *submit* to the languages of the empire, the languages of the enlightened species: Spanish, German, French, Dutch, and English. Then the colonialists crushed or suppressed the native languages. Why the language? If they could change the language, then they could change the native. Once they changed the way indigenous peoples spoke of their world, their food, their clothes, their relationships, even the way they spoke of their own bodies, they changed the way they saw their

---

[6] John Willinsky, "Language, Nation, World," in *Learning to Divide the World: Education at Empire's End* (Minneapolis: University of Minnesota Press, 1988), 189-211. Also see Benjamin Harshav, *Language in the Time of Revolution* (Stanford, California: Stanford University, Press, 1993).

world. The colonialist changed the world of the native.7 Grammar has always been about guerilla warfare.

Language has always been serious business. Your language announces the world you inhabit. The tongue you speak announces what people make a claim on your very life. Anyone who submits to another people's language is allowing their life to be interrupted. Whether by choice or circumstance, submitting your life to a tongue different from your native language alters your life, changes your path in life. There is a deep connection between language and kingdom, language and empire building. Today, empire building continues. All over the world peoples are being forced to submit to English as the essential language of commerce. There is a tower of Babel being built all around us.

On the day of Pentecost, however, God's people received power. They received power not to build nations but the power to heal nations. It is all about language. The disciples where clothed in languages not their own. We must underscore the significance of this divine action. The language given from heaven was the language of the nations. Through speaking in tongues the disciples of Jesus are brought into worlds not of their own making. They had no choice. This was God's doing. The disciples would not have chosen tongues foreign to their own. Their concern was the restoration of Israel, but God's concern was the re-creation of the world in the Son. The disciples were made to submit to languages and (worlds represented by those languages) worlds not their own, not of their own choosing.

The importance of this submission is exactly what we contemporary readers of Acts 2 often bypass in interpretation and resist in application. Speaking in tongues is an embodied activity. The *disciples of Jesus* speak in tongues. This signature of Holy Spirit baptism disrupts identity. The peoples from the nations gathered in Jerusalem hear their own native languages coming out of the mouths of foreigners, strangers to their worlds (Gk. *ta idia dialekto hamon en haegennathamen*. Acts 2:8b).

Clearly, all those gathered in Jerusalem already shared a fundamental point of belonging—they are part of Israel. They are with these Galileans bearers of covenant with God. Yet the presence of the disciples of Jesus speaking in tongues becomes a question to the other nations. Thus the reversal is complete. The question of national self-determination or ethnic authority transforms through the presence of the Holy Spirit into a new question. Why are Galileans speaking our languages? Through language, the disciples of Jesus become a question to the other nations of their own existence. The ramifications of this embodied speech act are revolutionary.

---

7 Eric Cheyfitz, *The Poetics of Imperialism: Translation and Colonization from The Tempest to Tarzan* (Philadelphia: University of Penn. Press, 1997), 59-82.

The submission to the languages of the nation, witnessed in this text, comes before the call to repentance. The call to the world to repent only comes after the disciples yield to the Holy Spirit and submit. Before the world can be invited to a life of repentance, Jesus' disciples must submit to its languages. But this has been our point of resistance. Indeed Acts 2 is commonly interpreted in profoundly segregationist ways. Preachers and teachers alike often interpret the event of speaking in tongues either as an intra-Jewish announcement of restoration or as symbolizing inclusion of the nations in the way of salvation in Jesus. Both interpretative trajectories are meaningful. Yet both trajectories move too quickly past the transformative moment of the world speaking through these Galileans. Their identity becomes confused by divine fiat. They are turned toward the world and joined to it as if they were the world's sacrament.

Jesus' disciples speak in tongues and ethnic boundaries get disrupted. The place of disruption is in their very bodies. They witness the world joined to a Jewish hope realized in Jesus. Speaking in tongues, I would suggest, does not primarily signify Jewish restoration or Gentile inclusion. It signifies a fundamental confusion of ethnic identity. The Holy Spirit enables this confusion, and it does not mean eradication. This confusion must precede restoration or inclusion. This act of confusion is a direct challenge to segregationist mentalities.

The Far Country: America the Segregated

Segregationist mentalities have always been powerfully at work in America. It does not require elaborate sociological analysis to conclude that Jim Crow "separate but equal" thinking is deeply engrained in the collective psyche and the collective imaginations of Americans. The vast majority of churches in America operate in homogeneous visions of ministry—that is, ministry focused on color, kin, or kind. We gear our visions of ministry toward our own peoples. We are fundamentally segregationists. Church life in America is not segregated by accident. Segregation results from the kinds of transformation of bodies that defined and continue to define America's social and cultural landscape. The history of this nation is a history of transformations. America is quintessentially the land of transformation. America transformed European immigrants and Africans into citizens and slaves respectively.

The story of immigrant transformations in America is the central story of the body in America.[8] Immigrants coming to America entered into a world shaped by race and slavery. In order to do well in America,

---

8 Matthew Frye Jacobson, *Whiteness of a Different Color: European Immigrants and the Alchemy of Race* (Cambridge, Massachusetts: Harvard University Press, 1998). Noel Ignatiev, *How the Irish Became White* (New York: Routledge, 1995).

immigrants had to participate in that shaping. The term White Anglo-Saxon Protestant (WASP) is not only a form of identity that summarizes a particular group in America; the term also summarizes a process of transformation that all immigrant groups were required to enter when they came to America.

From Barbarian to Citizen

Coming to America meant you were willing to tame the wilderness. Taming the wilderness meant much more than clearing land. It meant that you were willing to place your bodies in the unfolding drama of destroying the native inhabitants. Participating in the destruction of indigenous peoples was one of the primary ways immigrants signaled to the world and to themselves that they were part of the American landscape, the formation of a white nation in contrast to the "Indians." Yet taming the wilderness was also an analogy for stripping away their immigrant past—that is, those cultural artifacts that signaled indebtedness to the old country, the old cultural ways, and the primitive mentalities of lower classes of the Old World.

Barbarians were those not ready to participate in the formation of this new nation. Their appearance signaled their immaturity. To look like a native, either of the New World (the Indian) or the Old World (the lower class European) was to be deemed to be inappropriate to the new order emerging in America. This meant that transformation was the order of the day. And transformation could take place simply by moving from one place to another and by taking a posture in clear distinction from the natives. For example, an Irishman in the early 1800s could go from being considered an inappropriate Barbarian in Boston to being seen as the embodiment of an American on the frontier. Simply by moving to a different social space and placing his body next to a native he is no longer an Irish immigrant but a White American. Stripping away the Old World was necessary for entrance into the emerging idea of an "American" with its concomitant idea of a new nation made up of new people set on a hill. To go from barbarian to citizen required destroying native identity and destroying, or at least concealing, immigrant identity.

From Dark to Light

Along side this transformation of barbarian to citizen was the color caste system that gave it power. The fruit of the enlightenment is that race colors the world. The racial vision of people groups reached its greatest power in America. The realities of African slaves and a (European generated) slaveholding society existed at the foundations of America. These realities meant that racial difference was an organizing principle in the social/class structures of society. Racial difference helped order the world and make sense of America. The designations of black and white were never simply signs of Africans and Europeans. Black and white were the perimeters within which the world was defined. Black and white were dark and light. That is, they were signs of the deep connection of appearance to behavior. The darker skin (and the bodily features associated with darker skin) signaled the barbarian, the uncivilized, the dangerous. Lighter skin (and its associated bodily features) signaled maturity, citizenship, and purity.

Patterns and practices of assimilation have this point of difference as the dominant feature. This was the question: "Can you pass as white?" Dark and brooding was a designation for appearance sought by no immigrant. It was the personification of the African in the New World. The great fear of every immigrant, every would-be American was to be mistaken as having a body like an African and thus to be designated one appropriate for slavery.

From Property to Property Owner

Africans did not own property; they were property. There were very few Africans who did own property but they in no way challenged this social fact. This social fact faced every immigrant who came to America — either you came as property or you came to own property. The transition from one to the other became the primary motivation for labor and life in America. Property ownership was one of the central prerequisites for redefining one's life. Becoming a landowner had direct implications for the body. Owning land not only connected one to the land, but also connected one to the growing ideology of America as the land of free men. Clearly, this was an economic determination, but it also guided how one ought to appear in public and how that appearance was to be interpreted.

The body of a landowner is fundamentally different than the body of one owned. The body of the landowner is sacred space, bound to the land as its progenitor, its parent that brings forth its fruit in due season. The body of the one owned (the slave) is secular space, needing purification. The body of the one owned is already defiled and is a site of defilement. Touch the body of the owned and you become unclean. Moving from being property to owning property was very serious business. It meant you would move from being vulnerable to being invulnerable, from being one without voice to one with some measure of voice in society.[9] Immigrants transformed themselves into White Americans. Becoming such an American freed you from being a dark barbarian who is property, i.e. from being an African slave.

---

9 Thandeka, *Learning to Be White: Money, Race, and God in America* (New York: Continuum, 1999), 42ff.

This transformation of bodies in America nurtured segregationist mentalities. People in America segregate in two directions—toward being white Americans and away from being white Americans. These directions established through historic patterns of assimilation did not culminate in fixed points in the histories of ethnic peoples in America. We find evidence of these directions in the struggles of peoples in America to claim western prosperity while maintaining their ethnic identities. We find evidence of these directions in the moments where racial oppression or ethnic tensions mark our social interactions. Most importantly for our discussion, we expose these directions in the ways we construct church life in America. Churches in America are the great enclaves of cultural belonging and nationalistic hope. The peoples of America have needed such churches in the faces of social setbacks, class warfare, and racial oppression. Our churches are either havens from the pressures and problems of assimilation in America or they are nationalist bastions of successful transformations. American church life is not an isolated reality. Church life in this country mirrors the desires of the nations.

Among every people and in every nation the church faces the question that greeted an ascending Jesus. Risen Jesus, when will our people be restored? When will our people be freed from oppressors and determine their own destiny? Even if the nature of the nation-state mutates into global multinational corporations with vast networks of communication systems and their own military forces, this question will remain for all peoples not wholly subsumed within such a nationalist entity. Indeed this question is becoming acute for those peoples being pressed further out to the technological and economic margins of global capitalism. As the church faces that question today, America displays to all churches in the world what is at stake in our answer to that question. In America, the answer to the question raised by Jesus' disciples is nation-building.

The history of Afro-Christians in America is the history of a people forced into nation-building. African American Christians have participated in the building of America. The black church also continues to build a nation within this nation through time-honored strategies of racial uplift.[10] Such strategies have always been embraced and deemed essential given the history and continuing reality of racial oppression in America. Yet nation-building has always created a dilemma for the African in America. Ultimately they cannot be assimilated, and thus, African American hopes for freedom in America or the freedom of an American go unrealized. Such freedom comes only to those model minorities who become fully assimilated immigrants. Karen Brodkin in her book, *How Jews Became White*

---

10 Kevin K. Gaines, *Uplifting the Race: Black Leadership, Politics and Culture in the Twentieth Century* (Chapel Hill, North Carolina: North Carolina Press, 1996).

Folks, notes how African Americans have been construed as the bearers of a deficient culture that thwarts their assimilation. Such a construal was the context within which some Jewish intellectuals (among many other ethnic intellectuals) refashioned their identity to become acceptable in America.

> Model minorities and deficit cultures are like two hands clapping; they are complementary parts of a single discourse on race as a cultural phenomenon. The Jewish ethnicity that intellectuals claimed for themselves as model minorities was an immigrant version of bourgeois patriarchal domesticity characterized by values of hard work, deferred gratification, education, and strong two-parent families with the mothers full-time at home. It was the invention of a deficient African American culture that illustrated its exemplariness.[11]

Every people who come to the shores of America embody the disciples' question to Jesus. Every people who come to America enter the project of nation-building and become captive to the dynamics of assimilation. And every people who come to America enact segregationist mentalities. Church life in America is ethnically and racially segregated because that is the shape of America life. Indeed, we have mistaken nation-building with the work of God. We have clearly gotten the vision of the tower of Babel, but we have not gotten the vision of Pentecost. The vision of the tower of Babel is a vision of nation-building formed around a common language, common concerns, and a shared goal. Yet, as Walter Brueggemann reminds us, such a vision fosters "a self-securing homogeneity."[12]

Pentecost is about one people who will allow the power of the Spirit to change their alliances and their allegiances. Pentecost is about one people who speak in tongues, one people who call to all nations and peoples. The church needs to be a people who are serious about speaking in tongues. We need to be people who allow the Spirit of God to fuse and confuse our languages, to fuse and confuse our patterns of worship. We must allow the Spirit of God to fuse and confuse our patterns of life, our ways of eating, sleeping, loving, and living. So that the nations may see in us a people freed from the desire of any one people or nation, a people freed from their plans, their violence and wars. Jesus' disciples must be about the business of speaking in tongues. We must become one people who say with our lips, "the world has been changed and is being changed"

---

11 *How Jews Became White Folks and What That Says about Race in America* (New Brunswick, New Jersey: Rutgers University Press, 2000), 150-151.
12 Brueggemann, *Genesis*, 99.

--not through the calculus of nation-states nor the stratagems of multinational corporations nor by the plans for power of any people, but by the power of the Spirit of the Living God.

The church is fundamentally biracial. Its biracial reality began the moment Jesus told his disciples to eat his body and drink his blood. Those disciples who refused to eat his body and drink his blood could have no part of him (John 6:56). The biracial reality of the church emerges out of our cruciform existence within the body of Jesus. We are born anew in him and live through him. Yet this biracial reality extends to Pentecost. At Pentecost, biracial existence announced by the gift of tongues means that Jesus' disciples might now live "in-between" the nations and their classificatory schemas, their hopes and plans, and their desires. The church is in-between political struggle, ethnic belonging, and nationalist desire because only from this position can we witness the wonderful work of God in the world.

This is not a formula for political quietism or a form of ideological blindness. The church is never above the desire of the nations or outside the reach of the nations. Rather as Katya Gibel Azoulay suggests (regarding biracial reality in general) being biracial "is *to be* an interruption, to *represent* a contestation, and *to undermine* the authority of classification." The gift of tongues means that the church will not be dismissed as an outsider to any nation, but it will not be trusted to carry forward nationalist agenda because it also speaks the language of the outsider. Indeed the church is the place where nationalist confusion should be the order of the day and ethnic fusion should be the order of service.

I began this essay referring to what I learned in my Pentecostal church. It is to the lessons of that church that I wish to return in ending. The central lesson I learned about receiving the gift of tongues is twofold: First, wait on the Spirit and do not resist the Spirit of God. This simple lesson should instruct all Christians. We should wait together at the table of the Lord. Together we should eat the body and drink the blood of one who gave his life for the world. Be joined to his body and allow God to show us how to speak in tongues. This means no more churches that share a building with different "ethnic groups" having "different ethnic services." It also means no more white churches and black churches (of the same denominations!) occupying the same immediate geographic area yet having "different worship experiences." The second aspect of this lesson follows from the first. Do not resist the Spirit of God. Allow the Spirit to make your church a strange place filled with strange power. Allow the Spirit to take your mouth and to take your voice and fill it with a language not your own. Allow the Spirit to use you to call to peoples, to be joined to peoples not your own. Allow the Spirit to give your life to peoples not of your own choosing. If you don't know how to do that then I have one simple answer: Wait on the Lord.

David Gilliam

HUMAN CONSCIENCE, THE DIVINE COMMAND, AND THE ESCHATOLOGICAL COMMUNITY

I am deeply indebted to Professor Ray Anderson for his gracious assent to be my mentor at Fuller Theological Seminary, giving countless hours training me to think theologically. He did this with grace, sincerity of heart, and a great deal of patience. One of Professor Anderson's most enduring qualities has been his accessibility. Even during the busiest of schedules, he found time to converse with his students on a wide diversity of issues, challenging us to consider new ideas and approaches to old theological problems and issues. He never attempted to sway us to agree with him, but always challenged us to think critically. Seeking to blend theology and ministry as two sides of the same coin, he trained his students to relate theological endeavors to church ministry. This paper is an expression of my gratitude and appreciation for the gifts Professor Ray Anderson has afforded me.

"The goal of this command is love, which comes from a pure heart and a good conscience and a sincere faith" (I Tim. 1:5, NIV).[1]

God's command to humankind is love, love that comes from pure motives and authentic actions as judged by the conscience. This command of love is synonymous with the Word of God. Jesus, who is the Word of God (John 1:1), explicates in His own person and life the meaning and nature of this command. Jesus broke down the command into two parts: 1) the command to love God with all one's heart, soul, mind, and strength; and 2) the command to love one's neighbor as oneself (Mark 12:30-31).

The love commanded by God is never an idealized love. Love does not exist in a vacuum or hypothetical realm. It must be made concrete in the behavior and actions of people. It must stem from pure motives and be freely expressed as a conscious act of the person. Jesus exemplified love in concrete action and always within the context of human relationships. "Love is something you do. The feelings, expressions and words of love have little substance apart from being 'incarnated' into an act (James

---

[1] All Scriptural references are from the New International Version of the Bible, *The NIV Study Bible*, Zondervan, 1985.

2:15)."[2] The ultimate incarnated act of love was realized in Jesus Christ. His love was freely given. It was a conscious decision by God to re-establish his covenant relationship with humanity.

Love exists in the concrete action of Jesus Christ in and for the world. It is Christ's own love that establishes the nature and authenticity of love in human relations. Jesus was fully aware of the nature and purpose of His actions. This love of Jesus is the basis and the focus for our own acts of love in the world. Authentic love requires that we actively participate in the humanity of Christ and in the life of Jesus. Ensuring that our own humanity and acts of love are consistent with Christ's is paramount. It is the role of conscience that provides this critical capability. It provides the awareness of the continuity of our own lives and actions as consistent with Christ's. Conscience makes us aware of the morality of our actions and their consistency with the love of Christ, and through its awareness we can affirm our humanity as created in the image of God. It requires critical self-awareness and being conscious of our lives and actions and their coherence with Christ.

The relation of conscience to this command of love in Christ is that it functions as the human capacity for self-awareness and assessment of the congruence of one's own life and actions with the Word of God and the command of love in concrete form in Christ. The awareness and assessment of conscience includes the purity of our motives; it is an awareness and assessment of whether or not we are acting in love offered freely in our relationship with God and others.[3] How, then, do we assure that our actions are out of love and not self-interest? What is the role of conscience in this activity and by what criteria does the conscience make this assessment?

Self-Awareness and Personal Values

As children grow up, they are taught right from wrong behavior. What they are taught is based on the parent's values and beliefs, the values and beliefs of their community, and their assent in part or in total to these values and beliefs—the compendium of which forms their personal value system. This value system is the basis upon which the conscience makes its assessment of one's behavior and actions.

---

[2] Anderson, *God So Loved . . . A Theology for Ministry Formation*, Fuller Seminary Press, Pasadena, CA, 1995, p. 110.

[3] This paper expands on my previous research, a Ph.D. dissertation under the mentorship of Professor Anderson, *The Role of Conscience in the Collective Community of Christ*, University Microfilms International, 1987, by showing that conscience has always been an innate faculty of humans, but that it must be united with faith in order to re-achieve its appropriate purpose.

Sigmund Freud viewed the conscience as one of two components of the superego, the other being the ego-ideal. In this scheme, the conscience prevents people from doing things that are considered morally wrong, and the ego-ideal motivates people to do things that are considered morally right. This theory suggests that the conscience is developed by parents, who convey their beliefs to their children. They in turn internalize these moral codes by a process of identification with their parents.[4] However, the conscience of the parents is also developed and shaped by the community and society in which they live. There exists a link to the present and previous communities and their value systems, and these, in turn, shape the value systems of the current and future generations. In this sense, we are eternally linked to Adam and Eve on one end and to the ultimate destiny of humanity in the eschaton on the other.

Children are disciplined through an assessment of their behavior based on a moral code of conduct that they learn from early childhood on. Self-awareness and self-assessment may be gained concurrently, but there is a period of latency between being taught right from wrong and the ability for self-assessment. This ability certainly develops more as they grow (one hopes), and, in fact, may even be considered a sign of maturity. A sense of personal and communal or societal values is developed along with self-awareness. For some, this value system is stronger than in others and for everyone it is different. It is not only dependent on personal character, but also on the strength of one's religious persuasion and beliefs.

Conscience is generally understood to be self-awareness and self-assessment of our lives and actions against some standard. What that standard is depends on one's personal and societal values, including religious values, around which or toward which one's life is oriented and focused. It is developed in the context of human community in our interpersonal relationships with each other.[5] The 'good' or 'bad' is determined in the context of these values. It is related to being conscious of our behavior judged against one's system of values and beliefs. The contents of this system depend on the context and content of one's life. Conscience is defined in *Webster's Dictionary* as "the sense of the moral goodness or blameworthiness of one's conduct, intentions, or character together with a feeling of obligation to do right or be good," and "the part of the superego in psychoanalysis that transmits commands and admonitions to the ego."

If conscience is a human faculty of self-assessment, what is its role in the Christian life? And what is its relation to this command of love? First,

---

[4] *Gale Encyclopedia of Psychology*, Published/Released: 2000, Published by Gale, ed. 2 (http://www.findarticles.com/cf_dls/g2699/0000/2699000072/p1/article.jhtml).

[5] Anderson & Guernsey, *On Being Family: A Social Theology of the Family*, Eerdmans, 1985, p. 60f.

it is necessary to recognize that conscience is an integral part of the very essence of being human, and of being created in the image of God. It is not some capability that was acquired subsequent to the fall in the Garden of Eden.[6] It is an essential part of our humanity as co-humanity and participates in our dialogue with God and each other. Second, conscience must be grounded in Christ and His command of love. It must enable one to assess the authenticity and moral rectitude of one's behavior and actions. It has a critical role in keeping our actions and behavior aligned with Christ. It also ensures that we are in keeping with His love both in our dialogue with God and in our actions towards others. Third, conscience also has a proleptic role in that it spurs us to concrete action for our neighbors. It is an awareness that compels us to participate in the love of Christ and outwardly express it by helping our human neighbor in need. Through this activity we affirm our participation in the eschaton which, through our lives and actions, now reaches back into the present and establishes the final word of forgiveness, love and hope for all humankind in Christ.

Being Human and the *Imago Dei*

God created humankind in His own image (Gen. 1:26). This image includes freedom—freedom to respond to the command of God, freedom to respond to His Word, freedom to respond to Him in the fellowship of love, and freedom to walk with Him in the Garden of Eden.[7] It is the essential nature of being human that we respond to the Word of God with our own word. We were created for dialogue and fellowship with God and with each other. Hence, the essential form of the image of God is what Professor Anderson calls "co-humanity." It is the essential form of human person as *imago Dei*. [8] A solitary individual cannot fully express the authentic essence of being human as created in the image of God, as self-dialogue does not constitute co-humanity. It is only when we stand in dialogue with God and each other, in response to His divine Word that we affirm that we are created in the image of God.[9] It is a freedom of dialogue, of address and response characterized by the fellowship of love and commitment understood biblically as a covenant relationship.[10]

---

[6] Contra-Bonhoeffer, *Creation and Fall*, MacMillan, 1974, and C. A. Pierce, Conscience in the New Testament, Robert Cunningham & Sons, London, 1958.

[7] Anderson, *On Being Human: Essays in Theological Anthropology*, Eerdmans, 1982, p. 79f.; Dr. Anderson presents an excellent essay on the nature and reality of "Being Human in the Image of God" in this book (p. 69-87).

[8] Anderson, *On Being Family*, p. 32, 57ff., for a further detailed explanation of co-humanity.

[9] *Ibid.*

[10] Barth, *Ethics*, Seabury Press, 1981, p. 477f.

Human Conscience and the Divine Command

As created beings, we also participate in the natural created order of the world. The world is the concrete place of human existence, and we as co-human have been made caretakers of this world. Knowledge of and the facility for response to the divine Word implies responsibility for the world in which we move and breathe. Hence being in the image of God not only intends that we have a divine quality to our humanity but a creaturely quality to it as well. We have the freedom to uphold the created world as part of our response to the divine Word and affirmation of our being *imago Dei*.

One characteristic of this freedom is conscience. Conscience exists because humans were created with the freedom to choose to be in fellowship with God, to dialogue with Him in love and fellowship, and by extension with each other as co-human. That one might not choose to fellowship with God is not an appropriate choice as it is a negation of the *imago Dei*. It stands as a denial that God is the Source and Sustainer of humanity; and it denies our co-humanity, as it is also a choice against the 'other.' However, this choice nevertheless exists as a necessary corollary of our freedom for fellowship with God.[11] Conscience acts as a moral compass in this choice. If God's Word is the source of one's values and beliefs, then conscience makes one aware of whether or not one's actions are congruent with His Word. This is the distinction between an egocentric and a theocentric value system. It is also why Paul commands Timothy in the passage quoted above not to allow false teachers to subvert the Word of God by teaching their own philosophy. It strikes at our very ability to hear and know the Word and God's address to us in it. Without knowing the address of God in His Word, we are unable to provide an authentic response in our dialogue with Him and with one another.

In an egocentric value system, one's beliefs or values are determined by either one's self or by capitulation to another, including another person, organization, or social system (community, society, government, etc.). In a theocentric system God and His Word are determinative of one's values and beliefs. The difference is that in a theocentric value system, the person affirms being created in the image of God--that is, choosing God and His command as the Source and Sustainer of one's image as co-human. The Word of God is determinative for human dialogue. It is characterized by love, specifically the love of God exhibited in Christ. Christ establishes the framework for the authentic and appropriate response, and the appropriate response to God and each other is one of love freely offered as an affirmation of our being in His image. This love becomes the foundation of our relationship with God and our neighbor. In an egocentric value system, the 'I' usurps the role of God and affirms the role

---

[11] Berkhof, *Christian Faith: An Introduction to the Study of the Faith*, Eerdmans, 1979, p. 178-210, esp. pp. 188-190.

of being 'like' God. The individual 'I' elevates itself as the final arbiter of one's values and beliefs.[12] The difference can be seen in Scripture as early as the creation of humankind in the Garden of Eden when Adam and Eve make the fatal decision to be 'like' God, knowing good and evil premised on their own suppositions and finite knowledge.

The story in Genesis 3 tells us that when Adam and Eve ate of the "Tree of Knowledge of Good and Evil," their eyes were opened and they realized that they were naked. The implication here is that 'knowledge of good and evil' is the human attempt to be 'like God' (*sicut Deus*). It is the self-determination of the 'I' to decide, as the ultimate authority, what is good or evil with respect to one's own person and the other.[13] Here the *imago Dei* stands in sharp contrast with *sicut Deus*. As *imago Dei*, the true nature of being human is determined by God's Word.[14] As *sicut Deus*, self-determination breaks one's fellowship with God and others. It strikes at the essential nature of the *imago Dei*, of being co-human. The center of focus is one's own word over the Word of God. It is now the attempt to know, like God, and to self-determine the boundaries for human behavior.[15] It is a human word that even attempts to command God to accede to it. It is also the attempt to make others stand under our own individual human word, under our moral suppositions. It is this that leads to a breakdown in love in our relationships, and, thus, is destructive to co-humanity. It is a limited knowledge resulting in an imperfect capacity for self-awareness and assessment, and consequently incapacitates the ability to love God and one another in fellowship.

Knowledge of good and evil, out of autonomous human suppositions, results in death and despair. The continuance of the Fall is graphically portrayed in Genesis Four. Cain kills his brother Abel and justifies it to himself as necessary. Here Cain acts according to his own suppositions. His acts are based on what he believes to be right or wrong. When confronted with the Word of God, instead of acquiescing to the Word and repenting, he lashes out destructively. The focus of Cain's perception is his own word (his knowledge of good and evil or moral supposition) as opposed to God's Word, so he commits an act that is in fact destructive to humanity, both his and the other's. He then justifies his actions based on his own moral supposition. When Cain makes himself the final arbiter of good and evil (one's system of values and beliefs), he falls into chaos and disorder. Camus puts it well, "Once more I have found a height to which I am the only one to climb and from which I can judge

---

[12] The 'I' is still the final arbiter even when it capitulates this determination to another.

[13] Gilliam, *op.cit.*, pp. 20ff.; see Bonhoeffer, *Creation and Fall*, Macmillan Publishing, 1974, p. 81f.

[14] Anderson, *Historical Transcendence and the Reality of God*, Eerdmans, 1975, p. 134ff.

[15] *Ibid.*, p. 137.

everybody. . . How intoxicating to feel like God the Father and to hand out definitive testimonials of bad character and habits."[16]

Bonhoeffer states that conscience arises as a consequence of becoming like God (*sicut Deus* — that is like God, knowing good and evil). It arises out of the attempt of the 'I' to overcome its sense of guilt and despair that is aware of one's continual dying through fear and woe,[17] but in fact it is more than this. Conscience is an essential human faculty of self-awareness that acts as a moral agent in leading one to obedience to the command of love, within the context of the divine Word. It has a critical role in the affirmation of one's co-humanity and *imago Dei*. Thus, it is part of the very character of God Himself. He is the primary moral agent who determines for all creation and humankind what is 'good and evil.' As stated by Professor Anderson:

> God's character provides the moral basis for God's creation. As Creator, God is not an impersonal power but a moral agent to whom all creation is accountable for its meaning as well as its goodness. The biblical account of creation asserts the goodness of all that God has made . . . . The moral character of the created world is defined by the character of God.
>
> Second, the moral character of creation is revealed through human beings as the image bearers of God . . . to be made in God's image and likeness is to have a moral character like that of the divine. Humans are thus moral agents not because of adherence to abstract moral law but because they bear the very moral character of God.[18]

However, conscience is not simply reactive in its self-assessment. It also has a proleptic function. Positively, it leads one to behave or act in obedience to the Word and the command of love. Obedience is a conscious and continuous decision to respond to God and others in freedom and love. It has both individual acts and one's behavior as a whole in view and their continuity with the Word of God. The awareness of conscience prompts one to act in love toward God and others when it is focused on the Word as its moral guide.

Certainly, the conscience of Adam after the Fall was an accusing conscience, as Adam's first reaction to hearing the presence of God in the

---

[16] Camus, *The Fall, and Exile And The Kingdom*, Modern Library Book, New York, 1958, p. 142f.

[17] Bonhoeffer, *Act and Being*, Harper & Row, 1961, pp. 166-168; Bonhoeffer, *Creation and Fall*.

[18] Anderson, *The Shape of Practical Theology*, InterVarsity Press, Downers Grove, IL, 2001, p. 210.

Garden was to run and hide. It was an act based on fear and guilt,[19] but fear and guilt of what? It was fear and guilt for having broken a fellowship of love and freedom with God and others. The conscience became a guilty conscience as a result of Adam's choosing his own word over God's.

The fall of humankind became self-negation of the community and the individual in the sense that the knowledge of good and evil supplanted the divine Word and knowledge of one's relationship with God as the defining limit and focus of one's life. Prior to the Fall, humankind's experience was of one's existence primarily as part of a community with the love of God as the basis of that relationship. The experience of the 'I' is first that of being part of a community, and second as an individual within the context of community. After the Fall, knowledge of good and evil brought on a different type of awareness. It was the awareness of the individuality of the 'I' first and of 'I' as part of a community second.[20] Yet, God in his graciousness toward humankind re-established for humanity both a limit and a center for human life in the incarnation of Jesus Christ.[21] Jesus took our co-humanity and made it part of His own person, including his human conscience, and re-established the Word as the defining center for human existence ("Man does not live on bread alone . . . " – Matt. 4:4).[22] In his own person, Jesus brought the human word back into continuity with the divine Word. At the cross, He felt the full anguish of guilt of the sins of the world through the awareness of His own conscience. The awareness through His conscience of His total estrangement from God led Him to the cry of despair "My God, My God, why have you forsaken me?" (Matt. 27:46). However, this cry of despair was not the final word. It is important to note that it was through this act at the cross that Jesus cleansed the human conscience by His sacrifice and by re-establishing the divine Word as the center for fellowship with God and existence as co-humanity.

The boundary for human existence is the Law, and the center of human existence is the covenant relationship ultimately expressed in Christ's incarnate life. He establishes in His own incarnate life both the

---

[19] Bonhoeffer, *Act and Being*, p. 81.

[20] *Ibid.*, 52f., 68, 78.

[21] See Bonhoeffer, , *Christ the Center*, Harper & Row, 1966, p. 62ff.

[22] Jesus' cry "My God, My God, Why have you forsaken me?" shows the utter isolation from His Father that He experienced from the guilt and shame He felt in taking on the sins of the world and burying them at the cross. Did Jesus have a human conscience? The answer has to be a resounding yes! Else how could He have been tempted in all points as us. Else how could He have experienced the guilt of humankind at the cross? Else how could He have fully redeemed humankind from the depths of isolation, guilt and despair? Even more, this same human conscience provided Him the awareness of the continuity of His own life on earth with the Word of God and the command of love.

boundary and center for human behavior and action.[23] Christ as the center of human existence determines the meaning of a life of faith in the Father, but He also determines the meaning of the boundary of human existence. He gives new direction and meaning to the Law as set forth in both his Sermon on the Mount and through the actions of his incarnate life (Matt. 5-7).[24] Here Jesus does not set aside the Law. He affirms its validity for humankind, but only as a boundary for human existence. While the Law, acting as a boundary sets limits to human existence, it also points back to the fact that human existence is from and for God (Rom. 1:20ff.). The human conscience now has been provided a reference point for self-awareness outside of the individual 'I'. Consequently, conscience is no longer relegated to assessing one's behavior premised on one's own self-determination and human word. We are called to live focused on the divine Word as the center of our lives. We are to live in obedience and awareness of our lives and actions as a response to the divine command of love. The boundaries exist because it is imperative that the Law points us back to the true center, Jesus Christ, and sets limits for human relationships and actions. The boundaries exist because of our "hardness of heart," Jesus states when He is asked about the lawfulness of divorce (Mark 10:5). If we are focused on the divine Word and the command of love, then the boundaries have a relativized meaning for human actions.

Conscience and the Divine Word of God

While the Law serves as a boundary for human behavior and actions, the Word of God is the center. As established above, the Law of God is premised on love in relationships and is expressed in the Word of God who is Christ. Christ is the epitome of love and explicates it in his own life and actions on behalf of humankind. This Word of God is the command of love. It comes to us and requires a response in kind as the essential element of our co-humanity as the image of God.[25] Conscience is awareness of the divine Word that addresses us and self-assessment of the continuity and freedom of our response to it. When the human word stands in conflict with the divine Word, the command of love becomes distorted by one's own perception. The human word must be brought back under the divine Word in order for conscience to provide the positive assessment of the congruence of our actions with the divine command of love.

---

[23] Bonhoeffer, *op. cit.*
[24] *Ibid.*
[25] Anderson, *Historical Transcendence and the Reality of God*, p. 169f.

David Gilliam

The conscience is a moral force that helps us to ensure that we act in accordance with our true nature of co-humanity. It involves upholding others in our relationships with them through commitment and love. Without the conscience, we would not be aware of the moral character of our actions nor their effects. It is critical, then, that the conscience be attuned to the Word of God and His love. We only hear this Word as we spend time in prayer, worship, and reading the written Word first within the community of Christ and second individually as our human response to God. Only through this human activity and participation in obedient listening and dialogue together with God does the conscience have the orientation necessary to provide accurate self-assessment. Hence, only from this vantage point can we be corrected by the Word when our actions do not conform to it. It is crucial to hear the Word of God in the voice of conscience in our actions. Even more crucial is to subjugate our word when we act in disaccord with His Word and to repent and seek forgiveness.

In the story of David and Bathsheba, the activity of conscience is quite apparent. David steals Uriah's wife and she becomes pregnant by him. He then attempts to cover it up by sending Uriah into battle to be killed (2 Sam. 12). Nathan confronts David by telling him a story about a wealthy shepherd with many sheep who steals another person's single lamb to slaughter and eat with a friend. David is incensed by this story and immediately passes moral judgment on the behavior and actions of the wealthy shepherd. David exhibits an innate awareness of right and wrong and fairness in this story. However, Nathan pronounces God's verdict on David as being this very person, the wealthy shepherd. Being confronted by this Word and his own behavior, David immediately concedes that he has sinned. He has caused the destruction of co-humanity through acceding to his own unbridled passions and desires, elevating himself over the divine Word and over the lives and wholeness of others. David repents when he is confronted by these words and re-subjugates himself to the authority of the Word of God. David's ability and willingness to listen and respond to the Word of God is the reason why God calls David a person after His own heart. David's action stands in sharp contrast to Cain, who tries to excuse himself for his actions, and then flees into the wilderness. He refuses to let himself be brought back under the authority of the Word and the command of love. His life becomes one lived in fear.

Establishing our own word over God's Word puts us in direct conflict with God. Our only option is to flee and hide in vain from God. However, when we are confronted with the incongruence of our actions with the Word of God and we re-submit to its authority, then the broken fellowship can be re-established by God. When hearing of the divine Word, David's conscience causes him to acknowledge his violation of

God's Word. The prophetic Word of God breaks through David's own word. He re-affirms the priority of the Word of God and repents. Hence, God forgives him (though he still must suffer the consequences of his actions). Here, conscience in its role of self-assessment not only accuses but also promotes positive behavior as shown in David's repentance. In this latter activity, the conscience then becomes a 'good' conscience.

Besides being an accusing moral judge, an even more critical activity of conscience is that of a positive moral guide. It affirms what is right, hence the 'good' conscience which approves one's course of action or behavior in accordance with one's system of values and beliefs. Consider those who refuse to participate in an activity for conscience' sake—conscientious objectors. They not only refuse to participate but also take an active stance and speak out against what they consider to be ethically or morally wrong. Even more, there are those who actively work to right what they consider wrongs, such as actively working to change laws that are harmful to persons or society. They are led to positive acts for people and society for the 'common good.' In this sense the conscience remains 'clean' or 'good.' It leads one to positive action. Passive resistance may be an appropriate action at times. However, there are instances where this is not enough. We are commanded to act in love on behalf of our neighbors, and our conscience prompts us to take action when confronted by our neighbors in need. Thus, even if only for the sake of avoiding guilt for inaction, conscience can act as a positive force prompting one to appropriate behavior or activity.[26]

In the story of the cleansing of the temple, Jesus confronted the money changers because they were making a mockery of the religious observance of sacrifice for the expiation of sins. He became angry and drove them out (John 2:14-17). What led Jesus to do this? His indignity was over the fact that they were subverting the role of the temple as a central place of prayer, making it instead a place of commerce. For this reason Jesus was angry. How could the people hear the Word of God if the temple was subverted to be a place where the laws and words of the Pharisees and Sadducees re-interpreted the Law and Word of God for their own purpose and profit? The ability to hear the Word of God is critical. Without the ability to hear this Word, we are unable to offer an appropriate response.

It is in his life unto death that Jesus as the Word of God (John 1:1-4) brought the human word back from self-determination, bound by its own moral values and beliefs reuniting it with the divine Word in His simple but tremendous act of love for humankind. He re-established God and His Word as the center of human existence and the command of love as the

---

[26] In this key area, Bonhoeffer unfortunately never fully worked out the role of conscience in the community of faith.

guiding principle for human actions and behavior. In his actions, Jesus cleansed the conscience from guilt and service to dead works to serve the living God (Heb. 9:14). Christ re-oriented humanity in his own person to fellowship with God, bringing the human word back into congruence with the divine Word. He re-established the command of love as the focus for human behavior and actions in His own person and life.

Conscience and Living in Light of the Eschaton

In Jesus, the human word is brought back into conformance with the divine Word. Continuity is re-established where the human word is centered on the divine Word. It now has the capability to respond authentically to the command of love in Jesus. Jesus becomes the final Word for humankind in his own person. Re-uniting the human word and the divine Word is a sign of the eschaton reaching into the present. He re-establishes the person as the image of God and co-human, with the center of human existence bound to the command of God to love freely in one's relationships with others.

As already shown above, the conscience is a human faculty of conscious awareness that provides self-assessment of one's behavior and actions.[27] It is a self-assessment premised on one's system of values and beliefs. When the human word exists in continuity with the divine Word and exhibits the response of love freely given, the conscience is said to be 'good' and now serves the living God (Heb. 9:14f.). If this human word is indeed in true continuity with the divine Word, then self-assessment of one's behavior and actions will lead one to obey the command of love in one's fellowship with God and others. It leads one to positive action for the concrete neighbor in need--that is, to go to the side of the road and minister to the one lying there who was beaten by robbers (see the parable of the Good Samaritan, Luke 10:25-37).

In His own life, death, and resurrection, Jesus re-orients our humanity to a life of transcendent living where the command of love is the predicate of relationships and forms the new basis of human behavior and

---

[27] Barth, *Ethics*, Seabury Press, 1981, p. 480, states, "In conscience, our own voice is undoubtedly *God's voice*. Our own voice: naturally only from the very remarkable standpoint, which cannot be understood except eschatologically, that we find ourselves divided and confronting ourselves, as it were, in the process. When my conscience speaks to me, I am *addressed*. Someone *encounters* me, coming from outside into my present reality. But this someone is not another person, a fellow human. He may encounter me as a fellow human does . . . the other person is not the someone. The someone is myself. I judge myself. I command this and forbid that. I warn myself. I give myself this or that permission. I console myself. In relation to an approaching or past moment of action I set myself under a final truth by which my action is measured. When conscience speaks, I find that I am on both sides, both listening and speaking."

actions. The human word, which formerly judged all human behavior out of the individual assessment of the 'I' acting 'like God,' is brought back within the framework of the Word of God in Jesus. Its assessment now has the Word as that which explicates the command of God to love others. Christ as the Word of God, now encompasses our lives and actions in His own transcendent life of obedience to the command of God. He draws us into His life, and as He does so through the power of the Holy Spirit, we grow in maturity in sincerity of faith and the purity of our actions.

In practical terms, our conscience, now oriented in Christ to serve the living God, enables us to acknowledge whether our behavior and actions are consistent with the love of Jesus. Our self-awareness and assessment does not judge our behavior and actions as being right or wrong based on abstract or independent moral principles so much as whether or not they exhibit the character of Jesus' love.

The guilt we experience when we violate this command (which we seem to do all too frequently) is the voice of conscience. Whenever we act out of accord with the divine command, conscience makes us painfully aware of it. Judas' conscience made him distinctly aware of the enormity of his act of betrayal. Judas is the epitome of being so consciously aware of his sin, and because of his feeling of total estrangement from God, he committed suicide. His sense of guilt overwhelmed him.[28]

In Christ, the guilt of conscience is no longer the final word. The guilt of conscience we experience now stands within the forgiveness of Christ. This word of forgiveness is Christ's final word of love for humankind. The depth of human despair and guilt of even Judas now stands within this final ultimate word and act of Christ. In the *Gospel According to Judas*, Professor Anderson points out that "Christ is the final word for all humanity. No death can overturn that word, even death that is self-inflicted."[29] Thus, he can go on to claim that Christ Himself says to each of us, "*Judas come home – all is forgiven!*" for each of us has betrayed Christ in our betrayal of others.[30]

Only in Christ does forgiveness extend to "cleanse our consciences from acts that lead to death, so that we may serve the living God" (Heb. 9:14). Likewise, in Christ, we too are commanded to forgive one another

---

[28] Anderson, *The Gospel According to Judas,* Helmers & Howard, Publishers, Inc., Colorado Springs, 1991.

[29] Anderson, *op. cit.,* p. 21, 55.

[30] If only Judas had allowed himself to stand before the judgment of God and His Word, could he have accepted forgiveness from Jesus Christ for his betrayal? Even more, could we relinquish our judgment of him and stand with Christ in forgiveness of him? And in the same vein, can we accept the forgiveness of Christ and each other when we become conscious of our own acts of betrayal? Can this conscious awareness lead us to relinquish our own perception of morality and the law for the Law of God and the command of love? It can and must in the healing forgiveness of Jesus Christ who stands with us and for us.

and not lay the burden of human judgment and guilt on others, but to stand alongside His Word of compassion and forgiveness. Through our acts of love, others are visibly brought within the sphere of God's Word and command of love. It makes them participants with us in this activity and re-affirms our co-humanity as created in the image of God.

Purification of the heart and cleansing of the conscience is a continual process in Christ. It requires growth in Christ and knowledge of His Word as it relates to our relationships with God and each other. It is a process of maturing in Christ. The Apostle Paul speaks to this whole issue in 1 Corinthians in his discussion of the weak and strong with respect to conscience and our behavior.[31] It is not by coincidence that Paul writes his now famous discourse on the character of love shortly after discussing the character of our behavior and relationships with each other in the community of Christ (1 Cor. 13). The command of love we are given in Christ is to exhibit it in all human activity and action both within the community and in the physical world. It is this very love that maintains the purity of our motives and authenticity of our actions as we stand with Christ for one another and the world.

In its proleptic role, the conscience guides us to act positively toward one another in love with pure motives. It is just as much a violation of the *imago Dei* when we sit idly by when another is in need and refuse to assist that person. In the story of the Good Samaritan, Jesus fully explains the nature and depth of acting for another (Luke 10:25-37). In this story, it is interesting to note that the 'religious' elite used one excuse or another not to take any action on behalf of the neighbor lying in the road, beaten and covered in blood. Their own human perception of law caused them to avoid acting to assist this 'neighbor.' It was an action that was callous without love or regard for the life of another. They absolved their consciences through the subversion of the law to justify their actions; and so they passed him on the far side of the road and left him there, dying. In contrast, the Samaritan stopped and lent assistance. He took the beaten man to a hotel and spent his own resources in restoring him to health and wholeness.

In a graphic portrait, Jesus is pointing out that our own moral attitudes, mores, judgments, and laws can prevent us from seeing the true need of others and acting on their behalf as true neighbors. Again, Jesus makes this same point when He says that when we act to help those in need, we do it for those for whom Christ lived and died. In a clear moment of insight here, Jesus may even have been pointing to Himself on the cross. We must touch the one with blood on Him at the cross, Jesus, in order to be cleansed and made whole from the ravages of the human word

---

[31] Gilliam, *op. cit.*, "Conscience and Community," pp. 71-81, where I examine Paul's use of conscience in 1 Corinthians.

and barren law in our lives and be brought back under the law of love in Christ. Jesus wants us to understand here that we are commanded by His love to have awareness of others and their needs and to act towards them in love and compassion. 'And Jesus had compassion,' we are told repeatedly in the gospels, and we are 'to go and do likewise' (Luke 10:37).

When our conscience leads us to acts of love for our neighbor, we must do so in concrete form. We are called by God to love the neighbor next to us, the one we see on the side of the road and can concretely help. Then, when we do help, we must recognize that we do so imperfectly. Even our own acts of love must stand under the forgiveness in Christ. However, these acts are perfected by Christ as an element of the eschaton reaching into the present world, for Christ perfects them in his own person as the final act and Word of our own acts. It is characterized by Jesus who is confronted by the leprous man (Matt 8:2-4). Jesus reaches out and touches the man. There is an eschatological moment where Jesus becomes defiled before He heals. Jesus could have healed the man at a distant; but He knows that this person needed to know that God stood with him and for him in his time of need. When we love our neighbor concretely, we reach out to help those in need, we also stand in the eschatological tension of where the acts of love and compassion are incomplete, but look forward to their final act of completion and healing in the eschaton.

Not acting when a neighbor is in need may be an act against one for whom Christ died. It is refusal to stand with the other in the face of death and destruction of humanity. It is, in fact, an act of betrayal, a re-enactment and participation in Judas' act of betrayal. We must stand with Christ at the cross for others and for ourselves. When the conscience guides us to action, love must govern the purity of our motives. And then we must be willing to accept forgiveness for our imperfect acts of love. We must allow ourselves to be forgiven by Christ, ask forgiveness of others, and then respond in forgiveness to both others and ourselves for these imperfect acts of love.[32] Why? We must do so because we are in the process of maturing in Christ and, hence, our actions can only be either conforming or non-conforming actions with the love of Christ. They are never, in themselves, the perfect act of love. Only Christ can take them and perfect them in his incarnate, crucified, risen, ascended, and coming humanity. We must be aware of our human limitations in light of the human perfections of Christ. Only from this vantage can we have a positive and preserving force on human society as we draw it with us in Christ toward the eschaton and the final judgment of God, a judgment of forgiveness and love.[33]

---

[32] Anderson, *The Shape of Practical Theology*, p. 158f.

[33] See Anderson, *Minding God's Business*, Eerdmans, 1986, p. 23f.

It is crucial to understand the importance of not continually wounding the conscience, either our own or others. In wounding the conscience, the conscience becomes seared. Under constant bombardment, the conscience can no longer hear the command of Christ (as shown above). It is a movement away from Christ and the *imago Dei* and a move toward *sicut Deus*. Violating the command of love wounds the conscience. This is a negative action either against a person (including the self) or an organization. In either case, it can be just as dangerous. If one pilfers small amounts of office supplies from the company for which one works, it is usually ignored, and sometimes even accepted without comment from anyone. Stealing parts and equipment, however, is frowned upon and usually causes dismissal. Embezzlement can land one in jail. While most of us would not go quite that far, it is a progression of action. For this reason it is dangerous to start down this path. Just because the company does not have a human face associated with it per se, does not mean that it is any less a form of human organization.

If one neglects to maintain moral integrity in one facet of one's actions, then other actions that also lack moral integrity will become easier to carry out. It is a negation of one's participation in co-humanity, or another person's or both, for preservation and elevation of the individual 'I'. It is no different from the series of steps that David took with Bathsheba and Uriah. He first saw Bathsheba, and then he desired her leading to lusting after her. He created the condition for him to be alone with Bathsheba. When he could not cover up his actions, he put Uriah in harm's way, which led to his death—an action that in our court's today would be considered murder. It was an ultimate act of betrayal by both David and Bathsheba, and it strikes at the very heart of co-humanity as the image of God.

What is important is that we allow ourselves to be confronted by the Word of God and recognize through the activity of our consciences our need to respond in repentance for our actions. Without repentance, we ultimately end up in the same dire situation as Judas, overcome with guilt, despair and alienation. The basis of repentance is the command of love, not law. The command of Christ to love one another constrains us to be consciously aware of others, and to act in a manner that builds up co-humanity and the *imago Dei*. In the eschaton the final Word of judgment will hinge on our love for those for whom Christ lived and died. In speaking of the Day of Judgment to the disciples, Jesus speaks of the imminence of the kingdom of God. Whatever we do now for one another is a sign of the eschaton and the kingdom of God breaking into the present world. "The King will reply, 'I tell you the truth, whatever you did for one of the least of these brothers of mine, you did for me'" (Matt. 25:40). The final Word of Judgment is based on whether we have acted in love and compassion toward our neighbor, the traveler in need on the road of life, and whether we have acted as Samaritans crossing to the side of the road on which lie the oppressed and wounded. In the words of Professor Anderson, "The poor, the hungry, the dispossessed, the oppressed, as well as the oppressor, constitute the criteria for responsible moral action;"[34] and responsible moral action is grounded in the command of love, which itself is grounded in the person of Jesus Christ as the ultimate Word of God for humankind.

> Social repentance is grounded in human solidarity and therefore makes a positive sacrifice of self-interests for the sake of an investment in the promise and the future of relationships between those who are estranged. Consequently there is an eschatological perspective to social repentance as a form of moral action. This action is deeper and more prepared for a sustained involvement than the ethical enthusiasm that rises quickly to a high pitch and then diminishes just as quickly. The basis for this, of course, is love for God and for the neighbor as our selves.[35]

Repentance for inaction or actions out of character (or potentially even in character) with the command of love is requisite in both the community of Christ and in individuals. Without it, there can be no forgiveness and, consequently, no cleansing of the conscience. Cleansing of the conscience is critical if we are to continue to have perspicacious vision of the continuity of our actions, of our word with the Word of God. It is not that forgiveness and cleansing have not already been pronounced as the final Word in our lives. They have. It blocks our ability to receive forgiveness and cleansing and acknowledge its efficacy in our lives. Without that knowledge, we, like Judas, stand on the brink of despair and hopelessness. The imperfections of our actions are that for which we repent and for which we have already received forgiveness and cleansing through the final Word of God, the final judgment reaching from the eschaton back into the present. As Barth poignantly sums up in his discussion on conscience:

> The voice of conscience has its origin in our unconditional belonging to God, in the absolute kingdom of God. In conscience I hear my own voice as that of the redeemed child of God. It is thus the characteristic call to me to reach out for what is ahead [cf. Phil. 3:13], for my approaching eternal home. The

---

[34] Anderson, *The Shape of Practical Theology*, p. 158f.
[35] *Ibid.*

measure by which my conduct is measured by the command of conscience is not that it should be faithful to my calling, nor that I should submit to the claim of my neighbor upon me—conscience can and does require these things but they are not the distinctive thing in its own particular message—but whether and how far my conduct, my conduct at this moment, is a forward step, i.e., a step toward the future which is promised me by God's Word, the future of the Lord and his lordship over all people and things.[36]

Living eschatologically means that our consciences are informed by the Word of God to follow the command of Christ to love God and one another just as He has loved us. In the words of Professor Anderson,

> This present world and social order, though under the power of the new creative order established through Jesus Christ, continues to suffer a tension between the new and old order. This present and continuing ministry of Jesus Christ takes place through the provisional forms of the church and its organizations as a sign of the kingdom of God.[37]

---

[36] Barth, *Ethics,* p. 486-487.
[37] *Minding God's Business,* p. 34.

Appendix for Pastors and Teachers

✳ ✳ ✳

Sermons and Materials by Ray S. Anderson[1]

---

[1] Transcribed by Allen Corben.

ON BEING CHRISTIAN[1]
(Scripture: Philippians 1:27)

On being Christian. I know what some of you are thinking. You're thinking, "There's Anderson again. He has a whole list of titles, just waiting to find something to attach them to." That's true in a sense. I will admit more than once I've submitted a title to the church secretary to put into the bulletin without the slightest idea what the content would be. I suppose if I ask for a show of hands, I'm probably the only one that's ever done that.

Titles are very intriguing, and very useful. I was asked last spring to write a book for Blackwell on a theology of death and dying. So, I said yes and sent back a proposal with a nice title: "On Being Dead." Now, somehow they thought that maybe lacked a little pizzazz, and besides they wanted a little on ethics in there. So, I sent a new proposal back with a new title: "On Being Good and Dead." When the book comes out, you'll see that that title remains unused, so I bequeath it to you. If you send me a church bulletin someday where you have used that title, I'll send you a free copy of the book.

One of my colleagues, having heard that I was going to speak today, said "Ray, for goodness sake, make it simple." I said "Oh, simple. You mean you want me to strip away the syntactical opacity and lay bare the intrinsic semantical significance of verbal entities and their objective correlation to ontological reality? Sure! I can do that. I learned how to do that from Dan Fuller years ago in his class. I've since heard that Dan has gone on to more sophisticated things, but I like to stay with the ABCs.

On Being Christian

Note that it is not "on being *a* Christian." That's an entirely different matter; I'm not sure I'd have a sermon on that. As I read the New Testament literature, I find very little concern for that question: "on being *a* Christian." The emphasis is upon being Christian. If you want to know if I am a Christian, you can ask me and I will tell you. I have a testimony to give to you that I am a Christian. If you want to know if I am being Christian, you ask my faculty colleagues, and my students, and the people that live and work with me.

When the Apostle Paul wrote to the church at Philippi, and gave them that magnificent christological hymn that is so familiar to us: "Have this mind in you which you have in Christ Jesus. Though he existed in the

---

[1] Ray Anderson's baccalaureate sermon at Fuller Theological Seminary, June 4, 1986.

form of God he did not think it robbery to be equal with God, but he humbled himself, took upon himself the form of a servant, and, being found in human form he was obedient unto death, even death upon a cross." Now, preceding that is Paul's pastoral admonition to the church, verse 27 of chapter one: "Only let your manner of life be worthy of the gospel of Christ, so that whether I come and see you, or am absent, I may hear of you that you stand firm in one Spirit with one mind, striving side by side for the faith of the gospel, not frightened in anything by your opponents . . . ," and so on. Then, Paul comes to the christological content of that pastoral admonition: "Have this mind in you which you have in Jesus Christ." Being found in human form does not mean merely that he became human by himself, but that he took hold of humanity, our humanity. He lived humanly among us. He was obedient unto death; he saw his name on a cross, and so he lived among us redemptively. And he received his life out of death, for the joy that was set before him. Knowing that the Father will glorify him, he lived his life among us gloriously. Humanly, redemptively, gloriously, he lived. Jesus is the content of what it is to be Christian: it is being human when it really counts. Being human when it really counts.

The New Testament seems to have very little concern about the abstract issue of the humanity of Jesus Christ, which occupies volumes and volumes of theological reflection. Jesus wasn't human simply by laying aside a clerical collar and having a night out with the boys. You didn't discover his humanity in the playground; you found his humanity out in the streets where it counted. There are some people, and you hear them talk: "You want to see how human our pastor is, you get him into a game of touch football. He's really human after all." That doesn't count. Being Christian is being human when it really counts.

When the woman came in off the street and began to wash Jesus' feet, a murmur went up: "If he knew what manner of woman this was, he would withdraw himself from her." Jesus said "Let her alone; she has done a beautiful thing for me." He was human when it counted. When the children were brought to him and the disciples even did not want him to be bothered by this little domestic ritual of mothers wanting children blessed, he said "No, do not forbid them. For of such is the Kingdom of God," and he took them in his arms, his human arms, and he blessed them. After his resurrection, and it was the resurrection of his humanity, he first sought out Peter. Peter, who had denied him. The last look that Peter had of the living face of Jesus was in the framework of the words "I do not know the man." He swore by the name of Yahweh that Jesus was a stranger to him. Then Peter went out and wept bitterly, his own humanity shattered. Jesus, being raised from the dead, found Peter and humanly, when it counted, said, "Peter, you still belong to me." The best apologetic for the resurrection is Christ's Spirit-filled humanity. The best apologetic is the humanity of Jesus after the resurrection, because that's when it counts. It is not some ghostly apparition that convinces us, but the Holy Ghost living in real persons. That's being Christian, because it is being human when it really counts.

Being found in human form, Jesus humbled himself and was obedient, even unto death. This being Christian is not only being human when it really counts; it is giving your life for the right reason. One thing about Jesus is that he was crucified for the right reason. He had a hundred other opportunities to give his life away. There were other people crucified the same day. Jesus gave his life for the right reason; it was out of obedience to the Father. He was not obedient to death; he was obedient to God the Father. He was willing to take up his life, even to the point of the cross, through that obedience to the Father. He gave his life for the right reason. The torment of our lives is that there are a hundred voices crying out to crucify us, to be the altar on which we sacrifice ourselves. Our flesh will be stripped from us bit by bit, but it is our privilege, being Christian, to give our own humanity where it counts, for the right reason. To serve, with our humanity, so that our life and our death become the single destiny that we have here on Earth. To see our name on a cross. "Take up your cross, and follow me," said Jesus. "Don't take mine; take your own." Take your own life in your hands, and find a place for it. Give your life, for the right reason.

Nikos Kazantzakis, author of *Zorba the Greek*, wrote another novel called *The Last Temptation of Christ*. The entire novel is the story of Jesus of Nazareth, who began well, and with great vision called his disciples to him. They forsook fathers and mothers and houses and homes, and they became his disciples, but somewhere along the way it went wrong. As Kazantzakis' story unfolds, Jesus falls in love. He marries, he has children, he becomes burdened with the domestic affairs. There is little time to go out and preach the Kingdom of God. The story goes on and on, unmercifully, drawing us into a caricature of the Jesus of whom the gospels tell us. At the end of the novel, when there is only one page left, the disciples are still coming to him. They are old men by now, bitter, disillusioned, cynical, saying, "Betrayer, you have betrayed us! We gave everything for the Kingdom of God; you have given nothing for it." Jesus says, "For God's sake, have a little pity for me, a little human compassion for me." The disciples say, "We're sorry; we have none." Then, on the very last page, Jesus feels the shock of something put on his lips. He looks around and he begins to feel the crown of thorns, he feels the nails through his hands, and a deep abiding joy surges through him, and he cries out with joy, "I am really on the cross, all of this was a delusion." It was the "last temptation" of Satan himself to fill Jesus' mind with this lie. Jesus thinks to himself "I was faithful; I am on the cross; it is *my* cross. The nails belong to me." At this point Jesus shouts, "It is finished!" and the novel ends.

Dietrich Bonhoeffer, in 1939, came to the United States to escape military conscription and the onslaught of Hitler's terror in Germany. He was only here six weeks when he said, "I must go back" and he bought a one-way ticket back to Germany in 1939. And it was a one-way ticket. He said, "No one will have a right to participate in the reconstruction of Germany who has not entered into the suffering and torment. I am German. And I am Christian. And the two together must find their target, where it counts." Bonhoeffer stripped off his clerical robe and invested his humanity in a place where it counted. He took up opposition against Hitler; he took up the cause of the Jew, and invested his Christian humanity in the cause of the Jew, where it counted. In the end, of course, he died but he died for the right reason. He was crucified on the right cross.

One year ago, Aubrey Adams sat here, like you, to receive his master of arts in theology degree, and then with his wife to head back to his native country of South Africa, where his brother was already in prison for protesting the inhumanity of apartheid. He went back to be a colored Jesus in a land where God appears to be white, and no doubt, there is a problem of paternity. But he had no other place to go except to say, "I am colored, I am South African, and I am Christian. That is my cross, that is my place."

"And God therefore, has highly exalted him, and bestowed on him the name which is above every name, that at the name of Jesus every knee should bow in heaven and on earth, and under the earth, and every tongue confess that Jesus Christ is Lord, to the glory of God the Father."

Being Christian is not only being human where it counts, not only giving your life for the right reason; it is also living with the glory in your heart. For all of the desperateness of the situation with Jesus, you'll never find him without the glory in his heart. He spoke of his own death as his moment of being "glorified." He prayed in John 17, "Father, the glory which thou hast given me, I have given to them. I am glorified in them." The story of the passion of Jesus is a story of a man who had the glory in his heart, and he lived it.

Four years ago, Matt Reynolds sat here, where you are sitting. He received his Master of Arts degree in theology. Matt was a young man who had experienced some problems growing up that had left him with a slight speech impediment. He was weak of stature, but he was a terror on theology. He bit into a theology of the incarnation like you wouldn't believe, and he wouldn't let it go. "But where am I going to go?" he said; "Who will hire me? I have a speech impediment, I'm not fluent." He graduated; we said, "God bless him," and there it was. About three or four months later, he called me up and said, "Ray, you wouldn't believe it, but I have just been invited to become a pastor of a little United Church of Christ in Kansas, a town that nobody has ever heard of, and God has given me this call, and I am going. Will you come and preach my ordination sermon?" So, on a Sunday afternoon, in a church in Laguna Beach where his parents are co-pastors, it was my privilege to preach the ordination sermon for Matt.

Just a few months earlier, another Fuller student had been suddenly stricken, taken into the hospital, and was dead of cancer within two weeks. I had called on him in the hospital that first week, and he had said "It's incredible! I finally came to God; I came to my senses. I came to this seminary, over thirty years of age. I came here, now, finally, having gotten it right. And now, I'll be dead in ten days." In the silence, he thought a moment, and then said, "No, it is right. It is right. This is the right place. This is the right time. This is God's time. And it is finished. It is begun and it is finished." I told that story in the ordination sermon for Matt Reynolds, and said, "Matt, this call of God upon your life is not a guarantee of success or long life, but it is a deep assurance to you that nothing can ever happen to take you out of God's place. Neither height nor depth nor principalities nor powers. Whatever happens you are in the right place."

After the service, his father came to me and thanked me for the sermon, but he said, "I am truly sorry that you cast such a shadow over such a joyous occasion." I apologized. I said, "I had not planned to say that; it came to me. I am sorry." Six months later, his father called me and said, "I have bad news. The church leaders in Kansas called me. They went to the church on Sunday morning, but it was dark and cold. So they went over to the house where Matt lived alone, and he had died in his sleep. He was dead." Matt's father said, "Now I understand why you were led to say that in that ordination sermon. That is a comfort to us; that it is the right place, the right time."

Even as we are gathered here, your fellow student, our brother in Christ, Romeo Serto, is in the hospital, his life ebbing out. He may not live the day, this brother from India, whose wife we are not even able to contact. Who will say that this is the wrong place, the wrong time for him? No, it is the right time, and it is the right place. Even as we are gathered here today, if it is God's will to take him before the day is over, we have begun the processional that will lead him right up to the threshold of the Kingdom of God, because he has the glory in his heart. He is in God's place, and God's time.

You want it simple? Let me tell it simple. You are going out, and some of you are going to go into therapy, to heal people. You are going to use all of the therapeutic techniques you have been taught, and you are going to fail on certain occasions. You are going to be pushed to the very brink of your own humanity. You will find yourself breaking, you will find yourself weeping real human tears, not therapeutic tears. But because they are human tears, and they are your tears, and you will cry out, "My God, I'm not sure what to do." And the other person will say, "Did you say 'God'?" And dear God, you will even find yourself praying with that person. There will be a magnificent and marvelous revolution in that person's life and heart. There will be healing; there will be wholeness.

Then you will say, "That's what it's about! That's integration. That's being Christian. That's being a healer. That's being human." That lies ahead of you.

You want it simple? Let me tell it to you simple. Some of you are going into the church. You are going into pastoral ministry of one kind or another. You are going to find yourself with an unmanageable army. You are going to find yourself with recruits that no longer want to serve in God's army. You are going to find yourself up against obstacles that were only horror stories in a pastoral theology class. But now they will be real. You will preach one hundred or two hundred sermons, and it will be labor. One day, you will lay aside the notes, and you will take the word of God in your hand like Elijah took the mantle. You will say, "Where is the Lord God of Elijah?" and you will lay the word, and the water will divide, and you will never again be the same. You will have experienced the reality of the power of God's Word flowing through you. That's where you are going. You are going out for that.

You want it simple? Let me tell it to you simple. Some of you are going out and you are going to thrust yourself into the stark terror and inhumanity of this world, where the principalities and powers wear three-piece suits. You are going into the city which has uncreated humanity; you are going to stare that evil right in the face, and you are going to call upon the power of God. You are going to see the recreation of humanity in the city, in the villages, in the jungles. We are going out, brothers and sisters. We are going out. To be human. We're going out to live redemptive lives, to find the cross with our name on it. We're going out with the glory in our hearts. The way out is shorter than the way back. Many of us will never make it back. Some of us will never make it to a graceful and gray-haired old age, reflecting and basking in the success of our ministry. Some of us will never live to experience the cozy Presbyterian retirement.

We are going out. For many of us, there is no way back. No way back. We have ten days. Ten days. At the end of those ten days, something will happen that will tear us apart. Never ever again on the face of God's good Earth, after those ten days are over, will every single one of us be in the same place again. Never ever. Oh, there will be reunions, of a sort. But not of all of us, not ever again, on the face of this Earth.

The disciples, after the resurrection, were gathered in Jerusalem. Acts tells us they were all there in one place, until Pentecost. Pentecost was the end of that. Ten days from now is our Pentecost. It is the day of the anointing. It's the day of the sending out. We call it commencement, but it is really our Pentecost. We have ten days to have our reunions. Christians are unique; they have all their reunions before they go. You know what a reunion is like. The old scores are settled; the old grievances are gone. We throw our arms around each other and we are now friends simply because we have been a part. We have ten days to be human, to be Christian, to be reconciled, to prepare ourselves for this Pentecost. Brothers and Sisters, we are going out with the glory in our lives. Hallelujah!

THE EPISTEMOLOGICAL RELEVANCE OF LAUGHTER[1]
(Scripture: Genesis 17 & 18)

I have entitled the message today, "The Epistemological Relevance of Laughter." For the more faint-hearted among you, I would suggest an alternative title: "He who laughs, lasts."

Faith grows on the narrow ledge of disbelief. I commend unto you our father Abraham, the man of faith, a man who had a habit of falling on his face. In this Scripture reading we see two occasions, and certainly there would be more with a man who had this particular habit. The first time he falls on his face, we are told, occurred when God spoke to him of this covenant and its marvelous implications too incredible to be grasped. The second occasion, almost immediately following, is when he is told that it is Sarah, his barren wife of ninety years, shall be the one through whom God fulfills this promise. He immediately falls on his face again, and this time laughs. Or, we are told that he laughs. I think that he laughs every time that he falls on his face.

But the interesting thing is this: I do not discern here that in this laughter of Abraham there is anything offensive to God. I envision Abraham lying on his face, pounding the ground with laughter, expressing his willingness to hear and respond and receive, but in his disbelief. How else can he respond? Because there *is* disbelief. There is raw disbelief of its objective possibility. There is no possibility of this being fulfilled. He is forced to disbelieve that his wife can conceive. Yet, in his laughter, he is grasping hold of that reality, and I would suggest in the only appropriate way. For how would you like it for Abraham to have stood there, tugging at his beard, saying, "Yes, I see. All right, that's fine. Anything else you want to talk about, Lord?" Oh no.

I think God would assume that you hadn't gotten the point. You know the old saying, "If you can keep your head when others about you are losing theirs, you don't understand the situation." The enormity of this truth can only evoke this kind of response; I do not think that God is displeased.

Now Sarah also laughs, but she does not fall on her face. Where does Sarah laugh? She stands behind the door of the tent. The eighteenth chapter of Genesis, verses 9-15. Almost immediately after this event, we read, God comes to Abraham again as the three angels of Yahweh. They said to him, "Where is Sarah, your wife?" He said, "She is in the tent." And the Lord said to him, "I will surely return to you in the spring, and Sarah,

---

[1] Ray Anderson's chapel sermon at Fuller Theological Seminary on Jan. 20, 1977.

your wife, shall have a son." Sarah was listening at the tent door behind him. Now Abraham and Sarah were old, advanced in age. It had ceased to be with Sarah after the manner of women. So Sarah laughed to herself, saying, "After I have grown old and my husband is old, shall I have pleasure?" The Lord said to Abraham, "Why did Sarah laugh, and say 'shall I indeed bear a child, now that I am old?'" Is anything too hard for the Lord? At the appointed time, I will return to you in the spring. Sarah shall have a son." Sarah denied, saying, "I did not laugh," for she was afraid. And he said, "No, you did laugh."

Now, I suggest that this is the laughter of unbelief, not disbelief. It is the laughter that is tinged with cynicism, and some bitterness, not with astonishment and joy. We must understand that Sarah would have received this word of promise from a different perspective than Abraham. There was no question of Abraham's virility. He had a 13 year-old son standing by his side, constantly: Ishmael. "Is it possible for Abraham to conceive? Certainly; I have evidence of it." Here's a woman who has never conceived. How many years did she hope that she might, and be a mother of Israel? How often had she caused that hope to awaken again, only to be disheartened? Finally, past the age of bearing children, she could at least, with some relief, not have to take up that expectation again. "At least *that* does not torment me." We read in the fifteenth chapter that Abraham certainly must not have made it very easy for her, because when God had told Abraham earlier that he would have a son, and through that son the promise would be fulfilled, Abraham said, "Lord God, what would thou give me, for I continue childless?" I can hear Abraham almost saying that over and over again, every morning. "Lord, what are you going to give me, I continue childless." I suggest that he lamented that fact in the presence of Sarah.

Now Abraham is the father of faith because he laughed in God's presence. The angel rebuked Sarah, not for laughing, but for denying it. If she had brought her laughter out, and fallen on her face before the angel, and pounded the ground with her fist, God would not have rebuked her.

I am reminded of one of the Hassidic tales that [Martin] Buber liked to tell of the old rabbi who was sitting around the table when the Word of God was read, the passage being "and God said." The rabbi got up and ran out of the room, and stood in the hall pounding his fist against the wall, gesticulating and shouting, ". . . and God said, and God said," absolutely in hysterics over the phenomenon that God speaks. We are not astonished at that; we ought to be. Every time we hear that, we ought to fall on our face and pound the ground with astonishment. In disbelief, and yet, believing in that disbelief.

For Abraham, faith is growing even in his disbelief. I suggest to you two ways in which that faith grows. "Oh that Ishmael might live before you." There is, first of all, an unlearning that must strip away all of the human presupposition that we bring to sustain faith, an unlearning. "Lord, here is Ishmael, my thirteen year-old son. Thirteen years ago, we considered him to be an answer to prayer. Lord, every night, I have taken this young boy on my knee, and I have told him again and again of the promise that you gave to me. I have taught him that that promise belongs to him. With wide eyes, he has absorbed my teaching. He is the promised seed." And God says, "Then unteach him. Unteach him; pull up that plant by the roots. Go back and tell him that you misunderstood." The unlearning that must accompany faith. "Oh that Ishmael might live before you." No. We all bring assumptions to the task of theology. We fight for them; we debate them. How long does it take for us to accept the discipline of unlearning, that the Word of God might stand within us, on its own? "Oh that Ishmael might live before you!" "No; unteach him."

Then there is the relearning that must now demand new responses. Isaac will be the gift of God, but Abraham and Sarah must meet again, face to face, and make love in hope. Abraham must convince Sarah to relearn that hope, to rekindle that hope. He must take her face in his hands and turn her face toward him, and meet her in love and hope. For Isaac will be given out of that meeting. They must relearn that movement of love that produces hope. Do they laugh? Yes. Is there now astonishment in their love? Yes! Because their love is a way to grasp the promise of God, in disbelief, and yet in hope.

When we decided to move to Scotland for a few years of study, it was at the end of eleven years of parish ministry. Our daughter Ruth was born in August of the very year that we had graduated from Fuller Seminary, and had taken up our ministry. When she was almost eleven years old, we decided to make that move, with all its irrevocable implications of disposing of house, furniture, cars, and eleven years of accumulation. Moving to Scotland with no agenda beyond that, we made that decision several months prior to the announcement of it to the congregation in the spring of that year. But we did not tell Ruth, because we assumed that she would be unable to enter into those tentative explorations and discussions. The morning I was to read my letter of resignation to the congregation, at the breakfast table, I said, "Ruth, I have something to tell you. In August of this year, we are going to sell this house, we are going to leave this home, we are going to leave this church, and we are going to Scotland. Do you know where Scotland is?" And she said, "Yes, it's pink." She thought it was a geography lesson. I said, "Ruth, we are going to leave here and move to Scotland," and she laughed and kept right on eating. "No, we're not," she said; she thought we were kidding. It was the laugh of unbelief, because she thought we were kidding.

I said, "No, Ruth, we are going and never coming back. We are leaving." She looked at me, and over her face was that fleeting movement of something. Then she laughed. This time, the laughter was just as strong, almost hysterical. She said, "No, we're not," but she knew, and I knew that she knew. It was the only way she could let me know that she knew; the only way that she could absorb this was to laugh. The interesting thing, from that moment on, until August, as we made our preparations, she never questioned. She never really argued. So what did she know when she laughed the second time?

She knew that because she belonged to us, that was her fate. Belonging to us was a destiny over which she had no control. She could not possibly have understood; we made no attempt to explain to her the rationality of it. We simply insisted that she accept it as her fate, as being part of our lives, and that movement of our life. Because she accepted it, because she knew that--even in her disbelief she knew that--there was no argument. Even at the end, she could say goodbye to her friends and sell her toys at the garage sale, because she knew.

Michael Polanyi once said "Our believing is conditioned at its source by our belonging." I think of Peter. In John 6, when all others left because they could not abide that Word, they left in unbelief. Jesus said to his disciples, "Will you go also?" Peter said, "To whom shall we go? Only you have the words of eternal life." Did he laugh? I think so. "To whom shall we go? Our fate is being bound up with you, and we know *that*, though we understand nothing."

I think of Sarah who learned to laugh as a way of knowing. In chapter 21, when Isaac is born, what does Sarah say of this? Verse 6: And Sarah said, "God has made laughter for me. Everyone who hears will laugh with me." Not *at* me, but *with* me. And she reveled in that knowledge that as the news spread, there was laughter, astonishment. She liked to think of it. I mean imagine this ninety-one year old woman deliberately walking into the Women's Missionary Fellowship and saying, "Ladies, you'll pardon me if I have to leave early; I have to go home and nurse my baby." I can see Sarah deliberately splitting them up, creating the astonishment. Why? Because that is at the center of her faith. Abraham also laughed in Genesis 17:17ff., when the Lord promised him a son. "The Lord said you shall call him Isaac." That son, for Abraham and Sarah, was a constant joy because he was a constant astonishment to them.

Karl Barth once wrote in his essay "Theological Existence in Evangelical Theology" these words:

> A quite specific astonishment stands at the beginning of every theological perception, inquiry, and thought, in fact, at the root of every theological word. If such astonishment is lacking, the whole enterprise of even the best theologian would canker at the root. On the other hand, as long as even a poor theologian

is capable of astonishment, he is not lost to the fulfillment of the task.

If you have become barren, and it has ceased to be with you after the manner of a theological student, consider the God who gives life from the dead. If you have fallen on your face, it may not be the worst position. It may well be that that which has been stripped from you is for the purpose of causing you in astonishment to relearn, to now possess a faith that, in its constant astonishment, will constantly renew and inspire, and be a joy to you. I have seen no one fall on their face in chapel. We do not have that happen. But I have, figuratively speaking, seen bodies strewn all over campus, who have fallen on their faces, in unbelief, in despair, and in emptiness. I'm saying to you that somewhere there is a connection between that which drives you to that position, and that narrow ledge of disbelief in which faith can be born and thrive as a source of astonishment and joy. You will jump to your feet and praise God. Let us pray.

Our Father, astonish us, overwhelm us. Be an exciting and creative God to us, who delights in speaking to our barrenness to demonstrate your great power and Word.

CASE STUDIES[1]

The case situation approach attempts to create an integration and practical focus for basic theological themes, demonstrating competence in approaching life situations from a theological and biblical perspective. In order to keep the responses as relevant as possible to the situation presented, critical endnotes should be attached to each response in which more technical theological points are made and sources cited. You are free to discuss the questions with other members of the class, but what you write should be your own work. The exam will be evaluated on the basis of the precision and coherence achieved in dealing with the topic, depth of theological insight which goes beyond mere paraphrasing of other material, and the overall helpfulness of your responses for those to whom they are directed. Include at the end of each part a report of your reading, including page numbers.

ST512 THEOLOGICAL ANTHROPOLOGY AND THE REVELATION OF GOD [Systematic Theology I: Doctrine of God, Scripture, Humanity, Theodicy]

1. You have a friend who is doing graduate work in the social sciences at a nearby university. She/he is not sympathetic to the tenets of the Christian faith, and wants to engage you in a dialogue on the matter of the grounds for faith. From previous conversations you know that this discussion will center on the question of how one who is trained in the scientific method can possibly accept non-empirical evidence as valid for belief. In anticipating this discussion, you decide to write out an imaginary dialogue with this person in which you can test out your own thinking on the subject. You realize that you will have to deal with the nature of revelation and decide to do this through the "paradigm" approach, using biblical events as sources. Attach a set of endnotes documenting sources.

2. You have just come from a debate sponsored by the theological faculty in which two faculty members took quite opposite positions. One insisted that the truth of divine revelation is accessible to the human mind and can be established as truth without bringing faith in as an epistemological assumption. The other vehemently repudiated this position and insisted that the truth can only be known through faith, so that only a believer can know that a human word can become divine revelation. Words like "rationalism" and "fideism" are thrown around

---

[1] These cases constitute Prof. Anderson's take-home examinations.

rather freely. You are constrained to write a response for the *OPINION*, a student publication which solicits contributions of this sort. You decide to begin with a theological exegesis of Genesis 3:1, "Has God said . . . ," as a way of focussing on the matter of verification of the Word of God (then again, you may decide not to use that beginning-- but you do have to begin!). Attach a set of endnotes documenting sources.

3. You teach an adult class in a large church as part of your intern assignment while completing your seminary degree. On one particular Sunday, the class discussion focussed on the implications of Paul's statement in Romans 8:28: "We know that in everything God works for good with those who love him, who are called according to his purpose." You explained the verse in terms of our confidence in God's providence, so that we know that God is always in control, even over the power of evil. The following Sunday, Sara Smith, a member of the class, handed you a note in which she wrote, "As you know, my husband and I had a child who was born with a severe microcephalic condition, and died 18 months later, after much suffering. I tried to understand this as part of God's plan and purpose, but have given up. I no longer believe that God is all powerful and controls every event which takes place. I have found Rabbi Harold Kushner's book, *When Bad Things Happens to Good People*, to be more helpful. I think that he is right when he says, 'I can worship a God who hates suffering but cannot eliminate it more than I can worship a God who chooses to make children suffer and die.'" You decide to write a letter to her in response giving her what you consider to be the biblical teaching on God's sovereignty and the problem of human suffering. Attach endnotes documenting sources and interacting with some of the more technical theological issues.

4. Pastor Don Smith was challenged in his use of scriptures as a divine authority by a young college student one morning after the sermon. "The Bible was written by men, right?" said the young woman. "Then it is an imperfect book and only reveals the religious insights and feelings of the people who write it." "Yes, it was written by men," replied Pastor Smith, rising to the challenge, "but the authors were inspired by the Spirit of God, and therefore it is divine revelation. Inspiration protected the authors from their own imperfect knowledge and guarantees to us that the Bible is true. The Bible has the authority of God himself because he is the primary author through his Spirit; the human authors are only secondary authors. The authority of scripture is determined by its claim to be divinely inspired. You must accept that claim as being true before the Bible will have any authority for you. After all," he concluded, "The

Bible clearly claims to be inspired by God himself, and thus if that claim is true it is the Word of God and not of men, right?" "Wrong," she replied, as she turned away, "but I don't know why." Is this incident another case of the "rich young ruler," who turns away from Jesus, leaving us with a feeling of sorrow? If you feel that with some time to think about it, a better response could be made to this young woman's question, write a letter to her giving your considered response which you feel would be more convincing. Attach a set of endnotes documenting sources used and discussing some of the technical theological points.

5. You have accepted an invitation to speak on a university campus to a student group in the theme: "Good News for Modern People." The leaders of the group have told you that the topic came out of a discussion with some non-Christians who were majors in cultural anthropology, and that the subject of translating the Word of God into modern thought forms, relevant to different cultural and ethnic traditions, was a source of lively debate. Some asserted that the Bible was written from one cultural and ethnic perspective, but that in translating it into a modern culture, the ideas as well as the words must be changed. In preparation, you decide to write out a brief statement which expresses your own view upon which you can enlarge when you actually give the talk. You want to be sure that you are able to explain what the Word of God actually is in a non-technical way, and yet deal with the critical problems of cross-cultural communication. Attach endnotes to document sources and discuss technical points.

6. You are an intern on a church staff, asked by the Pastor to participate in a community seminar on human rights. At its first meeting, the question of the theological basis for a stand on human rights emerges. You are asked to prepare a brief paper dealing with this question for the next meeting. Someone suggests that you begin with the saying of Jesus already cited in the meeting found in Matthew 12:12, "of how much more value is a man than a sheep." Someone else also referred to the recent issue of *TIME* magazine which featured a cover story on the evolutionary origins of human life and somewhat facetiously remarked that you will probably have trouble showing how the image of God could have developed in this way! The Pastor won't let you off the hook, and you consider the alternative of finding another placement! However, you still have to write a paper for this class, so you give it a try! Attach endnotes documenting sources.

7. An adult Sunday School class of a church in your city is beginning a series entitled, "Relationships of Men and Women in the Bible," and

they have asked you to be a guest speak for the first session. Of course, they want you to talk about Adam and Eve! Your next-door neighbor began attending that church a year ago, and you have noticed some problems developing in their relationship. The wife has become more passive and even depressed, while the husband seems to be caught up with the challenge to be the "godly leader" of "his home." They have shown interest in this series and you expect that they will attend. In considering the needs of this group, you realize that your first talk could have major implications for their evaluation of subsequent sessions. Taking this opportunity seriously, you decide to write out your view of male/female relationships based upon the biblical account of creation, also drawing upon relevant texts from the New Testament. Don't worry that reading your paper to the class may only consume six or seven minutes--you know that its relevant content will generate lively discussion! Use endnotes to document sources and to discuss more technical theological points.

8. Betty is single, a college graduate, works as an appraiser in an insurance office, and attends the social functions of the young adult group in your church, but only infrequently the worship services. She has had several short, but intense relationships with men over the past few months, and recently moved to an apartment complex which advertises itself as an "adult community for singles," and is popularly known as a place for "swingers." In a candid moment, she reveals to you the fact that she has adopted a life style that includes sexual freedom. "My father is a minister," she said, "and I was brought up to feel that sexual desire outside of marriage was sinful. However," she went on, "I discovered that sexual desire is part of my physical nature and if it is wrong, then it is my nature that is sinful, and not a particular act. If what the church calls sin is part of my human creatureliness, then I will do what comes naturally and let the church go to hell." Despite the vehemence of her statement, you sensed that she was really seeking a better alternative. You decide to write her a letter in which you attempt to make clear the relation between sin and human creatureliness, focussing on the image of God and male/female relationships. Attach endnotes documenting sources and interacting with some of the more technical theological issues.

9. At an inter-church conference of lay leaders for your denomination, a discussion of human sexuality leads to the public acknowledgement of a homosexual life style by a staff member from a church in another city. You were impressed by the mature and thoughtful way in which the group handled this revelation, but could not hold back your own opinion that homosexuality was a fundamental disorder when

considered from the perspective of God's creation of humanity as male and female. The response was gentle but firm: "I have no other nature than an orientation to members of my own sex. I think that you are reflecting typical cultural patterns of hostility toward the homosexual person, which even the Bible contains, rather than a truth based upon divine revelation." You had no immediate response to this, but cannot shake the discussion from your mind. After returning home, you decide to write this person a letter and explain more fully what your views are on the subject after studying more thoroughly the issue from a theological perspective. Add endnotes documenting sources and interacting with some of the critical issues.

10. On a plane trip home, you are seated on a full flight. As the flight progresses, you strike up a conversation with a pleasant-looking man who occupies the center seat next to you. You take note that he seems very intelligent, and he subsequently identifies himself as the Chairperson of the Department of Comparative Studies at a large state university. As your conversation progresses, and you begin to discuss Christianity, he identifies himself as a gay Christian. You have just discussed issues of Christianity and homosexuality in class the previous week, so you pursue the issue of homosexuality and biblical authority. Your new friend is very polite, and very well prepared for this discussion. One of his main objections is quite thought provoking. "Some Christians only obey the Bible when it says what they want it to. The ordination of gays is prohibited by most churches because they say that the Bible condemns homosexual behavior. To me, it seems that Paul prohibits women's ordination also. When it comes to ordaining women, however, many Christians are willing to ignore what Paul says completely. How can they be so inconsistent?" You fumble for a quick and inadequate response which he does not challenge. Anyway, you were saved by the announcement that the plane is about to land! The gentleman had given you his card when you parted and suggested that you continue some correspondence on the issue. Later, you realize that your home Presbytery is struggling with this same issue, and you decide to write a paper which can be presented to your local church board of elders as a basis for discussion of the issue of the ordination of homosexuals. You write the paper for your board of elders dealing with the issue raised by your flight companion. You will also send him a copy of your paper, so you will want to include some discussion of the issue he raised. In your paper explain exactly what the issue is and write it so that it can be understood by laypersons. Attach endnotes documenting sources and interaction with some of the more technical theological points.

Case Studies

11. Peggy Smith, an active member of Christ the King Church and President of the singles organization in the church, called the Ambassadors, felt on the threshold of a nervous breakdown. She had been divorced from her husband of 10 years for two years now, and with two children in school, worked full time to support herself and to help make up the times when child support payments did not come from her former husband. When she confided in her Pastor and shared with him the periods of depression which came with increasing frequency, she was told that her problem was not emotional but spiritual. "If you really were obedient to the teachings of Scripture," the Pastor had said, "you would experience the comfort and strength of Christ and would not need any other crutch to lean on." You are a part-time intern on the church's staff, and when she related the conversation with the Pastor to you, your advice was to seek professional counseling, as her problem was probably one that required therapy and not spiritual platitudes. This was apparently reported back to the Pastor, who has sent you a note demanding an explanation! Because you had spoken rather impulsively, you decide to prepare for your discussion with the Pastor by thinking through the matter more carefully and writing out a statement expressing your understanding of the emotional and spiritual dynamics as related to Christian faith. You might write this out and send it to the Pastor ahead of time so that your position will be made more clear prior to the encounter. Attach endnotes documenting sources and discussing theological points too complicated for the Pastor to follow!

ST514 RECONCILIATION AND HEALING OF PERSONS
[Systematic Theology II: Doctrine of Christ, Atonement]

1. Marty is the teacher of an adult Sunday School class which you attend. During a class discussion on the relationship of Christianity to the Jewish religion, he made the statement that the Church is the result of God's action in rejecting the Jews and starting over again with Jesus. When one member of the class challenged him by saying that Jesus himself was a Jew, he responded by quoting Galatians 3:28, "In Christ there is neither Jew nor Greek. . . ." You respond by citing John 1:14, "'The Word became flesh and dwelt among us," and making the point that it was significant that in the incarnation God had assumed Jewish flesh for our salvation. The class ended at that point. However, Marty came up to you and asked you to make your point more clear. You agreed to write a brief paper on the subject and share it with him so that you could discuss the question further. Add endnotes documenting sources with additional critical comments interacting with the sources cited.

2. At a church Bible study for college students and single adults, the question came up as to whether or not it is proper to pray to Jesus or whether we should pray to God "in the name of Jesus." The youth minister spoke up and said that he remembers a professor of theology in seminary warning them against the danger of "Apollinarianism" in worship by making Jesus so divine that he becomes merely an object of worship. "Unfortunately," he adds, "I can't remember why this would be a problem, but I think that it does have something to do with the question of prayer to Jesus." Turning to you, he suggests that you prepare a brief response to the question to present at the next meeting as a basis for further discussion. In preparing this response, he asks you not to deal with the historical material concerning Apollinarius as much as the central thrust of his position with regard to the person of Christ, showing the practical implications for prayer and worship. Add endnotes documenting sources and including some critical interaction with issues and sources.

3. The minister of the church which you attend has preached a Good Friday sermon on the text: "My God, my God, why hast thou forsaken me?" (Matt. 27:46). In this sermon he stated that on the cross, the transcendent and divine aspect of Jesus' personality withdrew to the point that we have only a human person left. But that this makes it possible for there to be a complete identification of Jesus with our humanity, and so he can be our mediator. As you leave the service, you mention to the pastor that you were disturbed by some of the theological implications of his teaching concerning the doctrine of salvation. Because there is little opportunity to talk at the moment, he asks you to put your thoughts down on paper, setting forth the theological concerns which you have together with your own explanation of the text, with the promise to make an appointment with you to discuss the matter after he had read it. You do this in the form of a letter, adding endnotes documenting sources and elaborating on some of the critical issues.

4. The statement of faith subscribed to by Fuller Seminary includes the following statement on the atonement: "By his death in our stead, he [Christ] revealed the divine love and upheld divine justice, removing our guilt and reconciling us to God." An elder in the church at which you interviewed for a position as youth director challenged you at this point, having read the Fuller statement himself prior to the interview. "I was brought up on the doctrine of the substitutionary atonement," he said, "but I now find that this is inconsistent with the nature of God as a loving and forgiving Father. I don't want you to give our young

people the impression that God must be paid off by the blood of an innocent man before he will forgive us." You had not really thought much about this yourself, so you make a response. Fortunately (providentially!), you were taking a class at that very time in which the atonement was discussed. In preparation for your response to the church, you write out your own statement as an elaboration of the Fuller statement on atonement, dealing with this concern. Add endnotes documenting sources and interacting with the critical issues and sources.

5. At an inter-seminary retreat, you are engaged in a stimulating discussion with Joe, a Roman Catholic seminarian. At one point in the discussion, he challenged you on the Protestant doctrine of justification by faith. "It seems difficult," he argued, "to understand how one could hold that a righteous relation to God can be determined by simply believing that God has fully accepted you as a sinner. This would empty the doctrine of sanctification of all significance for, to the extent that you take seriously the command of God to live a holy life, you are compromising the principle of justification by faith." You had not really thought about that before, and are unable to give him an immediate answer. However, he asks you to write to him and state your position. Add endnotes documenting sources and interacting with the critical issues.

6. In reading through a portion of *Calvin's Institutes of the Christian Religion,* you come across the statement: "All things being at God's disposal, and the decision of salvation or death belonging to him, he orders all things by his counsel and decree in such a manner, that some men are born devoted from the womb to certain death, that his name may be glorified in their destruction" (*Institutes.*, III, 23, 6). Your first reaction was one of anger, then disbelief that anyone could have said such a thing. Then you remembered that a good many people do hold to the doctrine of double predestination and of the limited atonement. You decide that you will first of all attempt to understand what Calvin meant by this, and then formulate your own response. You know a professor of theology at Fuller, and decide to submit your brief paper to him for a critique! Add endnotes documenting sources and interacting with critical issues.

7. The church where you serve on the staff as director of parish renewal, would like to begin a healing ministry in connection with the monthly communion service. At the meeting of elders, where this was presented for discussion, one elder spoke up enthusiastically. "I have been waiting for this emphasis for some time. I visited a church where

people are being healed and heard the pastor say that God intends that we be healed of our physical afflictions because our healing is 'in the atonement.'" This provoked some strong reactions among the group but, as the pastor later commented, "There was more heat than light!" Because this ministry would fall under your supervision, the pastor asks you to prepare a brief paper on the subject of "healing and the atonement," for presentation at the next board meeting. "I'm not sure how I would answer this questions myself," confessed the pastor, "this was never covered in seminary and I'm not really a theologian. But give it your best shot! While you realize that your paper will need to be understood by the lay persons on the board, you also want to cover some technical theological issues and point the pastor toward some resources. Therefore, you add some endnotes documenting sources and interacting with the critical theological issues.

8. "Christians aren't perfect, just forgiven," read the bumper sticker on the dented and dusty pickup which swerved suddenly in front of Jill's car on the freeway. "Another one of those born again Christians," Jill thought to herself. "The sticker should read, 'Being forgiven means you never have to say you're sorry!'" That evening, as she is writing a letter to her formed college roommate who is now in seminary, she describes the incident, and writes, "You see! This is why I have so much trouble with you Christians. You told me the reason that you changed your major from biology to religion was that you had a 'conversion' experience and had become a born again Christian. Yes, you changed your vocational goals, but frankly you are the same person to me that you have always been--no better and no worse. I know that you have quoted the Bible to me about being born again and converted, but I really don't see that it makes much difference. Born again Christians still have problems don't they? And aren't converted people just acting out their neurotic patterns through different kinds of behavior?" Putting yourself in the place of Jill's friend, write a letter to Jill attempting to show her what the real meaning of conversion and being born again is. Put your discussion of technical theological terms and issues in the endnotes, along with documentation of sources used. Who knows, you might even get away with using this letter to fulfill a course requirement some day!

Case Studies

ST516 THEOLOGY OF CHRISTIAN COMMUNITY AND MINISTRY
[Systematic Theology III: Doctrine of the Holy Spirit, Church, Sacraments]

1. In an adult Sunday Class in which you are teaching on the "fruit of the Spirit" (Galatians 5:22-23), a member of the class offers the opinion that these characteristics are often found in non-Christians as well as in Christians. In fact, the class member adds, I know some non-Christians who exhibit more of these qualities in their life than many Christians. "What does Paul mean by 'fruit of the Spirit' and what are we to say about people who have this 'fruit' without having the Spirit of Christ?" You are saved by the bell, as the class is over. In preparation for class next week, you write out a brief statement of your response to share with the class, using endnotes to document sources and to discuss some of the more technical theological points in your discussion.

2. In a discussion with a member of the Greek Orthodox Church, you are told that the Western church, both Catholic and Protestant, has an inferior view of the Holy Spirit. He mentions the introduction of the *filioque* clause into the Nicene Creed by the Western church as a serious error, and a teaching which subordinates the Spirit to the Son. He argues that only when the Spirit proceeds directly from the Father can the Spirit have full parity with the Father and the Son, and only then will the church be liberated to experience the Spirit as the immediate presence and reality of fellowship with God. Your letter to this person should explain your own view of the relation of the Spirit to the Son, and how you respond to the argument that the *filioque* clause leads to an inferior view of the Holy Spirit. Attach endnotes documenting sources and discussing some of the more technical theological points.

3. On Pentecost Sunday in the church year, three members of the congregation are asked to read a brief sermon (5-6 pages) on the topic, "The Spirit as God's Gift to the Church." You are asked to be one of the participants, and as you write your sermon, you remember that during the past year, considerable uneasiness and some controversy has been occurring over the question of the "gifts of the Spirit" and the "charismatic" question. You hope to write a sermon that will provide a basis of understanding and unity for the church in this area. Attach endnotes documenting sources and interaction with some of the more technical theological points.

4. A young man in your church has returned home after spending a year at a Bible College. In an adult Bible class during discussion on the nature of the church, he makes the statement: "The church was born at Pentecost of the Spirit and exists by grace. Therefore, the promise of

God to Israel in the Old Testament as well as much of the early teaching of Jesus which relate to the Kingdom of God do not apply to the church." You challenge him at this point, but he is unable to do any more than repeat his statements without giving a theological basis for them. The teacher of the class asks you to prepare a brief discussion paper for the next class pointing out where you disagree with that position and giving a biblical and theological rationale for your own understanding of the relation of the church to Israel. Attach endnotes documenting sources and discussing some of the more technical theological issues.

5. A friend of yours who is Roman Catholic tells you that your church (Protestant) cannot be the true church because it does not have a bishop who can trace the office directly back to one of the founding apostles. "Without apostolic succession," you are told, "a church cannot be considered to be founded upon the apostles." You had not really thought much about this before, but now decide to do some studying and thinking on the question with a view to writing a letter presenting a Protestant view of what an apostolic church is. Write the letter not so much to argue as to inform, drawing upon some reading you have been doing as well as on biblical material. Attach endnotes documenting sources and interaction with some of the more technical theological points.

6. The church of which you are a member has recently created a stir in the community by sponsoring a half-way house for young people in trouble with the law on church property, located in an economically and socially blighted area of the city. Despite reasonable attempts at security and supervision, the police, through an undercover agent, have discovered that there have been some illegal use of drugs on the part of some of these young people at the half-way house, and made some arrests. At a congregational meeting of the church, the pastor delivered an eloquent argument for the continuation of this ministry on the basis of an "incarnational theology" which was prepared to take such risks for the sake of a Christian presence in the world. The editor of the local newspaper heard about this meeting and asked you to write an article for the religious section of the Saturday edition explaining the nature of an incarnational ministry and how it could be considered to be a ministry of the gospel of Jesus Christ (why wasn't the Pastor asked to write this? Who knows--perhaps she did not take this class when she did her M.Div. degree!). You consider this an excellent opportunity to present a witness to the community and agree. Before you send it to the newspaper, you submit it to your professor where you are taking a course in theology for criticism and suggestions. Include endnotes,

documenting sources and discussing some of the more technical theological points not appropriate for a newspaper article. (see question 9)

7. Bob and Sue come to Pastor Anderson with a problem which they share in common, and yet each has a different situation. Bob was baptized as an infant in the church to which his parents belonged. Last year he experienced a spiritual turning point in his life and made a profession of Jesus Christ as Savior. Sue, on the other hand, was baptized in a Baptist church when she was 12 years old upon her confession of faith, but now says that she doubts that she was really a Christian at that time. She too has come to personal faith in Christ during this past year. Both of them want to know if they are really baptized, or whether or not they should or could be re-baptized. They ask Pastor Anderson to write out a short paper on the meaning of Christian baptism as it relates to faith so that they can study it and make their decision. Write this paper, explaining the nature of baptism and suggesting to them what their options might be. Include endnotes to document your sources and to discuss more technical theological points.

8. Joe is an alcoholic who has made a profession of faith in Christ as Savior, but still struggles with the problem of drinking. He is not a member of the church, but attends frequently and counsels with the pastor regularly. On a certain Sunday, when communion is being held at the evening service, Joe meets the Pastor outside the church and says that he does not plan to come in because he has been drinking and, in fact, is somewhat intoxicated. The Pastor tells him that he should come on in and receive communion, and that this is just where he should be, embraced by the Body of Christ in a time of need. During the following week, the chairperson of the church talks to the Pastor and explains that the board of elders is quite concerned about this incident, and want to meet with the Pastor on Saturday and receive an explanation for this action. The Pastor decides to write out a brief statement setting forth the nature of the Lord's Supper and use the occasion to share with the elders the theological significance of this sacrament with regard to the life of the church. As you write this paper, include endnotes documenting sources and discussing some of the more technical theological points.

9. You are working as an intern in a church when you receive a call from a young woman who is a friend of a member of the congregation. She requests pastoral counseling due to a crisis she is going through, and is presently in the hospital. Upon talking with her, you find that she was recently involved in an automobile accident and as a result is paralyzed

from the waist down. Her boyfriend had been visiting her until recently when they broke up. He used to come and visit her at the hospital and pray with her for healing. He insisted that if she had enough faith God would heal her, quoting such scriptures as Matthew 8:8ff; 17:20; James 5:13ff. However, as she was not being healed, he suggested that she was weak in faith and needed to develop a more spiritual attitude. Breaking off the relationship with him, she had the feeling that her whole life was falling apart and that God had deserted her. She was in desperate need for support and counseling. Having set up a follow-up appointment with her, you begin to think about what you will say to her. Fortunately, you are currently taking a class on Christian Community, which enables you to think through the issues involved. Write this paper as a letter to send to her prior to your visit. Suggest ways in which she can understand the promises of answered prayer with respect to her boyfriend's position as well as your own. Attach endnotes to document sources and to interact with some of the more technical theological issues.

BIBLIOGRAPHY OF RAY S. ANDERSON'S WORKS (1964-2002)

1964 *Like Living Stones*. Minneapolis: Free Church Press.

1968 Marriage After Divorce. *Eternity* (May).

1973 Toward a Theology of Celebration. *Christian Scholar's Review* III (1).

1974 Society and Culture. *Westmont College News Publication* 26(1): (January).
The Lengths of God in Christian Involvement. *Reformed Journal* (July/August).
Theology as Rationality. *Christian Scholar's Review* 4 (2).

1975 *Historical Transcendence and the Reality of God*. Grand Rapids: Eerdmans; London: Geoffrey Chapman.
Review of *Incarnation and Immanence*, by Lady Helen Oppenheimer (London: Hodder & Stoughton, 1973). In *Scottish Journal of Theology* 28(2).
Review of *True Patriotism*, by Dietrich Bonhoeffer (edited by Edwin Henton Robertson. NY; London: Harper and Row; 1973). In *Scottish Journal of Theology* 28(4).

1976 Review of *Freedom Made Flesh: The Mission of Christ and His Church*, by Ignacio Ellacuria (translated by John Drury. Maryknoll, NY: Orbis Books; 1976). In *The New Review of Books and Religion* (June).
Review of *Theology for a Nomad Church*, by Hugo Assmann (translated by Paul Burns. Maryknoll, NY: Orbis Books; 1975). In *The New Review of Books and Religion* (June).

1977 Producing Doctors for the Church. *Theology, News and Notes* (October).
Review of *Space, Time and Resurrection*, by T.F. Torrance (Grand Rapids: Eerdmans, 1976). In *Christianity Today* (December).

Bibliography

1978 — Theologians in Life and Thought: Mark 2:27. *Education for Ministry: Theology, Preparedness, Praxis*: 15th Biennial Meeting, edited by Gaylord B. Noyce, Association for Professional Education for Ministry. Toronto: Trinity College (June).

1979 — *Theological Foundations for Ministry* (editor and contributor). Grand Rapids: Eerdmans; Edinburgh: T & T Clark.

1980 — *A Casebook for Theological Reflection*, Fuller Theological Seminary, Continuing Education Department. Date approximate.

1981 — Notations on a Theology of the Holy Spirit. *TSF Bulletin* (April).

1982 — *On Being Human: Essays in Theology Anthropology*. Grand Rapids: Eerdmans.
A Theological Basis for Social Justice: The Little Man on the Cross. *Reformed Journal* (November).
Real Presence Hermeneutics: Reflections on Wainwright, Thielicke, and Torrance with Some Implications of the "Real Presence" of Christ in the Hermeneutical Task. *TSF Bulletin* 6 No 2:5-7 (November/December).

1983 — Burnout as a Symptom of Theological Anemia. *Theology, News and Notes* (March/April).
Christopraxis: Competence as a Criterion for Theological Education. *TSF Bulletin* 7 (3): (January/February).
Son of God. In *International Standard Bible Encyclopedia*, vol. 4. Grand Rapids: Eerdmans.

1984 — *On Being Family: A Social Theology of the Family*, with Dennis B. Guernsey, Grand Rapids: Eerdmans.
Review of *Anthropology in a Theological Perspective* by Wolfhart Pannenberg (translated by Matthew J. O'Connell, Philadelphia: Westminster Press, 1985). In *TSF Bulletin* 9 No. 2:24-26, Nov-Dec.

1986 — *Minding God's Business*. Grand Rapids: Eerdmans.
Theology, Death and Dying. Oxford and New York: Basil Blackwell.
Karl Barth and New Directions in Natural Theology. In *Theology Beyond Christendom – Essays on the Centenary of*

the Birth of Karl Barth. Allison Park, PA: Pickwick Publications.

The Resurrection of Jesus as Hermeneutical Criteria: Part One. *TSF Bulletin* (January/February).

The Resurrection of Jesus as Hermeneutical Criteria: The Case for Sexual Parity in Ministry. *TSF Bulletin* (March/April).

Conversion: The Essence of the Christian Story. *Theology, News and Notes* (June).

South Africa: *Kairos* or Crisis? *Reformed Journal* 36(10): (October).

Review of *Theologies of the Body: Humanist and Christian*, by Benedict M. Ashley (Braintree, Mass: The Pope John XXIII Medical-Moral Research and Education Center, 1985) in *Christian Scholar's Review*, 16 No 1:79-81.

Review of *Human Life: A Biblical Perspective for Bioethics* by J. Nelson Robert (Philadelphia: Fortress Press, 1984) in *Reformed Journal* 36 No. 6:23-25, Je 1986.

Review of *The Majesty of Man: The Dignity of Being Human* by Ronald B. Allen (Portland, OR: Multnomah Press, 1984). In *TSF Bulletin* 9 No. 3:37, January/February.

Review of *Liberating Faith: Bonhoeffer's Message for Today* by Geffrey B. Kelley (Minneapolis: Augsburg Publishing House, 1984). In *TSF Bulletin* 9 No. 4:23, March/April.

1987　God Bless the Children and the Childless. *Christianity Today* 31(28):(August 7).

Response to D.Min. Report. In *Theological Education* 23:84-88, Spring 1987.

Barth Bashing [Replies to R.A. Muller, C. Brown and R.J. Mouw] in *Reformed Journal*, 37:6-8, May 1987.

1988　Socio-cultural Implications of a Christian View of Humanity. *Asian Journal of Theology* 2/2 (October).

The Family as Matrix of Character. *Theology, News and Notes* (Fall).

Toward a Post-Apartheid Theology. *Reformed Journal* (May).

Toward a Post-Apartheid Theology in South Africa. *Journal of Theology for South Africa* (June).

Review of *The Option for Inclusive Democracy* by Bernard C. Lategan, et al. (Stellenbosch: University of Stellenbosch Press, 1987) in *Journal of Theology for Southern Africa* No 63:88-93, Je 1988.

Bibliography

1989   *Mission Theology and Church Theology: An Integrative Approach.* Photocopied manuscript. Pasadena: Fuller Theological Seminary. Became *The Praxis of Pentecost.*

Evangelical Theology: Heirs of Protestant Orthodoxy (editor and contributor). London: Collins.

Christopraxis: The Ministry and the Humanity of Christ for the World. In *Christ in our Place: Essays in Honor of James B. Torrance*, ed. Trevor Hart and Daniel Thimell. Exeter: Paternoster Press.

Evangelical Theologians. In *The Modern Theologians*, vol. 2, ed. David Ford. Oxford and New York: Basil Blackwell.

Isomorphic Indicators in Psychological and Theological Science. *Journal of Psychology and Theology* 17(4).

1990   *Chrisians Who Counsel: A Theological Approach to Wholistic Therapy.* Grand Rapids: Zondervan.

Human Nature, Problems of. In *Dictionary of Pastoral Care and Counseling.* Nashville: Abingdon.

Image of God. In *Dictionary of Pastoral Care and Counseling.* Nashville: Abingdon.

The Love that God Is. Photocopied manuscript. Pasadena: Fuller Theological Seminary. Became *Soulprints.*

1991   *The Praxis of Pentecost: Revisioning the Church's Life and Mission.* Photocopied manuscript. Pasadena: Fuller Theological Seminary. Became *Ministry on the Fireline.*

The Gospel According to Judas, Colorado Springs: Helmers and Howard Publishers.

1992   Self Recovery: From Overcoming to Becoming . . . Living on the Growing Edge. Photocopied manuscript. Pasadena: Fuller Theological Seminary. Became *Self Care.*

Faith, Doubt and Commitment: An Analysis of D.M. Baillie's *Faith in God.* In *Christ, Church and Society: Essays on John Baillie and Donald Baillie,* David Fergusson, editor. Edinburgh: T & T Clark.

The Incarnation of God in Feminist Christology: A Theological Critique. In *Speaking the Christian God,* Alvin F. Kimmel, editor, Grand Rapids: Eerdmans.

The Humanity of God and the Soul of a City. In *Theology, News and Notes.* Pasadena: Fuller Theological Seminary, June.

Response to Paul Vitz: Perspectives From Biblical Anthropology. In *Journal of Psychology and Theology*, Vol. 20, No. 1.

Bibliography

1993
Ministry on the Fireline: A Practical Theology for an Empowered Church. Downer's Grove: InterVarsity Press.
La fede, la morte e il morire, Torina, Italy: Claudiana Editrice. An Italian translation by Romeo Fabbri of *Theology, Death and Dying*, listed above.
Anthropology, Christian. In *Encyclopedia of Modern Christian Thought*, Alister McGrath, Editor. Oxford, England: Blackwell Publishers.
Fundamentalism. In *Encyclopedia of Modern Christian Thought*, Alister McGrath, Editor. Oxford, England: Blackwell Publishers.
Death, Theology of. In *Encyclopedia of Modern Christian Thought*, Alister McGrath, Editor. Oxford, England: Blackwell Publishers.

1994
Don't Give Up on Me – I'm Not Finished Yet! Putting the Finishing Touches on the Person You Want to Be. New York: McCracken Press.
Liberating the Psalmist Within: Giving Your Past a Present. In *Steps*, Spring.
The Gospel According to Judas – Is There a Limit to God's Forgiveness? Colorado Springs: NavPress.
My Father Taught Me . . . Everything I Needed to Know. Photocopied manuscript. Pasadena: Fuller Theological Seminary. Became *Unspoken Wisdom*.

1995
God So Loved: A Theology for Ministry Formation. Pasadena: Fuller Theological Seminary. Became *The Soul of Ministry*.
Everything That Makes Me Happy I Learned When I Grew Up. Downers Grove: InterVarsity Press.
Self. In *New Dictionary of Christian Ethics and Pastoral Theology*. Leicester, UK: InterVarsity Press.
Unspoken Wisdom: Truths that my Father Taught Me. Minneapolis: Augsburg Fortress.
Self Care: A Theology of Personal Empowerment and Spiritual Healing. Wheaton: Victor Books.
Review of *Theology and the Practice of Responsibility: Essays on Dietrich Bonhoeffer* (ed. Wayne Whitson Floyd, Jr. and Charles Marsh. Balley Forge, PA: Trinity Press International, 1994) in *Calvin Theological Journal* #30.
Review of *The Other Bonhoeffer: An Evangelical Reassessment of Dietrich Bonhoeffer* (by Georg Huntemann, tr. Todd

Bibliography

Huizinga. Grand Rapids: Baker, 1993) in *Calvin Theological Journal* #30.

1996   *Soulprints: Personal Reflections on Faith, Hope, and Love.* Photocopied manuscript. Pasadena: Fuller Theological Seminary.

A version of *Ministry on the Fireline: A Practical Theology for an Empowered Church* translated into Chinese was published by the Evangelical Formosan Church in El Monte, CA (Sharmon Hsiao, translator).

Empowering Ministry. In *The Call to Serve: Biblical and Theological Perspectives on Ministry in Honour of Bishop Penny Jamieson*, edited by Donald Campbell. Sheffield, England: JSOT Sheffield Academic Press.

Homosexuality: Theological and Pastoral Considerations. In *Journal of Psychology and Christianity*, Vol. 15, #4 Winter.

1997   *The Soul of Ministry: Forming Leaders for God's People.* Louisville: Westminster/John Knox Press.

1998   *Living the Spiritually Balanced Life: Acquiring the Virtues You Admire.* Grand Rapids: Baker Books, 1998.

On Being Human: The Spiritual Saga of a Creaturely Soul. In *Whatever Happened to the Soul? Scientific and Theological Portraits of Human Nature.* Warren S. Brown, Nancey Murphy and H. Newton Malony, editors. Minneapolis: Fortress Press.

The Task of Grandparents in Families. In *The Family Handbook*, edited by Herbert Anderson, et al., Louisville: Westminster John Knox.

1999   *Theological Foundations for Ministry* (editor and contributor). Grand Rapids: Eerdmans; Edinburgh: T & T Clark. Reprint.

2000   Homosexuality and the Ministry of the Church: Theological and Pastoral Considerations. In *More Than a Single Issue: Theological Considerations Concerning the Ordination of Practising Homosexuals.* George Knight, ed. Australian Theological Forum.

2001   *The Shape of Practical Theology: Empowering Ministry with Theological Praxis.* Downers Grove: InterVarsity Press.

Bibliography

Call Me Judas: Amazing Grace for the Troubled Soul. Photocopied manuscript. Pasadena: Fuller Theological Seminary.

Spiritual Caregiving as Secular Sacrament. Photocopied manuscript. Pasadena: Fuller Theological Seminary.

Reading Thomas Torrance as a Practical Theologian. In *Theologians in Dialogue with T. F. Torrance: The Promise of Trinitarian Theology.* Elmer Colyer, editor. Landam, MD: Rowman and Littlefield Publishers.

The New Age of Soul. Eugene, Oregon: Wipf and Stock Publishers.

2002 *Dancing with Wolves while Feeding the Sheep: The Musings of a Maverick Theologian.* Eugene, Oregon: Wipf and Stock Publishers.

The Social Ecology of Human Personhood. In *On Being a Person: A Multidisciplinary Approach to Personality Theories.* Todd Speidell, ed. Eugene, OR: Wipf and Stock Publishers